MILITARY POWER, CONFLICT AND TRADE

MILITARY POWER, CONFLICT AND TRADE

MICHAEL P. GERACE

The Umbra Institute, Perugia

FRANK CASS
LONDON • PORTLAND, OR

First published in 2004 in Great Britain by
FRANK CASS PUBLISHERS
Crown House, 47 Chase Side
London N14 5BP

and in the United States of America by
FRANK CASS PUBLISHERS
c/o ISBS, 920 NE 58th Avenue, #300
Portland, Oregon, 97213-3786

Website: www.frankcass.com

Gerace, Michael P.
   Military power, conflict and trade
   1. Commercial policy – History – 20th century 2. Commercial policy – History
   – 19th century 3. International trade – History – 20th century 4. International
   trade – History – 19th century 5. Military policy 6. International trade –
   Political aspects 7. Great powers – History 8. World War, 1914–1918 –
   Economic aspects
   I. Title
   382.3'09041

ISBN 0 7146 5442 6 (cloth)
ISBN 0 7146 8448 1 (paper)

Library of Congress Cataloging-in-Publication Data

Gerace, Michael P., 1963 –
   Military power, conflict and trade/Michael P. Gerace
      p. cm
   Includes bibliographical references and index
   ISBN 0-7146-5442-6 (cloth) – ISBN 0-7146-8448-1 (paper)
   1. Military readiness – Economic aspects – History. 2. Mercantile system –
   History. 3. International trade – Political aspects – History. 4. Commercial
   policy – History. 5. Great powers – History. 6. World politics – 1900–1918.
   7. Internationla economic relations – History. I. Title.

HC79.D4.G47 2004
382.09'041–dc22

2003055546

Typeset in 10.25/12pt New Baskerville by FiSH Books, London WC1
Printed in Great Britain by MPG Books Ltd, Bodmin, Cornwall

Contents

Tables

Abbreviations and Acronyms

2SLS	Two-Staged Least Squares
3SLS	Three-Staged Least Squares
ACP	African, Caribbean and Pacific Countries
CAP	Common Agricultural Policy
CMEA	The Council for Mutual Economic Assistance
COCOM	Coordinating Committee for Multilateral Export Controls
EC	European Community
EU	European Union
GDP	Gross Domestic Policy
GNP	Gross National Product
MFN	Most Favored Nation
MID	Militarized Interstate Disputes
NATO	North Atlantic Treaty Organization
NNP	Net National Product
OLS	Ordinary Least Squares
OPEC	Organization of Petroleum Exporting Countries
WPI	Wholesale Price Index

Acknowledgements

This book was a long time in coming. I began thinking about the relationship between military spending and trade back in 1992. Since then, my thinking on the subject has travelled down countless pathways – not all of which were fruitful. The present book is a revised version of my dissertation, which was written between 1993 and 1995 in the Department of Political Science at Boston University, although it is not as different as were my initial plans for revision.

I would like to offer thanks to those who helped me over the years. I certainly owe a debt of thanks to my advisors David Mayers and William C. Green, whose time and advice I consumed lavishly when I was their student. I have also knocked on many doors of people who were willing to listen to my questions and offer advice, of whom some were political scientists, some economists and some historians. I have also benefited from the advice of several anonymous reviewers of article-length papers as well as the present book. I am quite sure that I became tiresome to some of these folks and some probably saw my chosen subject of study as being a bit curious, but I was treated with kindness nevertheless.

Michael P. Gerace
Perugia, Italy

Foreword

In this book, Michael Gerace explores the connections between military power and international commerce, taking as a case study the fascinating period before the First World War. Many traditional strategists in fact had very clear ideas about these linkages. Both Sun Tsu and Clausewitz, in their individual ways, recognised the importance of the national economy in producing the resources needed for war-fighting, and it was not a great leap from this to see that the war economy of the opposition would make a fruitful target for those military operations. This could either be direct (in, for example, the burn and destroy military campaigns of the Hundred Years War or General Sherman's [in] famous march through Georgia in the American Civil War) or indirect (in the attritional campaigns of the Western Front, which were intended to grind away not merely at the enemy's military forces but at the fragilities of the economy that supported them).

Before the advent of the air age, naval strategists like Mahan and Corbett took all this one stage further. For them, commerce depended in the main on the passage of merchant ships conveying goods and people from one area of the world to another. This afforded the countries best placed to exploit sea-based commerce, access to the world's riches and to its markets. This, in turn, provided the resources (sailors, ports, ships, a maritime-merchant class, a sophisticated financial infrastructure able to offer governments a means of raising and maintaining their fleets) that funded the naval power that in turn under-wrote maritime endeavour. It was in effect a virtuous circle. The countries able to exploit these synergies would prosper in peace and triumph in war. According to Mahan, this explained why the maritime nations were so successful:

> Control of the sea by maritime commerce and naval supremacy means predominant influence in the world... [and] is the chief among the merely material elements in the power and prosperity of nations.[1]

But of course there were vulnerabilities in the system. Sea-based trade seemed wide open to attack and it was surely the prime function of navies to protect it. Mahan indeed thought: 'the necessity of a navy... springs, therefore from the existence of a peaceful shipping, and disappears with it.'[2] In just the same way, the other side's commerce made a lucrative target for campaigns designed to undermine the enemy's war economy, hence the great maritime wars of the past often revolved around major campaigns to defend or attacks maritime trade.

As Michael Gerace argues, it was therefore easy, in the old days, to associate military power with economic competition, where the desire of one nation to 'trade with advantage' could almost be regarded by its commercial rivals as a form of war. This manifested itself in the closest of links between mercantilism (that is very competitive trading where the objective is to take the maximum short-term profit whilst hammering commercial rivals into the ground) and military power. Britain's infamous Opium Wars against the Chinese in the nineteenth century are the classic example of a country using military might to force an adversary to trade on disadvantageous terms.

But set against this, there arose in Britain, the Manchester School, who argued that prosperity need not be a zero sum game and that free trade, in which both sides could benefit and prosper would improve mankind, reduce tensions, develop the cooperative instinct in world society and ultimately lead to a situation where recourse to armed conflict as a way of resolving disputes would seem increasingly inappropriate – even counter-productive. Hence on the one side there was mercantilism and military force; on the other liberalism, free trade and pacifism.

Michael Gerace provides a much needed exploration of these themes at what was possibly the pivotal time in the transition from the one concept of international relations to another. He shows that this polarisation is far too simple, and that the notion that the utility of armed force would simply decline as nations and peoples traded more with each other was quite simply wrong. Indeed there are many who argue that seapower itself was, from the very start, deeply imbued with the trading values that underlay liberalism and free trade.[3] Military power, at least in the form of navies, seemed to lie at the heart not just of mercantilism, but also of the more liberal and co-operative visions of commerce that have largely superseded it. Nothing could more clearly demonstrate the need to study the continuing and varying links between commercial and military power Michael Gerace explores. Moreover, at the start of a new century, a time when an international coalition thinks of itself as defending a globalised trading system considered to be ultimately to the benefit of all, such a study could hardly be more timely.

Professor Geoffrey Till
Dean of Academic Studies
King's College London at the JSCSC

NOTES

1. Cited in William E Livezey, *Mahan on Sea Power* (Norman, OK: University of Oklahoma press, 1981) p 281–2.
2. Cited in A. Westcott (ed.), *Mahan on Naval Warfare* (Boston, MA: Little, Brown, 1919) pp. 16, 18.
3. See, for instance, Peter Padfield, *Maritime Supremacy and the Opening of the Western Mind* (Woodstock and New York: Overlook Press, 1999) and indeed my own *Seapower: A Guide for the Twenty-First Century* (London: Frank Cass, 2003).

Introduction

This book is about the interaction between military power and international trade among the Great Powers prior to the First World War. On the one hand, the book is about the behaviour of the Great Powers themselves up to 1913, with the focus being on how their conflict and rivalry behaviour was entwined with their commercial behaviour. I am most interested here in how patterns of conflict, which persisted in peacetime, both influenced and were influenced by the commercial activities of these countries. On the other hand, the book is about the larger issue of how military power and international commerce interact more generally. The era of the Great Powers, using a substantial amount of their statistical data, is used as a test case for the issues posed in this book. The interwar years and the postwar period, while generally excluded (except in cases where brief comparisons are made), would be the next logical blocks of time to examine.

The organizing concept of this work is that the military power and commerce of large and powerful states are inseparable. In times of major war the secure movement of commodities and military power are the lifelines of a state. In periods of relative peace, trade and strategy are bound together to form the heart of a state's foreign policy. While this book advances the argument that military power and commerce move together, the nature of this relationship, how it behaves over time, across states, and under conditions of rivalry remain to be understood. No study has attempted to explain the full relationship between military power and commerce, and the very question of their relationship has never been directly posed. In fact, the very idea seems like an anachronism in light of current trends in the literature.

The issue of how military power and trade are related is close to the surface of several debates, but no studies seek to answer the question directly. Yet common observations on world politics seem frequently to affirm that wherever the commerce of large countries flows, military power flows with it. The connection between the two often appears at the very heart of matters. Whether one hears of how trade routes require protection, of how international economic relations have become the main arena of conflict, of how raw materials have strategic significance, or even of a news item about how one country's navy has blockaded the trade of another – all of these issues imply some sort of relationship between military power and commerce.

The goals of this study are to advance an argument for the relationship between military power and commerce and then to determine how military power and commerce were related among the Great Powers. In building my argument, I delve into several related arguments that are connected in various ways to this issue. The core of the book is the empirical material, which uses the best data available on the Great Powers (most from their national statistical series). I fashion an argument that military power and commerce are directly related, which is motivated partly by realist and mercantilist reasoning and partly motivated by an attempt to understand in a very practical way how the variables interact. While this argument may find sympathy in some traditional bodies of work (discussed in Chapter 1), it is generally out of fashion with current trends in the literature.

It has been fashionable for some time to assert that the inter-dependent global economy has altered the nature of world politics to the point where military power is being, or has been, deprived of its role. Interdependence literature generally sees the military and the commercial as being mutually exclusive. This is also true of a good portion of the current globalization literature, which seems to rehash many of the themes of interdependence. While no systematic statements about how military power and commerce are related are available in this literature, the general implication is that the two are inversely related. The above view boils down to the idea that military power has a relatively narrow role in world politics – one of settling disputes that involve the traditional issues of sovereignty, territory, and conquest. If economic interdependence weakens sovereignty and makes territorial issues less relevant, then it seems reasonable that the military role will decline.

The idea that economic interdependence will make military power decline in its role has a great deal of intuitive resonance in the West. The traditional connection between mercantilism and militarism (hence liberalism and peace) is clearly rooted in the tradition of idealism in international relations. The application to international relations of the notion that an economy without government is the most prosperous has produced a complex of normative convictions that drive such reasoning: prosperous trading relations lead to peace, because all states can pursue their rational self-interest without hindrance; economic want breeds war; mercantilist practices breed economic want; mercantilist practices, therefore, lead to military competition and war; thus in a world of prosperity, where comparative advantage among states defines international relations, military power will have no role.

The same may be said of the notion that sovereignty is in decline. Changes in the world economy will inevitably lead to changes in the structure of the state system. As states are increasingly enmeshed in economic and related linkages, they are less and less able to control their environments and to achieve their goals. These economic changes will ultimately purge world politics of war by depriving war of the very environment within which it grows – that of the competitive system of sovereign states.

While these issues are addressed more fully in Chapters 1 and 2, I will state here that the above assertions seem to reflect normative preferences more than they reflect empirical findings. There was a tremendous amount of economic interdependence among the Great Powers prior to the First World War and, while they asserted their sovereignty, they readily attempted to interfere in each other's affairs and in the affairs of other countries. And the considerable economic interdependence among them did not prevent them from building large and aggressive militaries that seemed to have roamed the planet in search of acquisitive opportunities.

A key point of this issue, indeed of this whole study, is the peacetime role played by military power. The natural focus of any study on military power is, of course, on warfare. Our general perspective on military power in world politics is conditioned by its war-fighting functions. As is discussed in the chapters that follow, we tend to ascribe a rather narrowly defined role to military power. We assess the distribution of military power across states in terms of war-fighting capability and the potential for war, while relegating military power to somewhat of a peripheral role in the ordinary day-to-day relations among states. As such, there is no clear understanding of the systemic role played by military power in peacetime, one perhaps central to the structure of peace among the large states. As discussed in Chapter 3, military power has quite a broad role in world politics, going well beyond the confines of what are called traditional issues. Many of these roles operate during peacetime and many of these peacetime military activities involve international commerce in some way. These military actions that interact with commerce are evident in the ordinary peacetime behaviour and policies of the Great Powers and, I would argue, of the major states today.

Issues of international trade, on the one hand, and strategy and security, on the other, are not clearly separable. The connections between the two are manifold (see Chapter 3). The Great Powers focused much of their strategic and naval behaviour on their trading positions. Britain, for example, was the quintessential liberal trading state prior to the First World War. Its trade and financial relations were perhaps larger and more geographically dispersed than those of any other state during this period. And yet Britain maintained a large and aggressive navy, an army, as well as a colonial army, while advancing a global political, military and economic presence that acted to support and protect Britain's liberal trading system. A few cursory examples of other states would include how the French navy was often oriented towards a *guerre de course* strategy against British commerce (as its peacetime strategy), or how colonial armies secured territory through force for trade expansion, or how the American Asiatic Squadron bullied its way into Chinese waters to expand and protect American trading interests.

There are many of the same issues at work during the post-Second World War period, albeit largely absent of colonialism. The peacetime strategic interests of the United States (also the main liberal trading state of its time), for example, demonstrate many of the same concerns and connections between military power and commerce. Some examples would include the role of the US navy in protecting trade routes, or the fact that American allies after the war were also its key trading partners, and the periodic use of American naval power to blockade and disrupt the trade of other states (that is, sanctions). The connections between military power and commerce were also evident with the Soviet Union. Its allies during the Cold War (Eastern Europe and, for a time, China) were also its primary trading partners. That it could be argued that Eastern Europe was involuntarily allied to the USSR is quite beside the point. There was still a close association between military and commercial interests. If we look at smaller states in the postwar period as well, we would doubtless find countless examples of military actions that have some sort of connection to trade relations.

It is also true that trade and finance were frequently close to the centre of Great Power diplomacy. It is simply wrong to maintain that the importance of economic issues is new. The nineteenth century witnessed many examples of politically motivated lending between countries and numerous conflicts over tariffs and trade. Issues of trade and finance were often important aspects to diplomatic issues and conflicts, even when the initial question had little to do with commerce. A major example would be the role of French financing to Russia with the 1894 Franco-Russian Treaty, which was a defence pact against Germany. Another would be the role of trade and finance as it related to Anglo-German rivalry in Turkey during the Baghdad Railway issue. Perhaps most of the major diplomatic questions of the day had a trade or financial component to them.

The point here is that commerce is intertwined with matters of strategy. The commercial interests of a country and its military interests, or at least the peacetime uses of its military power, are not independent of one another. Understanding the interconnections between the military and commercial behaviour of countries is, as I hope to substantiate in Chapter 3, central to understanding peacetime patterns of conflict.

QUESTIONS OF THE STUDY

The primary questions for this study, then, reduce to three. How are military power and commerce related? How does this relationship vary across countries? These two questions will be developed by exploring the actual ways in which military power and commerce interact in a general sense and then grounding these interactions in an essentially realist argument to motivate the study. While the argument in the book is a realist one, this book is not about realism *per se*. Realism has little to say about the questions examined here in a direct sense. The focus on power relations between states and the corresponding element of mercantilist reasoning that resides in much realism makes this book realist. In fact, mercantilism is more directly relevant (though generally neglected and even frowned upon in contemporary literature). These matters are discussed in Chapter 3.

How does military rivalry in peacetime affect trade relations? This third question goes to the patterns of conflict that seem to persist in peacetime, or, at least, those patterns that did persist in the period before the First World War. The issue here reduces to a test as to whether trade expansion and conflict between states are mutually exclusive and, if so, under what conditions this is so. The most sophisticated body of literature related to this matter is that on conflict and trade (see Chapter 2). While the older literature in this tradition tended to find an inverse relationship between conflict and trade, the more recent findings are mixed.

While I do not build conflict and trade models in this work, this literature relates to the subject at hand through its association with interdependence theory. The empirical portion of this book relates to the conflict and trade literature in two ways. One is that conflict and war terms are tested in the regression models of Chapters 4 and 8. The other way is that I analyse the trade data of rival Great Powers under three scenarios of trade relations in Chapter 7: trade between the rivals themselves; their trade to a third Great Power market; and their trade to a third country that is not a Great Power, but is a target of their rivalry. In each of the three scenarios, the issue to be determined is whether the trade positions of rivals demonstrate polarization of any kind, where one country's position increases while the other's decreases. This focus is partly motivated by an attempt to substantiate British complaints about the Germans gaining in international trade markets at their expense (see Chapter 6).

These are seemingly simple questions, but the ways in which military power and commerce interact may very well prove to be complex. These questions are also important because the issue of how military power and commerce are related goes to central aspects of the relations among large states, such as the role and utility of military power in peacetime, the significance of interdependence for conflict among states, how trade and military behaviour interact, and the structure of peace among large states.

WHY THE PRE-FIRST WORLD WAR PERIOD?

To explore these questions, this study analyses the trade and military data of the Great Powers up to 1913. The countries studied include the United States, Britain, France, Germany, Italy, Russia, and Japan. Austria-Hungary is generally left out of the study, except for cases of brief statistical comparison. The reason for this is that Austro-Hungarian data seems to have a lot of difficulty owing to changes in currency units and separate counting of much data, such as budgetary data, as well as problems of data availability.

The starting date of this study is somewhat arbitrary, generally after 1850, but the ensuing period is generally thought to be the classical period of Great Power rivalry. While some of the data for the countries extend back to 1850, much of it is available in the 1860s or early 1870s. Data for a united Germany began in 1871, for example, and for Italy in 1861. British, Russian and French data are available without difficulty from 1850, however, and considerably earlier for some series.

There are several reasons why it is interesting to study the period before the First World War for an understanding of how military power and international commerce interact. The time period is the classical period of Great Power rivalry, which is interesting and important in its own right. In many ways, this period put its stamp on the modern system of competitive states. Aside from the fact that the countries in this study have been and still are of central importance in the world (although to varying degrees), their militaries and international trade have comprised the great majority of the subject of this study.

Most importantly, however, the period before the First World War offers perhaps the best opportunity in modern history to analyse the relationships in this study among a substantial number of major states, all of whom were involved in competitive commercial and military practices that persisted for a long period of time. The pre-First World War period was characterized by expanding trade and stable commercial ties among the Great Powers, the general persistence of stable trade relations (punctuated by mostly short-term disputes), and a variety of military, diplomatic, and commercial rivalries that involved all of the Great Powers to varying degrees. There is also a measure of strategic and commercial diversity among these states, which allows for some interesting comparisons. Some of the states are sea powers, some are land powers, some are resource-rich, some are resource-poor, some have pursued liberal trade policies, some have pursued mercantilist policies, some had overseas empires, and some expanded over land.

Another reason why the pre-First World War period is attractive here is that, from a data point of view, the period is long and stable enough to offer adequate time series to study the relationships at hand. Nineteenth-century statistical reporting was of high quality and it was stable. The quality and detail of what the various national series offer declines noticeably after the First World War. A description of the data and sources used can be found in Appendix 1.

The only other multipolar system in modern times was between the two world wars. The interwar years are less attractive than the previous period, however, being much shorter in length and being characterized by chaos and disruption. The aftermath of the war, the shock of the Depression, and the rise of communism in Russia and fascism in Italy and Germany all present problems for data continuity (though less so with Italy). In fact, the interwar years do not offer enough good annual data for all of the countries in this study.

A good deal of Russian data ceases to be useful, or even available, after the Soviet regime comes to power. Aside from the initial disruptions caused by the world war, the revolution and the civil war, there is the problem of political secrecy in Soviet statistical data. There is also the deeper problem of arbitrariness that permeates much Soviet data. Due to the nature of the Soviet economy (under war communism during 1918–22, and later under Stalin's collectivization from about 1930 onward), data that are denominated in monetary terms or are a reflection of price information are inherently arbitrary because of the way that prices and quantities were determined (centrally and administratively). There was no underlying market rationale for pricing and, therefore, the aggregated data do not reflect underlying economic conditions. At bottom, Soviet data may not be measuring what one thinks they are measuring.

Germany presents another major problem for data continuity in the interwar period. The first problem that one confronts here is the instability in the German price level in the early to mid-1920s, owing to hyperinflation. This instability ruins the data for a few years. Soon after, however, the Nazis come to power and a noticeable change in data reporting follows. German military data, for example, are no longer reported in Germany's national statistical series (*Stastisches Jahrbuch für das Deutsche Reich*) after 1934. There are some estimates of total German military spending up to 1938,[1] but the information available in the usual way is ended. At best, one can get a German military time series up to 1934 from the national statistical series, though it will be troublesome in the mid-1920s.

Italy does not seem to have the same problems. Despite the advent of the Mussolini regime in 1922 and the curtailment of the liberal order after 1925, Italian data retain a remarkable level of continuity for a long time afterwards. The Italian fascist state was, of course, far less centralized and radical than its German counterpart. Most Italian military and trade data are consistently available up to the late 1930s. Only total military spending is available in Italy during the 1930s, however, and the last year that military spending is reported in the national series is 1937.

The Cold War period is perhaps the most unique of the three blocks of time, primarily because this period left only two Great Powers for such a study (only one of which had military and economic data that could be reliably analysed). The post-Second World War data of Western Europe and Japan are certainly available and reliable, of course, but these states played very different roles during the Cold War than was true before the First World War or in the interwar years. Western Europe and Japan ceased to be actors with the First World War and became reactors to the policies of the superpowers. Western Europe and Japan became both security and trade partners with the United States after the war and the roles played by them were quite circumscribed. Britain and France certainly maintained out-of-area roles for their militaries, but Germany, Italy, and Japan did not.

It seems more reasonable that the militaries of the allies are better understood as being part of a larger collective security order that revolved around the United States. In addition, the trade expansion of Western Europe and Japan during the Cold War was largely within the confines of a US-centred world economy. The interaction between military power and commerce among the major states during the Cold War period, then, must be understood in terms of the collective security and trade associations of the allies. In terms of Great Powers, however, the United States remains the only candidate with adequate data for such a study.

It would probably be more fruitful to study the questions in this work cross-sectionally for the period after the Second World War. This is especially true of the period since 1960 because of the increase in the number of countries in the world. A study that includes all of the different states in the world today would allow for deeper understanding of how military power and commerce interact under any number of different conditions. From a data point of view, international organizations, such as the World Bank and the IMF, have made the data of many states widely available.

METHODS

The basic thesis of this work is that military power and commerce move together, and they do so for very good reasons. I also argue that the effect of military rivalry on trade polarization depends on the type of trade. There is no polarization of trade among Great Power rivals regarding their mutual trade, although rivalry does help fuel trade conflict (not necessarily the same thing). There is trade polarization among rivals in the trade of the rivals in third country markets, whether the third country is another Great Power or a target of rivalry itself. These findings hold for the major states before the First World War. I would not presume to extrapolate beyond 1913. The interwar years and the Cold War period are very different from the period before the First World War. I would argue, however, that the findings in this work do prompt questions about military and commercial expansion.

These findings were arrived at by employing a mixture of analytical and descriptive methods. Regression models are estimated in Chapters 4 and 8 using country-level data, although the models and variables are defined in the last section of Chapter 3. I estimate four single equation models for each of the seven countries studied in Chapter 4 and six additional regressions in Chapter 8 (for a total of 34). The regressions in Chapter 8 are based upon those in Chapter 4. While the models are single equation estimates, there is some argument for estimating them as a system of equations. I have chosen not to do this, however, for several reasons. While the basic models have been defined through the argument set down in Chapter 3, I nevertheless want to let the data speak for itself within those limits. In addition to all of the economic and military variables, there is a set of dummy variables for conflict, war, and those for important dates and turning points that I want to test. I also want to test certain independent variables for possible changes in their relationships to the dependent variables through the use of these dummy variables. Within the limits set by the argument and choice of regressors, then, I want each model to be as convincing as possible without being constrained by the requirements of estimating a system. While this decision may draw criticism, the models presented in Chapters 4 and 8 are both solid and provocative.

There is also extensive use of correlations and descriptive statistical data throughout the book. Most of the correlations are used in Chapter 7, though there are some in Chapter 5 as well. The primary use for correlations in Chapter 7 is to compare the relative positions of each country in the import markets of the others. While these correlations are of limited value in terms of providing explanation, they do summarize the general tendencies in the data rather nicely.

Descriptive statistical tables are relied on in Chapters 5, 6 and 7 to examine a good deal of commercial and military data. The general goal of using these tables is to integrate detailed trade and military information into the historical context of Great Power behaviour. This is especially true regarding military and commercial policies in Chapters 6 and 7. The description and analysis of Great Power behaviour relies on secondary literature, mainly from historical and related works. The story of Great Power rivalry is not presented in a comprehensive way. A good deal of diplomacy and alliances are left out of the discussion, or are referred to only briefly. Instead, the substantive discussion is focused in on military and commercial interaction alone.

While I rely on secondary literature to provide references for the substantive material, the statistical tables offer a degree of commercial and military detail that is frequently absent from Great Power studies and much data that is hard to get. The regional trade and commodity group tables in Chapter 6, for example, were mostly (though not entirely) compiled by myself from annual trade tables.

The term *military power* is used extensively throughout this book. The term is used synonymously with military spending in the regressions and for most of the descriptive uses of data. It is true that military power is a broad concept that can be indicated by any number or combination of elements. There is some truth to the idea that overall expenditures are not the best indicator of military power when comparing across states. One author maintains that the differences among militaries, which bear upon their level of capability, are not taken into account with overall expenditures. Instead, it is argued that the operations and maintenance budgets of militaries are a better guide to general capability because operations and maintenance budgets will grow as the amount of military equipment grows and as military technology becomes more sophisticated.[2]

This argument may have some truth to it, though it is not possible to obtain the detailed breakdowns of military expenditures for all seven states throughout the time period in question. While it is relatively easy to get subcategories of military expenditures for a few years with some countries, it is not possible to do so for all countries and all years. Therefore, overall military expenditures are used here. There may also be a flaw in the above argument due to the likelihood that the cost of technology and the cost of maintaining capital equipment will not remain constant, nor will there be a constant ratio between them, such that the magnitude of the operations and maintenance budget of a military may not accurately reflect how capital intensive a military is. The operations and maintenance budget of a military may decline in real terms over a long period of time, despite the technological improvement of a military.

The only breakdown of spending that will be used regularly in this study is that between army and navy expenditures. It should also be noted that the amounts actually spent on the military, both ordinary and extraordinary expenditures, are used here, not the amounts that were appropriated or voted for in the budgets (see Appendix 1).

The term *military power* is also used in this book in a rather practical way in that there is continual reference to the actual uses of militaries, rather than using the term to indicate a broader or more diffuse concept of military power. Given that military spending reflects the costs of these uses of military power, using the term synonymously with military spending should not unduly mislead the reader. This is addressed more fully in Chapter 3.

THE ARGUMENT

An important part of this study is to elaborate on the military dimension to mercantilism. The argument advanced in Chapter 3 is that the relationship between military power and commerce is grounded in the manifold connections between military power and trade and that these connections are aspects of mercantilist behaviour. These connections are evident whether or not a state pursues a free trade policy. I do not call the argument in Chapter 3 a *theory* because the argument is deliberately built from the bottom up, rather than from the top down.

What does this mean? Rather than starting off with general assumptions about state behaviour and then trying to theorize about the relationships, I attempt to motivate the proposed relationships at a lower level in Chapter 3. After a discussion of mercantilism proper (which may, unfortunately, appear to be a bit general), I then elaborate on the specific connections between military power and commerce with the goal being to expose the actual links between the variables in a concrete way. While aspects of these connections can be found scattered across a giant body of literature (see Chapter 1), there is no effort to look at all of these connections in a systematic way. After presenting the links between military power and commerce, then, I attempt to evaluate the ways in which these links might inform a relationship between the variables.

There are two reasons for pursuing this bottom-up approach. First, the question of how military power and commerce are related is actually not a question. That is, while the question is related to several bodies of work, the matter is not posed as a question anywhere. I would even say that the question itself lacks intuitive appeal. A reader may rightly ask: 'Just why should military power and commerce be related at all?' given the lack of a real precedent in the literature. As I hope to convince the reader in Chapter 3, however, there are so many connections between military power and commerce, many of which operate in peacetime, that there is extremely good motivation for expecting the two to have some sort of relationship.

Second, I want to stay away from grounding the relationship in generalities and, instead, construct the argument on hard, concrete and common-sense connections. The common-sense issue is crucial. Frequently research in international relations seems to sacrifice the common-sense connection for the (sometimes vague) generality. The literature in Chapters 1 and 2 will attest to this. While some of this literature is sophisticated in terms of its use of theory and methods, some of it tends to ignore the issue of how and why the variables interact in a very practical way.

This problem is actually wider spread than the present question. My lack of satisfaction about the prospects for building a genuinely convincing theoretical argument in the conventional way has caused me to think about the issue of common sense at length. Why is it that theories pointing to opposite conclusions can be equally reasonable? Even if a theory is very clear and even rigorous (perhaps even based in rational choice), it can be opposed by another theory that offers as convincing a point of view. This relates to the perennial question of why theory in international relations (and perhaps in political science more generally) does not progress – or, at least, does not produce a body of theory that is as well-built, analytically powerful and practically useful as is largely the case in economics. While there must be numerous reasons why this is so, it occurs to me that one elementary reason has to do with what I call common sense in the variables. In comparing political science with economics, for instance, I note that the majority of the variables used in economics appear to contain direct common-sense referents to their conduct while most variables used in political science do not. I use the term common sense here to refer to the very rudimentary meaning in a variable's conduct. If a variable contains a direct common-sense referent to it, then this meaning is self-evident to an observer and is true by inspection.

A few examples will clarify what I mean. Consider the interest rate, which is a macroeconomic variable (in truth the inter-bank lending rate is the key rate that seems to determine the others in the economy). This variable either rises or falls and when it does so, we know immediately what it means in a very basic sense. Suppose the interest rate rises, holding everything else constant. Considering no theory or any other change, the meaning of a rise in the interest rate is self-evident. It means that borrowing is now more expensive, given that the interest rate is the price of borrowing money, and that those who save money can earn a higher return. It does not mean anything else. This statement is common sense and it allows us to make further common-sense statements. Still holding everything else constant, we can assert that business will now be less inclined to borrow. We could quibble over the importance of the interest rate in governing investment behaviour, as Keynes would, but whatever its overall importance, a higher interest rate will influence borrowing adversely (still holding all else constant). This is common sense because as the interest rate rises, business must now earn that much more on an investment to pay back the loan and earn a profit, which raises the risk.

Another example would be the wage level at the macroeconomic level (or even the wage rate in a firm or an industry). If the wage level rises, and nothing else changes, then we know immediately what this means. It means that the costs to business rise and disposable income for workers rises. A further common-sense statement from the firm's point of view, still holding all else constant, is that the rising wage level exerts downward pressure on profits. This will incline business to cut back output, which, if severe enough, implies a recession and higher unemployment. All of this is straightforward common sense. No theory was invoked. It is true that the theory of the firm tries to provide a rigorous framework for these observations (and there are criticisms of this theory as well, including criticism of the assumption that the firm seeks to maximize profits), but it is true by inspection that profits equal revenue minus cost, such that if cost rises and nothing else changes, then profits fall.

The above examples are, of course, exceedingly simple scenarios that would surely be more complicated empirically (and would also be more complicated in the context of modern theory), but the statements are direct common-sense referents to the variables. It might be true that some of the statements made above were considered to be *theory* many years ago, but they appear to be common sense today because the meanings of the changes in the variables noted appear to be embedded in the very definitional composition of the variables themselves. The wage level is a component to the costs facing firms and the interest rate is the price of borrowing money.

It is also true that there are economic variables that do not have common-sense referents with this level of clarity, but most appear to. I am attempting to make a conceptual distinction here between theory and the common-sense referents in the variables. A characteristic of economic theory, even if it is very complicated and abstract and even if there is scholarly disagreement over the theory (there is much disagreement in macroeconomics), is that the logic of the argument inherent in the theory is connected in a sensible way to the common-sense groundwork in the variables. The economic theorist seeks to ensure that the theory is connected to the underlying common sense in the variables in order to make *economic sense*. No theory will predict that firms seek negative profits, or that as the wage level rises labour unions oppose this and firms support it. These statements make no sense. The common sense in the variables is the practical, nuts-and-bolts groundwork upon which theory rests.

There is no such thing as making 'political science sense' in any practical way. I can think of examples where a political variable's conduct offers a direct common-sense referent in political science, but these are few and far between. A trivial one is that, in an election for a single seat, the candidate who gets the most votes wins (barring complicated electoral rules). Another piece of common sense is that, in a parliamentary government, the more political parties there are the less any one party will be able to obtain a majority of the vote, necessitating coalition governments. Both of these examples may be trivial and there may be a number of additional trivial cases, but most of the variables that we have in political science do not contain direct common-sense referents to them. Instead, we have variables that contain either numerous common-sense possibilities or no common-sense referents at all.

Military spending is crucial to the present book and will make a fine example to illustrate my point. If the military spending of a state rises, holding all else constant, then what does this mean? Considering only the political (or non-economic) aspects of this change, we have a series of common-sense possibilities. An increase in spending might mean that the state bought more military capability, although it might also be that the state bought military goods that did not produce more capability (that is, that the state wasted its money, perhaps in response to constituency pressure on legislators for jobs). If the state did increase its military capability, however, it might be common sense to assert further that the state is now more secure in the world because it can better protect its interests. It is just as sensible to assert, unfortunately, that increasing military capability would make a state less secure because other states will react to this and spend accordingly. The connection between increasing capability and security can go either way. An additional possibility is that the state's spending is not defensively oriented. It is very possible that the increased military spending is on offensive capability because the state has plans for war or aggressive expansion. It is even possible that the state increased its spending for domestic political or economic reasons (such as a fiscal policy reason), having nothing to do with international relations.

The trouble with all of this is that we do not know which scenario is the likely one in any general way, because each is a common-sense possibility that can arise from an increase in military spending. And there are still others not mentioned here. We can only know which scenario applies after the fact when we investigate empirically. But if we are trying to theorize, we will be hard pressed to connect our proposed relationships to the common-sense referents in the variables in a manner that is truly more convincing than a well-constructed alternative. In addition, the different common-sense possibilities with military spending are not all mutually compatible. An increase in spending cannot simultaneously make a state more secure and less secure, whereas the different meanings of an increase in interest rates (borrowing is more expensive to business, savers look forward to higher earnings), or a rise in the wage level (costs to firms increase, disposable income for workers increases, sales of consumer goods rise when the money is spent) are all mutually compatible.

The only way to restrict the change in military spending to a single common-sense referent, or to a set of compatible referents, is to impose assumptions on the state or the variable (that is, assume that the state has no expansionary intentions, does not waste its money, has no known rivals or enemies who might respond to a spending increase, and does not respond to domestic pressures for military spending). We could then assert that a spending increase means that the state now has more capability and that this increase in capability provides more security. But we have deprived ourselves of a real understanding of the variable. The common-sense referents to variables are the tangible reasons why our theory might prove to be supported empirically.

Many of our variables are like military spending in that they simply contain multiple common-sense possibilities when they change, possibilities that are not mutually compatible with each other. Some variables, however, appear to have no common-sense referents at all. A good example is the variable polarity. Polarity – defined as the number of major states in the international system – has been at the centre of much theoretical and empirical work. This variable generally has three conditions – unipolarity, bipolarity and multipolarity, the definitions of which are self-evident. Repeating the same exercise as above, lets suppose that the system moves from a multipolar to a bipolar one. With all else constant and no use of theory, what can this mean? It appears that this change offers no direct common-sense meaning of any kind. The most we can do in trying to find a common-sense statement is to restate the definition of polarity – that is, because of this change, power is now more concentrated. But what this means in itself is unclear.

The lack of common sense here deprives us of a guide as to how to interpret the meaning of this variable in a consistent and convincing way. It should be no surprise, then, that we have theories that predict opposite outcomes about the same condition in polarity. Waltz argues that a bipolar system is the most stable, for example, while Singer and Small argue that it is the least stable and is prone to war.[3] Each provides an argument to support their respective viewpoints and each argument is sensible. The proposed relationships between the two variables – polarity and stability – contain some common sense, but these arguments do not reduce to common sense in the variables.

There is instead what I would call quasi-common sense in the polarity variable, however, which is a speculative form of reasoning about the condition of the variable (here, bipolarity). I do not mean that quasi-common sense is a speculative argument about a relationship (that is, how two or more variables interact), but is a speculative argument about a single variable itself. One might argue, as Waltz does throughout his book, that two major powers can more easily solve their mutual problems better than several can and that there are less commitments and hence less constraints on a state's behaviour in the bipolar world.[4] Here the salient features of bipolarity are that they reduce complexity in state-to-state interactions and lessen constraints on each state. Or one might argue, along with Singer and Small, that there are more alliances in a bipolar system and alliances are correlated with war. Having fewer alliances in the multipolar world and hence fewer constraints on behaviour, states are free to pursue their self-interest without conflict.[5] Here the salient features of bipolarity are that states are more constrained and tangled in alliances, which is nearly opposite to what Waltz sees in bipolarity.

These types of argument can guide our interpretation of the variable's conduct – that is, what is the salient meaning in the condition *bipolarity*? These arguments are not manifest in the variable, however, nor are they true by inspection. That rising wage levels push up the cost to firms, in contrast, and, all else constant, exert downward pressure on profits is self-evidently true or true by inspection, whereas the above reasoning on polarity is speculative in nature. Because the variable has no clear common-sense referent, the theorist constructs a speculative argument about what polarity means which then guides interpretation of polarity. Once we understand what polarity means – fewer constraints or more, and so on – then we can assert the hypothesis that bipolarity is more (or less) compatible with stability. It is the salient characteristic in the variable that the theorist is playing upon when asserting how this variable relates to the other variable. Each quasi-common-sense argument about polarity is sensible, but speculative, and each hypothesis about polarity and stability is sensible, but neither is grounded in direct common-sense referents in the variables. As Michael Sullivan states, 'not surprisingly, equally valid-sounding critiques exist of both bipolarity and multipolarity'.[6]

How many variables in international relations (or in political science more generally) have this characteristic to them? I do not know the answer to this, but if we took a census of all of the variables used in our discipline we would no doubt find many. The work on the causes of war, for example, is replete with these types of variables. This is true even when economic variables are employed in the explanation. The reason for this is that the economic variables – such as the GDP growth rate – are being used outside of their normal neighbourhoods and thus outside of their usual common-sense content. When using GDP growth as an explanatory variable in war, for example, one does not refer to the connection between economic growth and employment or inflation, or to any of the extended possibilities that arise from these items. It is irrelevant to the issue of what causes war to assert that, as economic growth rises, unemployment falls. The normal common-sense referents here are no longer the salient issues. Instead, in attempting to connect the variable to war, some quasi-common sense is required because straightforward reasoning about how economic growth could cause war will not lead to self-evident common-sense statements. Rather, we must construct a speculative argument about what could come out of growth – such as an increase in the demand for resources (which is common sense), which would then imply some type of state action that presumably leads to war (which is not common sense). The argument might be very sensible, but it is not a direct common-sense referent to the variable.

I do not want to carry this argument much further because there could be no end to this discussion. I do want to make the point that theory-building in our discipline tends to amount to constructing sensible arguments for relationships that either rest on quasi-common sense in the variables or relate tenuously to the multiple common-sense possibilities contained in other variables. In either case, whether the imputed characteristics of the variable are actually operating in one's data in practice is something of a lottery. Maybe the increase in military spending increased defensive capability, maybe it was a waste of money or maybe it was for aggressive purposes. Maybe the spending amount for one year did increase capability while the spending amount for the next year was a waste of money. It even appears to me that we actually do not consider the common-sense meaning in a change in the variable to begin with because we start off thinking in a rarified, abstract sense in our effort to build a theory right off the bat.

Rather than attempt to build a theory for the relationship between military power and commerce in the usual way, then, I try to provide as much common sense in the variables as possible – in particular, the connections between military spending and trade. While I do provide some argument in Chapter 3 about the relationships in a more general sense and how they reflect state behaviour, I also try to reason out the actual links between the variables and what they might mean in terms of a relationship.

This exercise may prove fruitless, but I am committed to exposing as much of the common sense in the variables as I can because the connections between military power and commerce are real in world politics. The danger is that the connections between the variables could be sufficiently numerous that my efforts will produce a messy story, rather than a relatively clean, single line of argument, but I am prepared to live with this.

The goal of Chapter 3, then, is to build an argument for the relationship between military power and commerce that is as grounded as possible in the nuts and bolts of military and commercial behaviour. Needless to say, the focus here will be on the actor level rather than the system level. The first part of Chapter 3 describes mercantilism proper, while the second part explores the actual connections between military power and commerce. The remainder of Chapter 3 attempts to evaluate these connections and presents the core models to be tested.

Why do I rely on mercantilism? As stated earlier, the manifold ways in which military power and commerce are connected are mercantilist features of state behaviour. I believe that realism (traditional realism more so than neorealism) is logically and historically associated with mercantilism. Mercantilism has something of a bad name today, perhaps because of the predominance of liberalism in the literature. Even modern realist studies, which may focus on power and conflict, can still have an underlying liberalism to them. Sometimes this is directly evident, as with discussion of hegemony and free trade, and sometimes it is more ingrained in the generalities of the theory, such as with the use of the market analogy and the firm to stand for the international system and the state.

Mercantilist behaviour is evident in numerous ways, even when a state has a preference for free trade. Even liberal trade arrangements, of course, are rarely unambiguous cases of free trade. The closer one looks at the detail of such agreements, the less one sees a policy of optimizing consumer surplus and the more one sees the interests of firms and the state. It also appears to me that a mercantilist point of view on state behaviour, as it relates to economic matters, is often visible in a wide body of literature without explicitly being termed *mercantilism.* I would even say here that many assertions about state behaviour that relate to the world economy that are made in radical literature are often disguised versions of mercantilism, without giving due credit to the mercantilists. One could even pick apart Marx himself and find glimpses of Antonio Serra or Thomas Mun or even Jean Bodin, let alone the classical economists that Marx made well-known use of.

SOME LARGER QUESTIONS

There are several reasons why exploring the issue of how military power and commerce are related is interesting. Discussions of state power and international economic relations, of course, are wide-ranging and the literature is enormous, but the military aspect of state power is relegated to a minor role in this discussion. There is a contemporary debate over national security issues and international economic relations, but the focus of these discussions is generally on how economic competitiveness can influence strategic capabilities.[7]

In addition, much of the literature in international political economy, which discusses the interaction between state power and the international economy, employs a distinctly non-military concept of state power. This body of literature will be discussed further in Chapters 1 and 2. Suffice it to mention here that an entire dimension of state power has been pushed to the sidelines in the debate over how state and trade interact. This study attempts to bring the military aspect of state power into the discussion. If military power and commerce are related, then how does conflict in one affect the other? What are the implications of this relationship for the role of militaries under conditions of economic interdependence? Does military rivalry affect trade relations (and vice-versa) and, if so, how? It is probably misleading to assume that trade rivalry and military rivalry are mutually exclusive. To what extent is stable commercial relations dependent upon stable military relations? These types of questions lead us to the larger role of military power in peacetime, an issue that is hard to overemphasize in this book.

Not only is it interesting to find out how military power and commerce interact, but it is also important to know why they interact and to fit this information into a meaningful framework. To what extent is the relationship between military power and commerce a function of the specific characteristics of the states in question, and to what extent is it a function of the overall distribution of power? Furthermore, to what extent are these relationships bound by history – that is, are they superseded by new developments? How is the relationship between military power and commerce linked to the interests of a state?

Not only would the full range of empirical links between military power and commerce be compared, but such an investigation would point to a multidimensional view of conflict. Patterns of conflict among states in peacetime are rarely one-dimensional. US–Soviet conflict was perhaps predominantly military, for example, but its economic component amounted to a global economic dividing line that changed only recently. By placing military power at the centre of peacetime relations of large states and connecting it to commerce, conflict becomes much more complicated. Estimating the relationship between military power and commerce among the Great Powers and then integrating these results into the story of their economic and military rivalry makes this point very clearly. The story is a complicated one.

Peacetime conflict among states, then, is understood here as reflecting patterned interactions between military power and commerce. These patterns may be geopolitical in nature in that they have a spatial component. One could very well focus on what regions of the world are most important to a state and why.

How does military power and commerce relate in other time periods, such as the interwar and Cold War periods? How does military power and commerce relate among other states, such as Third World states? Do the relationships hold only among large and powerful countries? In short, many questions are prompted by this study – certainly more questions than answers.

PLAN OF THE STUDY

Chapters 1 and 2 explore the relevant literature for the questions above. It seems that, while no body of literature deals with the relationship between military power and commerce directly, there are several that relate to the issue in some way. One such group of literature involves navalist and related military/strategic literature, some historical works (especially of the traditional variety), war potential literature, rise and decline literature, and some geopolitical literature. While this is a diverse group, most of this literature offers an array of nuts-and-bolts connections between military power and commerce. This is especially true of the navalist and military/strategic literature.

From a substantive point of view, the traditional literature lends support to the argument for a relationship between military power and commerce. In light of the absence of a pre-existing answer to this question, the traditional literature provides some (though not all) of the logical and actual points at which military power and commerce intersect. The areas where military power and commerce interact have largely to do with two related issues: the specific uses of military power and how those uses affect trade (intended or not); and the specific ways in which international commerce affects military power.

The discussion of relevant literature here is designed to be more than a mere literature review. The goal is to provide a picture of the commercially relevant aspects of military power in terms of the range of military actions that states engage in and to provide a picture of the militarily significant aspects of commerce. These connections between the two are expressed in the policies of states, but how they are expressed is no simple matter. Where possible, I try to be specific in drawing out the implications that these bodies of work have for the relationship between military power and commerce. The implied interactions are more complex than they may seem at first glance. Sometimes this literature is quite good at exposing connections, however complicated they may be, and sometimes it engages in grand generalizations that are less helpful.

Realist literature also offers some insights, but they are fewer than one might expect, and much of it engages in generalizations as well. Where realist works are specific about military and commercial matters, they tend to focus on material that is common to the above bodies of work. Indeed, much of the literature noted above may itself be termed *realist*. The theoretical aspects of realism appear to be relevant in a less direct sense. Aside from the power-centric nature of realism, the persistent view of economic matters in terms of state power (especially in traditional realism) is the area of obvious relevance. In much traditional realist literature, economic issues are evaluated from a mercantilist point of view.

This book is not about realism, however. Dissecting the niceties of realist literature would take us far afield. This work attempts to build an argument about the relationship between military power and commerce. To this end, my efforts in Chapter 3 are confined to organizing the numerous nuts-and-bolts connections between military power and commerce and placing these linkages in a mercantilist context, as well as defining the models and variables to be evaluated in later chapters.

Another group of literature examined is interdependence and the related globalization literature in Chapter 2. This differs from all of the above for its opposite implications. The literature in Chapter 1 tends to imply that military power and commerce should be directly related. These implications are arrived at in diverse ways, of course, and there are a few exceptions. Interdependence literature and the related work in globalization, in contrast, tend to imply that military power and commerce move away from each other. Interdependence literature does not pose the question in a direct way, but its implications for the relationship are straightforward. This is also true of some globalization literature. This body of work is very diverse and not all of it is relevant, but there is some globalization literature that seems to be old wine in new bottles. Some of it appears to be a more contemporary version of interdependence literature.

After the argument has been outlined in Chapter 3, regression models are estimated in Chapter 4 using a host of military, commercial and conflict variables. Twenty-eight models are estimated in Chapter 4 and the results are provocative, though mixed. I will state here only that there appears to be support for both arguments in the models.

Chapters 5 to 7 are empirical investigations of how military power and commerce actually interacted among the countries in this study. Chapter 5 is a straightforward examination of the magnitude of inter-dependence among the Great Powers focusing on price levels, inflation rates, trade dependence and mutual import dependence among the states. The goal is only to determine if there was interdependence among them and to what degree. The results stand in contrast to the common assertion that interdependence is new to the world. Chapters 6 and 7 examine more trade and military data in a descriptive way. There are several purposes here. One is to determine if there are any commercial–military patterns evident among the states that provide insight into the diversity of the results in Chapter 4. I am also interested in grounding the commercial–military behaviour of the states in a historical and an empirical context. Finally, I examine the import dependence of each state with the idea being to determine if rival states show different patterns in their trade dependence that do non-rival states. The policies of the Great Powers, of course, are well known. Therefore, I do not simply recount foreign policies. The goal is rather to compare commercial and military data of the states while relating this data to expansionary practices.

It is manifestly true that there are significant connections between military power and commerce among the states in this study. It is just as true that these connections reveal a terrifically complicated story, however. There is no single clean story revealed in any of the data. While Chapter 8 was intended to help clear up some of the complexity of the earlier story, the chapter actually ends up contributing to this complexity. I estimate six additional regressions using regional trade data to discover that the signs, magnitudes and significance of the trade terms in the military models themselves vary.

Because the goals of this study are both substantive and theoretical (theory with a small t), the study may be slightly untidy. Part of the reason for this is that this study is definitely interdisciplinary and stands among several bodies of literature, which usually ignore each other. The other reason for the untidy story here is that I am committed to letting the data be as complicated as it wants to be. The closer to the statistical detail that one gets, the more complicated the behaviour of the Great Powers appears to be. It seems that both arguments – one arguing for a direct relationship between military power and commerce and the other for an inverse relationship – find some support.

Despite the tentative nature of the conclusions reached here, I believe there is more support for a direct relationship than an inverse one. This study seems to have raised many more questions than it has provided satisfactory answers to, however. What could and probably should be done is a study of these questions among contemporary states. The entire postwar period offers many possibilities here.

NOTES

1. See, for example, Burton H. Klein, *Germany's Economic Preparation for War* (Cambridge, MA: Harvard University Press, 1959), p. 258.
2. Ron Huisken, *The Meaning and Measurement of Military Expenditures*, SIPRI Research Report No. 10 (Stockholm: SIPRI, 1973), pp. 15–17, 29–32.
3. See Kenneth N. Waltz, *Theory of International Politics* (New York: Random House, 1979) and J. David Singer, *Models, Methods, and Progress in World Politics* (Boulder, CO: Westview, 1990).
4. Waltz, *Theory*, pp. 165, 193 and passim.
5. Singer, *Models*, pp. 163, 242 and passim.
6. Michael Sullivan, *Power in Contemporary International Politics* (Columbia: University of South Carolina Press, 1990), p. 83.
7. Some of this literature is discussed in Chapter 1 below.

1

The Relevant Approaches to Military Power and Trade

While one could find a nearly endless amount of commentary that relates to the subject of military power and commerce, there are several bodies of contemporary literature and a substantial body of traditional literature that relate to this issue in some way. While I present each body of work separately below, it should be stated that these traditions are not as conceptually distinct as I might imply. Despite their differences, there are several areas in each that seem to mingle with one or more of the others. In addition, several of these traditions deal with a similar set of questions, although I will try to minimize repetition.

What follows, then, is an attempt to evaluate the relevance of each tradition for the questions in this study while also attempting to draw out, where appropriate, what these approaches would lead one to expect in terms of a relationship between military power and commerce. While none of these bodies of work has posed the question squarely or tried to investigate the possible systemic relationships between military power and commerce, they all have some implications for the relationship. In addition, much of the traditional literature offers a great deal of the substance of why a relationship between military power and commerce ought to be expected. The reason is that the traditional literature tends to focus on specific military activities, many of which operate in peacetime, while making direct connections between this activity and commerce. Finally I will try to confine the discussion below to the most pertinent points of the literature, rather than present a general evaluation of each approach.

REALISM

Traditional realism does not offer a ready-made framework for the questions in this study any more than do those below, but it does offer two general areas of relevance to the questions in this book. First, there is a strong tendency in realism towards mercantilist reasoning, which contrasts with the underlying liberalism in much of neorealism. This reasoning stems from traditional realism's view that conflicting interests between states are natural conditions in world politics and that this conflict can often enter into commercial relations. Second, realism, like the economic potential for war literature (see below), has a history of focusing on the elements of national power (to use Morgenthau's term). Without repeating myself too much, I will state that this aspect of realism is like the war potential literature. It focuses on all aspects of a country's economy, from its population to agriculture to industry, and tries to evaluate this in terms of a country's power potential.[1] We might derive the same types of connections between military spending and trade as those suggested in the economic potential for war literature below.

The focus on conflicting interests that are intertwined with the economy and the issue of war potential are byproducts of the assumptions in traditional realism that the state is a dominant actor in world politics, that it is rational in its behaviour and that it thinks and acts in terms of power. States pursue their interests, which are defined in terms of power. This is Morgenthau's language, but it communicates the long-held idea that the state has an autonomous system of values (centred on the goal of acquiring and retaining power) that governs its decisions.

These basic assumptions can be held very strictly where the state is a power maximizer, or more loosely where the state merely pursues its own interests, however defined. Stephen Krasner, for example, has a fairly loose definition of a state's interests. He states that the national interest is defined by what states say and do as long as the state's actions are tied to some general public goal and these goals persist over time.[2]

As stated earlier, however, this book is not about realism and it will not be discussed further. I felt it necessary to at least mention some of the general aspects of realism that relate to the questions at hand, but the literature below (some of which might actually be called realism) addresses the issues in a more substantive way.

NAVALIST LITERATURE

The most relevant traditional approach to the problems posed in this book is perhaps the oldest and is located primarily in the literature on sea power and its functions. From classical thinkers, such as Mahan and Corbett, to the present, sea power has been said to perform a host of functions that bear on both trade and shipping. These functions can be offensive or defensive, and be long- or short-term in duration; they can also be implicit or explicit in terms of how they relate to trade.

The most obvious area where sea power relates to trade is economic warfare. There are many definitions of economic warfare. Some view it as operating mainly under conditions of military war between states. Here it becomes a tool to aid in the defeat of an enemy by both strengthening oneself and weakening one's opponent.[3] Some see it as being an alternative to military conflict. Because commercial relations provide the opportunity for influence, economic coercion can take the place of military coercion.[4] From the military standpoint, however, economic warfare involves the use of military power to interrupt the flow and use of resources among countries, and is 'coercively oriented...against an adversary to diminish its power'.[5] This view sees modern economic warfare as being similar to past practices, except that, during the Cold War, it was waged during a period of general military stalemate.[6]

Others take a broader view of economic warfare as something that can involve both military power and many non-military methods, including policy restrictions on trade, credit and financial controls, and shipping regulations.[7] Thus economic warfare can encompass many types of state actions, not all of which involve military power. One could consider the postwar US trade control regime and its multilateral counterpart with CoCOM, for example, to have been a protracted state of economic warfare under conditions of peace.

The military aspects of economic warfare can involve nearly any type of military action, whether it is limited force during peacetime or a greater amount of force during wartime. The *guerre de course* strategy is perhaps one of the oldest examples. *Guerre de course* refers to a naval strategy that is aimed at raiding and destroying the commerce of an enemy as a primary war strategy, as opposed to the traditional goal of acquiring command of the sea.[8] The strategy presupposes a measure of inferiority on the part of the state that adopts it and, in wartime, is an effort to deny to the enemy what the enemy has already denied to oneself.[9] The French pursued this strategy towards Britain in the nineteenth century and part of the twentieth. Germany also pursued a commerce-destroying strategy in both world wars. *Guerre de course* is a strategy for an inferior naval power, whose own commerce is threatened with complete stoppage by a superior navy.[10]

The phenomenon of commerce-raiding, of course, has a long history. It reflects an older mercantilist focus on relative wealth between states, where one state seeks to impose economic injury on another while enriching oneself at the target state's expense.[11] Historically, the privateer was a key agent in this activity. The privateer would receive letters of marque from a sovereign to engage in private war at sea. Privateers began to lose their military value in modern times, however, due to the growth and specialization of naval power and due to the fact that merchant ships became distinct from warships. Indeed, privateers themselves came to require naval protection.[12] And even though privateers were outlawed by the Declaration of Paris of 1856, the phenomenon of prize money on the sea continued. The British navy, for example, continued to collect prize money until after the Second World War.[13] It should be noted that the United States did not ratify the Declaration, partly because it wished to reserve the option of using privateers for the future.[14] The practice of commerce-raiding from the Declaration onward, however, increasingly became a function of professional navies.

Technological changes have altered the status of *guerre de course* over the last century and a half. The advent of steam, for example, gave merchant ships more flexibility in avoiding commerce raiders because merchant vessels became less dependent on wind, and could thus deviate from their routes with greater ease.[15] On the other hand, the advent of the torpedo boat and the submarine, especially when employed on a large scale, made *guerre de course* much more formidable against countries that were dependent on maritime trade.[16] Geography can also be relevant to a *guerre de course* strategy. Mahan thought that the geographical proximity of France to Britain gave the French strategy of *guerre de course* an advantage because it was close to its object of attack. The French cruisers had ports on the North Sea, Channel, and Atlantic, where British trade passed.[17]

The goals of *guerre de course* strategies have been described variously. The immediate goals have to do with attacking merchant shipping, but the ultimate goal is financial disruption. The destruction of shipping and trade would have the effect of driving up maritime insurance and freight costs to the point where trade ceases.[18] This threat led Britain, for example, to anguish over the problem of war insurance before the First World War, as well as to fear the consequences of food shortages. Britain's dependence on overseas food supplies produced talk of 'starvation theory', which underlined Britain's sense of vulnerability in the event of war. There was also fear of the social and labour unrest that could result from food shortages.[19]

In addition to *guerre de course*, navies engage in blockades and embargoes. Blockades and embargoes, of course, are big methods employed by big navies. Bernard Brodie distinguishes between the naval blockade, which limits only the movement of military forces, and the commercial blockade, which aims at stopping trade.[20] The blockade is a total policy aimed at strangulation, while the attack on commerce is a strategy of irritation.[21] Blockades and embargoes, when employed, are the military means by which trade is controlled. Mahan believed that trade control at sea was the equivalent of the command that land powers exercised internally. He stated that the sea's value comes from it being a highway of commerce and communications with 'the concrete expression of this singular importance of the sea [being] the merchandise in transit, the increment from which constitutes the material prosperity of nations'.[22] Mahan even believed that the trade of private citizens, once it is on the sea, is really public property. Because 'money is the sinews of war', and trade is involved in making money for the state, merchandise looses its private character when it is in transit over the seas.[23]

Perhaps the control of trade is not the principal weapon of sea power, as Mahan thought, but it certainly is a long-standing function of sea power whatever its relative strategic value.[24] Michael MccGuire contends that three components of sea-borne trade deserve strategic attention. In addition to goods in transit, or the passage of the ship, he includes the availability of the goods and the availability of shipping as well. Strategic attention should be focused on all three of these elements because all are open to interference.[25]

In addition to these offensive actions that affect trade, there is the entire defensive side of sea power. The concept of command of the sea, or sea control, which is the ultimate strategic concept for the big navy, embodies the very assumption of defence of one's own trade. Definitions of command of the sea abound and I do not want to get too deeply into the niceties of the concept or its problems. It will suffice here to say that command of the sea aims at controlling the conditions under which other navies can operate, including the ability to choose battle or not. Older definitions imply a totality of control of the sea, while modern ones introduce more distinction.[26]

Regardless of the niceties of the concept, then, command of the sea implies the ability to protect one's trade. This includes a host of functions. In war, large navies may defend against *guerre de course* through convoys, where warships escort and protect merchant ships in transit.[27] Some argue that the convoy is the only reliable means of defending against commerce destruction.[28]

There is some controversy, however, about the naval requirements of protecting one's commerce. Commentators have often seen that their own country required more protection than that of others. The common British view before the First World War, for example, was that German naval policy was aimed not at protecting German commerce, but at unseating Britain. The German demand for commerce protection was quite overstated. Some in Britain did argue the unusual case that the German navy meant no harm to Britain and that Britain had no right to stand in Germany's way, but most saw Germany as a menace.[29] At the same time, however, British commentators applied a different standard to

Britain and its needs for protection. For Britain, command of the sea was required before British commerce could be protected.[30] The Germans, of course, maintained a mirror image of the British argument. Tirpitz thought that without battleships, German cruisers and torpedo boats meant nothing, because even they required protection.[31]

In peacetime, a state with a global trading position needs to assure itself of the ability to protect its trade from the very offensive actions noted above, as well as any others (including terrorism and piracy). This requires protection of trade routes, choke points, and access to critical areas.[32] Sometimes these needs are cast in terms of vital commodities, such as oil, and sometimes they are seen as being a more general requirement of an entire trading system.[33] Such a general level of control, of course, also yields a coercive tool against adversaries. Britain's famous 'five keys' were said to dictate European access to the planet, which was the very gate-keeping that Germany was trying to undermine.[34] There is also a large Cold War literature on the perils of the Soviet challenge to the West with specific reference to the need of assuring access to vital trading regions of the planet and the security of trade routes.[35] South Africa and the Cape Route, the Mediterranean, and the Middle East were usually seen as being the most prominent areas. Today the United States spends a considerable amount defending oil supplies from the Middle East, for example, though the estimates of this amount vary widely from between $6 and $60 billion a year.[36]

There is the argument, however, that sea lanes are becoming less important due to the fact that an increasing amount of world commerce, measured in value, travels electronically in the form of investment. Commodity trade is a decreasing component of world commerce.[37] While investment may make up a growing share of international commerce, the amount of commodity trade has grown in absolute terms. In addition, this argument ignores the fact that many commodities are vital to the maintenance of a country's economy, not to mention national security, regardless of what proportion of trade they reflect. Finally, foreign investment itself may produce a commercially relevant use of naval power because it produces property ownership abroad on the part of one's citizens, which may factor into a state's interests. Would Iran not have used military power against a smaller state in 1979 if a smaller state, rather than the United States, had frozen Iran's $12 billion in the wake of the hostage crisis?[38] Would a large country not do the same against a small country? There is some precedent for a large state using its military power to collect debts and punish financial recalcitrance as well.

Finally there are a host of naval actions that have some impact on trade at a smaller level. They include gunboat diplomacy, showing the flag, policing territorial waters, ensuring good order, and enforcing treaty rights and rights of passage. All of these functions are important factors in modern international politics.

James Cable defines gunboat diplomacy in fairly specific terms. He states that:

> Gunboat diplomacy is the use or threat of limited naval force ... in order to secure advantage, or to avert loss, either in the furtherance of an international dispute or against foreign nationals within the territory or the jurisdiction of their own state.[39]

In Cable's definition, gunboat diplomacy falls short of war, but involves more than simply sending the navy to a foreign port in order to show the flag, gain prestige, or serve some other non-coercive end. Gunboat diplomacy involves the coercive use of limited naval force by one nation against another in a dispute; it is used by a strong state against a weak state; and it is identical to coercive diplomacy, except that it always involves the use of naval force in some capacity, while coercive diplomacy is broader in scope.[40]

Cable's definition of gunboat diplomacy mentions nothing about a state's overseas commercial interests. It is probably true that an overt commercial interest in the offensive use of naval force, in the absence of a threat to commerce, is old-fashioned. A good deal of US naval thought in the second half of the nineteenth century, even before Mahan, for example, saw the navy's role as being a principal support to commerce.[41] The United States in the nineteenth and twentieth centuries also maintained an Asiatic Squadron in the Far East, which included gunboats, in part to advance American commerce and protect the lives and property of Americans abroad. The same can be said of other major powers with interests in the Far East at the time. Indeed, the American navy in peacetime was the real trade representative of the country. This was especially true in China, where American gunboats, along with those of various European states, patrolled the territorial waters and rivers of China.[42]

Instances of gunboat diplomacy, however, continued throughout the twentieth century and have not declined. Indeed, the ability of large states to use limited force against small states can also be carried out with air power, and in some cases, land power.[43] One author maintains that the number of states practising gunboat diplomacy may increase for two reasons. One is that there has been a growth in the number of navies with the ability to project power. The other is that the increasingly multipolar world may offer more opportunities for the use of limited force.[44]

The other types of naval activities noted above, such as showing the flag, are aspects of naval diplomacy that are designed to influence the behaviour of another state.[45] Showing the flag, as Cable states, is different from gunboat diplomacy in that gunboat diplomacy is always aimed at attaining some specific advantage; showing the flag can have a variety of outcomes. Showing the flag may just be a reminder of the power and interests of the state in question, or it could have a training or intelligence purpose.[46]

The economic value of the sea itself produces a host of issues that relate directly to naval power. One author notes that since the Second World War, there has been a trend of 'creeping sovereignty' over the seas, which refers to coastal states extending control further out from their coasts.[47] Today, littoral states claim up to a 200-mile exclusive economic zone, which includes territorial rights over the seabed and subsoil resources out to the edge of the continental margin, the fisheries in these waters, rights of passage, pollution control, and related matters.[48] States do have the right of innocent passage for merchant vessels, but the idea of freedom of the seas operates 'inasmuch as any nation may operate ships on them without the permission of other nations'.[49]

Historically, as Koburger indicates, major navies had no real trouble in the narrow seas of the world with respect to passage and the pursuit of their interests, unless the trouble came from another large navy. But modern technology, such as fast craft, submarines, missiles, shore-based defences, and others, have allowed smaller coastal states to deny access in narrow waters without having to develop superior surface forces.[50] It has been argued that this development has deprived the large navy of the ability to command the narrow seas adjacent to an enemy, or has at least made the job of doing so more difficult, and has given the smaller coastal navy a means of influence against the larger ones.[51] These conditions can produce conflict between states. In peacetime, the littoral state exercises its sovereignty, maintains good order, and controls the resources in its territorial waters; the non-littoral state seeks passage, access to local ports, and the use of local resources, such as fishing and mineral exploitation.[52]

There are several issues relating to exclusive economic zones that can lead to conflict. First, the heavy use of resources, including fisheries, may threaten these resources with depletion. This could lead to intensified control over territorial waters. Second, boundary and jurisdictional disputes exist over territorial waters, such as that among Japan, China, and Korea relating to oil and gas resources in the local waters.[53] There are also conflicts over the efforts of straits states to tighten regulation of passage, for reasons of pollution, accidents, and shipping. Coastal states seek to impose restrictions on warships for security reasons. The United States is interested in unimpeded passage of its warships, as was the Soviet Union prior to its collapse. And finally, conflict exists over deep seabed development issues.[54]

The growth in the importance of maritime resources to states underlines the need to ensure order at sea, which has been defined as 'the peaceful regulation of commerce and communications between states of diverse cultures and political structures'.[55] Even if good order always existed, however, larger states may still find it necessary to coerce smaller states to obtain their ends.[56]

The above description of the commercially relevant aspects of naval power shows that commercial and military interests on the sea are intertwined. The very concept of sea power usually includes a set of commercial interests. Even Soviet Admiral Gorshkov included an economic component to his concept of sea power. His definition of sea power is expansive and, aside from its ideological rhetoric, sounds very Mahanian. Gorshkov includes just about all military, commercial, and scientific uses of the sea in his concept of sea power. He states that 'the concept of sea power to a certain degree is identified with the economic power of the state'.[57] Gorshkov includes merchant, fishing, and scientific fleets in his concept of sea power. He states that merchant ships are not only important as a means of transporting cargo, but also have an important reserve role for the navy in time of war.[58]

Gorshkov's thinking, of course, is not very different from traditional Western concepts of sea power, most of which include its commercial aspects. It may be true, however, as one author notes, that there is a more complex relationship between merchant ships and naval power today than was the case in the days of Mahan. Today, many ships (especially American) fly under flags of convenience. In addition, there is an international division of labour in trade. While competition among states could produce change away from the interdependence and openness of the world economy, the current interdependent state of affairs may require that the idea of protecting commerce be put on a broader basis. Shipping has become internationalized and states can have large trading interests without a large merchant fleet. This means that the warships of one flag may have to protect merchant ships of another, which would be in the broader interests of all trading states.[59] To some extent, the extension of commerce protection from one country to another already occurs with the US navy, whose role in protecting trade routes and the flow of commerce benefits much of the world today.

The naval literature focuses on the use of military power on the sea for political, commercial, and military ends, with some set of assumptions about the political and commercial pay-offs to be obtained. The commercial and military aspects of the sea are not clearly separable. Geoffrey Till states that distinctions between economic and military operations, in terms of attacking maritime communications, have historically been blurred because the sea is a common arena for both activities.[60]

While the above literature provides the substance of interactions between military power and commerce on the sea, it does so from a navalist viewpoint. This means that the concepts discussed are assessed largely in terms of their naval and strategic utility. The purpose of the above, however, is to underline the fact that, regardless of the relative war-fighting value of any of the above concepts, they are crucial for trade. Their importance may be relative and subject to debate from the naval standpoint, but their importance from the trading standpoint is closer to being absolute. The power to control, destroy, or advance trade through military power is independent of market mechanisms. Indeed, the very survival of international trade markets is a function of the military environment, inasmuch as markets require protection from the aggressive acts of others.

ARMIES AND AIR POWER

With some qualification, it could be argued that much of the above also applies to land power and perhaps even air power. It is traditional to assert that armies are a less flexible instrument of statecraft than navies. One reason for this may be that the use of armies abroad implies political commitment, while navies can be employed and withdrawn.[61] This may be another way of saying that armies do not have the same fluidity of movement that navies have because the land areas of the planet are fenced off by sovereignty. Navies have the high seas as well as innocent passage in many parts of the world. Mahan thought that the superior mobility of the sea over the land gave countries with access to the sea an advantage in pushing their commerce forward, especially in Asia.[62] Despite this, however, land power has historically played a crucial role for a country's commerce in both contiguous and far-off areas.

The sovereign control of a state's own borders, guaranteed and sometimes administered by its army, gives the state the power to regulate, tax, and even interrupt trade. Nearly all states have this capacity and may use it in wartime or as a means of revenue creation, coercion, and influence in peacetime.[63] Similar to Mahan when he states that private property loses its private nature when on the sea, R. G. Hawtrey states that sovereignty confers what amounts to property rights over its territory. This gives states the power to grant and withhold these rights, especially with respect to development concessions.[64] In addition, dominant land states that occupy a hegemonic position in a region can prevent sea powers from gaining trading access to areas – such as with the Continental blockade of British trade by Napoleonic France. This may be a land power's equivalent to the command exercised by large sea powers.[65]

Among countries that are linked together by land routes, some cooperation is usually required with regard to national road and rail links, but such matters often become entangled in the power and interests of the states in question. This is especially true with the issue of access to sea and air corridors.[66] A corridor to the sea, which traverses another state's territory, implies a transfer of sovereignty to the inland state.[67] The granting of corridors has always been problematic. In some cases, notably Germany after the First World War, foreign access through a corridor can leave a lasting grudge on the part of the conceding state. For this reason the idea of transit rights was accepted at the Barcelona Conference on Freedom of Transit in 1921, where 40 countries signed a convention, granting inland states 'the same facilities for access to the sea...as if the journey had taken place on the territory of a single state'.[68] Despite the acceptance of transit rights, however, the practice of transit has diminished because states have used their ability to interfere with the transit of goods for their own political purposes.

The Cold War division of Europe also diminished the practice, despite the maintenance of the legal status of transit rights.[69] The Berlin Blockade in 1948 itself was a case study of this very problem over land. While this crisis is usually not viewed from this standpoint, it was indeed a case of land power stopping access to an exclave. The exclave was then threatened with commercial starvation, which was remedied only by the air power of the United States.

In addition, armies can be sent overseas to occupy territory. Armies enter foreign territory either by invitation or by force. The colonial armies of France and Britain acted as garrisons and police forces. The British Indian Army grew as a private arm of the East India Company. As the Company's trade on the continent spread, along with its system of treaties and acquisitions, the army established 'cordon sanitaires within which trade could prosper'.[70] As time wore on and the administration of India was taken over by the British government (after the 1857 mutiny), the Indian Army became a general tool of colonial policy. The French colonial experience reveals a similar story. Although there is a tendency to idealize French colonial and army policy as not being oriented towards 'crass commerce', but being the tool of a grand civilizing mission.[71] But the French too required order for the maintenance of commerce. The colonial army was also the ultimate guarantor of French colonial policy in the interwar years, which became increasingly protectionist.

Russian expansion into Central Asia and the Far East throughout the nineteenth century and earlier was also colonial in nature, housing the same mix of political, commercial, exploratory, and military objectives that were present in Western colonial expansion.[72] There has been a strong tendency to demonize Russian expansionary behaviour in the West, as if it were somehow driven by forces that were both sinister and different from those driving Western expansion, but Russian behaviour appears to be no different from the British movement into India or even the American movement out towards the Pacific Ocean. Each came with the same amalgam of motives (exploration, ores, hides and, later, trade) and each came with an ideology that justified the move. The Russians had a literary tradition of messianism that extolled the virtues of Russian civilization while justifying their expansion that was quite like Manifest Destiny in North America or the Rhodesian-style rhetoric on British civilization and the *civilizing mission.*

In fact the practice of demonizing Russian expansion probably began with the British, who feared Russian movements southward towards India. While idealizing the British Empire, British imperialists pointed to the Russian menace. In some ways, the geopolitics of Halford MacKinder may be just a massive exaggeration of this tendency to demonize Russian movements southward in defence of British movements northwards.

While colonial occupation is a thing of the past, it offers a wealth of experience regarding the relationship between security over land and trade expansion. All the colonial armies expanded along with transport infrastructures, soon followed by stable trade flows. The old school of political geography often portrayed the evolution of a political community as moving towards becoming an economic unit. This involved a territorial exploration and settlement process, followed by boundary evolution. Military force was thought to be a necessary instrument in this process.[73]

While colonial armies are gone, however, similar security functions are performed by alliances and occupation. Could Soviet trade control policies in Eastern Europe, which involved a coercive reorientation of East European trade away from the West and towards Moscow with the CMEA, have been implemented and sustained without long-term occupation by the Soviet army? Could Western Europe have rebuilt and participated in the US-centred postwar economic order without being subverted, in the absence of alliance with the United States? We may ask the same about South Korea in light of North Korea, and even about Japan. Could Japan's rehabilitation after the war (perhaps after the start of the Korean War) have been as successful if the Soviet army jointly occupied the country along with the American army in a manner similar to that of Germany?

Finally, air power has some bearing on commerce as well. The air power theorists of the interwar years, of course, tended to hold extreme positions on the future of air power. Most attributed capabilities to air power that had some bearing on trade, however. Douhet's notion of the massive air attack required the selection of industrial and urban targets. While this type of activity has been used in war, Douhet's reasoning that such bombing would exploit the fragility of civilian morale may have underestimated civilians. Douhet also thought that aircraft would remain general all-purpose weapons, as opposed to becoming functionally specialized, as between bombers and fighters,[74] whereas air power became much more complicated than he had envisioned it to be.

William Mitchell argued that bombing from the air could sink ships, both warships and merchant ships. Air power and submarines together would menace surface vessels to the point where they would decline in importance and become auxiliaries to armies and air forces.[75] Mitchell also thought that aircraft could control sea communications, which could be used to starve into submission a country dependent on maritime trade.[76] The strategy of *guerre de course*, then, would be carried on from the air. De Seversky also thought that 'air power has achieved primacy in modern warfare... [and] the first and decisive arena of modern conflict is neither on land nor on sea but in the skies, in the "air ocean"'.[77]

These views of air power, put forth in absolute terms, never fully materialized. Air power remains a support for land and sea power. Nevertheless, air power is also flexible in terms of its ability to strike and withdraw, especially when used in conjunction with sea power. It should be noted, however, that air power does not directly parallel land and sea power in terms of having a commercial component. While some commerce is carried through the air (varying from country to country), the majority of commerce goes by sea and then land. Commerce carried through the air is a fraction of that in the other two environments. People travel long distance by air more than by sea, but the commercially relevant aspects of its military uses are linked to sea and land movement.

While the naval and related literature above provides information about how military power and commerce interact, it does so from a traditional viewpoint. There is no effort to explore the full nature of this relationship, nor is there any attempt to find generalizations. In addition, this literature evaluates the above connections in terms of their role in strategy and war-fighting, not from the standpoint of trade. The literature remains descriptive and focused primarily on military debates. I will address in Chapter 3 what these naval and military activities imply about the relationship between military power and trade. The military connections above are so diverse in nature that the task of deriving possible relationships is difficult at best.

ECONOMIC POTENTIAL FOR WAR

Another school of thought related to the questions at hand is also an older one that finds only a modified descendant in the current literature. This school focused on the issue of economic potential for war and saw its high point in the 1940s. There is a vast literature dealing with war planning as it relates to resources, labour, industrial potential, weapons manufacture, and economic controls. Most of these early works also saw self-sufficiency in key items as being crucial for war potential,[78] which often produced calls for a variety of mercantilist policies to lessen wartime vulnerability, such as stockpiling materials that the home country lacked naturally, restrictions on exports, reductions of luxury imports and a host of related policies.[79] The United States very often ignored such concerns until a threat emerged that drove home the military significance of economic activity. This was evident in US policy towards the merchant shipping industry before both world wars. Free trade arguments for competition and a hands-off approach to shipping often won the day until a clear military threat emerged, which underscored the military significance of merchant ships.[80]

This approach focuses on the resource requirements of nations, but it often goes further to consider all relevant aspects of an economy as they relate to war potential, including the labour force. Klaus Knorr's work represents perhaps the major themes of this literature. He defines economic potential for war as 'the ultimate capacity of a belligerent to produce combat power',[81] although he later broadened the scope of the concept. Knorr notes a distinction between economic potential for war and military potential for war. The first is a broader concept that encompasses nearly every aspect of the economy that affects a nation's ability to fight a war, and the second is focused only on the military means.[82] This approach also sought to catalogue the various elements of national power, as a checklist or 'power inventory'.[83]

Knorr states that the concept of economic potential for war declined because of the expectation that future wars, involving nuclear weapons, would not be attritional. In a nuclear war the decisive blows would come in the beginning. The advent of nuclear weapons meant that 'there definitely is no future for World War II',[84] and the concept declined. But the oil shocks of the 1970s and the renewed awareness of the Soviet threat after 1979, along with its expanded navy, may very well have revived the notion. The oil shocks also created awareness of the need for peacetime security of access to oil and other raw materials among industrial countries. Contemporary anxiety about secure access to minerals has led to similar policy demands, such as stockpiling minerals that a country had a shortage of.

The United States, for example, maintains a strategic petroleum reserve. It was at a mere 7.46 million barrels at the end of 1977, but has increased enormously since then. During the 1990s, the United States maintained an amount that fluctuated between 500 and 600 million barrels (it was 567 million barrels in 1999).[85] Much of the modern concern about oil security, however, is also over price stability and the economy as a whole. Unstable oil prices are thought to be as significant a threat to an industrial economy as the loss of access is.[86] Perhaps sharply rising oil prices will produce another episode of stagflation. Fear of such a development reminds one of Britain's traditional fear of instability in insurance rates and food prices engendered by *guerre de course*.

The economics of stockpiling may be ambiguous,[87] but there are a variety of reasons why a country may stockpile commodities. These include constrained access to commodities, price suppression (especially if the commodity is controlled by a cartel), and military/strategic reasons. It has even been suggested that countries could begin stockpiling commodities in order to offset the effects of US sanctions directed towards them.[88] If this were true, then stockpiling could be a tool to defend against aggressive military actions that bear upon commerce.

From the standpoint of war potential, then, trade is relevant for military power as a means to address domestic economic short-comings, to overcome military vulnerabilities, and to feed war production. This may work as long as trade is secure. The possibility of constrained access just mentioned creates a vulnerability that also calls for a military role. This is classic mercantilist reasoning, which points to some form of trade control policy, such as seeking to maintain a favourable trade balance, importing commodities for stockpiling, or using military power to secure access to overseas supplies of minerals. This thinking is also criticized by liberal thought on trade (see Chapter 2).

The issue of economic potential for war may seem like an old-fashioned notion, but the idea never really went away and actually may be more relevant today than it was in the past. There is a contemporary debate over this very question, but the issues are couched in different terms. The current debate points to vulnerabilities caused by trade expansion – that is, the outflow of resources to other countries, technology transfer, the loss of capabilities, and so on. It focuses on the same question, but from the other end of the trade flow. It is generally the concern of the wealthy country – how it can stem the loss of manufacturing capability in critical items or stem the exports of materials to potential adversaries – whereas the earlier debates saw trade expansion as a means to acquire military resources (and thus reduce one's vulnerabilities), which, today, may very well be the perspective of the weaker country. A principal theme in this newer literature is how a country's economic potential for war has been influenced by economic interdependence, the opening of markets and changing comparative advantage. This sense of vulnerability is focused on the major economies in the world and their ability to obtain security.

Some of this work tries to assess the degree to which the United States has lost the ability to produce militarily significant items and what to do about it. Theodore Moran, for example, argues for a policy of 'sophisticated neomercantilism', which recognizes that when the supply of a specific military item is concentrated in too few foreign markets, then there is a need for the United States to maintain an ability to produce the item.[89] The traditional attitude on this matter was a call for a blanket policy of economic autarky in the areas vital to national security, but Moran recognizes that such a policy is both unnecessary and unreasonable in the modern world. He recognizes that counteracting comparative advantage imposes costs on a society. Thus a blanket policy of autarky in military items would be too damaging to an economy.

Others have argued on the other side of this issue, that the ready availability of military resources through ordinary market channels poses a security problem for the exporting country. Still others focus on how to maintain a national advantage in technology given the nature of free trade and interdependence.[90]

This literature is focused on vulnerability (and even decline) because of the loss of capabilities due to comparative advantage and to the acquisition of military capability by potential adversaries, and because it is concerned with the problems of advanced countries (such as the United States). But there are two sides to every coin. We could view this literature from the standpoint of the less developed, but ambitious, country. Such a country may be gaining access to military technology and resources through trade. In other words, from the viewpoint of the smaller countries, the vulnerabilities of the advanced countries are their opportunities, which actually speaks to the older tradition of literature above – that is, using trade as a means to feed war potential.

The current debate over the economic potential for war obviously relates to both the interdependence (see Chapter 2) and the decline literatures (below). The modern variants of this literature are actually part of a broader literature that deals with the connections between national security and the world economy more generally. This literature touches on many of the themes in the debates noted in this chapter.[91]

One of the dangers in this literature is that it is easy to overstate the presence of vulnerability or the resource requirements for security. Because of this, older literature had a clear tendency to be dramatic and indiscriminate in the call for a policy to address the problem at hand. While the connections between trade and military power appear to be straightforward in this literature, there is a good deal of ambiguity.

We can state generally, for example, that military power depends on trade if the country in question imports materials that are important for its military power. But here we have numerous possibilities, each of which may contain different forms of this relationship. If the country imports finished military goods, for example, then trade fuels military power in an immediate way. If the country imports capital goods that are used to develop its industry which, in turn, may produce military goods, then the relationship is less immediate and more long-term in nature. If the country imports raw materials that are important for domestic military industries that already exist, then the relationship is a longer-term one as well. And if the import of military items is thought to reflect a vulnerability, then this vulnerability could produce a military role to protect access to trade. If this is true, then we have an even more complicated relationship. Here military power depends on imports, but the security of imports depends on the employment of that military power.

If the country exports military goods, technology, or resources, then the relationship is more complex. If the exports threaten to deplete critical goods or resources that are needed for domestic military production, then exports could have a negative impact on military power (although this seems unlikely to occur). There could also be a negative relationship if one's exports fuel the military power of an adversary, which is a more likely scenario. As the adversary becomes more powerful due to the militarily significant imports, the exporting country becomes relatively weaker. This relative change in the balance of power between the two countries could, in turn, motivate the exporting country to increase its military power in response, which would make the relationship all the more compli-cated. At the extreme end, it is conceivable that an arms race could start between the exporting country and the importing country, all fuelled by the exports in the first place.

Might this not be at least partially true of the US–China relationship today? American exports to China include many militarily significant items. Up to the Tiananmen Square crisis in 1989, the

United States permitted a wide array of military technologies to be sent to China and offered military advisers as well. Throughout the Clinton years, some of the post-Tiananmen restrictions were lifted as well. The US also maintains a large overall trade deficit with China, which provides China with very large net inflows of income each year. US–China relations, however, are fraught with hostility and perhaps even competition. If US threat assessment of China, and any resulting war planning, are influenced by China's military capability, and if US exports to China have at least partly fuelled Chinese military power, then it is very reasonable to assert that US exports to China play a role in fuelling the military competition between them.

Exports of goods in general (military or not) may produce a role for military power more generally, however. The security of trade routes and access to export markets can generate a military role in the same way that access and security apply to imports. These issues will be addressed more fully in Chapter 3.

HEGEMONY AND RISE AND DECLINE LITERATURE

The rise and decline tradition is an old one, but the more recent work in this area seems most relevant to this study. In much of the contemporary work, military power is discussed not necessarily in terms of trade, specific commodities, or war production, but in terms of a country's economy as a whole. It is said that the size and capability of a state's military power, and thus its strategic position, is ultimately dependent on the size, productivity, and technological capabilities of its economy. This position is an old one, but is the basis of recent debates over decline in the United States. One may argue that this literature was unduly pessimistic, however, and may have been born of the stagflation and sluggishness of the 1970s.

Paul Kennedy's thinking, for example, is based on two propositions. First, change in history is driven fundamentally by economic and technological change. Second, uneven growth rates affect the military and strategic position of states, which reflects the view that military power is dependent upon an economy's ability to afford it. The rise and decline of states, then, is explainable in terms of this uneven growth. When a hegemonic state's military commitments begin to outstrip its economic ability to pay for them, coupled with the arrival of new and lean competitors, the hegemonic state begins to decline and is pushed down the path of history.[92]

Robert Gilpin puts forth a similar thesis, although in more theoretical terms. Gilpin wants to explain change in the international system as being a function of hegemonic decline (and usually hegemonic wars). He states that due to changing interests and uneven growth among states, 'the international system moves from a condition of equilibrium to one of disequilibrium'.[93] Disequilibrium emerges because of a change in the balance of costs and benefits between maintaining or changing the system on the part of the states in it. Gilpin's explanation is based on five assumptions: a system will remain stable if it is unprofitable for a state to change it; a state will seek change if the benefits of doing so outweigh the costs; a state will seek this change through territorial, political, and economic expansion until the marginal costs of any further change are equal to or greater than the marginal benefits; once equilibrium is reached between the costs and benefits of further change, the economic costs of maintaining the system rise faster than the capability to support the system; if this state of affairs continues, the system will change, with the hegemonic power declining and a new equilibrium emerging.[94]

Contemporary arguments about US economic decline and its security implications also note that the principal problem is consumption being larger than savings and investment. Trade deficits and rising costs are the superficial problems.[95] Others see US industrial and technological decline as having eroded the foundations of the postwar security system. The emergence of industrial innovation elsewhere is creating the basis for new security systems.[96] Literature in the 1980s and early 1990s tended to see Western Europe and Japan as being the main beneficiaries of this process. As the United States declined and the Soviet Union retreated, Japan rose to immense wealth and Western Europe stood poised for economic union and autonomy.[97] The future is said to offer two general alternatives for world trade relations: a managed multilateralism (the best option) or a regional mercantilism (the worst option), or vacillation between these two positions.[98]

While it is reasonable to assume that a state's military power depends on a country's economic ability to afford it, much of this literature (and interdependence literature as well) portrays the state as behaving like a rational consumer or even a firm. What does it mean when Gilpin says that the system will remain stable as long as it remains unprofitable to change it? How is profit, from the state's point of view, even calculated? While some of this literature may come under the umbrella of neorealism, there is an underlying liberalism in the reasoning here where the state is thought to be focused on maximizing welfare. Sometimes it is difficult to understand what is being said here because the notion of welfare is left vague in this literature. Does welfare refer to the economic well-being of a population? Does it mean net benefits in the sense of welfare economics? Or does welfare refer to non-economic, perhaps military, goals for the state itself?

The state may be concerned with welfare, or maximizing economic benefit and minimizing costs for its consumers, when it comes to many economic policies, but it is also concerned with matters of economic power in the old sense of the term. This means that the state will not always act in ways that are rational from the standpoint of welfare maximization or even some notion of profitability (if it could be calculated). The very presence of stockpiling policies that militate against efficiency, for example, shows that the state does not always behave like a value-maximizing consumer.

Mancur Olson puts forth a critique of mercantilist policy choices that is fully grounded in the liberal perspective. He demonstrates that concerns over war shortages and much of the above thinking are irrational from the standpoint of consumer choice theory. He looks at food shortages in Britain's history during three major wars and shows that much of the mercantilist thinking about shortages and their consequences is false.[99] Olson, of course, is trying to put forth a consumer choice approach to the issue against traditional mercantilist thinking. The basic idea is that it is arbitrary and wrong to consider some goods necessities and others luxuries from a consumer choice perspective because any good will bring about the same amount of satisfaction at the level of marginal expenditures. The composition of consumer expenditures on various goods will determine their overall importance. Thus a marginal increase in petroleum may be no more important than a marginal increase in wine.[100] Both bring about the same amount of satisfaction to the consumer.

The fact that states do behave in mercantilist ways shows that they are not just rational consumers. This was understood quite clearly in older literature, which juxtaposed the *economic power* approach and the *economic welfare* approach during the interwar years. While most of these works argued that the welfare approach was consistent with peace and the other with war, they understood that state policies on economic matters could be rational from the power approach and irrational from the welfare approach.[101]

If we are to look at a mercantilist policy choice as being irrational from a consumer choice point of view, then we assume that the state's decision-making is governed by the larger society's utility maximizing behaviour. The reason for this is that the mercantilist policy is either unnecessary or altogether fails to fulfil the utility maximizing goal. It may be a sub-optimal policy that keeps utility below its maximum, which makes it an irrational policy. But if the state is actually pursuing a mercantilist policy to begin with (which is presumably why we are criticizing the state in the first place), then the state is obviously not governed by a utility maximizing calculus that resembles the decision-making of the consumer. It is, instead, behaving like a mercantilist. If the state is trying to achieve power objectives, then, how can we say that the state's policy choices are irrational (provided that the policies do not also fail to produce power)?

Obviously the state is not just mercantilist. It also engages in behaviour that is designed to serve the welfare aims of society. When it comes to the debate over liberal versus mercantilist policies in trade, though, the above literature often seems to confuse the difference between what is and what ought to be. The criticism of state behaviour comes with advice on what policy should be pursued. This is the *ought* portion of the argument. But the analysis is usually cast in scientific-empirical terms, which is what economic theory claims to be. This is the *what is* portion of the argument. If the state is mercantilist in some of its decisions, then this *is* the fact to observe. How can we then say that the state is wrong or irrational? Are we trying to argue that the state is violating the laws of science? If so, then why are the facts of state behaviour not valid empirical observations on how states actually are? If we simply observe the facts, then we will develop a theory that says that the state is sometimes mercantilist in its behaviour. Perhaps this conflict is due to the idea that the state is a major portion of the economy in terms of resources and policies and, at the same time, not a welcome portion of the economy. The state is some non-economic force that intrudes into the economy which, if left alone, would operate according to the scientific principles reflected in economic theory.

More will be said about these issues in later chapters. Suffice it to state here that the militarily significant aspects of economic policies are not necessarily intelligible from the standpoint of liberal assumptions. If the state were just a 'consumer' there would be no problem with this reasoning. But the state is also a 'soldier' that thinks in terms of maximizing military values, not the enjoyment of income. Thus it may not be arbitrary for the state to impose the judgement that some goods are more important than others. Pursuing an economically inefficient policy, such as subsidizing the merchant shipping industry, may also be quite rational, despite the fact that those resources could be put to better use from the welfare perspective.

What does the rise and decline literature imply for the relationship between military power and commerce? Kennedy's argument may imply a different relationship at each stage of a state's career. When a state is rising, military expansion and trade expansion move together. When the hegemon is declining, they become inverse. In the case of the rising state, the direct association between trade and military power could reflect two different processes. One would be that the rising state enjoys a growing economy. Because the economy is growing, both trade and military power are expanding. Trade growth is led by growth in the productive capacity of an economy (with exports) and growth in domestic demand (with imports). Military expansion is supported by expanding wealth, which allows the state to afford it. If this were the association between the two, then it would be a spurious one if the composition of trade were not linked to the military. The real cause of the association would be the economy's growth in general. The association between military power and trade would be coincidental because each are caused by the same third variable. This association would not be spurious if trade were also fuelling military power, but this relates to the previous argument.

It is also possible to argue that military expansion in the rising phase is led by expanding state interests that are at least partly defined by trade expansion. Kennedy implies this when discussing the role of the British navy in the nineteenth century, for example. If this were the case, then the direct association would reflect the same sort of arguments that the navalist literature above points to. Generally we would see military expansion as acting as a support mechanism for commercial expansion.

In the decline phase of the state, we would expect military power and trade to be inversely related. The reason for this may be that when the state is declining its military commitments are thought to outstrip its economy. This could imply that trade is declining (or at least the trade deficit is growing), especially as the declining state confronts more efficient competitors. Thus the state tries to maintain its military commitments (where the costs of doing so may be growing), while its trade begins to suffer. This argument is related to the military spending and economic growth literature. The more recent hypothesis in this work is that military spending has a negative impact on economic growth, though there are a long list of reasons offered for this.[102] Most of this literature is grounded in conventional macroeconomics, although some of it is designed to substantiate the Kennedy argument.[103]

GEOPOLITICS AND RAW MATERIALS

Geopolitical literature offers several areas of relevance to the questions of this study, but the one that is most obvious involves the strategic and geopolitical significance of raw materials. While there is a massive literature on raw materials, not all of it is concerned with strategic issues. Much of this literature is simply economic and political. But the strategic significance of raw materials has been discussed since the emergence of geopolitical writing itself.

The strategic literature on raw materials often focuses on the problem of access in time of war or the need to control raw materials as a requirement for national greatness.[104] It was a long-standing conviction in the older geopolitical literature that all great countries possess a hinterland in order to complement the needs of an industrial centre (an ecumene). If a country lacked adequate raw materials, this was traditionally thought to bar a country from greatness.[105] Whether these assumptions are good ones or not (indeed, one can argue that they are not), they have informed geopolitical literature. This thinking was expanded by MacKinder, who saw Russia's resource potential as being the material to produce great military power.[106] Strangely, he did not see the United States in the same way.

It was sometimes said that the trend of the age was for smaller political units to disappear as larger units absorbed them. This was thought to be a function of the needs of modern industrialized warfare, because the larger units would provide larger populations and more raw materials.[107] This very issue was perhaps present in nineteenth-century European anxieties towards the United States and Russia. The victory of the north in the American Civil War, postwar reconstruction, industrialization, and tougher trade competition from the United States led to calls for a continental alliance against the United States. The European press saw American competition as being a menace and called for some type of concerted action against the United States.[108] These fears were only reinforced by near collisions between the United States and various European states, such as those with Germany in 1887 over Samoa and Britain in 1895 in a Venezuelan dispute. And the United States defeated Spain in 1898, which added to European fears.[109] Fears about the economic rise of the United States, of course, later gave way to the same fears over Germany's rise. The view that direct political control over raw materials was a necessity also drove calls for national expansion and the acquisition of colonies.[110] The concern for raw materials was frequently linked to the perceived need for population outlets as well.[111]

The pre-Second World War thinking on raw materials, of course, also had its critics. It was commonplace to hear that the central problem of raw materials was that the need for them was international while control over them was national. This disparity was thought to be a cause of war, which could be solved by creating some form of international control over them.[112]

The Cold War also spawned a wealth of geopolitical literature on raw materials. This literature tended to see the problem in terms of US–Soviet conflict and the need for secure access to raw materials for the West. The Middle East and South Africa were prominent areas of focus. The Soviet Union was often seen as attempting to expand its influence and control to areas of critical Western dependence on the raw materials in the area.[113] This concern was often linked to expanding Soviet sea power as well.

The above literature is perhaps the only area where geopolitics has discussed trade of any kind in more than a cursory way. Many traditional geopolitical works deal only superficially with economic matters, which has perhaps been a major limitation of the whole geopolitical tradition. As alluded to in the above description, however, geopolitics employs mercantilist reasoning in its approach to economic matters as well, one that recalls older discussions of *power economy* versus *welfare economy*, only it does so unsystematically.

Much geopolitical work has also engaged in massive generalizations without presenting sufficient evidence. The grand picture of the emerging Russian threat in the heartland, first outlined by MacKinder and later revived during the Cold War, for example, was perhaps a massive exaggeration that failed to take into account the economic, political, and logistical difficulties that stood in the way of Russia.[114] Russia could not even subdue Afghanistan in 1979, let alone invade India and take it away from Britain one hundred years earlier. MacKinder was perhaps a good British imperialist who turned Anglo-Russian rivalry in Central Asia into a grand call for opposition to any threat to British power.

Despite the weaknesses in geopolitical literature, its focus on raw materials and trade as a source of power and even vulnerability to states, which calls forth a military role, places this slice of geopolitical literature in the same camp as much of the above.

NOTES

1. See Hans J. Morgenthau, *Politics Among Nations* (New York: McGraw-Hill, 1985) 6th edn, revised by Kenneth W. Thompson, pp. 127–69.
2. See Stephen D. Krasner, *Defending the National Interest: Raw Materials Investments and US Foreign Policy* (Princeton, NJ: Princeton University Press, 1978), pp. 42–5. See also by Krasner, 'State Power and the Structure of International Trade', W*orld Politics* 28/3 (April 1976), pp. 317–47, where he employs a similar concept of the state.
3. Paul Einzig, *Economic Warfare* (London: Macmillan, 1940), pp. 1–2, and Neill H. Alford, Jr. and N. Neill, *Modern Economic Warfare: Law and the Naval Participant* (Washington, DC: GPO, 1967), p. 11.
4. Albert O. Hirschman, *National Power and the Structure of Foreign Trade* (Berkeley: University of California Press, 1945), p. 15. John C. Scharfen sees economic warfare as being the use of economic weapons or using economic force to achieve an end, just as the state uses military force. He calls for the same type of clarity regarding means and ends that exists when it comes to using military force. See his *The Dismal Battlefield: Mobilizing for Economic Conflict* (Annapolis, MD: Naval Institute Press, 1995).
5. Alford, *Modern Economic Warfare*, p. 11.
6. Ibid., p. 1.
7. Klaus Knorr, *The Power of Nations: The Political Economy of International Relations* (New York: Basic Books, 1975), pp. 138–9, and Yuan-Li Wu, *Economic Warfare* (New York: Prentice-Hall, 1952), pp. 6–8.

8. Bernard Brodie, *A Guide to Naval Strategy* (Princeton, NJ: Princeton University Press, 1944), p. 137.
9. Brodie, *A Guide*, p. 137.
10. Bernard Brodie, *Sea Power in the Machine Age* (Princeton, NJ: Princeton University Press, 1941), p. 103.
11. Nicholas Tracy, *Attack On Maritime Trade* (Toronto: University of Toronto Press, 1991), p. 17.
12. Ibid., pp. 18–19, 24.
13. Ibid.
14. Edwin B. Hooper, *United States Naval Power in a Changing World* (New York: Praeger, 1988), p. 101.
15. Brodie, *Sea Power*, pp. 103–4.
16. Brodie, *A Guide*, p. 139, and Eric J. Grove, *The Future of Sea Power* (Annapolis, MD: Naval Institute Press, 1990), p. 15.
17. Alfred T. Mahan, *The Influence of Sea Power Upon History: 1660–1783* (1890; reprint, New York: Sagamore Press, 1957), p. 27.
18. Geoffrey Till, *Maritime Strategy and the Nuclear Age* (New York: St. Martin's Press, 1982), pp. 150–1, 155.
19. Arthur J. Marder, *The Anatomy of British Sea Power: A History of British Naval Policy in the Pre-Dreadnought Era, 1880–1905* (New York: Alfred A. Knopf, 1940), pp. 84–6. For an in-depth study of this issue, see also Margaret L. Barnett, *British Food Policy During the First World War* (Boston, MD: George Allen and Unwin, 1985).
20. Charles W. Koburger, Jr., *Narrow Seas, Small Navies, and Fat Merchantmen: Naval Strategies for the 1990s* (New York: Praeger, 1990), p. 43.
21. Brodie, *Sea Power*, p. 329.
22. Alfred T. Mahan, *The Problem of Asia and its Effect Upon International Policies* (Boston, MA: Little, Brown, 1900), p. 51.
23. Ibid., p. 53.
24. Tracy, *Attack*, p. 2.
25. Michael MccGwire, 'Maritime Strategy and the Super-Powers,' in Jonathan Alford (ed.), *Sea Power and Influence: Old Issues and New Challenges* (London: IISS, 1980), p. 58.
26. Hedley Bull states that, due to modern technology, command of the sea today will be less than absolute, with sea control being the more likely. He also states that it is reasonable only to seek command of one's own territorial waters and their approaches, unless in cooperation with allies. Hedley Bull, 'Sea Power and Political Influence', in Jonathan Alford (ed.), *Sea Power and Influence: Old Issues and New Challenges* (London: IISS, 1980), p. 7.
27. For an overview of the nature and practice of convoys, see John Winton, *Convoy: The Defence of Sea Trade, 1890–1990* (London: Michael Joseph, 1983).
28. Grove, *Future*, p. 15.
29. E. L. Woodward, *Great Britain and the German Navy* (Oxford: Clarendon, 1935), p. 54.
30. Marder, *Anatomy*, pp. 97–8.
31 Peter Padfield, *The Great Naval Race: The Anglo-German Naval Rivalry, 1900–1914* (New York: David McKay, 1974), pp. 55–6.
32. See Robert J. Hanks, *The Cape Route: Imperiled Western Lifeline* (Cambridge, MA: Institute for Foreign Policy Analysis, 1981).
33. See Ewan W. Anderson, *Strategic Minerals: The Geopolitical Problems for the United States* (New York: Praeger, 1988).
34. Britain's Admiral Fisher stated that '5 keys lock up the world! Singapore, the

Cape, Alexandria, Gibraltar, Dover. These five keys belong to England, and the five great Fleets of England will hold these keys!' Quoted in Marder, *Anatomy*, p. 473.

35. See, for example, Hanks, *The Cape Route*; also by same author, *The Unnoticed Challenge: Soviet Maritime Strategy and the Global Choke Points* (Cambridge, MA: Institute for Foreign Policy Analysis, 1980).

36. For reviews of the literature on this and the difficulties in deriving estimates see Patricia S. Hu, 'Estimates of 1996 US Military Expenditures on Defending Oil Supplies from the Middle East: Literature Review' (August 1997), at www-cta.ornl.gov/Publications/military.pdf; and Mark DeLucchi and James Murphy, 'US Military Expenditures to Protect the Use of Persian Gulf Oil for Motor Vehicles' (April 1996), at www.uctc.net/papers/325.pdf.

37. Grove, *Future*, p. 179.

38. For a good discussion of the freezing of Iranian assets in the United States, see Benjamin J. Cohen, *In Whose Interests? International Banking and American Foreign Policy* (New Haven, CT: Yale, 1986), pp. 147–76.

39. James Cable, *Gunboat Diplomacy: Political Applications of Limited Naval Force* (New York: Praeger, 1971), p. 21.

40. Ibid., pp. 20–1.

41. For an excellent study of this, see Kenneth J. Hagan, *American Gunboat Diplomacy and the Old Navy: 1877–1889* (Westport, CT: Greenwood Press, 1973).

42. For a concise discussion of US naval policy and diplomacy toward the Far East, with specific attention to China, from the late nineteenth century into the 1920s, see Bernard D. Cole, *Gunboats and Marines: The United States Navy in China, 1925–1928* (Newark: University of Delaware Press, 1983), especially pp. 24–44.

43. The early air power theorists, of course, saw it as providing nearly unlimited force against transport and economic infrastructures. See references to Douhet, Seversky and Mitchell below. Also see below for the role of armies in securing trade over land.

44. Grove, *Future*, p. 196.

45. Till, *Maritime Strategy*, p. 209.

46. James Cable, *Navies in Violent Peace* (New York: St. Martin's Press, 1989), pp. 71–3.

47. Koburger, *Narrow Seas*, pp. 99–100.

48. Ibid.

49. A. D. Couper, *The Geography of Sea Transport* (London: Hutchinson University Library, 1972), p. 65.

50. Koburger, *Narrow Seas*, pp. xv–xvi.

51. Ibid.

52. Ibid., p. 101.

53. See, for example, Mark J. Valencia, 'Northeast Asia: Petroleum Potential, Jurisdictional Claims and International Relations', *Ocean Development and International Law* 20/1 (1989), pp. 35–61.

54. Robert E. Osgood, 'Military Implications of the New Ocean Politics', in Jonathan Alford (ed.), *Sea Power and Influence: Old Issues and New Challenges* (London: IISS, 1980), pp. 13–15.

55. Michael Howard, 'Order and Conflict at Sea in the 1980s', in Jonathan Alford (ed.), *Sea Power and Influence: Old Issues and New Challenges* (London: IISS, 1980), pp. 74–5.

56. Erik Moberg, 'The Protection of Resources,' in Jonathan Alford (ed.), *Sea*

Power and Influence: Old Issues and New Challenges (London: IISS, 1980), p. 19.

57. S. G. Gorshkov, *The Sea Power of the State* (Oxford: Pergamon Press, 1979), pp. 1–2.

58. Ibid., p. 28.

59. Grove, *Future*, pp. 40–1, 179–80, 222.

60. Till, *Maritime Strategy*, p. 150.

61. Edward N. Luttwak, *Strategy and History, Collected Essays* (New Brunswick, NJ: Transaction Books, 1985), Vol. 2, p. 79.

62. Mahan, *Problem of Asia*, pp. 40–2.

63. Hirschman, *National Power*, pp. 15–16.

64. R. G. Hawtrey, *Economic Aspects of Sovereignty* (London: Longmans, Green and Co., 1930), p. 23.

65. Colin S. Gray, *The Leverage of Sea Power: The Strategic Advantage of Navies in War* (New York: The Free Press, 1992), p. 85.

66. Patrick O'Sullivan, *Transport Policy: Geographic and Economic Planning Aspects* (Totowa, NJ: Barnes and Noble, 1980), p. 219.

67. Norman G. Pounds, 'A Free and Secure Access to the Sea', *Annals of the Association of American Geographers* 49/3 (September 1959), p. 256.

68. Ibid.

69. Ibid., pp. 256–68.

70. Gerald Morgan, *Anglo-Russian Rivalry in Central Asia: 1810–1895* (London: Frank Cass, 1981), p. 11.

71. See, for example, Jean Gottmann, 'Bugeaud, Gallieni, Lyautey: The Development of French Colonial Warfare', in Edward M. Earle (ed.), *Makers of Modern Strategy: Military Thought from Machiavelli to Hitler* (Princeton, NJ: Princeton University Press, 1943), pp. 234–59. Gottmann portrays French army policy in the colonies as being motivated by a grand civilizing mission.

72. Numerous motives have been attributed to Russian expansion. Many see a grand design behind nearly every Russian act. But there is no compelling reason to assume that Russian expansion was anything but a land power's equivalent to Western colonial expansion overseas, with boundaries being settled in a piecemeal fashion and with commerce and conquest being as significant there as they were elsewhere. See Morgan, *Anglo-Russian Rivalry*, who sees trade as being as important for Russian expansion as it was for Britain in India.

73. A classic view of patterns of expansion and the evolution of boundaries into an economic unit is Nicholas J. Spykman and Abbie A. Rollins, 'Geographic Objectives in Foreign Policy, I', *American Political Science Review* 33/3 (June 1939), pp. 391–410; and by same authors, 'Geographic Objectives in Foreign Policy, II', *American Political Science Review* 33/4 (August 1939), pp. 591–614.

74. For old, but excellent treatment of the three air power theorists, see Edward P. Warner, 'Douhet, Mitchell, Seversky: Theories of Air Warfare', in Edward M. Earle (ed.), *Makers of Modern Strategy: Military Thought from Machiavelli to Hitler* (Princeton, NJ: Princeton University Press, 1943), pp. 485–503, and, just on Douhet, Bernard Brodie, *Strategy in the Missile Age* (Princeton, NJ: Princeton University Press, 1959), pp. 71–106. For a good modern treatment, with an emphasis on Mitchell, see Russel F. Weigley, *The American Way of War: A History of United States Military Strategy and Policy* (Bloomington: Indiana University Press, 1973), pp. 223–41.

75. William Mitchell, *Winged Defense: The Development and Possibilities of Modern Air Power – Economic and Military* (New York: G. P. Putnam's Sons, 1925), pp. 4–5.

76. Ibid., pp. 5, 101–2, 126, 127.

77. Alexander P. De Seversky, *Victory Through Air Power* (New York: Simon and Schuster, 1942), p. 333.

78. There is an enormous number of works in this area. For a classic study, see Henry W. Spiegel, *The Economics of Total War* (New York: Appleton-Century, 1942). See also earlier works noted above on raw materials.

79. The British McKenna Duties, in the Finance Act of 1915, imposed duties of 33.5 per cent on a variety of imports. The alleged purpose was to cut down on luxury imports, strengthen the exchange rate, increase revenue, and decrease imports in order to provide cargo transport for war materials. The duties were maintained until 1924. This policy reflected classic mercantilist reasoning that some goods are necessities and some luxuries, and a positive trade balance aids in war production. Joseph M. Jones Jr., *Tariff Retaliation: Repercussions of the Hawley-Smoot Bill* (Philadelphia: University of Pennsylvania Press, 1934), pp. 215–16; Einzig, *Economic Warfare*, p. 55.

80. For a discussion of overall US policy here, see Rene de la Pedraja, *The Rise and Decline of US Merchant Shipping in the Twentieth Century* (New York: Twayne Publishers, 1992).

81. Klaus Knorr, 'The Concept of Economic Potential for War', *World Politics* 10/1 (October 1957), p. 49.

82. Klaus Knorr, *Military Power and Potential* (Lexington, MA: Heath Lexington Books, 1970), pp. 21–39.

83. See, for example, Stephen B. Jones, 'The Power Inventory and National Strategy', *World Politics* 6/4 (July 1954), pp. 421–52.

84. Klaus Knorr, *The War Potential of Nations* (Princeton, NJ: Princeton University Press, 1956), pp. 3–15. See also Knorr, 'Economic Potential', p. 51.

85. US Census Bureau, *Statistical Abstract of the United States* (Washington: GPO, 2000), p. 591, table 958.

86. Thomas L. McNaugher, *Arms and Oil: US Military Strategy and the Persian Gulf* (Washington, DC: Brookings Institution, 1985), pp. 8–9.

87. See, for example, Albert L. Nichols and Richard Zeckhauser, 'Stockpiling Strategies and Cartel Prices', *Rand Journal of Economics* 8/1 (Spring 1977), pp. 66–96.

88. This possibility was articulated in 'Terms of "Engagement": Lugar Anti-Sanctions Measure Could Preclude Important US Security Policy Options', Casey Institute Perspectives, no. 98-C 117 (William J. Casey Institute of the Center for Security Policy), 22 June 1998, at www.security-policy.org/papers/1998/98-C117.html.

89. See Theodore H. Moran, *American Economic Policy and National Security* (New York: Council on Foreign Relations Press, 1993).

90. Some examples are Rose Marie Ham and David C. Mowery, 'Enduring Dilemmas in US Technology Policy', *California Management Review* 37 (Summer 1995), pp. 89–107; Beverly Crawford, 'The New Security Dilemma Under International Economic Interdependence', *Millennium* 23 (Spring 1994), pp. 25–55; and David G. Haglund (ed.), T*he Defence Industrial Base and the West* (New York: Routledge, 1989).

91. For a good summary of this literature, see Michael Mastanduno, 'Economic Statecraft, Interdependence, and National Security: Agendas for Research', in Jean-Marc F. Blanchard, Edward D. Mansfield and Norrin M. Ripsman (eds), *Power and the Purse: Economic Statecraft, Interdependence and National Security* (London: Frank Cass, 2000), pp. 288–316; Michael Mastanduno, 'Economics and Security in Statecraft and Scholarship', *International Organization* 52/4 (Autumn 1998), pp. 825–54.

92. Paul M. Kennedy, *The Rise and Fall of the Great Powers: Economic Change and Military Conflict From 1500 to 2000* (New York: Random House, 1987). Kennedy summarizes his reasoning in the introduction, pp. xv–xxv.

93. Robert Gilpin, *War and Change in World Politics* (Cambridge: Cambridge University Press, 1981), pp. 14–15.

94. Ibid., pp. 10–11.

95. For a concise argument along these lines, see Moran, *American Economic Policy*.

96. Michael Borrus and John Zysman, 'Industrial Competitiveness and American National Security', in Wayne Sandholtz et al. (eds), *The Highest Stakes: The Economic Foundations of the Next Security System* (New York: Oxford University Press, 1992), pp. 7–8.

97. See, for example, Wayne Sandholtz and John Zysman, 'Europe's Emergence as a Global Protagonist', in Wayne Sandholtz et al. (eds), *The Highest Stakes: The Economic Foundations of the Next Security System* (New York: Oxford University Press, 1992), pp. 81–113.

98. Steve Weber and John Zysman, 'The Risk that Mercantilism will Define the Next Security System', in Wayne Sandholtz et al. (eds), *The Highest Stakes: The Economic Foundations of the Next Security System* (New York: Oxford University Press, 1992), p. 168.

99. See Mancur Olson, Jr., *The Economics of Wartime Shortage: A History of British Food Supplies in the Napoleonic War and in World War I and II* (Durham, NC: Duke University Press, 1963). Olson states that 'the view that a shortage of food or industrial raw material is particularly disabling to a nation is as clear an example of the "physiocratic fallacy" as the view that all wealth comes from the earth and that only products of the earth should be taxed', pp. 17–18. This thinking makes sense if the units of analysis are consumers, concerned with enjoyment of income, but not if they are 'soldiers', concerned with war potential.

100. Ibid., pp. 7–14, where he explains his reasoning.

101. See Eugene Staley, *World Economy in Transition: Technology Vs. Politics, Laissez Faire Vs. Planning, Power Vs. Welfare* (New York: Council on Foreign Relations, 1939), pp. 204, 206–8, 212. See also Eugene Staley, *Raw Materials in Peace and War* (New York: Council on Foreign Relations, 1937).

102. The literature on military spending and economic growth is rather large. Some of it argues for a positive relationship and some for a negative relationship. Some examples of the negative argument include the following: S. Deger and R. Smith, 'Military Expenditure and Growth in Less Developed Countries', *Journal of Conflict Resolution* 27/2 (1983), pp. 335–53; R.W. DeGrasse, *Military Expansion and Economic Decline: The Impact of Military Spending on US Economic Performance* (Armonk, NY: ME Sharpe, 1983); P.C. Frederiksen and R.E. Looney, 'Defense Expenditures and Economic Growth in Developing Countries', *Armed Forces and Society* 9/4 (1983), pp. 633–45; D. Lim, 'Another Look at Growth and Defense in Less Developed Countries', *Economic Development and Cultural Change* 31/2 (1983), pp. 377–84; M.J. Mueller and H.S. Atesoglu, 'A Theory of Defense Spending and Economic Growth', in J. E. Payne and A. P. Sahu (eds), *Defense Spending and Economic Growth* (Boulder, CO: Westview, 1993), pp. 41–53; C. Nardenelli and G.B. Ackerman, 'Defense Expenditures and the Survival of American Capitalism: A Note,' *Armed Forces and Society* 3/1 (1976), pp. 13–16; R.P. Smith, 'Military Expenditures and Capitalism', *Cambridge Journal of Economics* 1 (1977), pp. 61–76. For reviews of both sides of this argument, see S. Chan, 'The Impact of Defense Spending on Economic Performance: A Survey of Evidence and Problems', *Orbis* 29/2 (1985), pp. 403–34; S. Chan, 'The Political Economy of Military Spending and Economic Performance: Directions for Future Research', in A. L. Ross (ed.), *The Political Economy of Defense: Issues and Perspectives* (New York: Greenwood, 1991), pp. 203–22; and R. Ram,

'Conceptual Linkages Between Defense Spending and Economic Growth and Development: A Selective Review', in Payne and Sahu (eds), *Defense Spending*, pp. 19–39.

103. C. Huang and F. W. Hoole, 'Military Burden and Economic Hegemonic Decline: The Case of the United States', in A. Mintz (ed.), *The Political Economy of Military Spending in the United States* (London: Routledge, 1992), pp. 238–58.

104. See Derwent Whittlesey, *The Earth and the State: A Study in Political Geography* (New York: Henry Holt, 1939).

105. The hinterland provides the ecumene with industrial resources and defence-in-depth. It is common to ascribe the sheer size of large states as being central to their great power status. Geoffrey Parker, *The Geopolitics of Domination* (London: Routledge, 1988), p. 142. See also Saul B. Cohen, *Geography and Politics in a World Divided* (New York: Oxford University Press, 1973), p. 103, who sees the viability of a united Europe as depending on its incorporation of North Africa and the Sahara to provide it with a hinterland.

106. Halford Mackinder's classic statement, of course, became the basis for a long-standing literature on the issues of resources and the relationship between technology and geography. See his *Democratic Ideals and Reality, With Additional Papers* (New York: W. W. Norton, 1962).

107. Whittlesey, *Earth and the State*, p. 193.

108. T. Miller Maguire, *Outlines of Military Geography* (Cambridge: Cambridge University Press, 1899), p.148–9. See also Jacob Viner, *The Customs Union Issue* (New York: Carnegie Endowment for International Peace, 1950), pp. 22–3.

109. Raymond G. O'Connor, *Force and Diplomacy: Essays Military and Diplomatic* (Coral Gables, FL: University of Miami Press, 1972), pp. 4–5.

110. There are many such works. See Royal Institute of International Affairs, *Raw Materials and Colonies* (New York: Oxford University Press, 1936), especially for its treatment of Italy, Germany and Japan as dissatisfied powers on this issue. See also Helmer Key, *The New Colonial Policy* (London: Methuen, 1927); Brooks Emeny, *The Strategy of Raw Materials: The Study of America in Peace and War* (New York: Macmillan, 1934).

111. See previous note.

112. There are perhaps as many interwar works that are critical of the traditional thinking about raw materials and national policies. Most focused on the need to find ways of avoiding conflict over minerals through international mechanisms of some kind. See Sir Norman Angell, *Raw Materials, Population Pressure and War* (Boston, MD: World Peace Foundation, 1936); Herman Kranold, *The International Distribution of Raw Materials* (London: George Routledge and Sons, 1938); Benjamin Wallace, Bruce and Lynn Ransey Edminster, *International Control of Raw Materials* (Washington, DC: The Brookings Institution, 1930); and C. K. Leith, J. W. Furness and Cleona Lewis, *World Minerals and World Peace* (Washington, DC: The Brookings Institution, 1943).

113. There is also a large literature on the strategic significance of minerals during the Cold War with special attention to US–Soviet conflict and South Africa. See the collection in Cas de Villiers (ed.), *Southern Africa: The Politics of Raw Materials* (Pretoria: Foreign Affairs Association, 1977); W. C. J. Rensburg and D. A. Pretorius, *South Africa's Strategic Minerals: Pieces on a Continental Chess Board* (Johannesburg: Valiant Publishers, 1977); Alfred E. Eckes, Jr., *The United States and the Global Struggle for Minerals* (Austin: University of Texas Press, 1979); Charles K. Ebinger, *The Critical Link: Energy and National Security in the 1980s* (Cambridge: Ballinger, 1982); Hans W. Maull, *Energy, Minerals and Western Security* (Baltimore, MD: Johns Hopkins University Press, 1984); also Anderson, *Strategic Minerals*.

114. This view of Russian power potential has had a long tradition since MacKinder. For different versions of this, each inspired by MacKinder in some way, see John E. Kieffer, *Realities of World Power* (New York: David McKay Co., 1952); Nicholas J. Spykman, *The Geography of the Peace* (New York: Harcourt, Brace and Co., 1944); Colin S. Gray, *The Geopolitics of Superpower* (Lexington: University of Kentucky Press, 1988); and Zbigniew Brzezinski, *Game Plan: How to Conduct the US–Soviet Contest* (Boston, MD: Atlantic Monthly Press, 1986).

2

Interdependence Theory and Globalization

As argued thus far, perhaps the most important body of contemporary literature for this study is interdependence theory. The reason for this is that it is the only body of contemporary literature that gives a clear indication of what should be expected regarding a relationship between military power and commerce. It may be ironic that I am advancing an argument that I claim to be essentially realist in nature while also acknowledging that realism provides no specific guidelines. Interdependence also does not address the issue of military power and commerce directly, but its focus on what happens to military roles as economic interdependence increases offers a clear guideline.

In general, interdependence literature tends to see trade and military power as being mutually exclusive. The general tendency in this literature is to see military power and trade as belonging to separate and opposing worlds, with separate and opposing forms of politics, channels of influence, and methods of dispute settlement. This is not to say that this school sees state power and trade as being mutually exclusive – quite the contrary. All acknowledge the role of state power in trade relations to varying degrees. But the relevant concept of state power, as it relates to trade, is distinctly non-military. When it comes to military power proper, most interdependence literature sees it and trade as moving away from each other.

VARIETIES OF INTERDEPENDENCE AND GLOBALIZATION

David Baldwin, for example, defines military and economic statecraft as being quite distinct. He states that military statecraft involves influence attempts that rely primarily on violence, weapons, and force, while economic statecraft involves influence attempts that rely mainly on resources in a market setting.[1] John Conybeare sees trade wars among states as being essentially conflicts over economic objectives relating to trade and where the means used in the conflict are restrictions on trade.[2] Conybeare maintains that commercial rivalry and military conflict were closely related in the eighteenth century, due to the mercantilist association of power and wealth. But the decline of mercantilism by the late eighteenth century led to the delinking of military and commercial conflict, and, indeed, 'nineteenth century liberals saw a negative correlation between trade and military conflict'.[3]

The interdependence literature generally upholds the view that economic interdependence (among other things) has caused military power to lose its utility in the world. Military power, as a state tool to achieve desired outcomes, is no longer rational, efficient, and effective in an interdependent global economy. In critiquing traditional realism, Keohane and Nye maintain that military power is not fungible across all areas: it may be relevant for some issues, but not for others. The traditional realists saw power mostly in military terms and assumed that the differences in military power among states determined outcomes to conflict. Keohane and Nye state that, under conditions of complex interdependence, defined as a condition of multiple channels connecting societies with a large and diverse set of relevant issues, military force will not be used.[4]

Not only is there no longer a distinction between 'high' military issues and 'low' economic issues, but the utility of military power is limited because power resources have become both multidimensional and issue-specific. Nye states that the world today is more economically interdependent than in the past, especially because of communications technology, which causes power resources to change. He states that 'the ability of great powers to control their environments despite impressive traditional power resources is also diminished by the changing nature of issues in world politics', which reflects the fact that 'power is becoming less fungible, less coercive, and less tangible'.[5] This is similar to Baldwin's requirement that power analysis be accompanied by policy contingency frameworks so that we do not fall into the trap of seeing military power as being the 'ultimate power'.[6] This thinking also relates to the soft power argument, prominent is the recent debate over US decline and advanced by some of the same people here. This argument generally maintains that the declinist point of view is quite overstated due to the scale of soft power resources at the disposal of the United States.[7]

James Rosenau similarly states that 'the more societies, cultures, economies, and politics become interdependent, the less do the resulting conflicts lend themselves to resolution through military threats and actions'.[8] The rise of interdependence has narrowed the scope of military applications because the newer issues do not involve military security and territorial matters. Thus military capabilities have narrowed in scope and governments have experienced a decline in the capacity to mobilize domestic support for military issues. Interdependence issues, in contrast, are technical, decentralized, fragmented, and accommodative, such as those involving technological complexity, monetary stability, pollution, and resources.[9] It is interesting to note that Rosenau does not label interdependence issues as also being very political and, hence, fraught with conflict (even if that conflict is non-military in nature). It would not be a difficult task to find conflict over access to technology, conflicts over accepting responsibility for pollution, conflicts over monetary issues and, of course, conflicts over resources.

One of the starkest divisions of the military and commercial aspects of world politics is that of Richard Rosecrance, who puts forth two divergent models of state behaviour – the military/territorial and the trading. The trading world and the military world constitute two separate ways of operating internationally. Rosecrance equates the military world with sovereignty, territorial expansion, autarky (and mercantilism) and war. Its method of politics and dispute settlement revolves around the balance of power and hierarchical distinctions among states. The second world is one where the balance of power has been replaced by comparative advantage in trade, so that hierarchy no longer defines states, but economic function does. Here nations will cooperate and negotiate, and be focused on trade gains, not territorial. The lack of power hierarchy will also introduce a measure of equality among states, which goes hand-in-hand with peace and prosperity.[10]

While most states are really a mixture of the two modes of behaviour, the trading state is growing at the expense of the military/territorial state. This situation has grown throughout the postwar period, but has its early roots in Britain's nineteenth century trading system. As interdependence grows today, however, it will curb traditional sources of conflict. Indeed, economic interdependence will have a salutary effect on state relations. Rosecrance states that 'only the reciprocal exchange and division of labor represented by the trading world can prevent conflict in such an anarchic environment'.[11]

This thinking carries over to the more recent debates about the post-Cold War period. Here Rosecrance sees an economic multipolarity emerging in the world, absent of Great Powers 'jockeying for advantage'. The main objectives of actors in this system will be economic, not military, where 'all countries are possible customers, markets, or sources of raw material and technology'.[12] Here, 'each country can influence and even 'economically deter' others by granting or withholding access to trade and to foreign investment'.[13] In such a system, 'warlike countries generally do not prosper'.[14]

There is quite a variety of contemporary interdependence literature as well, most being in line with the above. One strand of this thought is that states can enhance their security through forming cooperative political and economic ties at the regional and sub-regional levels.[15] If interdependence mitigates conflict, then the goal should be to try and create interdependence. This literature appears to be a combination of interdependence and the multilateral conflict management literature.

It has also been argued that interdependence has had limited success in lowering conflict, not because of any flaws with inter-dependence *per se*, but because states continue to pursue their self-interest. As long as self-interest guides state behaviour, then there will be conflict.[16] This point of view may be in line with Rosecrance's concept of the military world, where states think and act in terms of the balance of power. At a deeper level, however, this concept of self-interest as itself being the problem breaks with the underlying liberal norm in much interdependence literature that the self-interest of countries are generally compatible.

The growing body of globalization literature is in many ways closely allied to the interdependence literature. In fact, much of this literature seems to be a rehash of the same sort of questions posed by interdependence. The debate over the decline of sovereignty in the globalization literature is a case in point. Sovereignty is thought to be threatened by a plethora of new forces in the world. Chief among them are the opening of markets, multinational corporations and the growing web of regulation between countries. These forces both constrain a country's ability to act and produce norms and structures that may make it more difficult for a country to use military force.[17]

Opinions vary, of course, regarding the desirability of sovereignty's supposed erosion. The view that the decline of sovereignty is an essentially good thing because it means the final end of the nation-state is normatively in line with most of the interdependence literature above.[18] This perspective often draws upon liberal economic analogies as well. There is also the point of view that sovereignty is indeed declining, but that this is a bad thing for a host of reasons. The erosion of sovereignty can deprive weaker economies of protection from stronger economies and it can weaken or threaten the survival of democracy itself. Instead, the maintenance of sovereignty is thought to be necessary for a country to prosper in the world economy and, according to some, to maintain democracy.[19]

Arguments in the globalization literature also debate the issue of economic and regulatory constraints which imply impediments to the use of military force. There is no overall agreement on this, however. Some paint a pessimistic picture of the world that, if correct, would lead us to expect an increased role for militaries in peacetime. Some of these points of view seem dramatically overdrawn, but they do underline the importance of economic interests and power differentials between states.

A case in point is the view expressed by George Soros, a market player himself. Soros has argued that the interests of the major Western states have narrowed in the post-Cold War period to focus increasingly on economic interests. This view is part of his general indictment of global capitalism. He maintains that the global capitalist system has failed on two grounds. One is the inherent instability in financial markets, which have wreaked havoc, and the other is the failure of politics. Politics, and a host of other professions, have become dominated by money and the values of money. In the past, he maintains, the West was more concerned with moral issues in foreign policy, but this has all but vanished today as economic self-interest has become dominant. He states in Chapter 6 of his book that: 'As long as capitalism remains triumphant, the pursuit of money overrides all other social considerations.' And again in Chapter 9, 'monetary values have usurped the role of intrinsic values and markets have come to dominate areas of society where they do not properly belong'.[20]

Soros, of course, is a poor reader of history. Aside from the ever-present moralism in current US foreign policy behaviour, he ignores the centrality of commercial interests in the traditional behaviour of the major states going right back to the sixteenth century, not to mention the utter brutality of these states in dealing with other states and peoples (and, frequently, their own peoples). While I would take his point of view as being an indication of the continued importance of economic interests, I would fault him for arguing that the centrality of such interests is new.

One might think that Soros' criticisms are those of a latent radical, but I think he is more of a mercantilist. His view of economic self-interest as being something incompatible with a general moral good is certainly a break with the liberal tradition and could reflect either a radical or a mercantilist point of view. What makes him more of a mercantilist, though, is that he sees money as being at the core of the economy (not to mention politics). To liberals, wealth and money are not at all synonymous, and class conflict lies at the heart of matters to radicals, whereas Soros echoes the classic mercantilist reasoning that sees money as being the driving force behind both the economy and the government.

In a similar vein, the argument of Singer and Wildovsky that globalization has really meant a bifurcation of the world into zones of peace and zones of turmoil seems artificial.[21] While their argument is designed to criticize the notion that the world is moving towards a single global order (a criticism that I tend to agree with), they also imply by their criticism that the past was somehow different from their characterization of the present. The division between wealthy and poor countries in times past was as stark as it is today, perhaps even more so. And the use of military power was more naked and in less need of moral cover than it is today. Just witness the aggressive role of the British and French colonial armies in conquered territories.

The idea that the past was different from the present in some fundamental way is common in much liberal literature. It would be hard to argue against this idea in the areas of science and technology or even in the expansion of the world economy, but it is easy to overstate the case when it comes to conflict between states. The centrality of economic interests, the use of military power to protect and advance those interests, and the stark inequality in the distribution of wealth and power do not appear to me to be much different today.

SOME PROBLEMS WITH INTERDEPENDENCE AND GLOBALIZATION

I will address only a few problems with the above literature. First, it was perhaps not such a revelation to hear that there was no longer a distinction between 'high' and 'low' politics in the 1970s due to economic interdependence. The literature of world politics from a variety of traditions (including the other trends of thought discussed in this work) gives the clear impression that none of the traditional writers assumed a distinction between high and low politics. In the nineteenth and early twentieth centuries, naval writers such as Mahan and Corbett, geographic and military writers such as MacKinder and T. Miller Maguire, traditional historians such as Langer, Woolf, and Marder, and many others across disciplines never seemed to have introduced such a distinction. Nearly every large diplomatic question had both a military and an economic component, and many issues of international trade and finance were enmeshed in the power rivalries of the Great Powers. If a distinction between high and low politics existed, with the implication that the military realm was always the most important and economic issues were unimportant, then it was perhaps among postwar realists alone – a relatively circumscribed body of writers. In the wider body of traditional literature, however, trade and strategy are discussed as if they are intertwined.

Second, the idea that sovereignty is declining seems unconvincing for several reasons. The above thinking tends to put forth a false picture of the past. There is the implication in this work that, in the past, sovereignty was more secure than it is today. Sovereignty was in a pristine state of near perfection in the past, but as we approach the present, the concept weakens due to modern elements of international politics. But a brief look at history will show that the origins and development of sovereignty from the late Middle Ages onward was a highly uneven phenomenon.[22] There was nothing pristine about it. Prior to the Thirty Years War, only a small number of states were thought to possess, it (France, Spain, England, and the Austrian Emperor). After the Thirty Years War, the idea of Great Powers emerged. The Great Powers were sovereign states that were more important than others. Most other peoples were either not sovereign or had partial sovereignty. The states within the Holy Roman Empire were given the power to make treaties with foreign powers, as long as they did not conspire against the Empire. While the emperor was fully sovereign, the others were partially so.

The Great Powers regarded other countries as being eminently violable and they violated each other on occasion. In the supposedly 'classical' period of Great Power rivalry prior to the First World War, when sovereignty was thought to be at its high point, the Great Powers routinely violated the integrity of countries that they did not recognize as being sovereign. And they routinely interfered with each other. There has never been a time period where the concept of sovereignty was so strong that it provided an impenetrable wall around all states.

In fact, all the wars of the Great Powers against each other are testimony to the fact that the sovereign states violate the sovereignty of their neighbours whenever they see a need to do so. Not only have states invaded each other, however, they have also occupied each other's territory, appropriated one another's property, and sought ways to entangle each other in dependent situations – whether through alliances and agreements or through calculated attempts at economic Machiavellianism.

Ironically, the concept of sovereignty has never been more respected among the major powers than it is today, in the era when it is said to be in decline. Today's major states demonstrate a respect for the legal authority of each other's governments and respect for the authority of smaller governments. The very growth of legal interaction among states, in areas such as trade, law enforcement, travel, and so on, is a good indication that sovereign states are apt to recognize each other's legal authority.

It could be misleading to assert that war and conquest were the primary modes of state behaviour in the past, but that there is less of a tendency to behave this way today. Today's major states were, with a few exceptions, the major states of the past who did indeed engage in much territorial acquisition through force. These states (the United States, Western Europe, Russia and Japan) may be less likely to engage in this behaviour today, but what about the rest of the world? China,

India, and a few other large states do not appear to have sworn off aggression as a method of acquiring territory. And then there are many smaller states who have been embroiled in wars throughout the postwar period. If we claim that the trend in world politics is to move away from using force, are we not just referring to the behaviour of today's major states? When we speak of trends in world politics, we may be ignoring the activities of the smaller states altogether and mistaking for trends the behaviours of the larger states.

There is also a problem with the picture that states were on a quest for economic self-sufficiency (thought to be the main cause of war) in the past, and were generally much more independent than they are today.[23] Because states were more independent in the past, sovereignty was stronger. The present is then contrasted from this picture of the past. We are told that sovereignty has declined or weakened because states are no longer independent. The state itself is either declining as well or transforming to adapt to the new world. This is a false picture.

The idea that states were somehow independent of one another when sovereignty was at its high point ignores the difference between legal ideas and factual conditions. Sovereignty is a legal concept. Its existence has never been predicated on the assumption of *de facto* independence from the influence of others (whether political, economic, or otherwise). Asserting a link between sovereignty and independence is perhaps an outgrowth of the notion that once a state has sovereignty, it is on equal terms with other sovereign states. Equality is being used to imply independence and autonomy. The presumption of equality in the idea of sovereignty has a legal sense only, however, and implies nothing about the *de facto* realities of world politics. A state may have sovereignty as a legal fact, but still be entwined in a web of political, economic and security dependencies. This link may also be due to the association (as in Rosecrance) of autarky and the old world of balance of power. If states were autarkic (which I do not think they were), then they were also autonomous from each other. As liberalism spreads, then, autonomy disappears and sovereignty is thus weakened.

A cursory look at modern history alone will show that a state's trade and finances have often been entangled in another's, trade policy has always been a central concern in traditional diplomacy, and a state's economic policies were often created with the impact that they would have on another country in mind. Witness British and European concern over Russian railway expansion into Central Asia in the nineteenth century; the use of French loans to Russia as a means of getting an alliance with Russia against Germany in 1894; the entanglement of economic, strategic, and diplomatic concerns of the

Great Powers with the growth of German influence in Turkey during the Baghdad Railway issue; the European protests and retaliation against the US Smoot-Hawley Tariff of 1930; predatory Nazi trade policies towards Eastern Europe in the 1930s; the Greater East-Asia Co-Prosperity Sphere. There are literally countless additional examples in modern history that could be cited in order to demonstrate plainly that in the period when sovereignty was said to be unassailable, states existed in complex webs of diplomatic, economic and strategic influences. It has never really been otherwise in modern history.

There tends to be a lack of clarity on what the relationship is between sovereignty and a state's wealth and power. Because of this, there is a lack of clarity on the relationship between sovereignty and both autonomy and independence. A state can be weak and dependent on another state, but still be sovereign, where the strong state respects the internal authority of the weak state, although the ability of a country to acquire sovereignty is itself related to power and wealth. The historical record reveals many variations on this issue. If the country is powerful and wealthy on its own, then its claim to sovereignty may be readily recognized or its claim may be supported with force or the threat of force. We might see the transformation of Prussia into the North German Confederation in 1867 and then into a fully united state after the Franco–Prussian War this way. Although a powerful state may recognize the sovereignty of a weaker state because of the implications this would have for itself and other states. Many of the smaller states in Europe, for example, were granted sovereignty because the Great Powers wanted buffer states between them. This was certainly the case for Belgium in 1830, for example.

In addition, impediments to a country's ability to act do not necessarily imply a decline of sovereignty for several reasons. Some impediments depend on voluntary acceptance by the state in question, such as in a treaty agreement. In such a case, the state still retains the right to opt out of it and can even violate the treaty. A treaty violation can lead to retaliation, but this does not imply that sovereignty is weaker. Treaty violations have led to conflict since the start of the modern state system itself. In addition, powerful states have depended on each other for security (through alliances) for as long as the state system has existed. Even in the European Union today, where members are giving up control over monetary policy and currency, a member country can opt out of the EU. Formally, states within the EU accept the irreversibility of the progress of integration, but there have been past examples where they have resorted to national solutions to problems in violation of the programme of integration. What would happen if one of the larger economies in the EU decided that it wanted to exit from use of the euro and go back to national currency?

To what extent does voluntary cooperation or even policy coordination imply limits to sovereignty?

Constraints that exist through a treaty would indeed be a limitation on sovereignty, however, if the treaty itself were imposed on a state by force. Peace treaties tend to have this character from the point of view of the defeated state. One thinks of German sovereignty and the Treaty of Versailles (1919) in this way, for example, or even the occupation and bifurcation of Germany after the Second World War. Treaties that are consentually entered into, however, do not militate against sovereignty, especially in light of the fact that sovereign states are generally the signatories to such treaties.

Other impediments emerge as unintended consequences, such as those due to economic weakness or even expansion of the world economy. These impediments involve constraints on a state's ability to act and constraints on a state's ability to achieve goals, but do not imply that the authority structure of a state is dissolving. There are two points to note here. One is that the ability of a state to get its way in the world is a function of its access to the relevant resources, whether economic, political, or military. A state can be sovereign and yet be weak. While a sovereign state may lack such resources, however, having sovereignty actually increases the ability to access such resources – witness a sovereign state's ability to build large conventional military power versus a revolutionary movement's guerrilla army. Second, every state in the international system today, as always, imposes a variety of regulations on the movement of people and commerce across its borders. While multinational corporations and the growth of capital markets have certainly complicated economic arrangements, their growth does not imply an end to the state's ability to regulate. States can still interfere, corrupt, and, on occasion, even sever economic connections.

If sovereignty were declining, would that not also imply a weakening of the state's ability to regulate people and commerce internally as some other authority structure assumes the role? We could argue that the state has an even greater ability to regulate its people internally due to modern transport and communications technology and, by implication, to control their entry into and exit from the country. Would it be contradictory if we argued that sovereignty was declining in international relations, but saw no internal corollary to this?

Finally, there is one clear threat to sovereignty, but this one has been around for a long time and is a byproduct of unequal wealth and power itself – that being the threat posed by other sovereign states. There are countless examples of sovereign states violating the sovereignty of other states, while upholding the notion for themselves. This threat is the obvious one, but is generally absent from the discussion over impediments to sovereignty. If a stronger state violates the sovereignty of a weaker state, this would not imply a general decline of sovereignty itself. Under these conditions, sovereignty would be weakened for the weaker country only. Iraq's invasion of Kuwait in 1990 is a simple example where one country violated the sovereignty of another. Had it not been for the power of other sovereign states (such as the United States), then Kuwait's sovereignty may have been permanently eclipsed. In addition, the UN's role in policing Iraq to prevent Iraq from manufacturing weapons of mass destruction is certainly a violation of Iraq's sovereignty, but could the UN do such a thing in the first place if it were not itself supported by the power of other sovereign states?

Despite the plethora of connections that cut across national boundaries, the distribution of wealth and power seem as central to a state's security and ability to act today as it has ever been. Although, in the era when sovereignty is said to be declining, the idea has probably never been more respected by the major states than it is today. Perhaps Thucidydes' refrain in the Melian Dialogue still applies – the strong do what they will, the weak do what they must.[24]

The above criticisms revolve around three general characteristics that are common themes throughout much interdependence literature. One is that interdependence is said to be new, a function of the postwar expansion of trade. The second is that interdependence is said to be of revolutionary significance because it will transform the way states and the world operate (or has already done so), thereby counteracting tendencies towards 'traditional' conflict. Third, interdependence is relatively permanent or irreversible – that is, interdependence is a long-term trend that represents the movement of progress itself, away from the old and permanently toward the new.

While there is certainly much about the postwar world that is new, interdependence itself is not new. As is demonstrated in Chapters 5 and 6, there was a high degree of economic interdependence among the Great Powers. Perhaps the magnitude of interdependence and the speed of economic transactions and political communication across states are new, but interdependence itself is not.

Finally, interdependence literature has a narrow understanding of military power. This issue is perhaps the most important point for this work. In general, military power is seen as being useful only for issues involving territory and expansion. New issues are said to be outside the purview of military power. Military power is thus narrow in scope, involving only a few types of issues, and its use is focused on particular issues with particular purposes. This means that military power is employed to achieve an outcome on a particular matter. This implies that there are no broader uses of military power. It also implies that the use of military power is temporary or even short-term because once the issue is addressed, the purpose of the military power is ended. There are three points to make here. One is that some of the new issues spoken of actually have direct military significance. At least three of the four new issues that Rosenau puts forth above have military relevance – nearly any type of technology has a military application, resource issues have strategic significance, and navies are involved in policing territorial waters to guard against pollution. Second, we could also argue that the so-called traditional issues are quite present in the modern world. Aside from the first Gulf War, there are many smaller conflicts in the world having to do with territory (many of which are bound up with ethnic and related conflicts).

The most important point, however, is that military power has a much broader range of uses in the world than interdependence literature would have us believe. Many of these uses are long-term and general in nature, some are short-term, and a large number of them have something to do with international commerce. While these links are explored in Chapter 3, the point here is that issues of trade are not clearly separable from military issues. One could expound upon any of the above points at length to demonstrate this. What I would like to draw attention to, however, is that military power has a broad role in world politics, one that goes beyond an issue-by-issue focus, and that this broad role has a great deal to do with trade. This last point will be examined more fully in Chapter 3.

CONFLICT AND TRADE

An allied body of literature is that on trade flows, which seek to measure the impact of conflict, diplomacy and alliances on trade, or conversely, to measure the impact of trade on conflict. This literature has grown enough in recent years in size and in sophistication to produce a diverse set of findings on how conflict and trade are related. A recent article by Barbieri and Schneider notes, for example, that the literature is characterized by differences in the definition of concepts, theoretical insights, and data, which may account for the diversity of findings.[25] Much of this literature frames trade as the independent variable and conflict the dependent variable, although some reverse the direction. Some have also tested the variables for causal direction with mixed results.[26]

A persistent finding in the liberal segment of this literature, especially the older literature, is that trade and conflict are inversely related, and that trade and cooperation are positively related.[27] Most of this literature employs some aspects of trade theory in the reasoning, which is usually focused on advancing the argument that free trade and cooperation between states go together. Most of it also employs gravity models, where political and conflict variables are simply added to the regressions.

Explanations for why trade should alter the behaviour of a state towards another state hinge on the set of incentives that are said to confront states. Polackek, for example, has argued that mutual dependence between two partners will raise the costs of conflict and decrease the levels of dispute.[28] This is straightforward liberal reasoning.

Pollins, in contrast, argues for politically influenced incentives on the part of both producers and consumers. Consumers may purchase the imports of a friendly country as a political gesture of friendship and refuse those from hostile countries, while importers may import from friendly countries in order to minimize risk. Importers are also said to be concerned with the state objective of international security.[29] This reasoning seems less convincing than Polackek's because there appears to be no good theoretical or empirical basis for asserting that consumption and production behaviour are influenced by political or diplomatic preferences, but this too is in line with liberal reasoning. The argument that importers take such information into account may be on firmer ground than that claiming the same of consumers, however, because firms involved in international trade do pay some attention to the problem of political risk. Sayers presents a good assessment of the economic assumptions in the work on trade and conflict.[30]

Recent literature on the trade and conflict debate tends to report more complicated findings. Mansfield and Bronson, for example, find that alliances and preferential trading agreements positively affect trade. This funding is based on post-Second World War data.[31] Oneal and Russett also continue to find support for the idea that trade promotes peace between states and even find that asymmetrical changes in dependence are unrelated to conflict.[32] Morrow, Siverson, and Tabares, however, do not find that alliances positively influence trade between states, although the presence of democracy does. The effect of alliances on trade can vary between multipolar and bipolar systems.[33] While Gowa also finds that while alliances positively affect trade, the nature of the relationship varies across different international systems.[34]

The idea that trade can change the behaviour of a country is common to much of the work summarized above. This notion is the intuitively obvious one because, after all, it is in line with traditional American foreign policy behaviour. Whether the United States employs trade sanctions against a country or accords trade concessions, the trade instrument is being used to influence behaviour. This behaviour was a key part of Cold War policy, such as the

Nixon–Kissinger policy of using trade to affect Soviet and Chinese behaviour. Expanding and contracting trade to the USSR and China remained policy behaviour right to the end of the Cold War (and continues today with China).

The policy focus assumes a certain direction in causality: policies are said to affect trade, which affect (or fail to affect) the behaviour of the target state. Very often, of course, it was the initial behaviour of the target state that caused the policies in the first place. US policies that tightened or loosened the trade embargo on communist countries affected trade with those countries, for example, which were thought to have some impact on the behaviour of those countries.

While the conflict and trade literature does not address the question of how military spending and trade are related, it has some implications. Like interdependence literature, we could expect military spending and trade to move away from each other based upon the liberal segment of the conflict and trade literature. We could argue that, as conflict rises between states, trade falls and military spending grows. The growth in spending would be a response to rising conflict. If we argue that trade affects conflict, then we could argue that as trade rises and conflict falls, military spending falls as well.

IMPLICATIONS FOR MILITARY POWER AND TRADE

While the above is only a cursory overview of what is really a predominant trend in international relations literature today, this summary does capture the main direction of the arguments. The interdependence line of argument, of course, is both idealistic and a reflection of basic liberal tenets. While these writers do not wish politics away, as a liberal economist might, many of them do see an 'economic multipolarity' as the framework of relevance and some see this as replacing the military balance of power, where comparative advantage and economic interests become the road to success in the future.[35] It is only the distortions of the outmoded military-territorial order that impede this process. There is the classic liberal assumption here that the basic self-interest of the units in question (here, states) are mutually harmonious. If states act as rational calculators of self-interests (or perhaps consumers) in a multipolar world, then a peaceful interdependence will result. Although cooperation may not always imply harmony, it could at least mean a tolerable state of friction.

Interdependence thinking (perhaps more so than the more recent conflict and trade literature) would lead us to expect a relationship (however specified) that might approximate the following:

$$\text{MILITARY} = \overset{-}{f}(\overset{+}{\text{TRADE}}, \overset{+}{\text{PROTECTIONISM}}, \text{WAR})$$

Where military power would be some negative function of trade or trade growth, some positive function of protectionism, and some positive function of war. Interdependence thinking is perhaps the only approach discussed in this work that suggests in a straightforward way any behavioural equation of the relationship between military power and commerce.

With the exception of war, of course, this work argues for an opposite set of relationships. I contend here (and hope to make clear later) that the separation of military power and commerce in interdependence literature is artificial. This artificiality, in turn, is based on a very narrow view of the role of military power. In this literature military power is a state tool that is designed only to settle disputes that revolve around 'traditional' issues. If new issues emerge, such as economic issues or pollution, then new methods of dispute settlement must emerge with them.

Despite the above criticism of interdependence literature, it should be said in its defence that the reasoning employed in this body of work is generally well-constructed and more rigorous than that reviewed in Chapter 1. While military power and commerce may not be artificially separated in the literature of Chapter 1, in contrast, this literature is nevertheless vaguer and less disciplined than that of interdependence and has traditionally acted as a poor guide for the formation of hypotheses and models.

NOTES

1. David Baldwin, *Economic Statecraft* (Princeton, NJ: Princeton University Press, 1985), p. 14.
2. John A. C. Conybeare, *Trade Wars: The Theory and Practice of International Commercial Rivalry* (New York: Columbia University Press, 1987), p. 3.
3. Ibid., p. 145.
4. Robert O. Keohane and Joseph S. Nye, *Power and Interdependence* (Boston, MA: Scott, Foresman and Co., 1989), 2nd edn, pp. 24–25.
5. Joseph S. Nye, Jr., *Bound to Lead: The Changing Nature of American Power* (New York: Basic Books, 1990), pp. 186, 188.
6. See, for example, David Baldwin, 'Power Analysis and World Politics: New Trends Versus Old Tendencies', *World Politics* 31/2 (January 1979), pp. 161–94.
7. See, for example, Joseph S. Nye, 'Soft Power', *Foreign Policy* 80 (Fall 1990), pp. 153–71.
8. James N. Rosenau, *The Study of Global Interdependence: Essays on the Transnationalization of World Affairs* (London: Frances Pinter, 1980), pp. 40–1.
9. Ibid., pp. 43–6.

10. Richard Rosecrance, *The Rise of the Trading State: Commerce and Conquest in the Modern World* (New York: Basic Books, 1986), pp. 15–28.

11. Ibid., p. 16.

12. Richard Rosecrance, *America's Economic Resurgence: A Bold New Strategy* (New York: Harper and Row, 1990), pp. 195–97.

13. Ibid., p. 197.

14. Ibid., p. 197. See also Richard Rosecrance, 'Regionalism and the Post-Cold War Era', *International Journal* 66/3 (Summer 1991), pp. 373–93.

15. See Lev Voronkov, 'Regional Cooperation: Conflict Prevention and Security Through Interdependence', *International Journal of Peace Studies* 4/2 (July 1999), pp. 83–93. See also Jean Marie Guehenno, 'The Impact of Globalisation on Strategy', *Survival* 40 (Winter 1998/99), pp. 15–19, who sees the European Union style of institutionalized interdependence rather than the American model as providing a better means of increasing security.

16. George Kaloudis, 'The Search for Global Order', *International Journal on World Peace* 15 (March 1998), pp. 3–21.

17. This erosion of sovereignty is called one of the novel aspects of globalization by Noel O'Sullivan in 'Concept and Reality in Globalization Theory', in C. P. Rao (ed.), *Globalization, Privatization and Free Market Economy* (Westport, CT: Quorum, 1998), pp. 11–27. Not everyone agrees that sovereignty is actually declining, though. For different points of view see Viktor Vanberg, 'Globalization, Democracy, and Citizens' Sovereignty: Can Competition Among Governments Enhance Democracy?' *Constitutional Political Economy* 11 (March 2000), pp. 87–112; Christoph Gorg and Joachim Hirsch, 'Is International Democracy Possible?' *Review of International Political Economy* 5 (Winter 1998), pp. 585–615; Peter F. Drucker, 'The Global Economy and the Nation-State', *Foreign Affairs* 76 (September–October 1997), pp. 159–71; Vivien A. Schmidt, 'The New World Order Incorporated: The Rise of Business and the Decline of the Nation-State', *Daedalus* 124/2 (Spring 1995), pp. 75–106.

18. Robert Gilpin summarizes these points of view in *The Challenge of Global Capitalism: The World Economy in the 21st Century* (Princeton, NJ: Princeton University Press, 2000), pp. 311–23.

19. This perspective comes in many guises. A representative sampling would include Peter Evans, 'The Eclipse of the State: Reflections on Stateness in an Era of Globalization', *World Politics* 50 (October 1997), pp. 62–87; Robert Marshall, 'Autonomy and Sovereignty in the Era of Global Restructuring', *Studies in Political Economy* 59 (Summer 1999), pp. 115–47; Carlo Jean, 'The Role of the Nation State in Providing Security in a Changed World', *International Spectator* 33/1 (January–March 1998), pp. 67–77; Samuel M. Makinda, 'Sovereignty and Global Security', *Security Dialogue* 29 (September 1998), pp. 281–92; Rebecca R. Moore, 'Globalization and the Future of US Human Rights Policy', *Washington Quarterly* 21 (Autumn 1998), pp. 193–212; M. Shahid Alam, *Poverty from the Wealth of Nations: Integration and Polarization in the Global Economy Since 1760* (New York: St. Martin's Press, 2000), who finds a direct relationship between how sovereign a country is and how well it has done in the world economy.

20. George Soros, *The Crisis of Global Capitalism: Open Society Endangered* (New York: Public Affairs, 1998), pp. 102, 106–7. Others, such as Henry A. Kissinger, *Diplomacy* (New York: Simon and Schuster, 1994), warn against advancing one's concept of values in the world, with the implication being that the US still does this. Ikenberry argues that this strategy is not idealistic, but a pragmatic approach to promote peace. See G. John Ikenberry, 'Why Export Democracy? The "Hidden Grand Strategy" of American Foreign Policy', *Wilson Quarterly* 23/2 (Spring 1999), p. 56, available at

wwics.si.edu/OUTREACH/WQ/WQSELECT/IKENB.HTM.

21. Max Singer and Aaron Wildovsky, *The Real World Order: Zones of Peace, Zones of Turmoil* (Chatham, NJ: Chatham House, 1993).

22. The question of the origins of sovereignty, conventionally attributed to the Conference of Westphalia in 1648, is also a matter of debate. In practice, the concept existed before the conference and was, indeed, formulated first by Jean Bodin in his *The Six Books on the State* in 1576. For a current debate, see the series of essays debating aspects of sovereignty in the special issue entitled 'Continuity and Change in the Westphalian Order' of *International Studies Review* 2 (Summer 2000).

23. Rosecrance, *Trading State*, pp. 14–15.

24. Robert Holton provides a critique of many of the assumptions about sovereignty, which he says amount to a myth. See his *Globalization and the Nation-State* (New York: St. Martin's Press, 1998), pp. 81–91.

25. Katherine Barbieri and Gerald Schneider, 'Globalization and Peace: Assessing new Directions in the Study of Trade and Conflict', *Journal of Peace Research* 36/4 (July 1999), pp. 387–404.

26. See, for example, Mark Gasiorowski and Solomon W. Polackek, 'Conflict and Interdependence: East–West Trade and Linkages in the Era of Détente', *Journal of Conflict Resolution* 26/4 (December 1982), pp. 709–29; Rafael Reuveny and Heejoon Kang, 'International Trade, Political Conflict/Cooperation, and Granger Causality', *American Journal of Political Science* 40 (August 1996), pp. 943–70; Rafael Reuveny and Heejoon Kang, 'Bilateral Trade and Political Conflict/Cooperation: Do Goods Matter?' *Journal of Peace Research* 35/5 (September 1998), pp. 581–602.

27. Mark Gasiorowski, 'Economic Interdependence and International Conflict: Some Cross-National Evidence', *International Studies Quarterly* 30/1 (March 1986), pp. 23–38; Gasiorowski and Polackek, 'Conflict and Interdependence'; Joanne Gowa, *Allies and Adversaries, and International Trade* (Princeton, NJ: Princeton University Press, 1994); Solomon W. Polackek, 'Conflict and Trade', *Journal of Conflict Resolution* 24/1 (March 1980), pp. 55–78; Brian M. Pollins, 'Conflict, Cooperation, and Commerce: The Effect of International Political Interactions on Bilateral Trade Flows', *American Journal of Political Science* 33/3 (August 1989), pp. 737–61; Brian M. Pollins, 'Does Trade Still Follow the Flag?' *American Political Science Review* 83/2 (June 1989), pp. 465–80; Lois W. Sayrs, 'Reconsidering Trade and Conflict: A qualitative Choice Model with Censoring', *Conflict Management and Peace Science* 10/1 (Spring 1988), pp. 1–19.

28. Polackek, 'Conflict and Trade.'

29. Pollins, 'Conflict, Cooperation', and Pollins, 'Follow the Flag'.

30. Lois W. Sayrs, 'Expected Utility and Peace Science: An Assessment of Trade and Conflict', *Conflict Management and Peace Science* 11/1 (Spring 1990), pp. 17–44.

31. Edward D. Mansfield and Rachel Bronson, 'Alliances, Preferential Trading Arrangements, and International Trade', *American Political Science Review* 91/1 (March 1997), pp. 94–107. See also Edward D. Mansfield, Jon C. Pevehouse, and David H. Bearce, 'Preferential Trading Arrangements and Military Disputes', in Jean-Marc F. Blanchard, Edward D. Mansfield and Norrin M. Ripsman (eds), *Power and the Purse: Economic Statecraft, Interdependence and National Security* (London: Frank Cass, 2000), pp. 92–118.

32. John R. Oneal and Bruce Russett, 'Assessing the Liberal Peace with Alternative Specifications: Trade Still Reduces Conflict', *Journal of Peace Research* 36/4 (1999), pp.423–42.

33. James D. Morrow, Randolph M. Siverson, and Tressa E. Tabares, 'The Political Determinants of International Trade: The Major Powers, 1907–90', *American Political Science Review* 92/3 (September 1998), pp. 649–61.

34. See Gowa, *Alliances and Adversaries,* Solomon W. Polackek, John Robst and Yuan-Ching Chang, 'Liberalism and Interdependence: Extending the Trade-Conflict Model', *Journal of Peace Research* 36/4 (1999), pp. 405–22, also find support for the idea that trade lowers conflict, but their results are complicated.

35. See Rosecrance, *Economic Resurgence* and *Trading State.* This thinking is also evident on the part of those who see a multipolar world as being most consistent with stability and economic prosperity. See J. David Singer, *Models, Methods, and Progress in World Politics* (Boulder, CO: Westview, 1990), p. 12, where 'a welter of crosscutting ties and such a shifting of friendships and hostilities [means] that no single set of interests can create a self-aggravating and self-reinforcing division or cleavage among the nations'.

3

Military and Commercial Linkages:
A Mercantilist Dimension

Despite the diversity of the literature in Chapter 1, a common thread running through much of it is mercantilism. Much of this literature has a tendency to view economic relations between countries and economic resources through a mercantilist lens. In fact, a general difference cutting across all of the literature thus far reviewed is a split between liberalism and mercantilism. The liberal view of economic matters is evident in early idealism, some geopolitical literature,[1] some neorealism (especially that dealing with multipolarity), inter-dependence and a segment of globalization literature. The mercantilist view is evident in most of traditional realism, some of neorealism, and most of the geopolitical, navalist, military, and war potential literature. What is interesting is that much of this literature employs liberal or mercantilist reasoning without explicitly saying so. These perspectives are so diffuse in the literature that one wonders what is really being debated across these approaches.

The strands of mercantilist thought in the above literature show a tendency to view economic issues, resources, and trade in terms of their influence on the production of power and international presence, and in terms of their role in engendering conflict among states. It is also true, however, that mercantilism and its role are left vague in these approaches, which may stem from the strong contemporary attitude that mercantilism is essentially bad and wrong-headed and is itself responsible for lower standards of living of people and conflict between states. But if mercantilist thought is prevalent in power-centric approaches to international relations, then it deserves some clarification.

There are also aspects to mercantilist behaviour that are often ignored. One of them is related to the larger question of the role of military power in peacetime. It is common practice to assume that military power has a rather narrowly prescribed role in the world. It is either a tool during war, or an increasingly outmoded tool of coercion during peacetime. In either case, military power is thought to be narrowly focused on achieving favourable outcomes in some issue area. This understanding implies two characteristics about military power. First, it implies that any given use of military power is related to a specific issue (which indicates the narrowness of its purpose). Second, it implies that its use is temporary, if not short-term. Once an outcome is achieved on some specific issue, then the military power has served (or failed to serve) its purpose. As explained below, while many uses of military power are narrowly defined, military power is also a tool that is broad in scope and performs functions that are both general and long-term in nature. These latter aspects of military power make it a constituent feature of peacetime relations between states, and this role is bound up with commerce. These aspects of military power are also essentially mercantilistic, and many exist whether a country pursues a free trade policy or not.

MERCANTILISM

There seem to be two broad orientations to mercantilism. One is focused on state power and the other on serving particular interests in the domestic economy or even on protecting the domestic economy from disruption. The distinctions that most authors make regarding the types of mercantilism seem to fall loosely in these two camps. Robert Gilpin, for example, makes the distinction between benign and malevolent mercantilism. The first seeks to safeguard national economic interests as a necessary minimum for security and survival. The second uses the international economy as an arena for imperialist expansion and engages in aggressive economic behaviour, such as economic warfare.[2] In interwar literature, Nazi economic policies were seen at the time as being a new and aggressive form of mercantilism, while the 'old type' was actually seen as being part of liberal society. Traditional mercantilism was thought to be motivated by a goal similar to that of liberal thought: securing domestic welfare and economic stability.[3] If this were true, then the only real difference between liberalism and the older type of mercantilism would be in the methods employed.

The focus on state power is very common in mercantilist thought. While writers differ in the specific types of policies they ascribe to mercantilism, the state is seen as using economic resources to maximize its power. This is where mercantilism's connection to realism is most evident. Here politics is said to determine economics.[4] Gustav Schmoller, for example, states that the main economic institutions of any period in history are dependent upon the nature of the political institutions of the time, which control the economy.[5] Schmoller sees mercantilism as being a stage of state-making, with the struggle for power and wealth among states being most important. He argues that the competitive mercantilist approach to economics was the original view of states. It was only through a slow evolution that states turned toward the liberal approach, which still houses the attempt to keep the weak states down.[6]

While Schmoller is correct in his historical chronology, in that mercantilism preceded liberalism, he is unwilling to take liberalism at its word. He believes that the same motivations inherent to mercantilism are embedded in liberalism, only they are hidden. These ideas were, of course, shared by others at the time. Because wealth and power are interdependent, mercantilism is oriented towards making the state wealthy.[7] Making the state wealthy is not entirely distinguishable from making the country at large wealthy, because the latter serves the state as well.

Heckscher's view of mercantilism seems to lean more towards the state power view. He describes mercantilism as being a system of power that employed two basic means. The first was to direct economic activity towards political and military ends, and the second was to create a reservoir of economic resources from which a policy of power could draw.[8] Hirschman's view of trade is similar to this, though narrower. He states that, from the standpoint of state power, trade has two effects – a supply effect and an influence effect. The supply effect of trade provides goods that strengthen the military power of a state. States thus seek to lessen their dependence or safeguard supplies by pursuing mercantilist policies, such as controlling trade routes, stockpiling, and directing trade towards friendly countries. The influence effect of trade stems from trade being used as a coercive tool, which Hirschman believes can be an alternative to war.[9] Similarly, Stephen Krasner argues that the state goal of maximizing power leads the state both to deflect economic resources toward specific political and military ends, and to create a reservoir of national economic strength to use for political goals.[10]

From the point of view of state power, then, the economic goals of states are to be assessed in terms of the power they produce for the state, not the level of welfare and standard of living they produce for society.[11] Some authors argue, like Schmoller, that countries oriented towards liberal economic thought are concerned with power as well. While the means employed may differ in kind and degree, the concern with power and wealth are common to both orientations.[12] Indeed, part of the goal of this study is to show that the association between military power and commerce cuts across ideological divisions and many mercantilist policies are practiced by modern states (stockpiling, redirecting trade, economic warfare, and so on).

Before proceeding, it should be noted that mercantilism could also be seen in terms of domestic interest group activity. Here the state's policies are a byproduct of lobbying activity, which leads policy-makers to produce protectionist and regulatory devices that serve the interests of certain domestic producers at the expense of the consumers. In this case, mercantilism is focused neither on state power nor on serving the ends of domestic welfare, but on serving the interests of specific producers in the economy. From this point of view, we could see mercantilism as being a form of rent- seeking that allows producers to coerce surplus out of the hands of consumers through state action.[13]

A traditional assumption that stems from mercantilist reasoning is that trade relations can be conflictual. An increase in the amount of wealth of a country could mean an increase in the power available to that state, as well as a relative decrease in the power of another state.[14] This reasoning was said to be behind the quest for self-sufficiency and colonies.[15] It has even been argued that military competition is the driving force behind a state's goal of industrialization and that trade rivalry itself may be a byproduct of this. Once a country reaches a sufficient level of industrial development, others follow in an effort to preserve the balance of power.[16] While there are several important goals to industrialization, the acquisition of military power is a primary one.[17]

The process of economic growth itself has even been pointed to as a cause of conflict. Choucri and North use the term 'lateral pressure' to describe the expansive behaviour of states: domestic growth causes an expansion in the external interests of states; this leads to competition for resources, markets and strategic advantage; and the crises that result acquire their own dynamic.[18] Liberal thought tends to point in the opposite direction on matters of conflict among states. Free trade is consistent with peace. But mercantilist thought sees trade itself as being a source of conflict. Alexander Hamilton thought that because the love of wealth was as powerful a motive as the love of power and glory, trade relations would likely be a source of war.[19]

Sometimes geographical proximity is thought to be a modifying factor. It is common to hear that regional trading agreements are often facilitated by proximity and ethnic and cultural similarity. While propinquity has often been the rule in such agreements, it is, to paraphrase Jacob Viner, based on a false association between close political and economic ties, on the one hand, and ethnic and political similarities, on the other. 'Neighborhood has never in international relations been a guarantee of, and often has been a detriment to, neighborly feelings, and often this has been not only a fact but one too freely acknowledged.'[20]

While many traditional types of mercantilist policies may no longer exist, such as acquiring colonies or hoarding bullion, mercantilist behaviour in a more general sense can be found in a wide array of contemporary policies. This study, however, is interested in the militarily significant aspects of mercantilism. There is common agreement among older mercantilist writers that military power was important for commerce before the nineteenth century. Heckscher notes, for example, that England used its economic laws to prepare for the land defence of the country in the fifteenth and sixteenth centuries.[21] Much like modern navalist writers, mercantilist writers also see the connection between navies and trade. Schmoller maintains that those states that understood how to employ their fleets and their customs and navigation laws in the economic interests of the state gained the lead in the struggle for power and wealth.[22]

The subject of economic blocs and trade control policies designed to influence the direction of trade have historically involved conflict among states and have had military significance. A traditional, but highly general, definition of an economic bloc describes it as 'an arrangement among certain nations, but significantly less than all nations, which tends to affect the quantities and prices of internationally exchanged commodities or factors of production'.[23] Economic blocs vary according to the degree to which countries economic policies and economies more generally are integrated. Thus there can be free trade areas, customs unions, a common market, and full economic integration.[24] There can also be tariff blocs, currency blocs, and developing-country blocs, and even commodity blocs that involve cartels. And there is a distinction between *antagonistic blocs* and *cooperating blocs*.[25]

It is common to portray the goal of economic integration to be the general improvement of the welfare of the participants, which is the liberal perspective.[26] There is certainly some truth to the idea that economic integration is motivated by welfare concerns. At the same time, however, economic blocs are also mercantilist in several ways. First, economic blocs may be focused more on protecting the interests of inefficient producers at the expense of consumers and non-member producers. Conflict between member producers and consumers, and conflict between member and non-member producers can translate into conflict between member and non-member governments. The uneven distribution of costs and benefits due to trade and related policies in a bloc may be the source of conflict in numerous possible ways. The Common Agricultural Policy (CAP) in the EU reflects this precise situation. The CAP awards surplus to inefficient member producers at the expense of consumers and non-member producers.

Second, economic blocs involve power relationships. Jacob Viner states that some of the more important movements towards customs union that involved a Great Power and a number of small countries were motivated by the political goals of the Great Power, while the economic consequences of the union were regarded as the necessary price to pay for the political objectives. The small countries, in contrast, were motivated by the economic gain of union and regarded the political consequences as a necessary cost.[27]

To what extent do economic blocs, involving a Great Power with small powers, become a sphere of influence of the great power and, thereby, reflect the interests of the Great Power? At the extreme end, we can see that economic blocs could be sought by a strong country as an economic hinterland to feed its war production. German trade control policies in eastern Europe in the 1930s were designed to serve German war production.[28] Soviet trade control policies in Eastern Europe after the Second World War served to cement Soviet domination of the continent, and Soviet industry became dependent upon supply from its satellites as well. A similar function can be attributed to Japan's Co-Prosperity sphere before the Second World War. Can a similar function be attributed to British imperial preferences between the wars or, indeed, to its entire colonial policy? Trade control policies might best be understood as being a function of the Great Power's grand strategy, which, in turn, reflects the nature of that power's interests.

An important element of trade blocs is whether they engender conflict with non-members – other blocs or states. Do economic blocs develop a special relationship with areas beyond its formal membership (for example, the EC with the ACP countries)? Saul Cohen thought that, for the EC to be viable, it must incorporate North Africa and the Sahara.[29] It is a traditional idea in political geography that, for a political unit to be viable, it must have economic viability. Economic viability means that the centre of power must have access to resources, which usually means control over territory.[30] This reasoning resembles the old call for autarky, especially in critical materials, but can easily lead to over-generalization and ignoring the role of ordinary market relations in providing reliable supply.

While the validity of the idea that autarky is a requirement for great power status can be dispensed with, there is a competitive element to blocs. In some cases we could see the creation of an economic bloc as being the attempt of a Great Power to either substitute for the absence of a hinterland or augment an existing hinterland. When the bloc develops special interests in external areas, conflict can result because these interests may come into conflict with another bloc or Great Power.[31] It is possible, however, that the quest for control over raw materials was more likely to lead to war in the interwar years than it is today.[32] Market mechanisms and political ties have proved to be effective instruments for assuring access today. But politically secured access and market mechanisms may themselves require protection from disruption, and smaller ambitious states may seek to disrupt stable market mechanisms. The role of OPEC in controlling supply to set prices and Iraq's war on Kuwait are different examples in the same commodity.

There is a traditional tendency to see the world in terms of emerging regional blocs. Some saw the emergence of regional blocs as reversing the trend towards global economic interdependence, with there being a greater amount of interdependence within blocs and a decreasing amount between them. The regional economic blocs are said to contain the seeds of economic warfare in them – such as the protectionist measures of the EC, as embodied in the CAP and the Common External Tariff.[33]

Part of the analysis of patterns of conflict among states involves an attempt to relate trade polarization to military power. The term 'polarization' is used here to mean a decline in trade between two countries or blocs in either absolute or relative terms. Chapters 6 and 7 partly attempt to determine whether the trade among Great Powers indicated any such changes.

MILITARY AND COMMERCIAL CONNECTIONS

There are two sides to the interaction between military power and commerce. One is when military power is employed in a way that affects commerce. These connections imply that trade is, in some way, dependent upon military power. As described below, states employ military power in peacetime to perform an array of functions, many of which involve a host of commercially relevant military actions. Trade expansion entails economic, political, and diplomatic interests, as well as strategic opportunities and vulnerabilities. Because trade is entwined with the manifold interactions of countries, we could even consider trade to be a dominant variable that acts as a central indicator of general peacetime interests. As a result, trade interests are bound up with the peacetime strategic orientation of a state.[34]

The other side to the interaction between military power and commerce is when trade affects military power in some way. These connections imply that military power is, to some extent, dependent upon trade. The role of trade in supplying military power points to the militarily significant aspects of economic policy, which are aimed at providing and ensuring resources necessary for the power and security of a state. This role of trade captures the array of mercantilist behaviours that direct economic resources towards military ends, which was indicated in some of the mercantilist thought above. One can, of course, debate the wisdom of trade policies that are influenced by military needs.[35] The point, however, is to note that trade takes on military significance because of its role in influencing military power.

If one were to list all of those uses of military power that have some impact on commerce, whether positive or negative, one would have a very long list indeed. These commercially relevant aspects of military power have been used by states in all manner of ways. Table 3.1 indicates some of the most common military actions that affect commerce. It is, of course, only a summary of what is really quite a broad area.

Table 3.1: Commercially Relevant Aspects of Military Power

On the Sea

Offensive	*Defensive*
Economic warfare, including blockades, embargoes, interdiction of trade, commerce raiding, capturing merchant ships, seizing contraband.	Maintenance of access/control of trade routes and critical waterways.
Guerre de course strategies.	Protect shipping.
Gunboat diplomacy.	Maintenance of access/control of sources of raw materials, overseas holdings.
	Security of allied territory, ports, harbours.
	Protect diplomatic representatives and lives and property of citizens abroad.
	Protect territorial waters and exclusive economic zones, fishing vessels and rights.

On the Land	**In the Air**
Occupation of colonial, allied, or satellite territory.	Control of air space.
Control of transport and communications infrastructure.	Destruction of economic and transportation infrastructure from the air.
Act as constabulary force.	Attack commercial shipping, rail lines, ports, etc.
Protect against commerce raiding by land.	
Police border (esp. when border trade exists).	

The above catalogues some of the primary points at which military power and commerce have, do, and possibly could, intersect. Taken together, the commercially relevant aspects of military power, though varying greatly in scope, intensity, and purpose, are the substantive reasons why we should expect military power to affect commerce. Applications of military power here can be offensive or defensive in nature, and be long- or short-term in duration; they can also be implicit or explicit in terms of how they relate to trade.

The broader commercially relevant uses of military power provide protective, regulative, and punitive functions for the state. The protective function refers to the use of military power to protect trade, shipping, trade routes, and access through waterways.[36] The protective function of military power also refers to the garrison on land that protects commercial and infrastructural assets from attack and interruption. Examples of the protective function over land are the old colonial armies of Britain and France, US overseas presence during the Cold War, and the requirement to protect transit rights (including those involving pipelines). It is ironic that much liberal literature in international relations upholds Britain in the nineteenth century as being the great example of liberalism, while tending to ignore the fact that Britain used both its naval power and land power (through its colonial army) in an illiberal manner forcibly to acquire territories that allowed Britain, to reuse the quote, to establish 'cordon sanitaires within which trade could prosper'.[37]

The protective function of military power appears to have some characteristics that are diffuse in nature and some that are very specific. Protection can exist continuously over time or be allocated at specific intervals or in response to specific events. It can also operate simultaneously in different geographic regions or can be focused on one place. It is also likely that all commerce that passes through protective channels is similarly protected. There is no need for discrimination among categories of commerce within a protective area. While any instance of protection will be specific in nature, such as protecting oil through the Persian Gulf, protection of commerce can exist in a more general sense as a threat to retaliate should commerce be interrupted.

Not all commerce requires an equal amount of protection or even protection in the same ways, however. Threats to commerce can be specific to a geographic area, such as a critical waterway, or vary with the political environment. The level of threat to commerce could be higher when a state confronts a specific adversary or during war and lower (and perhaps latent or non-existent) at other times. The level of threat to commerce may also vary with the importance of the commerce itself. Trade that is central to an entire economy or trade that has direct military/strategic value may be more sensitive than other categories of trade and could, by virtue of its centrality, draw fire from an adversary. Less important commodities, in turn, could escape such attention. Oil and other raw material imports, and even agricultural imports, can be highly sensitive targets for an economy, for example, but the disruption of toy imports appears to be decidedly less ominous. This distinction among classes of commerce may make sense in some circumstances where the transport channel in question is commercially specialized, while such a distinction may make less sense in other channels of transport where all classes of commerce commonly move. Geographically, however, military protection of commerce is given where and when it is needed and the form this protection takes (sea, land, and so on) depends on the context.

While the protective function would have a positive impact on trade, it is not easy to specify how this would be so. Protection supports commerce by providing a secure environment within which trade can flow. It prevents the interruption of commerce by a belligerent. The support offered to trade may be enjoyed by the country providing the protection and by other countries. All countries who use Persian Gulf oil, for example, benefit from American protection. Similarly, British domination of the Suez Canal came with the promise not to interfere with the passage of other states or to take sides during a conflict between two other countries (though this was violated during the Spanish–American War in favour of the Americans).

Because the need for protection is assessed by military planning, which takes the current, past and likely future situation into account, we could argue either that current trade is positively influenced by current and past military power or that current military power is positively influenced by current and past trade.

This issue could be further complicated by the nature of protection itself, however. It is possible that, due to the very nature of protection, we would not expect the magnitude of commerce to vary with the amount of protection. We might instead expect that some amount of protection will be provided, based on security considerations, and that, once reached, that amount will suffice for all quantities of commerce that travel through the channel in question. The character of protection appears to be absolute in nature. It is either there in a sufficient amount or it is not. If it is there, then commerce can flow and grow to any magnitude. If it is not there, then commerce can be interrupted and destroyed. While the amount of protection sent to a specific location can vary, it is possible that this variation will be determined by the magnitude of threat, rather than the magnitude of commerce.

There are three possible counters to this argument, each of which implies that the magnitudes of commerce and protection should co-vary. The first is the possibility that the magnitude of threat varies with both the composition and magnitude of commerce. The presence of threat in the first place may be totally unrelated to commerce and may be entirely military/strategic in nature, but the commerce itself becomes its actual or potential target. If the commerce is of central importance to an economy or represents a large portion of a country's trade, for example, then the level of actual or potential threat could rise with the commerce. Thus the bigger the target, the more protection it may require.

A second possible counter to this argument is that most states do not have a sufficient amount of protection in place to begin with. One state may have a sufficient amount (that is, the dominant power) and others may be vulnerable to that power, be in competition with it, or simply trade outside its protective confines. As a competitor's commerce expands, for example, the state in question may see a growing need for protection because its overall commercial interests are growing and these may be bound up with expanding interests more generally. Thus military power may expand with expanding commerce.

If NATO provided a secure environment within which American and west European trade could grow, for example, then perhaps a direct relationship between the magnitude of protection and the magnitude of commerce existed in the early years. Once NATO fully developed (perhaps after Kennedy's Flexible Response strategy), however, then the amount of protection in Western Europe proper may have been sufficient for all quantities of commerce and thereafter varied with the nature of the Soviet threat. It may also have been that the need for protection elsewhere increased, as commerce expanded geographically, although, as indicated above, the threat to commerce itself may have grown with the Soviet threat. If the threat grew as trade grew because larger amounts of trade posed a larger target for influence, then we would expect the magnitude of protection to have remained directly related to the magnitude of commerce in Western Europe.

Third, it is possible that the relationship between protection and commerce is really one between protection and the mode of transport that carries the commerce. With sea-borne trade, for example, it is reasonable to think that the magnitude of protection will grow with the number of merchant ships to be protected rather than with the amount of cargo they carry. Ten merchant vessels require the same amount of protection whether they are carrying full loads or not. The protection afforded to pipelines is also focused on the pipeline itself, rather than the oil flowing through it. If this is reasonable, then it might be that the connection between protection and commerce is moderated by the mode of transport. That is, as trade grows in magnitude, there is an increased need for more transport infrastructure (ships, pipelines, trains, and so on), which means that the need for protection will grow as well.

The regulative function of military power refers to the ability of major states to control commercial movement over land and sea. The ability of navies to control trade is, of course, a long-recognized function,[38] although only a few states have actually had this ability in a broad sense. The model example of this in the nineteenth century was the British navy. Britain's strategic positions around the narrow seas and littorals of Europe and Asia not only protected its own trade, but gave Britain the ability to regulate the commercial movements of the Continent.

The regulative function also appears to be diffuse in nature in that it involves a persistent and long-term role for military power that can exist simultaneously in different geographical regions, though any particular application of military regulation will be geographically specific. The regulative function would have a positive impact on the commerce of the state that has this ability in a few possible ways. One is that the regulative function positively affects the trade of the state in question because it amounts to the same thing as the protective function. That is, a regulative function may imply a protective function. Another way is that a country could use its ability to control movement to benefit its own commerce at the expense of others.

Related to this, the regulative function can also directly affect the commerce of other countries. The country with the ability to control the movement of others can do so in a manner that affects the commerce of the other state beneficially or adversely. It is hardly questionable that US naval power has benefited the trade flows of Western Europe, Japan, and probably a list of other countries in the postwar period.

The punitive function of large military power involves the ability of a major state to use force against another to enforce compliance and retaliate against aggression. In terms of commerce, this could involve retaliation against threats to commerce and shipping and other acts of economic warfare, threats to access and transit, a violation of treaty rights, or an attempt to control aggressive ambition. Pushing Iraq out of Kuwait was an American effort at controlling the expansive ambitions of Iraq. The British and French effort to punish Egypt in 1956, for nationalizing the Suez Canal and violating concession rights, was (from the British and French viewpoints) a failed attempt to control ambition.

The punitive function is specific in nature in that it involves the use of military power against a particular political or economic target when that target is deemed a sufficient threat. The application of military power here will be geographically specific and be related to specific events or acts of the target country. The punitive function will operate as long as the conflict between the respective countries operates. Punitive actions are probably mostly short-term in duration, unless the conflict in question lasts for a long time. There are some modern examples of punitive actions affecting commerce that seem to persist over long periods of time. One may say that American sanctions against Iraq are a long-term affair, but such acts appear to be the exception.

The list of punitive behaviours that relate to commerce are summarized in the naval literature in Chapter 1. These would include uses of limited force, such as gunboat diplomacy, which may be focused on destroying port and transport facilities and the local military assets of smaller states or landing forces on territory. Punitive acts can also include the military aspects of economic warfare, which may seek to impose an embargo or destroy the commerce of a state through *guerre de course,* or simply to cut off the flow of resources to an adversary. Punitive acts can be designed to change behaviour or they can be retaliatory in nature.

It seems clear that punitive military actions against commerce will have a negative impact on the commerce of the target. It is unclear, however, how such acts will affect the commerce of the state exacting the punishment. It could be that a threat to commerce posed by a state adversely affects the commerce of another state, causing the affected state to enact punitive measures that restore the commerce previously threatened. If this were true, we might also expect that punitive actions would have a positive impact on the trade of the state engaging in the punishment. It is likely, however, that such a scenario would not be easily distinguishable from other punitive actions, which themselves could have a different impact on commerce or none at all.

Coercive and intrusive military actions have also been used, not so much to punish an adversary or to respond to aggression, but to commit aggression itself in order to force an adversary to accept one's terms. China stands as one of the greatest historical examples of a country that has been the target of intrusive army and naval presence of most of the Great Powers at one time or another up to 1949, when the Communists came to power. The American Asiatic Squadron before the Second World War, for example, enforced American commercial rights in China and elsewhere in Asia.[39]

Intrusive military actions that relate to commerce are expansionary and acquisitive. They can range from colonial acquisitions to enforcing demands that involve smaller impediments to a recipient's sovereignty. Railway expansion throughout Asia in the nineteenth and twentieth centuries is another example of the intrusive demands of Great Powers, and the acquisition of overland transport involved both commercial and military expansion. The acquisition of military security and trade gains (and economic growth more generally) were prominent goals in railway expansion everywhere.[40]

While intrusive acts would have a positive impact on the commerce of the aggressor, at least in the short run, it is hard to find examples of the acquisitive use of military power among the major economies today. It may be easier, however, to find contemporary examples among smaller powers. There are many examples of this behaviour among the Great Powers prior to the First World War, though, as indicated throughout this book.

When taken together, the above uses of military power provide states with a fairly large menu of military actions that bear upon trade –

whether it is the control of trade routes, or the bullying of another state into concessions. The militaries of major states exert such influence in world politics on a steady basis – not solely on an issue-by-issue basis. The British navy before the First World War did not move into the Indian Ocean when a threat emerged and vacated it in the absence of a threat, but maintained a long-term presence there. An emerging threat might cause the presence of the British navy to increase in magnitude, but it also maintained a long-term presence. The German effort at undermining British control over sea access to Asia in the same period was a long-term effort as well. The US naval presence in various parts of the world during the Cold War was also a long-term affair.

Finally, we must make a distinction between military power and military spending. The above discussion of military functions refers to the state's use and employment of its existing stock of military assets, such as ships, soldiers, and guns, which were all purchased through past military spending. If we correctly argue that a threat to commerce (actual or potential) causes a state to employ some of its existing stock of military assets to a region, for example, then how exactly would this influence military spending? How are the stock of military assets and military spending connected more generally? The issue here is the degree to which variation in the use of the current stock of military assets influences variation in military spending, and perhaps in the opposite direction. Understanding this issue will aid in better understanding the degree to which changes in military spending reflect changes in military power. This is a crucial issue here because the primary military measures used in the analysis in Chapter 4 are army and navy spending.

It is clear that past military spending is responsible for the current stock of military assets, such that variation in past military spending will, at least partly, account for variation in the current stock of military assets. The difficulty here is that variation in past military spending will also reflect a welter of other influences (see my speculation on this in the introduction). It also seems clear that a dramatic increase or decrease in the use of the current stock of military assets will influence military spending in the next period. If a war occurs in one year necessitating a dramatic increase in the use of military assets, for example, then there will likely be an increase in military spending recorded for the next year. When a war ends and the current need for military assets decreases, conversely, there is likely to be a decrease in military spending in the next period. This has been true in the modern American experience and it also appears evident from the visual inspection of the military spending series used in this book. Dramatic changes in using military assets can, of course, occur below the level of war and encompass any variety of threat or necessity that decision-makers believe important enough. It is just as likely that minor variations in employing military assets will not influence future military spending because they occur within the expectations of planners.

If we put these two channels of influence together, we have a chain of mutual influence. Perhaps a threat emerges to commerce or a general need for protection is articulated by policy-makers. This will cause an employment of military assets out of the current stock. If the threat or need is thought to be large enough or if the existing stock of assets is thought to be insufficient to handle current or future needs, then military spending will increase in the next period. This, in turn, will drive up the future stock of military assets. If the presence of threat subsides or if the need for protection is thought to have decreased, or even if military needs unexpectedly become less than what was planned for, then this will lead to less employment of military assets out of the current stock. The decreased need for the current stock of assets will exert downward pressure on military spending next period. The decrease in spending, in turn, will imply a smaller stock of future assets as replacement of old stock and development of new assets decreases.

We could even generalize this relationship between the stock of military assets and spending to account for military spending in general (that is, beyond its connections with commerce). It might be convenient to think of the state as having some idea of its current needs for military assets, which would reflect information from military planners. Perhaps decision-makers expect to use a certain quantity of military assets on a regular basis in order to handle the threats and needs that have been perceived by planners, while keeping a certain quantity of military assets available but unemployed for unexpected emergencies (that is, a reserve). If the current needs turn out to require the employment of more assets than was anticipated, this would draw down the current stock below the reserve level. Military spending would then increase in the next period to replenish the reserves needed for national security. If the current needs turn out to require the employment of fewer assets than anticipated, in contrast, this would increase the size of unemployed military assets. Military spending would then decrease in the next period to adjust the quantity of military assets down to the level thought necessary.

It might even be reasonable to expect that increases in military spending due to increased needs for military assets will occur, on average, at a faster rate than decreases in military spending that are due to decreased needs for military assets. The reason for this could be that when there is an increased need to employ military assets, the rate of loss of those assets due to conflict, wear and tear, and technological obsolescence (which may be accelerated during conflict and war) will be higher, which puts additional pressure on military spending. This states only that the stock of assets shrinks more rapidly when they are being employed, requiring faster replacement.

This discussion implies a distinction between the actual uses of military assets, which draw from the current stock, and the level or total stock of existing assets. The actual uses of military assets could even be thought of as a flow concept, in contrast to the total stock of assets. The functions of military power above refer to the use of these assets, such that a measure of the level or stock of assets would probably not capture these military actions well. Changes in the use of military assets (reflecting changes in military needs or changes in the nature and magnitude of threats), however, would influence changes in the stock of military assets, as argued above. A measure of fluctuations in assets or of fluctuations in military spending, then, may be adequate inasmuch as fluctuations in either of these variables reflect changes in the use of assets and in military needs.

The only real difficulty here is that there are bound to be lead–lag relationships between changes in the use of military assets and changes in the stock of assets that will be difficult to determine. If an increased need for naval ships were articulated because current needs turned out to be higher than expected and policy-makers believed that future needs were also going to be higher, then this would lead to an increase in military spending next period and an increase in the stock of naval ships. When do the naval vessels come online and add to the stock of assets? It could take one or more periods into the future before the spending increase translates into an increase in assets, which means that there could be two or more periods into the future between the increased need for assets and their actual arrival. It seems likely that there will be different lags involved with different kinds of military assets as well due to differences in the time it takes to produce the assets or even to buy them from other countries.

Despite these difficulties, this reasoning implies that variation in military spending will partly reflect variation in military power, with reference to the functions outlined above. Because military spending will reflect numerous other influences and there will be different lags across different types of assets, however, there will be some disconnection between the behaviour of military assets and the behaviour of military spending. If this is true, then the process of employing military assets in response to commercially relevant issues will be imperfectly approximated by the connections between military spending proper and trade. There are certainly additional reasons why these connections will be imperfectly approximated (see below), but this problem may be lessened by specifying the models adequately such that most of the variation in the dependent variables is accounted for.

What implications do the militarily significant aspects of trade have for the relationship between military power and commerce? These issues address the other side of the coin, which refers to how trade can influence military power. Table 3.2 summarizes the connections between military power and commerce where military power is thought to depend on trade in some way. These summary indicators are gleaned from the literature reviewed above.

Table 3.2: Militarily Significant Aspects of Trade:

Trade as Supplier of Military Power	
Directly relevant	*Indirectly relevant*
Import of military hardware and other finished military goods, such as uniforms.	Import of raw materials, capital goods and technology for domestic production of military power.
	Import of commodities for stockpiling, or import commodities for consumption while stockpiling domestically produced goods.
	Purchase of foreign militarily sensitive corporations to access technology and resources.

Military vulnerabilities arising from trade

Loss of capacity to produce military items due to changing comparative advantage.
Purchase of domestic militarily sensitive industries by foreign corporations, which can transfer technology and capability to potential adversary.
Export of raw materials, military hardware, technology, etc., which could weaken the exporting country and/or strengthen the importing country.

The top half of Table 3.2 refers to the role of trade in supplying military power to a country. Here I distinguish between items that are directly relevant and those that are indirectly relevant. The directly relevant category is the one that will have a clear impact on state military spending. Finished military goods, whether weapons, uniforms, communications, or even food items for soldiers, are purchased by the state for its own military. Under this category, then, we would expect military spending to increase when imports of this type increase.

The indirectly relevant items in the top half of the table refer to relevant effects on the domestic economy due to trade, rather than on state spending. If a country gains the ability to produce weapons, then state spending may either increase to purchase the weapons or be redirected away from a foreign supplier to the domestic supplier with no corresponding change in spending levels. We might speculate that once a country acquires the ability to produce weapons domestically, then it may become more aggressive, which would suggest a spending increase. If a state actively seeks to create a military sector to its economy, then we might surmise that it has long-range plans for its role as a power. There would also be a time dimension here. The impact on military spending due to an increase in military production, made possible by capital imports, would occur one or more periods after the imports.

In addition, if a country imports raw materials that are significant for military industry, this would act as a source of supply to military power, but there may or may not be a corresponding impact on state spending here. The state's decision to purchase hardware from a domestic supplier is separate from the supplier's ability to import the raw materials, which suggests no impact on military spending. It could actually be that an increase in military spending drives the increase in the import of raw materials or other relevant goods for domestic military production, rather than the other way round, in order to meet the increased demand from the state to begin with. In addition, state spending may be guided in part by ensuring security of access to the raw materials as well, which would bring us back to the protective function of military power above. As with some of the arguments above, we could fashion an argument here that military power could be either a dependent or an independent variable. These items are labelled indirectly relevant because their influence on military power is not straightforward and may be of a longer-term nature than when the state directly purchases finished military goods from abroad. Stockpiling sensitive commodities has the effect of increasing the security of a state and/or economy (even if there are ambiguous welfare effects), for example, but there seems to be no direct implication for state military spending here unless the stockpiling itself were included as a category of military spending.

The bottom half of the table refers to the vulnerabilities that can occur due to trade. All of these items are indirect in nature because all of them relate to the larger economy of a country and have no direct implications for state military spending. In fact, if there is any state action at all regarding these items, it would be by way of trade policies designed to lessen vulnerabilities. The threat of the loss of capacity to produce a military item due to changes in comparative advantage, for example, could lead a state to use protectionist measures to retain the ability to produce the item.

Changes in military power under this category, then, are broader than those implied by changes in military spending. A possible exception in the bottom half of the table is when a country exports military goods or technology to another country. As mentioned in Chapter 1, it is possible that the resulting increase in military power on the part of the importing country will cause the exporting country to increase its military spending in response in order to redress any perceived imbalance in capability between itself and the importing country. The US–China trade relationship could contain such a dynamic.

The above linkages between military power and trade are very diverse. The operation of any of these connections is likely to vary by country and context. Generally, one may look at the global distribution of a major state's trade as being a geographic picture of its overall interests. This idea is in line with the geopolitical concept that both the economic potential of a country and its economic interests produce security requirements and competitive opportunities,[41] which informs its military behaviour. Trade indicates regions of the world that are most important for a state and the economic conditions that confront a state (by virtue of the commodity composition of trade, which indicates the nature of a country's dependence). These connections also lend substantive support to the navalist notion that trade and strategy go hand-in-hand because a country's trade is a barometer of its strategic interests.[42]

THE STRUCTURAL ROLE OF PEACETIME MILITARY POWER

The primary difficulty with the above connections between military power and commerce is their very diversity and the likelihood that the relevance of any mix of these connections for a given state will depend greatly on circumstances. The variety of different political, economic, and military conditions that confront states could generate such a welter of influences between military power and commerce that no obvious direction of influence or behavioural relation is evident. The connections above are real ones, however, and must relate in some measurable way. Some of the connections are long-term, some are short-term, some are defensive and some are offensive. Further, some of them imply a direct connection between commerce and state spending and some do not.

We could advance the argument that the commercially relevant aspects of military power, many of which operate on a regular basis, exert a structural presence in world politics. The protective, regulative and punitive functions of military power reflect steady levels of influence in world politics. Major states build military infrastructures that persist in peacetime. The term *infrastructure* is used in the sense implied by Thompson, which includes treaties, informal agreements, control of dependents and satellites, an alliance system, bases and other points of support, economic and military aid programmes, arms sales agreements, and similar items. Such a network allows a major state to project power and influence into other regions.[43]

With a few exceptions, I would also argue that the role of trade in providing support for military power is embedded in this structural role because these supports to military power themselves call forth military power to protect them. Regarding the immediate connections here, we would see military power as depending on trade (even if most of these links are indirect). But we can also see that military power can be employed to protect these supports, such as with access to raw materials.

Susan Strange's concept of structural power is similar to this aggregate picture of military power. Strange outlines four types of structural power to include control over security, production, credit, and knowledge. Structural power is defined as being 'the power to shape and determine the structures of the global political economy within which other states, their political institutions, their economic enterprises...have to operate'.[44] The application of military power that affects commerce is a contextual force that can vary from being a competitive spoiler of order to that of a stable presence acting as the linchpin of order itself and a bedrock for peacetime relations among states. This concept of military power is far broader than seeing it as being only a tool with which to achieve favourable outcomes, although it is certainly this too.

As a structural characteristic of peace, military power is understood here not as being a function of the macroeconomy, but as part of the milieu of the relations between states within which economic relations operate. Military power is understood here as forming the bedrock upon which peacetime relations rest. This aspect of military power would be lost if we tried to explain military power as being a demand relation in the economy or if we just focus on military power as being a tool of war (although such perspectives may be appropriate for other questions).

It could be argued that the structural role of peacetime military power represents an effort of the state to provide a semblance of the security that domestic commerce enjoys to the international commerce of its people. To some extent there is a parallel to be made here between the domestic and international environments. Commerce within a country could not survive if the state were not committed to protecting it. On the one hand, domestic police pose a threat to the robber. On the other hand, a legal system exists to process criminals into prison and to adjudicate commercial contract disputes and enforce their results. The domestic legal structure thus exists to provide a stable environment within which commerce can prosper. The defensive and protective aspects of military power that bear upon international commerce are analogous to the domestic police function of the state, only a state's military power exists in a competitive environment. The parallel breaks down, however, with the more aggressive military actions. There seems to be no modern domestic corollary to the aggressive use of military power in peacetime to coerce a favourable result, such as an act of gunboat diplomacy. In modern times, no domestic party uses the police to coerce another party into a commercial arrangement. The above parallel does hold with the defensive and protective aspects of military power, however.

One possible caveat to the above may be the argument that major states have shown a reluctance to use force to settle disputes in the contemporary world due to the constraint of international law.[45] While this is debatable, we could also ask to what extent it can be said that the strength of such laws themselves is a function of the major powers. It is true that large states make concessions to small states in treaty bargaining, as has happened with the law of the seas. But acceptance of the bargaining process itself and its sponsoring institutions are prerequisites for its effectiveness. It is a cliché to hear that the United Nations would have no influence without the support of the United States.

The ability to regulate commercial movement through military power has, at least twice in the last century and a half, been accompanied by a stable legal environment that grew out of the activities of the dominant states: before the First World War and after the Second World War. An international legal environment, composed of rules, customs, institutions, and treaties, amounts to a set of constraints on newcomers. Mahan observed that the rise of Britain in the seventeenth and eighteenth centuries was aided by the lack of a pre-existing international legal environment. He states that 'the very lawlessness of the period favored the extension of their [Britain's] power and influence',[46] because British ambition was uninhibited by legal and institutional fetters. Mahan's view is similar to the classic mercantilist view put forth by Schmoller, who saw international law as being the opportunistic creation of strong states, which justified their ambition and maintained the status quo.[47]

The dominant state becomes a major influence on the nature of the laws that accompany its rise, which serve to maintain its position and inhibit the mobility of others by establishing the terms of acceptable competition. Mahan states that 'law itself...is, in last analysis, simply force regulated'.[48] Not only does law require force to be effective, but the dominant states are the primary creators of the law and its main policemen.

The application of international law itself, then, presupposes an ability of major states to use force. Whether force is accompanied by law or not, however, the various military actions noted above are still quite evident in world politics. Despite the vast changes in the nature of world politics over the last half-century, the use of military power has not changed all that much. While military technology has changed, and with it the military doctrines that guide its use, the range of offensive and defensive military actions that have operated during peacetime have been strikingly stable for the last few centuries. Major states still engage in protective, regulative, punitive, coercive, and intrusive peacetime military activities.

MODELS AND VARIABLES

The above arguments suggest that military power and trade are directly related, but the nature of this relationship is unclear. Because some connections are long-term, some short-term, some specific, some diffuse, the nature of the relationship could vary considerably. The relevant connections between military power and commerce that apply to a given country would reflect that country's particular economic and military circumstances. It would be unlikely that the United States would be concerned with agricultural imports, for example, while the opposite would apply to Britain.

It is also likely, however, that the mix of relevant connections between military power and commerce for a country would be composed of short-term connections, the importance of which will vary from period to period, and longer-term connections. At one time, security of access to raw materials from a specific region could acquire heightened importance because of the emergence of a local threat. At another time, a country may pursue economic warfare against a target. And at still another time, a country could face a challenge to its military role in a region. In addition to all of this, there can still be certain connections that are long-term and relatively constant over time, such as protecting trade routes. The importance of the import of agriculture into Britain, for example, remained a constant theme in British policy, producing the 'starvation theory' posed by the *guerre de course* strategy of others.

In cases where there is an overriding and long-term concern with a specific commercial–military connection, there may be a correspondingly dominant policy rule for military behaviour that overrides others for a long period of time. British command of the sea was a predominant policy rule prior to 1913, for example, and it was clearly linked to import dependence (as will be discussed in later chapters). On the other hand, the nature of threats confronted by Britain changed (and grew) over time, which probably added considerable complexity to the connections between military power and commerce. France was the primary rival on the sea to Britain prior to the advent of the German challenge. Russia was also a rival in the area north of India. From approximately 1890 onwards, Britain faced challenges from all but Italy and Austria-Hungary. Britain is a good example of how long-term concerns can mix with new and changing circumstances to produce a complicated story.

An additional point to note is that the specific strategic and economic circumstances of countries imply that emphasis will vary by branch of the military and by imports and exports. It seems reasonable to expect that armies will be most important for land powers and navies for sea powers. Although there is some ambiguity here because sea powers still use their armies as foreign policy tools, which can be carried overseas by their navies. Even if the army of a sea power remains within its home territory as a tool of national defence, however, its level of readiness for war, its capability level and the defence policy posturing of decision-makers are themselves tools of influence. In addition, land powers still trade with non-contiguous parts of the world, which may call forth a naval role. Finally, imports or exports or both could be the focus of interest for countries. A country's dependence on external supply for resources may imply that imports are the focus. Protecting access to overseas markets or security of trade routes could imply that exports are more important.

A reasonable way to capture this diverse mix of connections may be to cast the relationship in terms of a country's dependence on military power where the variables of interest would be army and navy expenditures as percentages of national income. If we define imports and exports in the same way, then we could argue plausibly that the complex connections above imply that a country's dependence on military power grows with its dependence on trade and (depending on our specification) vice-versa.

When thinking specifically about what sort of relationships should be expected, however, the possibilities are complicated. The issue of protectionism is a case in point. If we rely on the average tariff level (customs revenue as a percentage of imports), then we could fashion an argument for either a positive or a negative relationship between this variable and military power. The motivation for including a protectionism variable in the model has been indicated above, though the tariff level of a country may be connected to military spending in several ways.

We might infer from interdependence literature that, if there is any relationship at all between protectionism and military power, it should be positive. The reason for this is the traditional connection between militarism (aggressive military behaviour of states, evidenced by military expansion) and mercantilism (evidenced by high amounts of protectionism and predatory economic behaviour). This could very well be true with the Great Powers.

It could also be argued, however, that the lower the level of protectionism of an economy, the more that economy is integrated into the world economy. The more liberal the trade policy, the more involvement with the economies of other countries, and thus the more interests there are to protect. Thus when protectionism is falling, the military is expanding as well. One might be tempted to say that the more liberal the state, the more of a need for peacetime military presence in the world it has.

There may be several other possible motivations for including protectionism in the proposed relationship, however. First, tariffs create revenue for the state. It is possible, though unlikely, that tariff revenue feeds military spending. If there were a direct budgetary connection, then we would expect the two to move together. This connection lacks a behavioural component, however, and is an insufficient motivation for including protectionism in a model.

Second, tariffs can be applied to military goods (finished or unfinished) at a different rate than other goods. If tariffs are high on military goods, then the state may seek to protect its military industry at home. Rising tariffs on military goods here do not directly imply a relationship between protectionism and military spending, but the tariffs could be low elsewhere. If they were low on non-military goods, then we might argue that as tariffs fall, the military expands in a manner noted above. If tariffs are low on military goods, however, then the state may seek to import military goods at a low price, which could lead to an increase in military spending and a heightened sense of dependence on external supply. This last connection might be a valid one, although it is still unconvincing.

A likely connection is that tariff policies, which are properly part of trade policies, influence trade relations between countries, which in turn influence the state of conflict between countries. Trade rivalry and military rivalry, while probably separate processes, may interact in complex ways. If we find that the average tariff rate is directly related to military spending, then, it could indicate that the trade conflicts of a country are connected to its military rivalries. It might be that the trade rivals of a country are also its military rivals (which is the case in some Great Power conflicts). An inverse relationship between the average tariff and military spending, in contrast, could imply that the state is not in trade rivalry at the time with any other state. Under these conditions, military expansion may follow trade expansion (which also implies that tariffs are falling).

It is also possible that, while a trade rivalry exists, it does not interact with an existing military rivalry, although this is probably untrue of any of the Great Power cases. Finally it is also possible that there is a trade rivalry, but no military rivalry at the time (though this is also untrue of the Great Powers).

The connection between military spending and the average tariff might also reflect a state trade policy that serves military/strategic ends (outside of the case of military goods). Perhaps the state maintains low tariffs on imports that are militarily significant (such as, raw materials and manufactures), but high tariffs on imports that are not militarily significant in order to maintain the tariff revenue. If this were the state of affairs, we might expect the relationship to be inverse with militarily significant items, but direct or nil elsewhere. In aggregate trade data, where these influences are combined, the relationship could net out to nothing or be significant in either direction, depending on which influences were stronger in the data.

Whatever the actual connections are between the average tariff and military spending, including the average tariff in the proposed relationship may be a way to establish a connection between trade policy and military spending in a manner not captured by the inclusion of trade variables alone.

The main problem with this is that the average tariff is related to trade, especially imports. As the tariff rises, imports fall. One might argue that the relationship between the average tariff and military spending exists because of the connection between imports and military spending, which would make the relationship spurious. This is unlikely because the influence moves from tariffs to imports, not the other way round. If we also argue that the influence moves from the average tariff to military spending, and that influence may be bi-directional between imports and military spending, then the spurious connection (if there is one) would be between imports and military spending. There is good reason to expect imports and military spending to be related, however, so that a spurious connection seems unlikely.

Before discussing imports and exports specifically, I will present the possible complexity that could result from the models. Table 3.3 lists the possible outcomes in the relationship between military spending and trade, where T is trade (either imports or exports), M is military spending (either army or navy), the subscripts indicate the period, and the arrows indicate whether the two variables are directly or inversely related. The first four cases describe the possibilities when military spending is the dependent variable and the last four cases show the possibilities when trade is on the left-hand side. The cases where no relationship exists are excluded.

There are 16 possible outcomes when we consider both variables as dependent variables. When considering each of the eight cases individually, of course, the meaning is obvious – there is either a direct or an inverse relationship between the variables. When considering both variables – military spending and trade – as dependent variables (that is, in separate models), then there are 16 possible outcomes, the results of which can be complicated. Six of the 16 outcomes are potentially contradictory and may indicate more complexity than initially expected, but the remaining possibilities argue for either the hypothesis developed above or the interdependence point of view.

Table 3.3: Possible Relationships between Trade and Military Spending

Cases	Dependent variable	Independent variable
1	M_t ↑	T_t ↑
2	M_t ↓	T_t ↑
3	M_t ↑	T_{t-1} ↑
4	M_t ↓	T_{t-1} ↑
5	T_t ↑	M_t ↑
6	T_t ↓	M_t ↑
7	T_t ↑	M_{t-1} ↑
8	T_t ↓	M_{t-1} ↑

Generally, the hypothesis above would be supported if the models showed that either cases one and five, one and seven, two and seven, three and five, three and seven, four and five, or four and seven existed. Each of these pairs are possible outcomes that would support the argument that military spending and trade move together. The confusing pairs here are two and seven, four and five, and four and seven. Case four alone indicates that as trade in period t-1 rises, military spending in period t falls, which appears to support the interdependence point of view. Alone, this would be the case. But if case four exists while the same country's data shows that case five or seven exists (when trade is a dependent variable), then we could interpret case four differently. Alone, we would see case four as arguing that increasing trade causes a decline in conflict and thus a decline in military spending. But we could also interpret four as indicating that falling trade motivates an increase in military spending because the fall in trade increases insecurity (with import dependence) or indicates the loss of export markets (which could entail aggressive use of military power for acquisitive ends). If cases four and five occurred, for example, then falling trade in period t-1 would lead to rising military in period t, which would lead to rising trade in period t.

Cases four and seven offer a similar story, but cases two and seven are less convincing. We could argue that these two cases together would support a direct relationship between military spending and trade, but the story appears to be less convincing than either cases four and five or four and seven. With cases two and seven, for example, the only reasonable interpretation of this would be that trade in period t falls, causing military in period t to rise, which would then cause trade in period t + 1 to rise. If this interpretation is unconvincing, then cases two and seven together may reflect contradictory information.

The interdependence point of view would be supported if the models showed that either cases two and six, two and eight, four and six, or four and eight existed. Each of these cases argues that military spending and trade move away from each other without ambiguity. Cases two and six together probably reflect the strongest case, but the others are also clear. No other interpretation of these cases appears at all likely, in the absence of additional information. If cases two and eight occurred, for example, then we would have rising military in period t-1 leading to falling trade in period t, which would lead to rising military in period t as well.

Finally, there are some potentially contradictory pairs that do not suggest ready interpretation and may require further information to understand them. These include cases one and six, one and eight, two and five, three and six, and three and eight. I will not explore these cases here, but if the statistical output reflects these cases, then more detailed information is needed.

Imports represent the goods supply to a country and thus indicate a country's dependence on other parts of the world and dependence on specific classes of goods. Imports also represent an outflow of income from a country, which also may have implications. I will confine the discussion below to the goods flow, however, because most of the relevant arguments reviewed above relate to this. An issue when imports are the independent variable, then, is whether import dependence calls forth a military role to reduce vulnerability (a support function) or whether import dependence either lowers conflict or occurs because conflict has decreased, each of which thus lessens the need for the military. If imports are the dependent variable, then the issue appears to be whether expanding military power supports or even advances imports or whether expanding military drives imports down because expanding military power is bound up with increasing conflict (military spending and conflict may be bi-directionally related), which then affects imports adversely.

A direct relationship between imports and military spending would likely reflect the significance of import dependence for an economy. This may imply a military/strategic significance (raw materials, military goods) or an overall economic one (such as with manufactured and food imports). If the important goods supplied were concentrated on specific regions of the world, then this would also indicate the importance of trade with those regions. Here military power would be a support for import dependence. This argument would be consistent with a positive relationship with or without lags and regardless of which variable was the dependent variable. In comparing the pairs above, this argument would also be consistent with cases one and five, one and seven, three and five, three and seven.

What if the relationship between imports and military spending was inverse? If this were true, then we might actually have support for the interdependence point of view. If military spending is the dependent variable and imports are an unlagged independent variable (case two), an inverse relationship would imply that falling imports drive military expansion (and perhaps conflict) and rising imports lead to declining militaries. If imports were on the left and unlagged military spending on the right and the relationship were inverse (case six), we could see military expansion (and perhaps conflict) driving down imports and falling military spending (and perhaps less conflict) as leading to increasing imports.

The story may be more complicated than this, however, when we consider lagged terms. If military spending is the dependent variable and imports are negatively related to military spending when they are lagged (case four), this could reflect either argument. We could still interpret this result in interdependence terms, where rising imports in period t-1 leads to falling military spending in period t (and perhaps decreasing conflict). We could, however, argue that a negative sign on a lagged import term would reflect the argument that military expansion in period t is motivated by acquisitive reasons, that is, is motivated by the insecurity caused by declining imports in period t-1. This possibility becomes more convincing when it occurs with either cases five or seven.

If case four occurred with cases six or eight, then we would have support for the interdependence point of view. If we reversed the variables and placed imports on the left and lagged or unlagged military spending on the right, and found military spending to be negatively related to imports (cases six or eight), this result would be consistent with the interdependence point of view.

On the other hand, if the military term were on the right-hand side and positive (cases five or seven) while occurring with case four, we would have support for the other point of view. If case four occurred with case seven, for example, we might interpret the result in the following way. Imports in period t-1 fall, leading military spending in period t to rise, which causes trade in period t + 1 to rise. If one examines cases four and seven above, this appears to be the only likely interpretation of this pair. It would make no sense to argue that as imports in t-1 rise, military in period t falls, which causes trade in period t + 1 to fall.

Exports are different from imports because export markets represent income earnings. Exports also represent a goods supply to another country, which can have direct military significance and may produce an export control policy. In most cases of exports, however, it appears that the income flow is the most relevant issue. A country's dependence on export earnings, then, can call forth a protective function. Also the movement of exports to their market, like imports, may require protection. If we find a direct relationship between exports and military spending, then we might infer that the state uses its military to protect (and perhaps even advance) its export markets. In comparing the above pairs, this argument would also be supported with cases one and five, one and seven, three and five, three and seven.

A positive relationship when exports are the independent variable (cases one or three), would indicate that military expansion occurs in response to export growth. This may reflect a support function for exports. If military spending were the independent variable and were directly related to exports (cases five or seven), then exports would grow in response to military expansion. This could also reflect the support function or it could reflect the aggressive use of military power for acquisitive ends. This might support the idea that states used their military power to advance their exports, not to merely support them.

What if exports and military spending are inversely related? If military spending is the independent variable and it is inversely related to exports (case six or eight), then we might also have support for the interdependence point of view because this would imply that expanding militaries drive exports down and vice-versa. But if exports are the independent variable and there is an inverse relationship, then the interpretation could go either way. It could be that rising exports drive down militaries because of the salutary effect that export expansion has on conflict and threat (as implied by interdependence). And it could be that falling exports lead to military expansion for the opposite reasons. Cases two or four support this view when they occur in conjunction with cases six or eight.

If exports are the independent variable and there is an inverse relationship between exports and military spending (cases two or four), however, it could also be that falling exports lead to military expansion because the state seeks to use its military as an aggressive tool to acquire export markets (that is, to reverse its loss of export markets). This behaviour was not unknown among the Great Powers, especially in the area of colonial acquisition, and may very well have played into trade conflicts where complaints arose over one country's loss to another in an export market (for example, British complaints about German trade gains from 1885 onward). Case four in conjunction with cases five or seven would support this view, as would cases two and seven.

If cases four and five existed, for example, this would imply that as trade in period t-1 falls, military spending in period t rises, which causes trade in period t to rise. If this were true then falling exports in the previous period motivate the aggressive use of military power in the current period to acquire more export markets in the current period. A similar scenario would be apparent with cases four and seven or two and seven.

If cases two and five occurred, however, we would have an apparent contradiction because there would be an inverse relationship when military was on the left and a direct one when trade was on the left, all in period t. Understanding this situation might require more detailed data.

The above possibilities are further complicated when considering the individual relationships between both imports and exports with military spending in the same model. Table 3.4 reflects these possibilities (without considering lags), where I = imports, E = exports, C = the average tariff (customs), and the arrows indicate how each is related to military spending by showing how that variable changes with rising military spending. The top part of the figure indicates how each commercial variable could be related to military spending when military spending is the dependent variable and the bottom shows how imports and exports could be related to military spending when military spending is the independent variable.

In the top part of the figure, the section labelled A reflects the possibilities for imports and exports (barring the cases where there are no changes and thus no relationships and ignoring the issue of lags), while section B reflects the cases that C can have with I and E. Each pair in the top row of section A can go with either rising or falling C, which makes four possibilities. The same is true of the bottom row of A and the bottom row of B. In the case where military spending is the dependent variable, then, there are eight possible outcomes for significant relationships between military spending and the three commercial variables (ignoring the problem of lags).

The hypothesis above points to the first pair in A (where both I and E are rising with military spending) and either pair in B. The pure interdependence case would probably be with the second pair in the bottom row of A (where both I and E are falling as military spending rises) and perhaps with rising C, all of which might show that falling trade, rising protectionism and military expansion go together. If we consider lags and the case where trade is on the left, of course, then the meaning of the results will depend upon how both sets of models compare (that is, which pairs of cases emerge).

Table 3.4: Possible Relationships between Commercial and Military Variables

---

Military spending as a dependent variable

A		B	
I ↑ E ↑	I ↑ E ↓	C ↑	C ↓
I ↓ E ↑	I ↓ E ↓	C ↑	C ↓

Military spending as an independent variable

I ↑	I ↓
E ↑	E ↓

The difficult cases are in the cross diagonal of section A, where one trade variable moves up and the other down while military spending rises. Is it likely that the interdependence argument would work on one trade variable while the above hypothesis works on another? If interdependence exerts the influence on trade that is suggested above, then there is no reason in interdependence theory to believe that only one variable would be so influenced and not the other. With the hypothesis developed above, however, we do not get much guidance either.

We might think that imports are more significantly connected to military spending than exports because of the vulnerabilities associated with import dependence, but there are reasons to expect exports to be similarly related. Is it possible that imports and exports are substantively different in terms of how they relate to military spending and in terms of how they influence conflict among states? If exports reflect income earnings, then maybe rising exports are more apt to make statesmen happy because of the increase in national income or maybe rising exports increase the costs of conflict. Thus, as exports rise, conflict declines and military power declines. Maybe statesmen will see rising export earnings as increasing the risks of disruption, however, and employ military power for protective purposes. Perhaps rising imports will increase the costs of conflict because of the increase in vulnerability in the goods supply, which implies that imports lead to a fall in conflict and perhaps military spending. Although the increase in vulnerability with imports might also call forth a protective role for military power, which would lead us to expect the opposite.

There may actually be considerable differences among states. If it is true that import dependence calls forth a military role for protection (implying an increase in military spending), for example, and if it is also true that rising imports lead to a fall in conflict (implying a fall in military spending), then which influence is more dominant in the data and why? It appears reasonable that the answer depends on the specific circumstances confronting a country.

The bottom half of Table 3.4, which reflects the possible relationship between each trade variable and military spending when military spending is an independent variable, is straightforward. Either trade variable could be positively or negatively related to military spending, with the negative outcome probably reflecting the interdependence point of view and the positive outcome the hypothesis here. In the presence of lags, and in comparison to the above cases, however, the meaning of the results will depend on the comparisons.

Once we consider lags in the independent variable, then Table 3.4 becomes more complicated, as cases one through eight can be applied to both imports and exports simultaneously. I will, of course, resist mapping these possibilities out here. Another complication here is that each branch of the military will be examined separately, which means that the results could vary by branch as well.

A potentially significant complicating factor here is the presence of conflict and war itself. We might generally think that trade and conflict or war move away from each other (a reasonable, but certainly not indisputable, possibility), but the presence of conflict and war may also change the relationship between trade and military spending. It could be that, in the absence of conflict, rivalry or war, military spending and trade are directly related because military behaviour is focused on protecting commerce (or being used aggressively for commercial reasons), but that during conflict, rivalry or war the relationship becomes insignificant or negative because military behaviour becomes focused on the conflicts at hand (where conflict and military expansion could have a combined effect of driving trade downward).

Unfortunately, the opposite could also be possible. It could be that, in the absence of conflict, rivalry, or war, military spending and trade are inversely related (for reasons suggested by interdependence), but that they become directly related during heightened states of conflict either because of the greater need for protection of commerce or because militaries during conflicts are used aggressively for commercial ends.

A potentially important theoretical issue here is the question of how a conflict process is connected to a trade process. One starting point to understanding this issue would be to fashion conflict (or its absence) as something endogenous to a trade process, where expanding trade either lessens or increases conflict (depending on the argument). Much of the conflict and trade literature (though certainly not all) appears to view conflict this way as does interdependence literature. If conflict is endogenous to a trade relationship, then there appear to be two explanations. One is that the conflict is itself over trade matters in a direct sense, such as with tariffs, trade balance issues, or conventional arguments for protection (such as job protection). In this case the role that trade plays in either creating or ameliorating conflict will likely depend on the nature of trade agreements. Further, the presence or absence of this type of trade conflict can have significance for the general relations between states (as a force for cooperation or conflict).

The other explanation when conflict is endogenous to a trade process is that the trade relationship itself could be significant for essentially non-trade issues, such as national security, or the general state of amity between countries. In this case it could be argued, for example, that expanding trade leads countries to seek cooperation and avoid conflict in other areas of policy because trade increases the costs of conflict. That is, we could employ conventional reasoning here. The basic point, though, is that the state of conflict (increasing or decreasing) is theoretically framed as being rooted in the trade relationship proper where the influence emanates from the trade relationship to the state of conflict.

The other starting point is that conflict can be framed as being exogenous to the trade relationship altogether. Here a conflict process would emerge for whatever reason (perhaps an arms race or a crisis event) and its presence then exerts an influence on trade. We can also think of the absence of conflict in the same way, though exerting the opposite influence on trade. The nature of this influence itself could operate through several channels. It could be that the general state of conflict (or its absence), while unrelated to trade in particular, nevertheless exerts downward pressure (or upward) on trade because of the hostility (or amity) between the trading countries. It could also be that trade becomes a relevant factor in an essentially non-trade conflict because of its potential strategic role in fuelling the power of an adversary, thus producing a policy of trade control. Here trade becomes a target of policy for reasons related to the conflict. It could even be that the presence of conflict heightens the threat posed to trade (for example access, dependence, export earnings) because it is a potential source of influence for an adversary (that is to inflict injury or control) which could either disrupt trade or call forth a military role for protection (which would support trade).

It is likely that mapping out all of the theoretical links between a conflict process and a trade process would produce a plethora of possible connections (very much like the connections between military spending and trade above). Different types of conflict can exist at the same time, some related to trade itself and some not, which could generate influences moving in different directions.

In the models below, conflict and war variables enter the models as independent variables. The goal is to determine whether the presence or absence of conflict or war modifies both the trade and military terms themselves and the relationship between military spending and trade. While the theoretical issues just noted are not mapped out in this work, we could likewise find mixed results. Perhaps the influence that conflict, rivalry, and war have on the relationship between military spending and trade varies by type of conflict. Perhaps conflicts among Great Powers are different than those between Great Powers and others. Perhaps proximity of the conflict to commercial centres or trade routes is the issue.

Because the focus of this study is on the relationship between military power and commerce, the trade and conflict dimension to these variables will play a smaller part than the rest. Despite this, the presence of the conflict and war variables in the trade models below will provide some insight into whether these variables influence imports and exports themselves.

With the above in mind, two core models are defined below (and tested in Chapter 4). For the case where military spending is the dependent variable, the central model, along with the expected signs on the independent variables, is:

$$\overset{+\qquad\ +\qquad\ +/-\qquad\ +\qquad\ +\qquad\ +}{ARMY_t/NAVY_t = f(IMP_t, EXP_t, CUST_t, WAR_t, CON_t, RIVAL_t)}$$

where the dependent variable is either army or navy expenditures. For the argument that military power should be an independent variable, the central model is:

$$\overset{+\qquad\ +\qquad\ -\qquad\ -\qquad\ -}{IMP_t/EXP_t = f(ARMY_t, NAVY_t, CUST_t, WAR_t, CON_t)}$$

where the dependent variable is either imports or exports. The variables for the above two models are defined as follows:

$ARMY_t$ = the annual growth rate of army expenditures as a percentage of national income

$NAVY_t$ = the annual growth rate of naval expenditures as a percentage of national income

$IMPt$ = the annual growth rate of imports as a percentage of national income

EXP_t = the annual growth rate of exports as a percentage of national income

$CUST_t$ = the annual growth rate of the average tariff level, where the average tariff is customs revenue as a percentage of imports

$\text{WAR}_t =$ a dummy variable for war (1 = war, 0 otherwise)

$\text{CON}_t =$ a dummy variable for conflict, derived from the Hostility Level variable in the Militarized Interstate Disputes (MID) data set.[49] CON_t takes the value of 1 if there is conflict (excluding war), 0 otherwise, and reflects the presence of conflict below the level of war. War is tested separately.

$\text{RIVAL}_t =$ the annual growth rate of military expenditures as a percentage of national income of a rival state. This could involve the army, navy or total military spending of one or more rivals.

Each independent variable has been specified in period t, but both period t and t–1 will be examined. An independent variable will be included in a model if it enters lagged, unlagged or in both forms. Whether imports in period t, t–1, or both fit into a model may vary by country and will be left as an empirical question.

WAR_t will actually be broken into two separate war variables when possible. The first war term will reflect major wars that each state has had and the second will reflect smaller wars, including colonial wars. Britain, for example, participated in the Crimean War (1853–56), and the two Boer Wars (1880–81, 1899–1902), while also participating in a series of smaller engagements with the rest of the world, such as the Sudanese War (1881–85), the Samoan Civil Wars (1887–89, 1893–94, 1898–99). I am interested in determining if these two classes of war influenced the military and trade variables differently. In the American case, the distinction in types of wars is that between wars outside the US (in Asia and the Western Hemisphere) and internal wars with Native Americans. There were many years of wars with Native Americans after the US Civil War, which may very well enter into the US army model.

CON_t is also a dummy that takes on the value of 1 if there was conflict during a given year that was below the level of war, as indicated by the Hostility Level variable in MID. If there was no conflict during a year or if there was war (even if war coexisted with conflict below the level of war), then CON_t takes on the value of 0 (1 otherwise).

Additional Variables

In addition to the core variables above, a series of dummy variables that reflect large events will be tested in the models. The dummy variables will be based on the following significant dates:

1871: Franco–Prussian War ended; a united Germany emerged
1878: Russo–Turkish War ended
1882: Triple Alliance signed
1890: Wilhem II emphasized the navy; Anglo-German naval rivalry
        started in earnest
1894: Franco-Russian Alliance signed; Sino–Japanese War began
1896: Italy defeated at Adowa
1898: Spanish–American War
1904: Anglo–French Entente; Russo–Japanese War began
1907: Anglo-Russian Agreement signed

In each case, the dummy will take the value of 0 on one side of the date and 1 on the other side. For example, D1871 would have the value of 1 up to 1871 and 0 from 1872 onwards. The issue is whether the relationship between any of the commercial variables and military spending changed from the above events onward. Generally speaking, each of the above dates marks the onset of greater competition, rivalry and aggression for the states involved. Germany certainly became a major competitor to France after the Franco–Prussian War, and the United States became a more serious competitor on the sea after the Spanish–American War. The last two dates are exceptions. The Entente between France and Britain marks cooperation over colonial questions in Africa, but is generally bound up with the larger rivalry at work. The Anglo-Russian Agreement of 1907 marked the (possible) end to Anglo-Russian rivalry over Afghanistan, but may be best seen as part of the British attempt to decrease the number of competitors it faced in order to concentrate more on the German problem.

The dummy variables will be manipulated slightly as well to determine whether the significant break-point occurred before, during, or after the above dates. Perhaps 1872 is more important for France than 1871, or perhaps 1877 is more important for Russia than 1878. The above dates merely mark the relevant events to be tested, but the actual break-points (if they exist) could be the year before or even after the event. In addition, an event above can have relevance for countries not directly involved. The advent of united Germany, for example, may be strongly relevant for France, Britain, and Russia.

A relative price measure will also be included in the import and export models when it makes a contribution as well. I decided to construct this measure because the trade models do need relative prices in them to capture the influence of domestic and foreign demand. The measures were constructed by taking the average of the wholesale price indexes of all of the countries in the study (not including Russia), except for the WPI of the country of interest. A ratio was then formed by placing this average WPI in the numerator and the national WPI of the country of interest in the denominator and then the percentage change of this ratio was taken. The resulting ratio would reflect the growth rate of the foreign price over the domestic price, or the growth rate of PF/PD. The percentage change of this ratio should be directly related to exports. For imports, the measure is the percentage change of the reciprocal of the ratio, or the percentage change of PD/PF (not the reciprocal of the percentage change of the other measure). The larger this measure is, the higher domestic prices are relative to foreign and the more imports there should be.

These relative price measures are crude in that they do not take into account the total number of countries that each of the countries in this study traded with, but these data are not readily available. We could include the WPIs of more countries, but we would generally not be able to get all of the relevant ones. In addition, this measure is not weighted in any way. Despite these weaknesses, the measure may still capture some variation in trade because the included countries are major trade partners of each other to begin with.

The annual growth rate of national income will be included in those models where it makes a contribution in order to absorb any economic influences on the dependent variables not accounted for by the commercial variables. The exceptions here are for Russia and Japan, both of whose national income data are available back to 1885 only. The only shortcoming with the national income data here is that GNP is the measure for Britain, Italy and the United States, while GDP is the measure for France and NNP for Germany. These are all different measures of national income. Despite this, the growth rates of these measures may serve a productive role in the models. For simplicity, they will all be designated as GNP_t in the models.

The growth rate of non-military government spending (GOV_t = total spending less military spending) will also be included in those military models where it makes a contribution. Non-military spending may reflect fiscal and budgetary influences on the military variables. I would expect that the more active a country's military is as a tool in foreign policy, however, the less related military spending will be to non-military spending. The reasoning behind this is that if the military is not very active in foreign policy and external conflict, then the same range of influences that generate non-military spending may exert influences on military spending. We might also expect armies to be weakly related to non-military government spending when armies are also used as domestic constabularies in their home countries, which implies that internal security considerations (as opposed to fiscal and budgetary ones) influence army spending. Generally the more active the military is in foreign policy or domestic police work, then, the less it will be influenced by non-military spending.

The growth rate of each country's merchant shipping tonnage ($MERC_t$) will also be included in those navy models and trade models where it makes a contribution. Merchant shipping tonnage may also reflect the connections between military spending and commerce in the navy models. I would expect this variable to enter a navy model positively. It may be, however, that the larger the trading position of a country, the less likely it is that merchant tonnage will enter its navy model. The reason for this could be that the large trading position is carried by ships under different flags, not necessarily the national flag. The smaller the trading position of a country, the more likely it may be that its navy is closely associated with its national merchant tonnage. Merchant tonnage may also help to capture some variance in the import and export models and so will also be tested in them. Finally, AR1 terms will also be included in the models when they make a contribution as well.

Generally, all military and economic data have been prepared in an identical manner.[50] Each series was deflated with the WPIs of each country (1913 = 100) and made percentages of national income, and then the percentage change of each was taken. The exceptions are the average tariff variable, which is the percentage change of customs revenue as a percentage of imports, and Japanese and Russian data. In these cases, percentage changes have been taken on each variable without first using national income. Finally, Russian data is all nominal because the Russian WPI is available back to 1885 only.[51]

Preliminary investigation shows that the military and trade variables as percentages of national income, and the average tariff level, have unit roots. Most of the variables do not have obvious trends up or down, but meander up and down over long enough time periods to prevent them from being stationary in their levels. Growth rates (the numerators of which are the first differences of the variables) purge the unit roots from the data. In addition, the focus on percentage changes allows comparison across all countries without confronting the problem of exchange rates. Finally, the relationships will be on a firmer basis if they are found in the annual fluctuations of the data rather than in their levels.

The first model above argues the straightforward case that military power is a positive function of trade, war, conflict, and rivalry and is either a positive or a negative function of protectionism. War and conflict may measure much the same thing, though war will be far more concentrated on a few years than conflict will be.

The conflict variables were initially going to be used in ordinal form, but it was decided that making dummies of them was a better option. Initially, I had defined two conflict variables from the Hostility Level variable from the MID data set. The first was ordinal and measured the highest level of conflict that a country had during a given year (regardless of the number of conflicts it had), on a scale of zero to five, where five was actual war. The second variable measured the number of conflicts a country had during a given year, regardless of their level. Instead, I have decided to separate war and conflict and make simple dummy variables out of each.

Times of war and conflict (as well as periods of heightened rivalry) may cause changes. When war erupts, three changes can happen regarding the variables above. First, military expenditures can increase dramatically. Second, if the war is large enough, trade can decline – sometimes drastically. Third, if the war is large enough, protectionism can increase.

The possible changes to the commercial variables due to war, and perhaps conflict and general threat, might cause a change in the behaviour of military power. What if military spending and imports are inversely related, for example, but become positively related under conditions of conflict? This could imply that the military support of imports exists when there is conflict, but not otherwise.

It is also possible that states pursue basically liberal trade policies, but abandon them during war, either to use trade policy to aid in war production at home or to use trade policy to weaken an adversary. If trade during war is sought and expanded in order to feed war production or to supplement domestic consumption in some way, then the relationship between military power and trade during war is more complex. Changes along these lines could be indicated if the relationship between the average tariff level and military spending undergoes changes during conflict and war.

The second model argues that trade is a positive function of military power and a negative function of protectionism, war, and conflict. The sign on WAR_t reflects the possibility that war causes trade to fall, which could reflect national security issues or the devastating effects of war. The negative sign on CON_t indicates that conflict could have a negative impact on trade, but this is uncertain. It is possible that the two are positively related for several reasons. Conflict could be used as an opportunity for trade gains. If conflict reflects Great Power rivalry, then it could be positively related to trade because aggressive trade expansion and conflict may move together with the Great Powers. The sign on $CUST_t$ reflects the traditional, though not guaranteed, expectation that trade and protectionism are inversely related. The $CUST_t$ variable will be excluded from the trade model when exports are the independent variable. There is no compelling reason to include this variable in the export model. It is possible that a country's exports fall when its average tariff level is high due to the retaliatory behaviour of other countries, but if such a connection exists in the data it is probably not straightforward. It may be that the relationship between a country's tariff level and its exports varies from one trade relationship to another and from one time period to another.

In each case, single equation OLS will be used. The reason for this is that I want to give each dependent variable full freedom to be related or not to any of the regressors that will be tested, and I want to test each model for possible changes in the relationships using the dummy variables. While the above argument (and that of interdependence theory) suggests some general outline for a relationship, as indicated in the core models above or the model in Chapter 2, the details of any such relationship are unknown. Thus the models above, along with the additional regressors to be tested, will be built in an exploratory fashion. The reader may accuse me of data-mining because of this, but the relationships have been derived generally from the above arguments and it is their details and differences across countries that are unknown. While I have defined a set of regressors based upon my argument, then, I want also to let the data speak for itself within those limits and to allow my argument every opportunity to be wrong.

My goal is to produce the most convincing models possible with each country, given the variables under consideration. This might very well mean that the trade variables simply do not enter the military models and I am totally incorrect. It may mean that the trade variables do enter the military models, but in complicated ways. Generally, there will first be four models for each country estimated, one for each branch of the military and one for each trade variable. This will produce 28 models in total. After estimating and evaluating these models, I will then estimate a second set of single equation models using more detailed trade data. This second set of regressions is in Chapter 8.

NOTES

1. While the bulk of the geopolitical literature is excluded from this discussion, an example of a geopolitical work that draws on liberalism is Daniel Deudney, *Whole Earth Security: A Geopolitics of Peace* (Washington, DC: Worldwatch Institute, July 1983). For a discussion of the different themes in geopolitical thought along these lines, see Geoffrey Parker, *Western Geopolitical Thought in the Twentieth Century* (New York: St. Martin's Press, 1985).
2. Robert Gilpin, *The Political Economy of International Relations* (Princeton, NJ: Princeton University Press, 1987), pp. 31–3.
3. Michael A. Heilperin, *The Trade of Nations* (New York: Alfred A. Knopf, 1947), pp. 94–6.
4. Robert Gilpin, *US Power and the Multinational Corporation: The Political Economy of Foreign Direct Investment* (New York: Basic Books, 1975), p. 27. See the table on p. 31 for a brief comparison of the liberal, Marxist and mercantilist approaches.

5. Gustav Schmoller, *The Mercantile System and its Historical Significance* (1897; reprint. New York: Augustus M. Kelly, 1967), p. 2.

6. Ibid., p. 63.

7. Charles W. Cole, *French Mercantilist Doctrines Before Colbert* (1931; reprint. New York: Octagon Books, 1969), p. 223.

8. Eli F. Heckscher, *Mercantilism*, revised edn, E. F. Soderlund (ed.), Vol. 2 (London: George Allen and Unwin, 1955), p. 31.

9. Albert O. Hirschman, *National Power and the Structure of Foreign Trade* (Berkeley: University of California Press, 1945), pp. 14–15.

10. Stephen D. Krasner, *Defending the National Interest: Raw Materials Investments and US Foreign Policy* (Princeton, NJ: Princeton University Press, 1978), p.38.

11. R. G. Hawtrey, *Economic Aspects of Sovereignty* (London: Longmans, Green and Co., 1930), pp. 26, 105.

12. Hirschman, *National Power*, p. 9. David Baldwin, *Economic Statecraft* (Princeton, NJ: Princeton University Press, 1985), p. 83.

13. See Robert B. Ekelund, *Mercantilism as a Rent-Seeking Society: Economic Regulation in Historical Perspective* (College Station: Texas A and M University Press, 1981).

14. Hirschman, *National Power*, pp. 4–5. Robert L. Schuyler, *The Fall of the Old Colonial System: A Study in British Free Trade, 1770–1870* (London: Oxford University Press, 1945), pp. 9–10.

15. Heckscher, *Mercantilism*, pp. 40–44.

16. Gautam Sen, *The Military Origins of Industrialisation and International Trade Rivalry* (New York: St. Martin's Press, 1984), pp. 6–8.

17. Ibid., p. 71.

18. Nazli Choucri and Robert C. North, *Nations in Conflict: National Growth and International Violence* (San Francisco: W. H. Freeman and Co., 1975), pp. 14, 16–17.

19. Edward M. Earle, 'Adam Smith, Alexander Hamilton, Fredrich List: The Economic Foundations of Military Power', in Edward M. Earle (ed.), *Makers of Modern Strategy: Military Thought from Machiavelli to Hitler* (Princeton, NJ: Princeton University Press, 1943), p. 136.

20. Jacob Viner, *The Customs Union Issue* (New York: Carnegie Endowment for International Peace, 1950), p. 19.

21. Heckscher, *Mercantilism*, p. 32.

22. Schmoller, *Mercantile System*, p. 72.

23. Ernest H. Preeg, *Economic Blocs and US Foreign Policy* (Washington, DC: National Planning Association, 1974), pp. 8, 23.

24. Ibid., p. 24.

25. Ibid., p. 7.

26. Bela Balassa, *The Theory of Economic Integration* (Homewood, IL: Richard D. Irwin, 1961), pp. 10–11.

27. Viner, *Customs Union*, pp. 91–2.

28. A good discussion of German trade policies in eastern Europe is David E. Kaiser, *Economic Diplomacy and the Origins of the Second World War: Germany, Britain, France, and Eastern Europe, 1930–39* (Princeton, NJ: Princeton University Press, 1980).

29. Cohen, *Geography*, pp. 151–3, 190.

30. Richard Hartshorne, 'Political Geography in the Modern World', *Journal of Conflict Resolution* 4/1 (March 1960), pp. 61–5.

31. Preeg, *Economic Blocs*, pp. 143–4.

32. While the major states in the postwar period have required security, they have

also demonstrated reluctance to use force when access has been threatened. In addition, political agreements and existing international law seem, in most cases, to assure access, although there are examples showing both the reluctance to use force (e.g., OPEC in 1973, closing of Suez in 1967) and the willingness to do so (e.g., US naval presence in the Straits of Hormuz, the Persian Gulf War) on matters that have to do with access. It seems unlikely that a trend in either direction on this question exists.

33. Preeg, *Economic Blocs*, pp. 55–6. Douglas Evans, *The Politics of Trade: The Evolution of the Superbloc* (New York: John Wiley and Sons, 1974), pp. 15–16.

34. We could even see peacetime trade as being a feature of a state's grand strategy. Edward N. Luttwak's definition of grand strategy here is insightful. See his *Strategy: The Logic of War and Peace* (Cambridge, MA: Belknap Press, 1987), pp. 179–80. Luttwak states that all the military aspects of state behaviour at lower levels of strategy produce results in international politics, which interact with all the non-military transactions of states. He includes diplomacy, propaganda, intelligence operations, and the economic transactions between states in the non-military component of grand strategy.

35. It is common for economists to decry such policies as being wasteful and unnecessary. A classic statement on this is Mancur Olson Jr., *The Economics of Wartime Shortage: A History of British Food Supplies in the Napoleonic War and in World War I and II* (Durham, NC: Duke University Press, 1963).

36. Most navalist works deal with these issues in some capacity. Some good discussions can be found in Robert J. Hanks, *The Cape Route: Imperiled Western Lifeline* (Cambridge, MA: Institute for Foreign Policy Analysis, 1981); by the same author, *The Unnoticed Challenge: Soviet Maritime Strategy and the Global Choke Points* (Cambridge, MA: Institute for Foreign Policy Analysis, 1980); Charles W. Koburger, *Narrow Seas, Small Navies, and Fat Merchantmen: Naval Strategies for the 1990s* (New York: Praeger, 1990); Nicholas Tracy, *Attack On Maritime Trade* (Toronto: University of Toronto Press, 1991).

37. Gerald Morgan, *Anglo-Russian Rivalry in Central Asia: 1810–1895* (London: Frank Cass, 1981), pp. 11.

38. Some argue that the main goal of naval power itself is to acquire surface control over the sea and the movements of others. See Chapter 1 for extended discussion and Koburger, *Narrow Seas*, p. xiv, on this particular point.

39. A concise discussion of US naval policy and diplomacy towards the Far East, with specific attention to China from the late nineteenth century into the 1920s can be found in Bernard Cole, *Gunboats and Marines: The United States Navy in China, 1925–1928* (Newark: University of Delaware Press, 1983), pp. 24–44.

40. Maurice Pearton, *Diplomacy, War and Technology* (Lawrence: University Press of Kansas, 1989), p. 65. An excellent discussion of railroad expansion and geopolitics can be found in Milan Hauner, *What is Asia to Us? Russia's Asian Heartland Yesterday and Today* (Boston: Unwin Hyman, 1990).

41. Most classical geopolitical works, such as those of MacKinder and Spykman, deal with resources, raw materials, colonies, and related matters in terms of strategic opportunities and vulnerabilities. More recent geopolitical works that deal with some of these issues are Ewan W. Anderson, *Strategic Minerals: The Geopolitical Problems for the United States* (New York: Praeger, 1988); and Colin S. Gray, *The Leverage of Sea Power: The Strategic Advantage of Navies in War* (New York: Free Press, 1992). Among other issues, Gray discusses *guerre de course* strategies in various contexts.

42. Patrick O'Sullivan, *Transport Policy: Geographic and Economic Planning Aspects* (Totowa, NJ: Barnes and Noble, 1980), p. 203.

43. Scott W. Thompson, *Power Projection: A Net Assessment of US and Soviet Capabilities* (New York: National Strategy Information Center, 1978), pp. 7–8.
44. Susan Strange, *States and Markets* (London: Pinter Publishers, 1988), pp. 24–5, 26–9.
45. In addition to norms against force, however, there is also an enormous supply of resources on land, and there are usually several alternative sources for a state. See, for example, Erik Moberg, 'The Protection of Resources', in J. Alford (ed.), *Sea Power and Influence: Old Issues and New Challenges* (London: IISS, 1980), pp. 22. Moberg asks whether it is likely that a state will attack another in order to control its maritime resources. He answers in the negative, except perhaps in the case of oil. It is more likely that a state will attack the maritime resources of another to influence its behaviour, however.
46. Alfred T. Mahan, *The Interest of America in Sea Power: Present and Future* (1897, reprint. Port Washington, NY: Kennikat Press, 1970), pp. 70.
47. Schmoller, *Mercantile System*, pp. 70–1.
48. Alfred T. Mahan, *Armaments and Arbitration: Or the Place of Force in the International Relations of States* (New York: Harper and Brothers, 1912), p. 106.
49. Note on MID data set. The Militarized Interstate Disputes (MID) data set of the Correlates of War project was accessed on the web at pss.la.psu.edu/DATARES.HTM.
50. For a complete discussion on the sources of the data and data preparation issues, see Appendix 1.
51. The Russian WPI and national income data are available back to 1885 in Paul R. Gregory, *Russian National Income: 1885–1913* (Cambridge: Cambridge University Press, 1982).

4

Models of Great Power Military Spending and Trade

This chapter explores the relationship between military power and commerce before the First World War by estimating a set of models for each country. The data indicate a complicated story. There is substantial evidence in the models below that, for the period before the First World War, military power and trade move together and that these relationships cut across differences in size and geographic orientation. There is also evidence of the opposite in the same models, however. In some countries, there are significant negative coefficients on some of the trade and military variables and significant positive coefficients on others.

After discussing the models and related matters, the following three chapters then examine descriptively the commercial and military data of the Great Powers to gain greater depth of understanding of the statistical results. Some main military and economic indicators of each are compared in order to see whether an overall pattern is present that helps explain the diversity in the findings. This will include a discussion of the trade and military expansion of the states. Special attention is given to the geographic and commodity-wide distributions of trade and Great Power movement through the Suez Canal. These indicators are related to the expansionary practices of the states. Then the trade relations and conflicts of known military rivals are compared in order to gain insight into how military rivalry affects trade. The areas of importance here include the relative positions of rivals in each other's trade, and their positions in the trade of third areas or countries. A final set of models is then estimated in Chapter 8.

The statistical results below are divided into two groups. All variables are those defined in Chapter 3. The first group includes regressions that test for relationships where army and navy expenditures are the dependent variables. The second group tests for relationships where army and navy expenditures are independent variables and imports and exports are dependent variables. The tabular presentation of the models in all cases may present some confusion because some terms are lagged and some unlagged, and only in cases where both forms entered a model is that evident in the table. The presence of lags is discussed with each model, but the reader can refer to Appendix 2 for the full specification of each model.

MILITARY POWER AS A DEPENDENT VARIABLE

The first group of models (Tables 4.1 and 4.2) offer some interesting results. Each country's army and navy data was regressed against import, export, tariff, conflict, and military data. The growth rate of national income was also included in those models where it made a contribution and the growth rate of merchant tonnage was included in those navy models where it made a contribution. Dummy variables, reflecting possible changes that occurred at specific times, were also tested (see Chapter 3 for the description of variables and dates). Three basic procedures were followed in testing for possible changes here. The Chow break-point and forecast tests were each conducted on the models, using a series of possibly significant dates. These tests yielded conflicting results in a number of cases, however, which is not uncommon. The presence of change was also tested with the use of intercept dummies and slope dummies with the commercial and military variables.

There were a few cases where the Chow tests suggested a significant change, but where this change could not be corroborated with slope or intercept dummies. There are quite a few cases where a significant (or near significant) intercept dummy was included in a model, where the dummies measured either possible change after a significant event or during conflict more generally. There were actually a larger number of cases where it appeared that significant slope dummies existed, but many were ultimately rejected. In these cases, the possible changes indicated by the slope dummies were simply not convincing enough to include in the models.

In cases where significant slope dummy terms were included, two types of change are reflected in the results. One type of change is when the relationship between the dependent variable and the independent variable of interest is generally statistically significant, but then loses statistical significance altogether in a certain block of time (such as after a major war) or when a certain condition is present (such as conflict). The other type of change is when there is a significant change in magnitude or even in the sign of the terms in question. In these cases, there is statistical significance both before and after the break-point and the relationship in question may change either in magnitude or direction.

The actual direction of the relationship appears to change significantly in a few cases, while in others the change is actually one of magnitude.

Table 4.1: Regressions with ARMY as Dependent Variable

	Britain 1854–1913	France 1858–1913	Germany 1875–1913	Italy 1865–1913	Japan 1875–1913	Russia 1864–1913	US 1869–1913
Constant	3.441	−10.341	4.122	−0.867	1.11	31.658	−5.24
IMP	2.295	1.215	−0.782	−1.232	−0.468	−1.582	−1.057
	(3.225)	(3.721)	(−2.403)	(−4.329)	(−2.674)	(−8.512)	(−2.295)
IMP(−1)	−0.873					−0.375	
	(−1.596)					(−3.312)	
EXP			0.83	0.318			0.33
			(2.91)	(1.548)			(1.336)
EXP(−1)	1.982	−0.711			0.196		−0.93
	(2.839)	(−3.016)			(1.256)		(−2.991)
CUST	1.147	0.92	−0.361		0.327	1.943	1.073
	(2.534)	(5.171)	(−2.278)		(3.069)	(9.265)	(3.145)
GNP	1.012	−1.426		0.913			1.048
	(1.456)	(−2.781)		(1.64)			(2.197)
GOV		−1.216		0.733	0.235	0.334	−1.326
		(−9.295)		(2.503)	(1.905)	(2.277)	(−3.21)
Navy	0.469			0.541	0.128	−0.839	1.153
	(2.331)			(4.9)	(2.008)	(−2.805)	(6.741)
WAR1	22.844	98.034		9.099	−18.485		
	(2.51)	(9.239)		(2.874)	(−2.287)		
WAR2		12.563					
		(2.113)					
CON	−11.679	0.969	−0.624	−10.134			
	(−2.2)	(0.191)	(−0.206)	(−2.739)			
DTIME	−0.143		−4.947		−0.192	−29.165	−1.992
	(−0.021)		(−1.802)		(−0.028)	(−4.598)	(−0.42)
RIVAL1		−0.756	−0.734		−0.251		−0.783
		(−4.011)	(−2.681)		(−2.526)		(−2.573)
RIVAL2			0.268				
			(3.897)				
SLOPE1	−2.257	−2.389	1.058		1.21	0.65	−1.498
	(−2.742)	(−4.565)	(3.205)		(3.351)	(2.016)	(−2.348)
SLOPE2						1.515	
						(6.37)	
SLOPE3						−1.902	
						(−7.128)	
AR1	0.32	0.55	−0.434	−0.627	0.201	0.457	−0.372
	(2.11)	(4.834)	(−2.508)	(−5.004)	(1.077)	(2.907)	(−2.382)
AdjR²	0.583	0.748	0.529	0.605	0.601	0.81	0.603
DW	1.929	2.091	2.084	2.093	1.955	2.023	2.048
n	60	56	39	49	39	50	45

Note: t values in parentheses.

Table 4.2: Regressions with NAVY as Dependent Variable

	Britain 1854–1913	France 1857–1913	Germany 1874–1913	Italy 1864–1913	Japan 1874–1913	Russia 1864–1913	US 1869–1913
Constant	15.162	–26.824	25.056	–2.731	–16.621	2.081	–0.007
IMP	–1.651	0.75	–0.985	0.761	–0.164		–1.98
	(–2.783)	(2.811)	(–3.829)	(3.347)	(–0.579)		(–7.821)
IMP(–1)				0.404		–0.006	
				(1.871)		(–0.052)	
EXP	–0.623	–0.796	–1.556			0.312	0.39
	(–2.23)	(–2.544)	(–3.666)			(1.589)	(2.659)
CUST	0.456	–0.786	–1.11	0.559			0.286
	(2.348)	(–3.223)	(–6.735)	(3.219)			(1.292)
GNP	–0.444		–1.302				–0.686
	(–1.685)		(–3.169)				(–2.896)
GOV		0.248		–0.559	0.417		
		(1.742)		(–2.049)	(2.234)		
Army	0.547	–0.575		0.348	1.888		
	(5.622)	(–3.628)		(3.986)	(5.197)		
WAR1		33.847					
		(3.503)					
WAR2	–11.252	12.952	–5.319			–6.717	
	(–3.17)	(2.594)	(–1.486)			(–1.942)	
CON	0.997				30.767	8.771	1.388
	(0.378)				(4.481)	(2.72)	(0.353)
MERC	–1.28	–0.814	1.634	–0.819	1.914		3.609
	(–1.932)	(–1.27)	(2.463)	(–2.267)	(9.743)		(6.07)
DTIME1	–0.905	22.475	–10.816	6.479	–13.212	1.792	–5.927
	(–0.321)	(3.781)	(–2.331)	(1.82)	(–1.937)	(0.467)	(–2.021)
DTIME2			–6.461				
			(–1.365)				
RIVAL1		–0.663	0.302			0.344	–0.371
		(–3.186)	(1.355)			(1.99)	(–4.115)
SLOPE1	–0.526	0.519	1.301		–2.041	0.794	1.126
	(–4.611)	(2.931)	(2.61)		(–5.25)	(2.847)	(3.533)
SLOPE2	1.645	1.639	1.754		1.034	–0.632	
	(2.557)	(2.786)	(5.982)		(2.468)	(–2.733)	
SLOPE3	1.312	0.517					
	(3.515)	(1.523)					
AR 1	0.18					–0.318	–0.54
	(1.344)					(–1.982)	(–3.89)
AdjR²	0.722	0.499	0.695	0.493	0.747	0.338	0.655
DW	2.228	1.946	2	2.013	1.996	1.783	2.054
N	60	57	40	50	40	50	45

Note: t values in parentheses.

Finally, AR1 terms were included in models when they made a contribution as well. It seems that the AR1 terms made contributions to each of the army models, but only two of the navy models. The resulting models also contain some collinearity among the regressors, though none of it appears to unduly degenerate the models.

Military and Conflict Variables

Generally, accounting for the variance of the army variables was more straightforward than the navy variables. There is a tendency for some of the navy models to fit less well than the army models, which was unexpected. The French, Italian, and Russian navy models are the poorest fits, but the Russian model is poor enough to be unconvincing. The key variable that is missing from the Russian navy model is probably merchant shipping tonnage, which is only partially available over the sample period. It is not terribly surprising that the Russian navy model is such a poor fit, however, given the land orientation of Russia.

Despite the poorer overall fits of some of the navy models, however, the commercial terms enter them as convincingly as they do the army models. The obvious differences in the overall fits, though, could indicate that army and navy spending share only moderate similarities. It is certainly true that more significant changes in the relationships between the independent and dependent variables were detected in the navy models with the dummy variables (13 compared to eight in the army models). This may reflect the fact that navies were generally more flexible an instrument of foreign policy than armies. That is, the presence of changes in the nature of these relationships may reflect shifts in the roles played by these militaries. It may also be that navy spending responds to more specific information than general commercial data. It may be that a subset of the trade variables enters the models more convincingly, such as the trade to a specific region or the trade of a specific commodity group. This issue is addressed more fully below.

It is also interesting that the navy variable enters five of the army models (excluded from those of France and Germany), while the army variable enters only four navy models (excluded from the German, Russian, and US navy models). Where both military terms enter the model of the other term positively, there may have been a strong similarity in how the respective branches of the military were used, or even an interdependence where each supported the other. Where one branch enters negatively into the equation of the other (the navy term in the Russian army model, the army term in the French navy model), this may indicate that the country has shifted its emphasis from one branch to the other over time.

Such a shift in emphasis appears to be evident in the French navy model, for example. In this model, the dummy variable D1872 enters positively and significantly (although it does not enter the army model). D1872 takes the value of 0 from 1856 to 1871 and one thereafter. This indicates that French naval spending (as a percentage of national income) grew, on average, at higher rates after the Franco–Prussian War and the advent of a united Germany. One might have expected the opposite, that French army spending would have been higher due to French rivalry with Germany (given that the war between them was mostly a land war), but France may have relied more on its naval power as a way to address the German threat – already having had a significant lead in naval power over the new Germany.

An examination of the French army and navy data used in the models supports these results. The army variable grew at an average of 9.8 per cent a year up to 1871 (this is strongly influenced by the extreme value for 1871 itself) while the navy grew at an average of 1.3 per cent per year. From 1872 onward, however, the army variable grew at an average of –0.55 per cent per year while the navy averaged nearly 1.7 per cent per year. Given the closeness in the two percentages for the navy variable and the dramatic difference between the two for the army variable, however, the data may also reflect more of a de-emphasis on army spending rather than a decided shift towards navy spending.

There is also a counter-intuitive result in the Russian army model where the dummy variable D1878 enters negatively and significantly, while being insignificant in the navy model (as an intercept dummy). D1878 takes the value of 0 from 1863 to 1877 and one thereafter. This indicates that Russian army spending grew, on average, at lower rates after the Russo–Turkish War than beforehand. We might also have expected the opposite to be true here, given the existence of the Austrian and German problems to the West, but the end of the war may very well have signalled a greater focus on sea power in light of the fact that Russo–Turkish conflict involved the Black Sea and the Turkish Straits.

An examination of the Russian military variables also supports these results. While the Russian army variable grew on average at 15.2 per cent per year up to 1877, its average growth rate from 1878 onward was 1.3 per cent. The navy variable reflects the opposite pattern, going from an average of 1.6 per cent to just under 7.1 per cent over the same periods.

It is a surprise that neither German military variable enters the model of the other, given the German shift towards naval power after 1890. The reasons for this may very well reflect the way the data are prepared. The levels of German army and navy spending do produce a clear negative scatter plot, which appears to capture any trade-off between the two branches of the military. The data in the models, however, reflect period-to-period fluctuations in national economic dependence on army and navy spending. These results suggest that the shift in German military policy may have been a longer-term affair that is captured in the trends in the data rather than in the fluctuations. This observation, if true, accords well with the traditional understanding of the shift in German *Weltpolitik* under Wilhelm II because such a shift in the geostrategic orientation of Germany was long-term in nature.

Another general difference among the models is the role of the war and conflict variables. Generally, the first war term reflects the major wars of the country in question and the second reflects smaller engagements (including colonial wars). The conflict variable is a dummy for conflict below the level of war, as noted.

Among the navy models, the first war term enters only the French model, whereas it enters all but three army models. In the case of Germany, of course, there were no major wars in the period. In the US case, the Spanish–American War (1898–99) is the only major war, which does not offer enough years to stand alone convincingly as a dummy variable. There were smaller engagements in Asia and a few in the Western Hemisphere (such as the Panamanian Revolution of 1903 and the Nicaraguan Civil War of 1909–12). When all of these conflicts are included in a single dummy variable, the result is insignificant. The second war term for the US included the internal conflicts with Native Americans, which, quite surprisingly, was also insignificant for the US army model.

The Russian army model remains the only case, then, where the war term remains conspicuously absent. If the first Russian war term excluded the Crimean War and the Russo–Japanese War and included only the Russo–Turkish War, then a significant result would be detected. With these other major wars, however, the result is insignificant. Also the slope dummy using D1878 may serve to absorb some of the change in the Russian army model. If so, then this would indicate a change in the nature of the relationships due to the war, but not the average level of military spending here.

The other unusual case is that the war term in the Japanese army model is significant and negative, which is wholly unexpected. This could reflect actual problems with Japanese army data, as the extreme value for 1895 was replaced with the average of 1894 and 1896, and that the higher amounts spent during 1904–05 were estimated (see Appendix 1). It is also possible that the dummy variable D1904 (DTIME in the table) in the Japanese army model, which contains the value 0 from 1873 to 1903 and 1 afterwards, reflects the point at which change occurred (with the Russo–Japanese War), and thus absorbs some of that change.

The remaining terms for major wars are positive. There is some difference regarding the terms for smaller wars, however. In the army models, only the French contain a term for colonial wars. The absence of the term in the British army model is not surprising, given that the British maintained colonial armies, but the absence of this term for the other armies is interesting. All of these countries were involved in a series of skirmishes and wars outside of Europe (and inside the US with Native Americans), but none of them appear to be strong enough to account for any meaningful variance in army spending.

These terms do enter four of the navy models, however, all being negative except for the French. In the British navy model, for example, colonial wars enter negatively and significantly. These negative terms in the navy models could reflect a trade-off between lower spending on the navy and higher spending on colonial expenses during such conflicts. France is the only case where colonial conflicts enter the navy model positively, which may imply the active use of the navy in such conflicts. The French case is more intuitive than the British here because the British navy was certainly a crucial instrument in the maintenance of Britain's colonial empire, which would lead me to expect colonial wars to enter the British navy model positively as well.

Conflict below the level of war enters four of the army models (two significantly as intercept dummies) and four of the navy models (two significantly as intercept dummies as well). In the case of the army models, all are negative except for France. In the two significant and negative cases (Britain and Italy), army spending grew at a lower average rate during such conflicts. Why might this be? It could be that naval spending was generally relied upon in dealing with conflicts below the level of war in these cases. Added support for this is that all four of the conflict terms in the navy models are positive (although only two are significant as intercept dummies).

The sign and significance on the conflict and war terms indicate whether a particular branch of the military is a meaningful tool in addressing those issues (or is sacrificed for the other branch if the term is negative). At issue here is the actual mix of conflicts and wars that are in each variable and how they involve each branch of the military. An answer to this would depend on the details of each case. A different scheme of organizing these conflicts could show a very different pattern. The conflict and war terms also play a role in producing significant slope dummies, however, which is more interesting (see below).

A curious fact in the models is that most of the military spending of known rivals did not enter the models. With the army models, Britain, Italy, and Russia do not have rival military spending in them, whereas rivalry terms are absent from the navy models of Britain, Italy, and Japan. There were a handful of cases where the military spending of rivals entered, either significantly or with near significance, but the terms went to 0 when other variables were included (in a manner not due to collinearity).

There are two interesting features to the rivalry terms that I will address. First, of the nine rivalry terms in the models, two are different branches from the dependent variable and four are the growth rates of both branches (total spending). The second issue is that six of the nine terms enter negatively.

In the French and US army models, for example, British navy spending enters significantly (RIVAL1 in both tables), but the British army does not. In addition, both branches of the Russian and French militaries enter the German army model (RIVALs 1 and 2), while total British military spending enters the US navy model (RIVAL1). It is common practice to expect that rivalry between countries will play out with navy against navy or army against army, but the relevant branch of the military in any given rivalry may vary. It may make good sense that German army spending responds in part to French and Russian navy spending. British navy spending is obviously the relevant branch for both the French army and navy.

The larger issue here, however, is that most of the rivalry terms have unexpected signs on them. Why does the British navy enter the French army and navy models significantly and negatively (RIVAL1 in both tables)? We can ask the same of the British navy in the US army model, or the British military in the US navy model (RIVAL1 in both tables). There is a positive sign on the Russian military spending term in the German army model (RIVAL2), and a positive sign on the British navy term in the Russian army model (RIVAL1), as well as an insignificant positive French army term in the German navy model.

One possible reason for the unexpected signs is that the sign on the term is sensitive to the specification. All of the terms are in percentage changes and some of them are lagged one time period. It should be noted, however, that the sign could be the same with and without a lag (as is the case with some of the variables) and there is no consistent pattern where unlagged terms have one sign and lagged terms another.

We should probably not interpret negative coefficients to mean that the relationship was insignificant or coincidental, because there is a good deal of history to support their inclusion. It may be that a more general model of rivalry itself actually underlies all of the connections among the military spending variables of the countries in this study.

A related issue is that the sample sizes in the models are all different. The relevant periods of rivalry were different with each. It is probably true, however, that most of the rivalries were more relevant for the data after German unification and, even more, from 1890 onward. Some clearly were not, though, such as Anglo-French naval rivalry (more relevant prior to German unification), and the Italo-Austrian rivalry (more relevant prior to 1882), the Anglo-Russian rivalry (relevant for the whole period at least up to 1907) and possibly the Austro-Russian rivalry (perhaps relevant for the entire period). It is very possible that the relationship between a rivalry term is positive in one period and negative in another, or even significant in one period and insignificant in another. In this case, the coefficient on the total sample would reflect the net effect of these contrary influences.

I must also admit here that, in the British case, I did not check to determine whether German military spending was relevant because this would have forced 20 years of data out of the British models. French or Russian military variables were the only ones tested for Britain in order to preserve as large a sample size as possible.

Commercial Variables

The commercial variables in the army and navy models are the real variables of interest here and offer some intriguing, though complicated, results. I will confine my discussion first to imports, then exports, merchant tonnage, and the growth rate of the average tariff.

There are four army models (Britain, Germany, Italy, and Japan) and three navy models (France, Germany, and Italy) where no change in the coefficients for imports appears evident. Imports enter the British army model and French and Italian navy models positively with the remaining terms in the above-mentioned models all being negative. There is a lagged import term in the British army model that is negative, but just below significance.

The relationships between these import terms and military spending were tested with a variety of important dates, as well as with conflict and war variables, and no convincing changes in slope coefficients were detected. It would appear, then, that imports enter the British army and French and Italian navy models positively (all case one), while they enter the Italian and Japanese army models and both models for Germany negatively (all case two).

The remaining seven models all demonstrate a significant change that occurs either during a certain condition (conflict, war) or after a certain date. In the French army model, imports enter positively and significantly (case one), for example, but become significantly negative (case two) during time of conflict (SLOPE2 in the table). The coefficient during conflict (being the sum of the original and that on the slope dummy) is –1.174, which is close to the magnitude on the positive term. Imports enter negatively in the US army model (case two), but actually become even more negative from 1898 onward (SLOPE1). Finally imports enter negatively (case two) in the Russian army model, but become insignificantly related to army spending from

1878 onward (SLOPE2), with the sum of the import and slope dummy coefficients being –0.067. Lagged imports also enter the Russian army model negatively (case four).

Change in the import terms is also evident in the remaining four navy models. While imports enter the British navy model negatively (case two), the relationship becomes insignificant during time of colonial wars (SLOPE2, where the coefficients sum to less than 0.0001). Similarly imports enter the US navy model negatively (case two), but change during time of conflict (SLOPE1). The magnitude of the relationship weakens during conflict, but is still negative. Imports enter the Japanese navy model negatively (though insignificantly), while becoming positive and significant from 1895 onward (SLOPE2), which reflects case one. Lagged imports also enter the Russian navy model insignificantly, but become positive during time of conflict (SLOPE1), which reflects case three.

There appears to be no general story with imports across the above models. Some reflect a positive relationship between military spending and imports, some a negative relationship, and some demonstrate a mixed result. While the full meaning of these results will await further evidence below, any particular argument for a relationship outlined in the previous chapter finds only partial support. If we think in terms of import dependence, for example, then why do imports enter the US and British navy models negatively? Could it be that import dependence was irrelevant to the naval policies of these states and, instead, the real issue was that, with falling imports, there was an increase in conflict and thus in naval spending? If this was the correct story, however, it is not supported by the absence of war terms in the US navy model and the negative war term in the British navy model, nor by the insignificant conflict intercepts in both navy models. If we think in terms of interdependence, in contrast, then why are some of the terms positive?

Exports also appear to reflect a varied pattern in the military models, though they also appear to be less connected to military spending in that exports do not enter some models at all (Russian army, Italian and Japanese navies) and are insignificant in several others (though included because some variation was evident and because a significant change may have occurred).

Exports enter the British army model lagged and positively (case three), but the slope dummy D1889*EXP$_{t-1}$ (SLOPE1 in the army table) is negative. D1889 takes the value of one from 1854 to 1889 and 0 afterward. The relationship appears to be weakly negative up to 1889 (the sum of the two coefficients is –0.259, which is case four), but positive thereafter during the period of heightened rivalry. Lagged exports enter the British navy model negatively and significantly (case four), but become positive and significant during time of conflict ($CON_{t-1}*EXP_{t-1}$, SLOPE3 in the navy table), which reflects case three.

Exports enter the French army model lagged and negatively and do not change (case four). Exports enter the German army model positively (case one), however, and enter positively but below significance in the Italian (case one) and Japanese (case three) army models. There is some weak evidence in the Italian army model that unlagged exports may change direction in the 1890s (perhaps after the defeat at Adowa in 1896), and that lagged exports may change during times of conflict, but none of these possibilities was significant. It may very well be that a subset of exports (for example, to a particular region) is where the relationship resides. The US army model shows unlagged exports entering positively (case one), though below significance, and lagged exports entering negatively and significantly (case four).

The navy models of these states show different patterns. Exports simply do not enter the Italian and Japanese models convincingly. There is some support for the idea that exports might change their relationship to Italian navy spending in the 1890s, but it was not significant.

Exports enter the US navy model positively without change (case one). In the French, German, and Russian navy models, however, there are some changes. In the French case, exports are negative (case two), but become positive during time of war ($WAR1_t*EXP_t$, SLOPE2), which reflects case one. Lagged exports also enter the German navy model negatively (case four), but appear to become weakly positive from 1882 onward (SLOPE2), which is case three. The negative sign on the coefficient must not be taken too seriously, given that the German navy model begins in 1874. The term from 1882 onwards, however, is more reliable. Finally the Russian navy model shows exports entering positively (case one), though insignificantly, but becoming negative from 1878 onwards (SLOPE2), which is case two.

The results with exports complicate the story with imports. It appears that there is more evidence for a positive relationship with exports and military spending than with imports. While there is some evidence for a negative relationship, most of it occurs in cases where a change in the coefficient is detected. Could it be that protecting export earnings was a dominant influence among the Great Powers (as opposed to the idea of protecting imports)? The idea of supporting exports through military power was, as indicated above, a prominent idea in American naval thought.

It is interesting to note that the intercept for D1882 (DTIME1) in the German navy model is significant and negative, which implies that the growth of naval spending was generally lower after 1882. The Triple Alliance of 1882 clearly had implications for the German army, given that France was a key rival of Germany, but the intuition of the result is not clear because D1882 does not enter the army model significantly. In addition, the same situation applies in the German navy model with D1890 (DTIME 2). Both time dummies were used for Germany because exports and the average tariff rate each appear to change during different times. The trouble with this is that, while we might expect D1882 to be negative with the navy we might also expect D1890 to be positive because of the heightened state of naval rivalry.

With the German army model, D1894 appears to be the most significant date for possible change and it too enters negatively, though insignificantly, which implies that there may have been less army spending on average after the Franco-Russian Alliance. This may be true because Germany was also focused on its navy at the time, but we do not get clear intuition on the signs of the time dummies for Germany. Perhaps German military dependence grew at lower rates after the above dates, but its spending levels in general (straight growth rates) would show a different result. The figures used here reflect national economic dependence on military spending.

As with the case of imports, a clearer idea of what these cases imply must wait for the results of the trade models. Judging by the mixed results thus far, however, the trade models will likely complicate matters even further. Taken alone, however, these results appear to prevent any single story-line from emerging in the data.

A difficult case in point is the export term in the British navy model. If we think that the negative sign on exports in the British navy model reflects the interdependence point of view, for example, then we must account for why the coefficient becomes positive during times of conflict (as is indicated by the slope dummy). If we try to account for the inverse relationship between exports and navy spending by arguing that it reflects the role of conflict in either driving navy spending up or in driving imports down, we will be contradicted by the fact that the actual relationship between exports and navy spending here becomes positive during times of conflict. If we argue instead that the absence of conflict reflects cooperation (which may or may not be true) and that cooperation exerts upward pressure on exports and downward pressure on navy spending, then we have accounted for the inverse relationship, but not the other result. The positive term during times of conflict is, in turn, compatible with the argument outlined in Chapter 3, but the negative term is not. More is said about these issues below.

The growth rate of merchant shipping tonnage ($MERC_t$) enters every navy model, except the Russian (Russian merchant tonnage not available). In the British, French, and Italian cases, merchant tonnage enters negatively (lagged in the French and Italian cases). The French term is also below significance, while the British term is borderline. It is not clear why this should be so. In the Italian case, for example, lagged merchant tonnage enters significantly and implies that as merchant tonnage grew in period t-1, navy spending fell in period t. If we choose to interpret this result as implying that military spending and commerce moved away from each other, where merchant tonnage represents commerce, then this result contrasts with the positive signs on lagged and unlagged imports in the Italian navy model. The same can be said of the British and French merchant tonnage terms.

In the remaining three navy cases (Germany, Japan, US) merchant tonnage enters the navy models positively and significantly, with large coefficients and very high t values for Japan and the US. These are the most intuitive results and suggest that these navies expanded along with their commerce. The differences between these results and the above negative results for merchant tonnage, in turn, might reflect differences in policy behaviour and in protectionism as it relates to their merchant fleets. The conspicuous strength of the terms in the US and Japanese models may reflect a combination of strong maritime orientation in trade and aggressive commercial practices (which, in Japan's case, may have been truer after 1895). It so happens, however, that all three of these states were highly aggressive challengers of the British position. It is traditional to focus in on the German challenge to Britain, but the Americans and the Japanese were also very aggressive in trade expansion and otherwise, especially from the 1890s onward.

Each of the three states began the period with relatively small trading and naval positions, but grew over time to acquire increasingly global trading positions that were accompanied by very aggressive foreign policies. Chapters 6 and 7 explore these issues in greater detail. It could very well be that the navies of these three states were more closely attuned to their merchant fleets for competitive reasons (such as to protect their shipping against interference from Britain). It could also be that these states used protectionist legislation to protect their merchant shipping industry more so than did the other states. These two possibilities are speculation on my part, but policy differences relating to merchant fleets and naval behaviour may help explain the differences among these states here.

The growth rate of the average tariff ($CUST_t$) enters every model except for the Italian army and Japanese and Russian navies. Strong positive relationships between $CUST_t$ and military spending exist in both British models, the French army model, the Italian navy model, and the US army model. There is a weak–positive relationship between $CUST_t$ and US navy spending.

In the remaining cases, there is some change in the relationship. In the French navy model, lagged $CUST_t$ enters negatively and significantly, but becomes insignificant from 1872 onward (SLOPE3).

In the German army model, $CUST_t$ enters negatively and significantly, but during conflict (SLOPE1) becomes significant and positive. There is a similar story with the German navy, where $CUST_t$ enters negatively up to 1889 and then becomes positively related to navy spending from 1890 onward (SLOPE2).

The opposite case appears in the Russian army model, where lagged $CUST_t$ enters positively and significantly, but becomes insignificant from 1878 onward (SLOPE3). Finally, the Japanese army model also has lagged $CUST_t$ entering positively and significantly, but here $CUST_t$ becomes more steeply positive from 1904 onward (SLOPE1).

It was argued that either positive or negative relationships would be found between military spending and the $CUST_t$ terms and, as with the trade variables, a complicated picture is evident. These results certainly appear to be confusing and there may be some inconsistency here when we compare these results to the signs on the import terms. What is curious about the signs on $CUST_t$ is that in the 11 models that include both the import and customs variables, $CUST_t$ and IMP_t enter with the same signs in two of them without change (British army, Italian navy). The remaining cases show mixed results where there is a change in one or both variables.

In the British navy model, IMP_t and $CUST_t$ enter with opposite signs, but imports become insignificant during war (SLOPE2). Similarly IMP_t and $CUST_t$ enter lagged with opposite signs in the French navy model, but $CUST_t$ becomes insignificant from 1872 onward (SLOPE3). $CUST_t$ and IMP_t enter the Japanese army model with opposite signs, where $CUST_t$ retains the same sign (but more strongly) from 1904 onward (SLOPE1). In the Russian army case, $CUST_t$ and IMP_t also enter with opposite signs, though both become insignificant from 1878 onward (SLOPEs 2 and 3 respectively). In the US army case, the two also enter with opposite signs, and maintain this with IMP_t becoming more negative from 1898 onward (SLOPE1). The US navy case is a weaker example of this, where both terms enter with opposite signs, but $CUST_t$ are insignificantly positive and imports retain their negative sign during conflict (SLOPE1).

The remaining three cases (French army, both German models) show the two variables entering positively, though one variable actually changes direction. Both terms are positive in the French army model, but imports become negative during conflict (SLOPE1). Both terms enter negatively in the German army and navy models, but imports become positive during conflict in the army model (SLOPE1) and $CUST_t$ become positive from 1890 onward (SLOPE2) in the navy model.

In five cases, then, IMP_t and $CUST_t$ generally have the same signs (with a change occurring in three cases). Two of these five cases are navy models and three are army models. In three of these five, the same signs are positive (British army, Italian navy, French army), where only the French army has a change (with imports). The two cases where the same signs are negative are both German models, where the change is that $CUST_t$ becomes positive both times. There are six cases where the two variables enter with opposite signs, three in navy models and three in army models. In five of the six, the import term is negative and the $CUST_t$ term positive. The French navy model is the exception.

Opposite signs on these two variables are the most intuitive results. Generally if we expect that $CUST_t$ and IMP_t are inversely related, then we should also find that they have opposite signs in the military models. The reason is that the military variable will have a similar response to the opposite movement of $CUST_t$ and IMP_t. As imports increase and the average tariff falls, for example, army would then increase. It so happens that $CUST_t$ and IMP_t are inversely related across all seven states (as the import models in Table 4.3 indicate). In addition, these two variables produce negative simple correlations as well, with the British, Japanese, and Russian cases being the strongest ($-0.521, -0.626$, and -0.586 respectively). The French and Italian correlations are weakest at -0.141 and -0.28 respectively. Negative relationships between $CUST_t$ and IMP_t appear to be inconsistent with cases where $CUST_t$ and IMP_t enter the military models with the same signs.

How do we interpret these results? The positive signs on $CUST_t$ suggest that military power and protectionism move together, while the negative signs suggest the opposite. It is very possible that these results reflect differences in trade policy, particularly in areas relevant for conflict, rivalry, or war. In comparing the two French models, for example, the navy model suggests an inverse relationship between the navy and $CUST_t$ until the advent of serious rivalry (1872), where the relationship becomes insignificant, while the army model suggests a direct relationship between $CUST_t$ and army spending without change. Though in the army case, imports become negative during conflict. Why might this be?

It could be that during times when conflict and rivalry were relatively absent (for example, prior to unified Germany), the navy and $CUST_t$ moved away from each other (as imports and the navy moved together), which might indicate that the French navy was an instrument of trade expansion (and even of free trade). Then the connection between navy spending and tariff policies changed or became insignificant as the navy turned increasingly toward matters of rivalry with the emergence of united Germany. In the French army case, the two variables are directly related, which suggests that while army spending expands with import dependence, protectionism does as well. Only during conflict (below the level of war) do imports and army spending become inversely related.

Why is the average tariff positively related to the French army and negatively to the French navy? One possibility is that the French army was more closely associated with protectionist behaviour in France than was the navy. The intuition underlying this might be that armies in general are most associated with their home territories than are navies, which is also where most of the production of militarily significant goods occurs. Planning for army needs may generally produce a preference for protectionism, which would reflect the very traditional idea of maintaining self-sufficiency in items that are thought to contribute to defence. Navies, on the other hand, roam the sea. Naval defence planning may increase as trade flows increase (and hence, increase when protectionism falls). This possibility is pure speculation, and does not accord with the other cases. Why, for example, does British navy spending rise as its imports fall and its $CUST_t$ rises?

It is more likely that the diverse results (which may make more sense after examining the trade models below) reflect differences in the use of trade policy. Trade policy may have different implications for armies and navies, or the relationship between trade policy and military spending may depend on the specific context in which trade, military power, and relevant conflicts all combine.

Both branches of the German military show a similar pattern to the French navy. $CUST_t$ was inversely related to German navy spending up to 1889 and positively from 1890 onward (which marks the heightened state of naval rivalry), while imports and navy were inversely related throughout. The German army model also shows that $CUST_t$ was inversely related to army spending in the absence of conflict (that is, conflict below the level of war), but positively related during conflict (SLOPE1, CONt*CUSTt), while imports were also negatively related throughout. In the German case, military expansion grows as the average tariff falls in the absence of conflict and rivalry, but becomes decidedly positive during conflict and rivalry.

There still remains the problem of $CUST_t$ and IMP_t having the same signs in some of the models. While the common signs on $CUST_t$ and IMP_t appear to be contradictory, they may actually not be so. The above models contain aggregate trade and average tariff figures in them. It could very well be that the increases in protection are directed towards one group of commodities or even certain regions of the world while the growth in trade dependence is focused on another group or region, with this distinction being hidden in the aggregate figures. I will not investigate this possibility because it would take us far afield and this issue is not a crucial one.

TRADE AS A DEPENDENT VARIABLE

Tables 4.3 and 4.4 present regressions where the military variables are now independent variables and imports and exports are the dependent variables. The logic of arguing that the trade variables should be the dependent variables is as plausible as is the opposite.

The regressors have a tendency to fit the import models better than they do the export models. While most of the export models offer convincing results, the Russian export model is very inadequate. The lack of national income, relative prices, and merchant tonnage data for Russia is a serious constraint on the quality of both of the Russian models. While more variance of Russian imports is captured than exports, both models should be viewed with caution. The Japanese models might also be viewed with caution, also lacking national income data. National income across all seven countries, however, did not enter each model significantly.

Finally there was one intractable problem of multicollinearity, that between the army and navy variables in the US import model. One solution was to use the growth rates of total military spending, given that the army and navy terms had coefficients with the same signs on their own. But the army contains a significant change, indicated with a slope dummy, while the navy term does not. In the US import model, then, I have decided to use a transformed version of the navy variable. The transformed navy variable was obtained through the following procedure: I regressed the navy term on all other independent variables in the model and used the error term of that model, which would reflect variation in naval spending unrelated to the remaining regressors. This is defined as NAVYPROXY in Appendix 2.

Commercial Variables

Before getting to the military and conflict variables, a few words will be said about the commercial terms in the models. The relative price measure entered all of the trade models, except for the Russian where the data were not available. Despite the crudeness of the measure, it appears to capture some of the variance of the dependent variables. The measure works better in the export models, where it is significant with all models, except for Japan's. The term also has the expected sign in all of the export models. The measure works less well in the import models, and has unexpected signs in the Italian and French models (though still significant in the Italian model). It is unclear why the price measure is negative in these two import models, although the price measures in the French and Italian export models are significant and positive as they should be. The two price measures for each country are growth rates of the reciprocals of relative prices (that is, PD/PF for imports and PF/PD for exports), which have a correlation of –0.99 and –0.988 for France and Italy respectively. It is very possible that the price information used is simply too far from the correct data with the import models, and it is possible that the signs on these price terms are being influenced by some collinearity in the models, although that does not explain why PF/PD appears to enter the French and Italian export models properly, not to mention the models of the other countries.

Exports entered all of the import models except for that of the US, but the French term is negative, a few are borderline significant, and one is below significance. Imports fail to enter three export models (France, Russia, US). In the remaining four export models, the Japanese term is negative and the German, while positive, is below significance.

The average tariff rate enters each import model negatively and significantly. The $CUST_t$ term was excluded from the export models, being only weakly related in a few and lacking a compelling reason to be included to begin with. We might think that $CUST_t$ should be inversely related to exports, especially with a lag, because high levels of $CUST_t$ might evoke reactions on the part of one's trade partners, which would lead to a fall in one's exports. Unfortunately this was not reflected in the export models, with the sole exception of the Japanese model. In all other export models, the term was insignificant.

The growth rate of national income entered five import models and five export models. National income enters the British and French import models negatively and it enters the others positively, whereas national income enters negatively in all five export models. These signs do not offer a consistent pattern. While I am not terribly concerned with this, we might expect positive signs on the national income terms in the export models and negative signs in the import models, but this is not the case.

Finally, the merchant tonnage figure was entered into those models where it made a contribution, although it enters only three import models and two export models. I had hoped that $MERC_t$ would capture more variance of the trade variables than it did, but it appears to be relevant in only a few models.

MILITARY AND CONFLICT VARIABLES

The military and conflict variables in the trade models are the real variables of interest here. Before discussing the military spending terms, however, I will mention a few points about the war and conflict variables first. Where the war and conflict variables are excluded from the model, they made no contributions either as intercept or slope dummies. In a few cases, they were insignificant as intercept dummies, but they produced significant slope dummies.

Table 4.3: Regressions with IMPORTS as Dependent Variable

	Britain 1854–1913	France 1857–1913	Germany 1875–1913	Italy 1865–1913	Japan 1874–1913	Russia 1864–1913	US 1869–1913
Constant	−0.162	3.943	−0.291	3.116	4.525	9.562	−1.996
EXP	0.215	−0.194	0.199	0.288	0.373	0.115	
	(3.578)	(−1.845)	(1.913)	(3.362)	(3.599)	(1.315)	
CUST	−0.354	−0.275	−0.297	−0.153	−0.233	−0.72	−0.444
	(−7.514)	(−4.794)	(−4.907)	(−1.843)	(−3.836)	(−6.069)	(−3.685)
GNP	−0.468	−0.735	0.434	0.377			0.642
	(−6.285)	(−3.648)	(2.758)	(1.535)			(4.063)
PD/PF	0.176	−0.277	0.252	−0.304	0.396		0.74
	(2.184)	(−1.666)	(1.286)	(−2.501)	(1.592)		(3.992)
MERC		−0.524	0.535		0.185		
		(−2.116)	(2.214)		(2.153)		
Army	0.063	0.109		−0.188			−0.289
	(3.003)	(4.057)		(−3.861)			(−5.559)
Army(−1)	0.076		0.201	−0.101		−0.708	
	(4.218)		(3.029)	(−1.951)		(−3.731)	
Navy	0.082		−0.1447	0.079			−0.079
	(2.881)		(−1.825)	(1.288)			(−1.468)
Navy(−1)	−0.292	−0.102			0.183	0.075	
	(−3.474)	(−2.38)			(2.539)	(1.779)	
WAR1	−3.037	5.082					
	(−3.085)	(1.847)					
WAR2	0.29						0.77
	(0.326)						(0.514)
CON	1.695	−2.335		−5.545	−10.882		−2.912
	(2.724)	(−1.338)		(−3.751)	(−3.541)		(−1.517)
DTIME			−2.952			−5.431	
			(−2.042)			(−2.07)	
SLOPE1	−0.091		0.198			1.027	0.377
	(−2.715)		(1.407)			(4.97)	(4.976)
SLOPE2	2 0.291						
	(3.358)						
AR1	−0.298		−0.514	−0.684	−0.399	−0.257	−0.534
	(−1.911)		(−3.263)	(−5.095)	(−2.479)	(−1.704)	(−3.706)
AdjR²	0.868	0.527	0.665	0.627	0.672	0.679	0.609
DW	1.966	2.207	2.143	1.931	1.853	2.047	2.23
n	60	57	39	49	39	50	45

Note: t values in parentheses.

Table 4.4: Regressions with EXPORTS as Dependent Variable

	Britain 1853–1913	France 1856–1913	Germany 1874–1913	Italy 1865–1913	Japan 1875–1913	Russia 1863–1913	US 1869–1913
Constant	−1.414	6.918	5.02	3.044	16.426	5.111	1.524
IMP	0.503		0.113	0.558	−0.512		
	(3.354)		(1.084)	(3.078)	(−3.35)		
GNP	−0.266	−1.017	−1.173	−0.647			−0.421
	(−1.606)	(−5.704)	(−5.87)	(−1.742)			(−1.822)
PF/PD	0.369	0.686	0.841	0.544	0.388		1.337
	(2.458)	(3.789)	(2.752)	(2.21)	(1.084)		(6.396)
MERC		0.278		0.594			
		(1.288)		(2.281)			
Army	0.192	0.269	0.157	0.131			
	(3.205)	(3.502)	(2.953)	(1.976)			
Army (−1)	−0.066			0.236	−0.722	0.883	
	(−2.772)			(3.555)	(−3.009)	(2.848)	
Navy	−0.277	−0.322	0.07			−0.654	0.2
	(−3.798)	(−5.439)	(1.058)			(−1.736)	(2.931)
Navy (−1)				−0.221			−0.274
				(−2.319)			(−4.188)
WAR1	6.381	7.471					
	(3.329)	(2.156)					
WAR2	2.018		−3.559	−3.459			10.143
	(1.197)		(−1.944)	(−1.722)			(2.028)
CON		−2.088					
		(−1.211)					
DTIME1	−0.116	−3.455	3.342		−4.912	0.474	
	(−0.094)	(−1.7)	(1.782)		(−1.438)	(0.076)	
DTIME2						−0.334	
						(−0.058)	
SLOPE1	−0.227	−0.354	−0.275		0.557	−0.806	
	(−3.331)	(−4.273)	(−2.283)		(2.154)	(−2.437)	
SLOPE2	0.331	0.266				0.53	
	(2.56)	(2.271)				(1.248)	
AR1				−0.407	−0.18		−0.367
				(−2.974)	(−1.083)		(−2.296)
AdjR²	0.634	0.572	0.455	0.45	0.423	0.104	0.616
DW	1.918	2.18	2.162	2.355	2.162	2.094	1.98
n	61	58	40	49	39	51	45

Note: t values in parentheses.

The first war term, which measures the major wars, enters two import and two export models (Britain and France in both cases). $WAR1_t$ is significant and negative with British imports, but positive though near significant in the French import model. The same war term is positive and significant with British exports and positive and significant with French exports as well. The Italian and US war terms have been placed in the second war category ($WAR2_t$) for the trade models because most of their wars were of the smaller variety. In the US case, the Spanish–American War was the only major war in the term, and the internal skirmishes with Native Americans would not relate to trade.

While the second war term enters the British import model insignificantly, it has a positive and significant impact on exports. The same is true for the war term in the US export model. In the German and Italian export cases, the war terms enter negatively (significant in the German case). Where conflict enters the models, it is negative everywhere except in the British import model.

Why is there such diversity in how conflict and war influence imports and exports? Where war and conflict have no influence alone, there may simply be nothing in the variables that meaningfully interacts with trade or some portions of the data may pull in one direction and other portions in another direction. There are two possible issues here. One is that conflict could be broken into different categories altogether, which could produce different results. The other issue is that the levels of conflict and war might each affect trade differently. Perhaps only some conflicts or wars affect trade and others do not. This could relate to the level, location, and multilateral involvement in the wars or conflicts in question. Perhaps the proximity of conflict and war to trade centres or trade routes is an issue. Given the definitions in the variables for conflict and war included here, there is no uniform influence from them to trade.

In cases where there are positive coefficients during war or conflict, it could be that the state seeks to increase the import of critical goods (such as raw materials and agriculture), as in the case of British imports with conflict or French imports with war. In such a case, though, we might also expect that the trade and military spending variables would be positively associated (that is, assuming that military spending rises with conflict and war), which may not be the case. It could also be that the positive war terms in the British, French, and US export models imply that these states gained by war or sought to increase export earnings during war. This possibility is not unreasonable, although it generally contrasts with conventional assumptions about conflict and trade. The United States, for example, gained in trade during both world wars because of its role as a supplier to the allies.

The negative signs on the war and conflict terms are more intuitive and imply that war and conflict drive trade down. Trade may fall during war for a host of reasons. Exports could fall because of a disruption in the military protection to export markets or perhaps (at least in very large wars) exports could be curtailed in order to serve internal war production needs. In an extreme case, exports could fall because the export markets themselves are where the war is and the countries in question undergo severe economic harm. There are no clear cases of this occurring on a wide bases prior to 1914, though this was certainly the story of Europe in the world wars (and Japan in the second). Imports could also suffer from disruption or insecurity during war as well.

The military spending variables offer results that are as diverse as those for the military models. There are five convincing cases where a military term interacts with a dummy variable in the import models. In the British import model, both army and navy terms enter in unlagged and lagged forms. Collinearity does not appear to interfere with the signs and significance of the terms. Both army terms and the unlagged navy term enter the model positively (case five and case seven for lagged army), while the lagged navy term enters negatively (case eight). The magnitudes on the military terms (especially those for the army) are generally small in comparison to the magnitude on the import terms in the British military models. This is a reasonable result, given that trade is generally much larger than military spending.

The British army term also interacts with conflict (CON_t*$ARMY_t$, SLOPE1), to become negative (case six). The coefficients for the army term and SLOPE1 sum to a small amount (–0.039). Given the small nature of the army coefficient to begin with, however, it is likely that British army spending becomes negatively related to imports during conflict. Finally the lagged navy term interacts with war (the second war term, which captures colonial conflicts), producing a negative coefficient whose absolute value is nearly the same as that on the lagged navy term (SLOPE2). The sum of these terms is very small (0.003) and much smaller than the magnitude on the lagged navy term itself, which indicates that lagged navy spending becomes unrelated to imports during these minor and colonial wars.

The story with British imports then presents some diversity, but the results tend to point to a positive relationship between military spending and imports. The lagged navy term may suggest the opposite, but this must wait for the overall comparison between the two sets of models.

Only two military terms enter the French import model and no convincing changes are detected. French army spending is positively related to imports (case five), while lagged navy spending is negatively related to imports (case eight). The German case is also simpler than the British. Here the lagged German army term is positively related to imports (case seven), while the unlagged navy is negatively related to imports (case six). It is possible that the navy term interacts meaningfully with the dummy D1890 (SLOPE1), which contains the value of 1 from 1890 to 1913 and 0 beforehand, but the change is below the level of significance. It is possible that the significance on the coefficient is influenced by collinearity, in which case we could argue for a positive relationship between navy spending and imports from 1890 onward (case five). Otherwise, the change in the relationship is too weak to be significant.

The Italian case shows that both unlagged and lagged army terms are negatively related to imports (cases six and eight respectively), while both unlagged and lagged navy terms are positively related (cases five and seven respectively). The lagged army term is borderline significant and the unlagged navy term is below significance, which may be due to collinearity with $CUST_t$. There is some indication that army spending interacts with conflict, but the effect appears to be weakly positive. The navy terms also appears to interact with war, but the effect is also slight (though still positive). These slope dummies were excluded entirely.

In the Japanese import model, only lagged navy appears to enter the model convincingly and here it is positive (case seven), though just below significance. Any changes detected with either military terms and any of the dummies for conflict and important dates were unconvincing. The Russian model suggests that lagged army spending is negatively related to imports (case eight), but becomes significant and positive from 1878 onward (case seven) with a magnitude of approximately 0.32 (SLOPE1). While the Russian model lacks price and national income information, the significance of these army terms appears to survive alternative specifications. Finally, the US import model indicates that both army and navy enter negatively (case six), though the navy term is below significance. The army term changes during war (WAR_t*ARMY_t, SLOPE1), however, where the magnitude becomes approximately 0.09.

Like the import models, military terms enter some of the export models in both lagged and unlagged forms. Unlagged army is positively related to British exports (case five), while lagged army is negatively related (case eight). Unlagged navy is negatively related to British exports (case six). Two changes are also detected here. The unlagged army term interacts with the dummy D1882 (SLOPE1), which contains the value of 1 from 1882 to 1913 and 0 beforehand. The slope dummy term is negative, but the sum with the army coefficient is −0.032, which is negative. The navy term also indicates a change with D1882 (SLOPE2) and becomes positive (the coefficients sum to 0.06). These coefficient values appear to be small, but it should be noted again that the general magnitudes on the military terms in the trade models are smaller than those on the commercial terms in the military models owing to the relative size differences between the military and trade variables.

The French army term is also positively related to exports (case five) while the navy is negatively related (case six). Both terms indicate change as well. The army appears to be negatively related to exports (case six) from 1870 onward (SLOPE1). The dummy D1870 contains the value of 1 from 1870 to 1913, and 0 beforehand. Similarly, the navy term interacts with conflict (SLOPE2), producing a positive term. The sum of the coefficients is still negative (case six), however, though flatter (−0.057). While the magnitudes on these changes are small, they are also in line with the generally smaller magnitudes on the military coefficients.

Both army and navy terms enter German exports positively (case five), although the navy term is below significance. The navy term is significantly negative (case six) in its relationship to exports from 1890 onward (SLOPE1), however. Both unlagged and lagged Italian army terms are positively related to exports (cases five and seven), while lagged navy enters negatively (case eight). The navy term does not enter the Japanese export model, but lagged army enters negatively (case eight). The relationship between army spending and exports changes from 1895 onward (SLOPE1) in that the slope coefficient becomes flatter, but it remains negative.

Lagged army enters the Russian export model positively (case seven), while navy enters negatively (case six), although it is below significance. Both terms also indicate a change. The army term remains positive from 1878 onward (SLOPE1), but becomes flatter. The navy term, while probably insignificant, may also become flatter (SLOPE2). While the navy term in general fails to enter significantly, it appears to account for some variation, which might indicate that a subset of exports is the relevant variable. Finally, army does not enter the US export model convincingly, but navy does. Here unlagged navy enters positively (case five), while lagged navy enters negatively (case eight). No changes appear to exist in these navy terms as well.

COMPARING MILITARY AND COMMERCIAL MODELS

The final exercise here is to compare the results of both sets of models in terms of the cases outlined in Chapter 3. This information may provide some clarity regarding the results, but I must also recognize that the comparison below is truly tentative. While there is no technical problem in making the comparisons, one might rightly expect that such comparisons should be made in the context of simultaneous equations. As explained earlier, I decided against using 2SLS or 3SLS because I wanted the models to be exploratory in nature and as convincing as they could be given the variables. To that end, I wanted to be able to include as many or as few of the initial set of variables defined as would convincingly enter the models and I wanted to be able to test the military and commercial terms for possible changes with the use of the dummy variables. A system of equations in this context would be unusually difficult or, at best, a much simpler set of variables in each equation would have to be settled on because rank and order conditions would have to govern the specifications.

There seem to be moderate differences between armies and navies in terms of how they relate to trade. In comparing the cases, most of the army cases appear to support the idea that military spending and trade move together, although there is some support for the opposite point of view. The navy cases offer more support for the view that military spending and trade move away from each other, although there is some support for a direct relationship here as well.

Armies and Imports

In the relationship between armies and imports, the British, French, and German cases support a direct relationship. Cases one and four appear in the British army model, though case four is below the level of significance, while cases five and seven appear in the import model. Even if we accept case four, though, its combination with either case five or seven argues for a positive relationship as well. The French army model reflects case one with imports, while the import model reflects case five with the army. The German case is less straightforward because the army and import models reflect cases two and seven respectively. Unless we consider this to be contradictory information (see Chapter 3), then we might argue that the German case indicates that as imports in period t fall, army in period t rises, which causes imports in period t + 1 to rise. If this is unreasonable, then we have to accept the idea that imports are inversely related to army spending (case two), but army spending is positively related to imports (case seven).

The Italian and Japanese cases support an inverse relationship, while the Russian and US cases offer mixed results. Case two appears in the Italian army model with imports, while cases six and eight appear in the import model with the army. The Japanese army model also reflects case two with imports, while the army does not enter the import model. All information in these two models, then, supports an inverse relationship between army spending and imports.

Cases two and eight generally appear in the Russian army and import models respectively, which argues for an inverse relationship, but case four is also in the army model and case seven defines the relationship in the import model after 1878 (SLOPE1). For the period prior to 1878, then, Russian imports and army spending appear to be inversely related, while they are positively related afterward. The US army and import models generally show cases two and six, but during war the army is positively related to imports in the import model (case five, SLOPE1). The change in the import term in the army model still reflects case two (SLOPE1). While the US cases generally support the idea that army spending and imports are inversely related, they appear to be positively related during times of war.

Armies and Exports

A complicated set of comparisons exists in the British army and export models. Up to 1889 (SLOPE 1), exports in the army model reflect a negative relationship (case four, though the coefficients sum to –0.275), but reflect case three since then. The army in the export model, on the other hand, reflects case five up to 1881, but changes from 1882 onward. The coefficients sum to a small quantity (–0.035) which would reflect case six. The army term also enters the export model under case eight with a small, but significant coefficient. There appears to be evidence of both a positive and a negative relationship with army and exports in the British case.

The French army and export models reflect cases four and five respectively, which argues for a positive relationship. The army term in the export model changes to case six from 1870 onward (SLOPE1), but the sum of the terms is small (–0.085) compared to the coefficient on the army term alone.

The German case is straightforward. The army and export models reflect cases one and five respectively, which argues for a positive relationship without any complications. The Italian case also argues for a positive relationship between army spending and exports. The army model reflects case one, while the export model reflects both cases five and seven. The export term in the army model is insignificant, however, which leaves only cases five and seven in the export model.

The Japanese case reflects case three in the army model (insignificantly) and case eight in the export model, which appear to be contradictory, although the army term in the export model changes to case seven from 1895 onward. The Russian case is also straightforward, given the absence of the export term in the army model. The army enters the export model under case seven, which argues for a positive relationship, but the change indicated by SLOPE1 suggests an insignificant relationship from 1878 onward (the coefficients sum to –0.077, which is considerably smaller than the original army coefficient).

Finally, the US case offers a bit of ambiguity. While the army term does not enter the export model at all, unlagged exports enter the army model positively (case one, though insignificant) and lagged exports enter negatively (case four). The stronger evidence here is for an inverse relationship between the US army term and exports.

Navies and Imports

The British navy and imports demonstrate mixed results. Imports enter the navy model as case two, which argues for an inverse relationship, but undergo a change during times of the small wars (second war term, SLOPE2 in the navy model) where the sum of the two terms is 0.001, which is insignificant. The navy term enters the import model as case five, however, and the lagged values also enter as case eight. The change in the lagged navy term during small wars (SLOPE2) also sums to insignificance with the coefficient on lagged navy (−0.001, which is identical in absolute value to the case with the navy model). The evidence here, then, tends to suggest an inverse relationship. Despite British dependence on imports for food and other commodities, then, the evidence does not support the idea that the British navy was focused on protecting its imports.

While the French case is straightforward, with no apparent changes, the results are potentially contradictory. The French navy model reflects case one, suggesting a direct relationship between French naval spending and imports, while the import model reflects case eight, indicating that lagged navy spending is inversely related to imports.

The German case appears to suggest an inverse relationship between navy spending and imports without ambiguity. The import term enters the navy model under case two, while the navy terms enters the import model under case six. The change in the navy term (SLOPE1) reflects case five, but is insignificant.

The Italian case reflects a positive relationship between navy spending and imports, which contrasts with the opposite finding for the relationship between Italian army spending and imports. Imports enter the Italian navy model under both cases one and three, while the navy term enters the import model under cases five and seven (case five is insignificant).

Imports enter the Japanese navy model under case one from 1895 onward (SLOPE2), but are insignificant beforehand, while the navy term enters the import model under case seven with no changes. Both of these situations suggest a positive relationship. The Russian case offers one piece of information only, although it suggests a positive relationship. Lagged imports enter the navy model under case seven during time of conflict (SLOPE1), but are completely insignificant otherwise. The navy term also fails to enter the import model altogether.

The US case reflects an inverse relationship between navy spending and imports. Imports enter the navy model under case two (retaining their negative values even with a slope dummy as well), while the navy term enters the import model under case six, although it is below significance).

Navies and Exports

The Japanese case drops out of this section altogether, given that navy spending and exports show no convincing sign of a relationship. Lagged exports enter the British navy model negatively (though just below significance), which reflects case four, but become significant and positive during times of conflict (SLOPE3), which reflects case three. On the other hand, navy enters the British export model under case six, which suggests an inverse relationship, but becomes very flat (through case five) from 1882 onward (SLOPE2). The strongest evidence here suggests a negative relationship as well. The French case also offers mixed results. Imports enter the navy model under case two, but reflect case one during war. The navy term enters the export model under case six, but becomes flat (through case five) during conflict.

The German case appears to support a negative relationship. Exports enter the navy model under case four, but become case three from 1882 onward (SLOPE1). The coefficients sum to a flatter quantity under case three. The German navy term enters under case five in the export model, but is insignificant, and changes to case six from 1890 onward. While the evidence here is mixed, the weight of the evidence supports an inverse relationship.

The Italian case offers one piece of information, that the navy term enters the export model negatively under case eight. The Russian case is least reliable here, in terms of the quality of the models, but exports enter the navy model under case one (insignificantly) and change to case two from 1878 onward (SLOPE2). The Russian navy term is insignificant in the export model, but enters as case six and then changes to case five from 1890 onward.

Finally, the US case largely supports a positive relationship, although there is some ambiguity. Exports enter the navy model as case one, with no change detected. The navy term enters the export model under case five as well, which indicates a positive relationship, but the lagged navy term reflects case eight.

CONCLUSION

From the above results, which are admittedly confusing, it appears that most of the results lean towards a positive relationship between military spending and trade, but there is some support for an inverse relationship and there are also cases with mixed results. The British, French, and German cases regarding their armies and imports appear to be straightforward positive cases. This also appears to be true with French, German, Italian, and Russian cases regarding their armies and exports. The Italian, Japanese, and Russian cases regarding their navies and imports, as well as the US navy and export case, also suggest a positive relationship.

The negative relationships, without any contrary evidence, are five in number. The Italian and Japanese army and import cases, the German and US navy and import cases, and the Italian navy and export case all suggest clear negative relationships. The remaining results are all mixed, with some leaning more in one direction than the other.

What is interesting is that the positive relationships with armies and imports involve Britain, France, and Germany, among the most powerful and wealthy of the seven states, while the clear negatives are Italy and Japan. The Russian and US cases are also mostly negative. If interdependence is operating here, then why is it focused on the lesser of the Great Powers? With the other cases, the line up of positive versus negative cases differ.

It is also interesting that, regarding navies and imports, Germany and the United States are the clear negative cases. Germany is typically thought of as being belligerent, expansionary, and ambitious, while the United States was very protectionist in this period as well. Britain, while having mixed results, does not show a clear positive relationship as we might expect. The tendency in the case of the British navy and imports is to suggest a negative relationship. Why is the role of the British navy as a protector of British trade not evident here?

If we look at the results by country, comparing the relationships across military branches and imports and exports, the results are also mixed. Each country shows a range, from positive to negative to both, with no clear pattern being evident.

We cannot make too much of these results here. These models are a first pass and are thus tentative. The trade terms are also in their aggregate forms. We might be able to estimate better models by substituting into the equations the commodity groups or regions that are most relevant. Data availability may make estimation of such models less than satisfactory with some countries and impossible with others. While the regional trade samples for Britain, the United States and France are adequate, other countries have problems and the commodity group breakdowns of their trade vary in quality as well. French commodity group imports are available back to 1866, for example, but exports only to 1877. All of the German commodity group trade reaches back to 1880, while Italian is available back to 1878. These issues are discussed again in Chapter 8.

It is also important to find an adequate context for the above results. The argument outlined in Chapter 3 needs to be investigated substantively with each country in order to place the above results in some context. Thus Chapters 6 and 7 will examine the trade, military, and some related data of the states in this study while attempting to integrate patterns in the data to the military, commercial, and strategic behaviour of the states.

5

How Interdependent were the Great Powers?

This chapter examines the price and trade data of the countries in this study in order to clarify the record of interdependence among them. The investigation of the data is not exhaustive here because additional interdependence data is presented in later chapters in the context of conflict and rivalry among the states. The goal here is to determine the degree of economic interdependence among these countries in terms of price, inflation, trade dependence, and trade interdependence data.

Generally, if economic interdependence is a new phenomenon in history, then we should see little of it among the countries in this study. Each country should not be very dependent on the outside world for goods and services and, among themselves, each should not be dependent upon any of the others in key economic measures. If there is a degree of interdependence among the states, however, and if conflict and interdependence are inversely related, then we should expect to see either little interdependence among the countries that became enemies and more among those that were allies or we should see a lessening of interdependence over time among enemies as the war approached and, perhaps, the opposite with the allies. This last issue will be addressed more directly in the next two chapters.

The methods employed to determine the presence and extent of economic interdependence among the countries are descriptive. I use correlations on price level and inflation rate data, as well as percentage figures on trade dependence. In Chapter 7 the issue of interdependence is explicitly examined in the context of rivalry and conflict.

As noted in Chapter 2, interdependence thinking and, to some extent, globalization literature have a tendency to be ahistorical. This statement was based upon the three general themes found throughout interdependence literature. The first was that economic interdependence is said to be new to history. It is seen as being produced by the postwar expansion of trade. The second was the idea that interdependence is of revolutionary significance to the world because it will change the way states and the world operate. This change in the nature of world politics will foster peace because it will counteract tendencies towards 'traditional' conflict. The third was that inter-dependence is thought to be a permanent or irreversible feature to world politics (and the international economy). This third feature of interdependence thought is imbued with the general Western notion of progress, where the world moves away from the bad old world and marches towards the new and better world. This assumption, of course, is characteristic of much social science, including economics.

While there is certainly much about the postwar world that is new, the data below show that interdependence itself is not new. Again the magnitude of economic interdependence among countries, the growth in the diversity of goods and services that cross borders, the growth in cross-border corporate ownership and the complexity of production and distribution schemes, and the speed of economic transactions and political communication across states may be new, but interdependence itself is not. All of these items, including multinational companies, existed in the period before the First World War (and, very likely, well before that). The general magnitude and complexity of these items may be new, but their presence is not.

INFLATION SHARING: PRICE LEVELS AND INFLATION RATES

One can attempt to measure interdependence in a variety of ways. A simple way is to focus on prices. James Caporasso defines interdependence simply as a condition where at least two states rely on each other to acquire some of their wants and needs.[1] Despite the massive generality of this definition, he notes that one indicator of inter-dependence is the transmission of economic disturbances across countries, such as inflation. He states that the success of postwar trade liberalization has been a main contributor to inflation in Europe and North America and that the cyclical sharing of price movements among them is so strong that it produces extremely high correlation coefficients of consumer price indexes from one country to another.[2]

If simple correlations of price indexes are an adequate measure, then historical data shows that this state of inflation sharing, as he calls it, existed in the period before the First World War among the major countries. Tables 5.1 and 5.2 show simple correlations of both wholesale price indexes (WPIs) in their levels and the growth rates of these indexes (which would be an inflation rate) in three periods of history among the countries in this study. Russia and Austria are excluded after the First World War.

Table 5.1: Correlations of Wholesale Price Indexes (levels)

	Britain	France	Germany	Italy	Japan	US	Russia
1871–1913 (Russia, 1885–1913; Austria, 1871–1909)							
Austria	0.826	0.908	0.867	0.818	–0.112	0.898	0.888
Britain		0.959	0.701	0.816	–0.448	0.881	0.758
France			0.824	0.867	–0.262	0.926	0.872
Germany				0.805	0.155	0.825	0.826
Italy					–0.043	0.763	0.815
Japan						–0.221	0.711
US							0.822
1918–39 (Japan, 1918–38)							
Britain	–0.133	0.033	0.497	0.63	0.962		
France		–0.111	0.519	–0.146	–0.047		
Germany			0.184	0.037	0.062		
Italy				0.505	0.519		
Japan					0.488		
1949–88							
Britain	0.988	0.982	0.986	0.936	0.995		
France		0.975	0.985	0.923	0.985		
Germany			0.946	0.976	0.989		
Italy				0.875	0.973		
Japan					0.954		

Data sources: B. R. Mitchell, *European Historical Statistics: 1750–1975* (New York: Facts on File, 1980) and *International Historical Statistics: Africa and Asia* (New York: New York University Press, 1982).

There are several features to note about the correlations among the levels of the WPIs in Table 5.1. First the correlations are strong in the first period among all countries except Japan, although Britain and Japan show a moderate negative correlation. The British–French correlation is particularly strong, though there are several other very high correlations. Even Russia (whose WPI is available only back to 1885) is strongly associated in its levels with the others, including Japan's. Russia was among the least developed of the countries in this time period, though rich in natural resources, and it was politically and geographically remote from the major economies. Even under these conditions, the Russian WPI is strongly associated with the others. At least in their levels (and thus in their trends), then, the WPIs of the major states show a strong degree of association in most cases.

The story changes dramatically for the period 1918–39. The associations among Britain, France, and Germany disappear, though Britain has moderate to strong positive correlations with Italy, Japan, and the United States. Britain, Italy, Japan, and the United States, in fact, all maintain significant correlations with each other. All others (except that between France and Italy) are insignificant. The weaker connections during the interwar years are obviously due to the instability of the period. The chief sources of that instability are the disruptive effects of the First World War, the German hyperinflation, the Depression in 1929 and the outbreak of protectionism in the 1930s. Regarding the trends in wholesale prices, then, some associations remained or were strengthened and the others were weakened. The weakening, of course, indicates that interdependence (at least in price levels) was reversible.

The final period shows a return to close association among all of the states, but to a far greater degree than in the first period and without exception. All of the states included show very close associations in the levels of their wholesale prices. These close associations are obviously due to connections among these countries established in the US-centred postwar economic order. The wholesale prices among these countries moved together with very little deviation from their common trends (which were basically flat) until the period between the late 1960s and the 1973 oil shocks.

The prices of the major countries have all gone up since 1973, but at varying rates. The closer we come to the present, the greater is the divergence in the trends of these WPIs, which reflects differences in the national experiences of these countries since 1973. Germany has generally had the lowest level of inflation of the countries in Table 5.1, while Britain and Italy have had the highest. Does the divergence in inflation levels since the oil shocks indicate a reversal of interdependence in price levels? It is likely that the answer is no, given the close trade interdependence among these countries and the advent of the euro and a single monetary policy today, although the price levels of these countries have certainly diverged since the early 1970s.

Correlations in the inflation rates of the countries, measured as the percentage change in their WPIs, are shown in Table 5.2. These data indicate a slightly different story than the levels of the data. In the period before the First World War, Britain, France, Germany, and Austria have closely associated inflation rates. Italy, the United States, and Russia are moderately associated with the above four (the US–Austrian correlation is strong), and there is only a moderate association between the United States and Russia. Further, Japan has weak to moderate associations only with France and Germany.

In the interwar period, Britain and France retain the association between their inflation rates and, surprisingly, both show stronger associations with Italy and the United States. All of the correlations for the German and Japanese inflation rates become insignificant, however. The German case may be explained as being a byproduct of the hyperinflation, but the Japanese case is unclear. The lack of association in the Japanese rate may be caused by their economic remoteness from the major economies or by differences in the levels of protectionism among the countries. While all countries were relatively more protectionist in the interwar years than they were in the period before the war, the timing of these changes as well as their levels may vary considerably.

Table 5.2: Correlations of Wholesale Price Indexes (percentage change)

	Britain	France	Germany	Italy	Japan	US	Russia
1872–1913 (Russia, 1886–1913; Austria, 1872–1909)							
Austria	0.714	0.734	0.659	0.417	0.102	0.489	0.688
Britain		0.766	0.766	0.545	0.165	0.555	0.538
France			0.762	0.534	0.318	0.532	0.581
Germany				0.532	0.41	0.52	0.436
Italy					0.045	0.191	0.277
Japan						0.099	0.222
US							0.416
1919–39 (Japan, 1919–38)							
Britain		0.716	0.028	0.651	0.077	0.808	
France			0.278	0.78	–0.029	0.608	
Germany				–0.011	–0.025	0.127	
Italy					0.142	0.556	
Japan						–0.285	
1949–88							
Britain		0.694	0.711	0.802	0.622	0.791	
France			0.683	0.552	0.535	0.588	
Germany				0.713	0.412	0.727	
Italy					0.246	0.812	
Japan						0.287	

Data sources: See Table 5.1.

Finally, all correlations in the inflation rates during the postwar period are significant, except those between Japan and both Italy and the United States. While it is not surprising to see high correlations here, the weak link between Japan and the United States is unexpected.

It should be stated here that the above correlations merely tell us whether there is a degree of 'inflation sharing' among the countries. There is no attempt to explain the inflation of the countries above, but only to get a measure of interdependence. No other variables have been brought into the issue and no lags among the variables have been specified. While lags between the levels or rates of one country and another might be expected, there is no apparent guidance about what those lags should be like. In addition, the data above are annual in nature, while price movements operate continuously. The transmission of inflation from one country to another through trade prices, for example, will operate on the receiving country as soon as the imports become part of domestic supply and demand. The lag length, then, would be between the time that firms in the exporting country purchased and/or produced the goods and services in question and the time they entered the receiving country's domestic market. The length of time that it would take for this to occur must vary considerably and, in a bilateral trade relationship, the direction of the transmission will be both ways.

In addition, price levels and inflation rates may be correlated because these countries pursued similar macroeconomic policies at similar times. If this were true, then we might think of economic interdependence as also including a policy component as well. It is not far-fetched to argue that countries that are so densely interconnected economically would have a tendency to pursue expansionary policies at the same time (though not necessarily to the same degree) or will be similarly affected by an adverse shock to their aggregate supply curves (as with the oil shocks). This is not to say that there has been genuine policy coordination among these states (with the possible exception of those who belong to the European Union) and there is good historical evidence to show substantial policy differences among countries as well. Countries with the higher inflation rates in the last 30 years (for example, Italy and Britain) may have engaged in more expansionary macroeconomic policy than countries with lower rates (such as Germany).

It can generally be stated from the above that, whatever the underlying reasons, prices have moved together across countries for a very long time and the strength of association among them has risen and declined. It is interesting to see that correlations before the First World War are comparable to those after the Second World War. The first period does show slightly weaker correlations than the later period, but the price movements were strongly associated in the nineteenth century. The decline in the strength of association among price movements in the interwar period shows that interdependence is not irreversible.

TRADE DEPENDENCE

Table 5.3 shows total merchandise trade (exports + imports) as a percentage of national income. Austria is excluded from the table due to a lack of national income data. While the national income values do differ across countries (see Chapter 3 on the variables), the figures below provide a rough comparison of overall trade dependence.

The degree of dependence on trade varies considerably across all countries in the table, but there appears to be four groupings. Britain clearly stands alone with trade as a percent of national income hovering around a mean of 44 per cent. There were some years in the first half of the time period when British trade was over half of national income. France and Germany were also very dependent upon trade and have similar levels of trade dependence, with the German percentages generally being a few points above the French. Both were well below the British amounts, however. Italy and Japan also have similar levels of trade dependence from about 1895 onward. The Italian and Japanese percentages, of course, have generally increased during the period, hovering around 25 per cent of national income during the last decade before the war.

Finally, Russia and the United States have similar amounts. The US percentages have generally dropped by a few points from their high of 14.9 per cent in 1878, however, while the Russian amounts have generally fluctuated around a mean of 13.6 per cent. The physical size of both Russia and the United States, as well as their wealth of natural resources, may help account for their lower levels of trade dependence. These features may indicate less of a need on the part of both countries for external supply.

It may also be that the two countries have similar levels of trade dependence for opposite reasons, however. Russia may have had a low level of trade dependence because of its relative economic backwardness, where trade simply grew slowly in comparison to others, while the United States may have had lower levels of dependence due to internal economic dynamism. That is, the United States may have experienced more rapid domestic economic growth than trade growth in this period. This appears to be the case, as indicated in Table 5.4, where US national income grew faster on average than did US trade from about 1886 until 1913. It is the opposite case for Russia.

There is also somewhat of a common pattern occurring across time from about the early 1870s onward on the parts of Britain, France, Germany, and Italy in terms of the general movement of their trade dependence. There was a general increase in the level of trade dependence among the four from the early 1870s (after a decline with Britain and France), reaching a high point between the late 1870s and early 1880s. The British peak was about 46 per cent in 1881, though France and Germany both saw their peaks in 1879 (34 per cent and 40 per cent respectively). Italy peaked somewhat later in 1887 with 22.6 per cent. These countries then saw their levels of dependence decline somewhat, reaching a trough in the 1890s. Italy's trough was first in

1891 (15.7 per cent), while France and Germany again troughed in the same year (1894) with 24.4 per cent and 30.1 per cent respectively. Britain troughed latest in 1899 at 38.2 per cent. The trade of the four countries generally increased after these troughs right up to the war. These general similarities in the movement of trade dependence may reflect common macroeconomic influences among the states. They also probably reflect the fact that each was a substantial trade partner of the others.

Table 5.3: Trade as Percentage of National Income, 1865–1913

Years	Britain	France	Germany	Italy	Japan	Russia	US
1865	51.65	27.4		16.8			
1870	52.77	23.66		16.45			12.42
1875	43.58	28.24	33.63	19.88			14.11
1880	45.7	33.46	35.36	18.72			15.36
1885	42.82	28.59	30.32	21.63	8.67	13.96	13.2
1890	44.14	28.31	32.45	17.85	13.12	14.29	13.23
1895	39.27	26.11	30.37	18.03	17.1	15.89	12.3
1900	39.64	26.84	33.27	20.28	20.37	12.25	12.99
1905	41.01	30.22	34.15	21.99	26.27	13.7	11.39
1910	46.14	32.77	35.84	24.68	23.51	14.72	10.1
1913	47.62	30.87	39.79	24.39	27.17	14.28	11.46

Sources: For trade, see various national series in Appendix 1. For national income, see Table 5.1 and United States, Dept. of Commerce, *Historical Statistics of the United States: Colonial Times to 1970* (Washington, DC: GPO, 1976), Vol. 1.

While we can state that there is a moderate to high degree of trade dependence among most of these countries (except for the United States and Russia), the amount of overall dependence on trade may hide certain facts that could be quite telling, however. The composition of a state's trade in terms of commodities or the geographic distribution of trade, for example, will show specific areas of dependence that may be an important element of a state's strategy (see Chapter 6).

Finally, there are meaningful differences among the states regarding the growth of trade relative to that of national income. From this information we can determine whether the economy as a whole is expanding faster than trade or if trade is expanding faster than the economy as a whole. Table 5.4 indicates whether national income or trade grew faster. The calculations were performed on national income and trade (exports + imports) data that were deflated with WPIs (1913 = 100). To determine which grew faster, I calculated the growth rates of the two deflated series for each country and then subtracted the growth rate of trade from the growth rate of national income (National Income Growth – Trade Growth). The larger the values are, the more national income is growing relative to trade. If one or both of the two values is negative and thus contracting, then we can state that the larger the value is the less national income is contracting relative to trade.

Table 5.4: Average Relative Growth Rates (national income – trade)

	Britain	France	Germany	Italy	Japan	Russia	US
To 1885	–0.84	–2.29	–2.59	–2.82			–5.67
1886–1913	–0.15	–0.28	–0.07	–0.27	–1.09	–0.99	0.11

In the first period: Britain 1852–85; France 1852–85; Germany 1873–85; Italy 1863–85; US 1867–85.

The figures in the table are also averages in two periods. I chose 1886 as the start of the second period because Japanese and Russian income data start in 1885 (their growth rates in 1886). It is also convenient that 1885 marks the start of commercial tension between Germany and Britain (see Chapters 6 and 7), and perhaps is the early beginning of a more competitive period for the Great Powers more generally.

We can interpret negative values in Table 5.4 (especially the larger ones) as indicating more trade expansion relative to economic growth as a whole. In the first period, for example, we can state that British trade grew faster than national income by an average of 0.84 per cent a year. All but one of the values in the table are negative. French, German, Italian, and US trade growth relative to national income growth in the first period was quite large compared to British. This may reflect the rise of competitors against Britain in international trade markets. All five of these countries show much smaller differences in the second period.

The most rapid trade expansion relative to national income in the second period is Japanese. This may reflect the fact that the Japanese national income data coincidentally start in a more competitive period for Japan, which included the Sino–Japanese War (1894–95), the Russo–Japanese War (1904–05) and the colonization of Korea (1910). Japanese expansion after 1885 may have assisted trade expansion. We cannot, of course, compare Japan and Russia between the two periods.

TRADE INTERDEPENDENCE: IMPORT DEPENDENCE

The import dependence figures of eight states are examined below to evaluate the record of their mutual dependence in terms of imports. The import figures are defined as each state's imports from the others as a percentage of its total imports. The import figures could have been measured as percentages of national income, but I wanted to look more directly at the role of each state in the import position of the others and I wanted to include Austrian data, as well as the full sample available of Russian and Japanese data. British imports from the United States as a percentage of British imports represent the most dramatic change among the trade partners in Table 5.5 below. The American proportion of British imports grew from 16.4 per cent in 1870 upward to a high of 26 per cent in 1880, with a slight decline to a low of 20.7 per cent in 1895. From 1895 to 1913, the American portion of British imports would fluctuate, resting at 18.4 per cent in 1913. British exports to the United States as a percentage of total exports also declined during the 1870s, but they fluctuated up and down throughout the rest of the period. France shows a general downward trend in its share of British imports, wavering between 11 per cent and 12 per cent in the 1870s and declining to 9.6 per cent in 1885. British imports from France would then waver upward between 10 per cent and 11 per cent, but then take a sharper decline, going from 9.8 per cent in 1901 to about 6 per cent in 1913. British exports to France, however, would also decline as a percentage of total exports, going from between 8 per cent and 10 per cent of British exports in the beginning of the period and declining to between 5 per cent and 6 per cent toward the end.

Table 5.5: British Imports (percentage total), 1870–1913

Years	France	Germany	Italy	Japan	Russia	US
1870	12.4	5.08	1.27	0.03	6.78	16.42
1875	12.49	5.84	1.24	0.1	5.54	18.61
1880	10.21	5.92	0.82	0.13	3.9	26.04
1885	9.63	6.22	0.81	0.13	4.77	23.31
1890	10.66	6.2	0.74	0.24	5.65	23.12
1895	11.39	6.48	0.75	0.27	5.94	20.77
1900	10.25	5.96	0.65	0.28	4.2	26.53
1905	9.39	6.34	0.59	0.33	5.91	20.45
1910	7.57	6.07	0.55	0.71	6.39	17.69
1913	6.03	10.46	1.06	0.57	5.24	18.43

Source: Central Statistical Office, *Annual Abstract of Statistics* (London: HMSO), various years.

In addition, the German proportion of British imports wavered between 5 per cent and 6.9 per cent during the whole period, except for 1913 when it reached nearly 10.5 per cent of British imports. Whereas British exports to Germany as a percentage of total exports were routinely higher than the percentages for imports from

Germany, wavering between 9 per cent and 13.7 per cent (with a low of 8.4 per cent in 1912). British trade with Russia as a percentage of British imports and exports is relatively stable throughout the entire period, with British imports from Russia never exceeding 7.1 per cent and exports 4.9 per cent, and both generally wavering well below these figures.

British dependence on imports from France generally declined over the period, while its dependence on Germany and the United States grew. The growth in dependence on German imports was pronounced only in the last few years before the war, although the US occupied the largest position in British imports. From an interdependence point of view, the relative positions of Germany and the United States in British imports are not very intuitive. One would expect to see the German position decline, especially prior to the war, and the US position grow. In fact, the US position in British imports declined by a few percentage points in the years before the war. The dominant position of the United States in British imports, compared to Germany, also contrasts sharply with British complaints during this period about German trade gains at Britain's expense (see Chapters 6 and 7).

Table 5.6 below shows German imports from the other states as percentages of German imports. German imports from Russia, the United States, and, to a small extent, Japan, did increase as percentages of German imports, which could reflect the gain of these states at the expense of the British position. While the movement of German imports away from Britain and France may make sense in terms of their rivalry, that towards the United States and Russia does not.

Table 5.6: German Imports (percentage total), 1880–1913

Years	Britain	France	Italy	Japan	Russia	US
1880	12.33	9.13	2.22		11.69	6.41
1885	15.44	7.43	2.58		11.74	4.16
1890	14.99	6.25	3.29	0.11	12.68	9.49
1895	13.62	5.41	3.44	0.18	13.4	12.05
1900	13.91	5.06	3.08	0.27	11.86	16.89
1905	10.55	5.5	2.9	0.27	14.67	13.51
1910	8.58	5.7	3.07	0.41	15.52	13.29
1913	8.13	5.42	2.95	0.43	13.23	15.89

Source: Germany, Kaiserlichen Statistischen Amt, *Statistisches Jahrbuch für das Deutsche Reich* (Berlin: Puttkammer and Muhlbrecht), various years.

While the time period of Austrian trade data is limited, Austria shows a strong degree of import dependence on Germany and a moderate degree of dependence on Britain and the United States. In addition, the magnitude of dependence on Britain falls as 1913 approaches, while dependence on Germany grows. There also appears to be a slight decline in Austrian import dependence on Italy in the latter years as well.

Table 5.7: Austrian Imports (percentage total), 1891–1913

Years	Britain	Germany	Italy	Russia	US
1891	10.51	36.51	5.54	4.56	3.83
1895	10.45	35.85	6.57	6.51	5.19
1900	8.79	37.44	6.72	5.25	9.02
1905	7.32	37.47	4.99	6.43	9.51
1910	8.03	40.45	4.59	5.5	8.31
1913	6.37	40.12	4.96	5.93	9.48

Source: B. R. Mitchell, *International Historical Statistics: Europe, 1750–1988* (New York: M Stockton Press, 1992).

Russian imports begin the period with pronounced dependence on Germany and Britain. While Russia decreased its import dependence on both countries over time, its movement away from Germany was very slight. Also Russian imports shifted only moderately towards the United States. Most of the shift in Russian import dependence was outside the sample of countries. It is interesting and perhaps even surprising that France did not increase its position in Russian imports given the Franco-Russian Agreement of 1894 and French financial concessions to Russia in the making of that agreement. Despite the anti-German nature of that agreement, Germany continued to have a substantial role in Russian imports (and an increasing one in France's, as indicated below).

Table 5.8: Russian Imports (percentage total), 1870–1913

Years	Britain	France	Germany	Italy	US
1870	33.58	5.96	42.68	2.06	1.55
1875	26.16	6.44	43.15	2.17	1
1880	26.78	3.75	48.93	1.13	1.82
1885	25.01	3.69	37.92	1.63	6.48
1890	25.73	4.7	31.82	2.46	14.77
1895	22.28	4.27	32.68	2.15	5.47
1900	20.28	4.95	34.64	1.43	7.05
1905	15.27	4.09	37.79	1.49	6.43
1910	14.21	5.63	41.51		
1913	9.9	3.28	37.26		

Source: Tawsawentral Nyi Statisticheskii Komitet, *Statistika Rossiiskoi Imperii* (Petrograd), various years.

While French trade with Russia did experience an increase in value after 1893, there was no tendency for either country's import dependence on the other to increase. French total trade with Russia never reached 5 per cent of French trade. Britain remained France's primary trade partner, although Britain's portion of total French trade would generally decline from over 24 per cent in 1870 down to 16.8 per cent in 1913. Germany and the United States had significant portions of French trade as well. French trade with Germany wavered between about 8 per cent and 12 per cent of total French trade during the entire period from 1871 to 1913, with a slight upward movement from the early 1890s onward (1870 saw a sharp decline to 3.6 per cent due to the Franco–Prussian War). French trade with the United States wavered between about 4 per cent and 9 per cent in this period as well, with no general trend up or down.

Table 5.9: French Imports (percentage total), 1870–1913

Years	Britain	Germany	Italy	Japan	Russia	US
1870	18.33	3.59	8.19		6.57	7.59
1875	17.72	9.87	9.12		5.56	5.38
1880	13.2	8.71	7.91		6.24	14.52
1885	13.14	9.15	6.43		3.99	6.65
1890	14.13	7.91	2.75		4.39	7.15
1895	13.34	8.34	3.08		5.24	7.61
1900	14.37	9.09	3.17		4.92	10.85
1905	11.97	9.64	3.11		5.55	10.35
1910	12.98	11.99	2.63		4.7	8.56
1913	13.25	12.69	2.86	1.48	5.44	10.62

Source: Annuaire Statistique de la France (Paris: Institut National de la Statistique et des Etudes Economiques), various years.

French imports also show a general decline in dependence on Britain, but French dependence on Germany actually grew considerably. The decline of Italy in French imports might be explained by the tariff war between the two countries after the French acquisition of Tunisia in 1881. We also do not see a general increase in French import dependence on Russia after the Franco-Russian Alliance of 1894.

One can see the general decline in Italian import dependence on France after 1880 in Table 5.10. Italy also demonstrates the common story thus far of a general movement away from Britain as well and a dramatic shift towards Germany, the United States, and, to a lesser extent, Russia. There was also a small degree of shift in Italian imports toward Japan. Data on imports from the US include imports from Canada, but they are quite small.

Table 5.10: Italian Imports (percentage total), 1870–1913

Years	Britain	France	Germany	Japan	Russia	US
1870	26.84	25.14	1.44		3.9	4.36
1875	24.5	30.43	3.07		3.82	3.54
1880	21.15	21.77	7.17	0.05	6.92	6.18
1885	19.9	18.31	7.56	0.03	5.81	4.6
1890	23.15	11.89	10.19	0.13	8.67	5.93
1895	19.64	13.56	12.06	0.1	8.69	10.4
1900	21.1	9.84	11.97	0.69	7.97	13.38
1905	17.26	10.19	14.24	0.81	10.15	11.92
1910	14.67	10.29	16.16	0.87	8.16	11.49
1913	16.14	7.73	16.71	1.66	6.47	14.65

Source: *Annuario Statistico Italiano* (Rome: ISTAT), various years.

Table 5.11: Japanese Imports (percentage total), 1880–1913

Years	Britain	France	Germany	Italy	Russia	US
1880	53.58	10.26	4.76	0.43	0.02	7.29
1885	38.08	4.08	5.11	0.29	0.04	8.41
1890	32.53	4.73	8.38	0.16	0.94	8.4
1895	34.95	4.01	9.46	0.11	1.1	7.18
1900	24.94	2.81	10.17	0.16	2.1	21.85
1905	23.95	1.05	8.75	0.1	0.56	21.58
1910	20.4	1.16	9.47	0.13	0.04	11.78
1913	16.82	0.8	9.37	0.15	0.01	16.78

Source: Imperial Cabinet, *Résumé Statistique de l'Empire du Japon* (Tokyo: Bureau of General Statistics), various years.

Japan began the period with a massive dependence on Britain, which may have related to the unequal treaties and the limitations on Japan's taxation and tariff policies. Over time, however, Japan shifted away from Britain and towards both Germany and the United States. Japan's imports also shifted away from France to the point where they almost ceased to import from France at all.

Finally, the United States repeated the familiar pattern of decreasing its reliance on Britain (and, to a very small extent, on France), while increasing its reliance on German and Japanese imports. This was true despite the role of the United States in British imports and their later allied status and despite the competitive relationship between the United States and Japan.

One common pattern in the above figures is a general decrease in reliance on Britain for imports. This was true for friend and foe alike. The United States, Germany, and, in a few cases, Russia experienced general increases in their import positions in other countries. Part of the movement away from Britain must certainly be due to trade growth outside of the major economies, as each country saw its proportion of trade to Africa, Asia, and South and Central America generally increase. But the United States, Germany, and, perhaps, even Russia may have picked up where Britain left off. The major complaints of Britain over losses in trade markets due to Germany might be supported in the shifts away from Britain above, but these complaints are certainly not reflected in British–German mutual trade itself. Instead the US trade position in Britain appears to reflect the complaints against Germany. With a few exceptions then, the trade of the Great Powers with each other did not show any polarization. The only unambiguous case of this is the French–Italian case.

Table 5.12: US Imports (percentage total), 1870–1913

Years	Britain	France	Germany	Japan
1870	34.86	9.86	6.19	0.69
1875	29.08	11.26	7.5	1.5
1880	31.59	10.33	7.78	2.25
1885	23.7	9.86	10.9	2.08
1890	23.57	9.89	12.55	2.66
1895	21.72	8.47	11.07	1.91
1900	18.82	8.59	11.41	3.88
1905	15.74	8.05	10.55	4.65
1910	17.41	8.48	10.85	4.24
1913	16.33	7.56	10.42	5.07

Source: US Department of Commerce, *Historical Statistics of the United States: Colonial Times to 1970* (Washington, DC: GPO, 1976), Vol. 2.

Chapter 7 revisits this data in the context of rivalry in order to examine the degree to which (if at all) the trade of countries known to be in rivalry stood in opposition to each other. Three general trade scenarios are examined: each state's imports from the other; each states position in the import market of the other states in this study; and each state's import position in a third country's market where the third country is the focal point of rivalry. This last scenario is limited to a case study on Turkey and Egypt during the Baghdad Railway issue.

NOTES

1. James A. Caporaso, 'Interdependence and the Coordination of Foreign and Domestic Policies in the Atlantic World', in Wolfram Hanrieder (ed.), *Economic Issues and the Atlantic Community* (New York: Praeger, 1982), p. 3.
2. Ibid., pp. 5–6.

6

Patterns of Military Power and Commerce Among the Great Powers

Are there any patterns evident in the behaviour of the Great Powers that will shed some light on the differences in the models in Chapter 4? How did military power and trade actually interact among these states in terms of policies, actions, and conflicts? This chapter examines a series of stylized military and commercial facts among the seven states, as well as their trade behaviour, in order to gain a deeper understanding of the results seen in Chapter 4.

While I have argued that the interaction between military power and commerce is linked to the expansionary policies of the Great Powers, the details of commercial and military behaviour can be daunting. The expansionary policies of the Great Powers before the First World War reflect the array of large and small commercially relevant aspects of military power outlined in Chapter 3. While there may be good reason for expecting military power and commerce to be related, it is actually in the detail of military and commercial behaviour that one might find the reasons for the differences. As the above results suggest, the story is not a tidy one.

This section first looks at several economic and military indicators of the seven states in order to determine whether patterns exist among them that shed light on the nature of military–commercial interactions. The geographic and commodity-wide distributions of trade for each of the states are also compared in order to relate commerce to the strategies and rivalries of the states.

PATTERNS OF MILITARY POWER AND TRADE

It could be argued from interdependence theory, and the liberal point of view more generally, that large trading states should have small militaries and those with large militaries should have weaker trading positions. We might also expect to find that countries that pursue mercantilistic trade policies are militaristic as well because we would expect more aggressive military behaviour to be associated with smaller trade positions. Liberal states would exhibit the opposite pattern. They would have large trading positions relative to their militaries and would not engage in aggressive military behaviour. The economic and military data below, as well as the story of Great Power behaviour more generally, suggest the opposite situation with some exception. Russia may exhibit a situation where a state with a relatively weak trading position has a large military, but the other states tend to reflect the opposite.

Table 6.1: Military Expenditures (percentage national income), 1865–1913

Years	Britain	France	Germany	Italy	Japan	Russia	US
1865	3.06	2.91		2.75			
1870	2.26	2.51		1.86			1.08
1875	1.79	2.44	2.88	1.91			0.76
1880	1.82	2.96	2.44	2.01			0.49
1885	2.2	3.62	2.26	2.63	1.92	3.91	0.55
1890	2.11	2.7	3.34	3	2.43	4.14	0.51
1895	2.16	3.33	2.5	3.62	1.52	4.43	0.58
1900	3.39	3.19	2.55	2.41	5.51	3.83	1.02
1905	3.02	3.1	2.43	2.17	4.42	3.96	0.97
1910	2.62	3.12	2.76	2.68	4.72	3.76	0.89
1913	2.67	3.66	3.17	3.17	3.91	4.74	0.85

Source: See Appendix 1.

Military expenditures as a percentage of national income are all quite low for the countries (Russian and Japanese national income data are from 1885 only and Austrian are not available). As Table 6.1 indicates, the percentages have gone above 5 per cent generally during time of war only with a very few exceptions, and none of the percentages exceed 6 per cent of national income. The Boer War, the Franco-Prussian War, the Italian war with Austria in 1866 and its war with Turkey in 1911–12, and the Spanish–American War all push the percentages up, but none goes above 6 per cent of national income.

Britain, France, Germany, and Italy generally have amounts that tend to be higher than 2 per cent but lower than 4 per cent of national income. Japanese and Russian figures, in contrast, have a tendency to be above 4 per cent of national income. It is likely that Japanese amounts were significantly lower before 1885, but the data are not available, and the general tendency for spending to be above 4 per cent of national income begins in the 1890s. The US figure appears to be substantially different from the others. After the high levels of spending in the Civil War, US spending as a percentage of national income fell such that it was below 1 per cent for the majority of years up to 1913 (where it was just 0.85 per cent). As a result of the Spanish–American War, spending only reached 1.69 per cent of national income in 1899.

This information can be compared to Table 5.3, which reports trade as a percentage of national income of the seven states. There is no general correspondence between levels of trade dependence and levels of military dependence. When one breaks these trade and military spending indicators into their component parts (imports, exports, armies, and navies as percentages of national income), the pattern does not change much. Simple correlations between these military and trade variables across each country show generally weak, non-existent or even moderately negative correlations, with Japan's data being positively correlated.

If we rank each of the four variables of the seven states according to their magnitudes, where each variable is compared across all seven states and given a rank from 1 to 7, where the higher the number the larger the value with respect to those of the other countries, a slightly different pattern emerges, but one that is still not very telling. The rankings for the French, Italian, Japanese, and American military and commercial indicators are positively correlated, but the others are generally not. With the US variables, for example, imports and exports generally ranked low as percentages of national income in comparison to the others, as did US army and navy spending. At least with the levels and thus the trends, then, there is no general correspondence between trade and military dependence.

The pattern in trade places Britain alone, with the highest trade dependence levels. British trade also tended to receive among the highest rankings, while there was generally a lower ranking for its army and a high one for its navy. France and Germany also had similar levels of trade dependence that were high, but certainly lower than the British amounts. Both states also saw each variable ranking change considerably over the years. Italy and Japan also had similar levels of trade dependence from about 1895 onward that were lower than the French and German amounts. And Russia and the United States had similar amounts, generally being the lowest, yet they were very different from each other in terms of military dependence.

Military expenditures as a per cent of government expenditures are also relatively low for all states in this period, except for Germany (see Table 6.2). Aside from Germany, the percentages exceed 50 per cent of total government expenditures only during wartime. The mean percentages for six of the states are also below 40 per cent. Germany and Russia are the only states whose general percentage declined over this period as well. All the other states experienced varying amounts of increase by 1913. This is especially surprising in light of the fact that Anglo-German rivalry really began in 1890.

Table 6.2: Military Expenditures (percentage government expenditures),
1865–1913

Years	Britain	France	Germany	Italy	Japan	Russia	US
1865	38.6			27.2		37.64	
1870	32.04	18.99		17.28	10.44	29.27	25.65
1875	33.56	21.83	82.71	19.94	18.92	33.27	22.8
1880	30.92	22.36	75.06	21.2	19.02	30.12	19.3
1885	33.9	26.23	66.45	22.96	25.38	27.11	22.56
1890	36.09	23.77	58.45	24.37	31.28	25.43	20.94
1895	35.08	26.36	48.36	26.62	27.59	22.36	22.63
1900	48.43	27.92	40.25	21.84	45.47	22.31	36.62
1905	44.15	27.82	42.7	19.74	32.41	15.44	42.95
1910	40.15	29.58	41.85	25.05	32.52	23.02	45.13
1913	39.4	35.82	47.25	30.23	36.42	24.42	46.93

Source: See Appendix 1.

One is also tempted to question Paul Kennedy's notion of imperial over-stretch. How can military commitments outstrip a country's ability to pay for them when total military expenditures for six of the states have a mean that hovers approximately between one-quarter and one-third of total government expenditures? In addition, the high German amounts also appear to argue against the idea of over-stretch because Germany spent the entire period before the war rising both economically and militarily, not declining. With the other six states, though, non-military government expenditures were the majority of spending for most years. A much greater amount of money was taken out of the national economies of these six states for non-military purposes than for military. If government spending has a negative impact on economic growth (as most neoclassical growth models imply), then should not the non-military expenditures have an even greater impact on the national economies than the military? And should we not focus on total spending rather than a specific category of spending?

The focus on military spending levels as a cause of decline is a bit suspicious. If the argument for decline is that military spending exerts downward pressure on savings and investment, and thus growth, then why is the even greater downward pressure of total spending not the issue? In this framework, it is arbitrary to assert that military spending is somehow different from other categories of government spending. Justification for assuming that military spending is somehow different would have to come from the actual spending side of the budget. Whereas the decline argument (perhaps implicitly) draws attention to the revenue side of the budget due to its focus on how military spending outstrips an economy's ability to pay for it.

This is actually the case in most growth models as well. Most growth models employ the assumption that total spending equals total revenue, in order to avoid the complications of debt in order to make their point. But here too, the focus is on how revenue, drawn through taxation, draws down savings and investment, which then draws down growth. The actual goods purchased on the spending side are basically irrelevant to this argument. Thus if we focus on how spending may draw down savings and investment, we have no justification for treating military spending differently than any other category of spending. An argument seeking to show that military spending adversely effects the economy would have to demonstrate how government purchases of military goods affect the economy differently from other purchases.

There is also two general patterns regarding the merchandise trade balances of the seven states. It appears that Britain, France, Germany, Italy, and Japan have many years of negative merchandise trade balances. Britain, of course, has had a negative merchandise trade balance for each year from 1851 to 1913. The general pattern with these five states is that, while some have positive values, the tendency to have a negative value increases as time goes on and the magnitudes of the negative balances tend to grow as 1913 approaches. Russia and the United States, in contrast, appear to have an opposite pattern. While each have some years of negative balances, their tendency is to have a positive balance as time goes on and the magnitudes of the positive balances also tend to get larger as 1913 approaches.

It should be noted that the trade balance figures referred to exclude re-exports and services. Nevertheless, the differences are interesting to note. Britain and the United States show basically opposite situations here, yet these two states are usually grouped together. The United States had a trade surplus for most of the period. There appears to be nothing obvious in these trade balance figures that points to differences among the states regarding the models in Chapter 4.

Another pattern to note is in the relative growth rates between trade and military spending. Table 6.3 shows average relative growth rates in two periods (much like Table 5.4). The growth rate of trade (exports + imports) less the growth rate of military spending (army + navy) was calculated. This difference was then averaged in the period up to 1885 and then from 1886 to 1913. The year 1885 was the same break-point in Table 5.4 and the period from 1885 is generally one of greater rivalry among the states.

Table 6.3: Average Relative Growth Rates (trade – military)

	Britain	France	Germany	Italy	Japan	Russia	US
To 1885	–0.004	–0.33	3.25	1.99	–0.02	–0.98	14.52
1886–1913	–1.94	0.07	–1.63	–1.29	–5.13	–0.33	–3.73

Britain, 1852–1913; France, 1856–1913; Germany, 1873–1913; Italy, 1863–1913; Japan, 1873–1913; Russia, 1862–1913; US, 1867–1913.

The figures indicate very small differences between average trade and military spending growth rates in three of the seven states in the period up to 1885, which suggests that trade growth and military spending growth kept pace with each other. Russia's military spending grew faster than trade by nearly 1 per cent in the first period as well. Germany, Italy, and especially the United States each show that trade grew considerably faster than military spending up to 1885.

All states, except for France and Russia, show that military spending grew faster on average than did trade from 1885 to 1913, with the Japanese and American cases being particularly high. Britain, Germany, and Italy also show more military expansion than trade expansion. The negative values in the period after 1885, then, probably reflect the heightened state of rivalry and military expansion of the period.

The degree to which a state's trade travels by sea or land is, in itself, not a perfect indicator of the orientation of a state toward sea or land power. As Table 6.4 indicates, even Russia had a majority of its trade travel by sea before the First World War, while Austria-Hungary was perhaps the most land-oriented in terms of trade during the period. The sea was decidedly of secondary importance for Austrian commerce. Russia is uniformly considered to be a land power, but not only has Russia consistently had a large navy, its trade has relied heavily on sea transport as well. Yet the army was Russia's most active tool in foreign policy at the time. Interestingly, Mahan thought that improvements in sea transport would not help Russia's commercial position because of Russia's overwhelming land orientation.[1] He thought too that strategic orientation towards land or sea automatically aligned with the orientation of commerce towards land or sea as well.

The Russian case indicates how both sea and land environments can interact. While most of its trade travelled by sea, Russia was mostly oriented towards its army. When we consider the fact that the majority of Russia's trade also went to western Europe (see regional trade figures below) and that western Europe was also the location of the primary land threats to Russia, then we have a consistent story.

Table 6.4: Percentage of Trade by Sea, Select Years

Years	Austria		France		Germany	
	Imp.	Exp.	Imp.	Exp.	Imp.	Exp.
1868	12	17.2	66.3	71.9		
1876	18.4	14.7	66.5	65.8		
1883	18.7	18.1	65.9	68.1	34.7	37
1886	23.7	20.8	67.6	69.1	35.2	38.5
1887	23	20.3	67.9	67.1	35.1	40
1889	22	18.5	69	67.6	34.9	38
1890	21.5	18.5	70.1	68.2	37.7	39.2
1895	20.7	12.8	70.3	69.4		
1900	19.8	15.6	68.1	65.8		
1905	19.6	16.9	68.4	62.3		

Years	Italy		Russia		US	
	Imp.	Exp.	Imp.	Exp.	Imp.	Exp.
1868	68.22	55.36	67.9	79.6	100	100
1876	60.2	41.9	54.5	70.7	97.5	100
1883	57.5	48.8	57.6	71.4	93.1	93.3
1886	59.8	44.3	60	72.7	90.7	87.8
1887	58.9	44.5	62.4	74.5	88.4	92.4
1889	65	46.7	61.3	72.9	91.3	85.1
1890	66.9	45.9	61.6	72.1	91	90.7
1895	66.5	46.1	53.4	71.5	88.6	82.3
1900	66.5	50.3	66.5	70.5	86.7	85.7
1905			57	77.4	86.7	81.6

Source: See Appendix 1.

While the German numbers for sea-borne trade are scanty (Germany did not distinguish trade by mode of transport after 1890), the majority of its trade was by land (at least up to 1890). Perhaps this is one reason why the German navy weakly enters Germany's import model (though trade enters both of its military models). It is curious, though perhaps coincidental, that Austria-Hungary and Germany were the most land-oriented in terms of trade among the states here while also having been allied since the Dual Alliance (1879). Aside from their contiguity and mutual importance as trade partners, each also traded heavily with the countries around them, which were all accessible by land.

Italian exports before the First World War were periodically dominated by land transport, but most of Italian trade was by sea. French trade, however, has shown a steady pattern of dominance by sea transport. Finally, American trade was almost wholly by sea in this time period. American trade over land, which indicates trade through the land borders with Canada and Mexico, has steadily increased. The two countries missing here, Britain and Japan, are both islands, of course, and their trade was 100 per cent by sea.

We should also keep in mind that Britain and Japan, while islands, had armies that were active tools in foreign policy. Britain had an army for home defence and a colonial army in India, and Japan had an army that would become the primary means of expansion on the mainland. Yet the trade of both Britain and Japan was wholly by sea.

THE ROLE OF THE ARMY AND THE SHIFT TOWARDS NAVAL POWER

It would seem that armies can have a greater variation in roles than can navies. While the roles played by navies do vary considerably, all of their roles are oriented toward the world outside of the respective territory. Even if a navy operates in its territorial waters, it is focused on what is occurring in the water, not on the internal society. Armies can have domestic and international roles. It is also possible that the international roles played by armies, at least in terms of how they relate to commerce, are subtler than they at first appear to be. It is also probably true that the connections between armies and trade are not as straightforward as those between navies and trade. Are there variations in the roles of the armies of the states in this study that would shed some light on the differences in the models in Chapter 4?

Up to the Crimean War, the armies of the Continent were long-service professional armies that reflected the social structures of their societies. These armies were oriented towards being domestic policemen, acting as bastions of the social order. But the wars during the second half of the nineteenth century demonstrated a need for a peacetime army ready for war. The wars of Italian and German unification and the Russo–Turkish War showed that armies that could not rapidly mobilize large numbers of men for war were at a disadvantage.[2] The long-service army, however, retained utility for overseas engagements. The short-service army could not send troops abroad for long periods. Britain maintained its Indian Army exactly for the purpose of a long-service overseas force that could be used in far off engagements. Russia and France had nothing like a colonial army, but France maintained volunteer units in Africa and Asia and had the Foreign Legion.[3] Army reforms, however, were the order of the day from the 1880s up to the war.

While Britain is routinely considered to be a sea power, its army was also an active tool in British foreign policy, except that British policy towards the army went through some changes. During the second half of the nineteenth century, there was an ongoing debate about the relative role of the army in British defence. The experiences of the Crimean War, the Indian Mutiny in 1857, and the Anglo-French measures against China in 1860 all fed the army school with arguments for the value of the army as a tool of home defence. The belief at the time that the navy could not stop an invasion of the country by a foreign army produced a school of thought that argued for a strong home defence, based on fortifications, which dominated in Britain after 1860.[4] What is odd about this debate is that external wars, where the British employed forces far from home, became the justification for a strong army that could be a bulwark against an invasion of Britain.

In the 1880s, however, the navalist school gained the upper hand, especially because of the arguments of Admiral Fisher. The navalist school saw that the navy's control of the sea was what prevented an invasion of Britain. Naval thought maintained that an enemy would not invade the country until it gained control of the sea, and thus, as long as Britain kept such control, no invasion would occur. The army, then, was thought to be a secondary tool in home defence. The navy was the primary defence tool for the Empire and the army should only consolidate the results of naval victories.[5]

The domestic defence orientation of the army remained the policy of Britain up to the Boer War. The weaknesses of the British army in the Boer War, coupled with the fact that the war itself was an opportunity for German ambition in Europe (not to mention Russian ambition in Central Asia), led to a series of reforms under Minister of War Haldane from 1905 to 1912. The reforms were designed to prepare the army for a major war.[6] The British war in South Africa gave Germany a freer hand in Europe. Germany responded by producing the Navy Bill of 1900, which expanded the German fleet and added additional weight to German world policy.[7] The result was that Britain reorganized its army as an expeditionary force, and created a host of administrative changes such as the creation of a General Staff.[8] The British army, then, changed from being oriented towards domestic defence to being focused on rapid deployment overseas. In both cases, however, the British army could be said to have been a tool in foreign policy. One must also question whether the home defence orientation was really how the army was used, given the strong and obvious connections between British army spending and trade.

The above developments regarding the British army indicate that it was orientated towards external threats, whether the specific issue was to defend against an invasion or to deploy the army far away. In addition, reforms and the resulting readiness for war of the army were obviously influenced by emerging threats from rival states. It is interesting that there was an interaction between the British army and the German navy here, as opposed to the usual story of the navies of the two states interacting, in that German naval expansion led to British army reforms. The responsiveness of the British army to the changing circumstances of threat is a likely channel of influence between the army and trade because British trade was obviously vulnerable to those threats as well (such as *guerre de course*). This might imply that a home defence orientation is connected to commerce more generally because the responsiveness of army spending and readiness to external threats is linked to the vulnerability of trade flows.

The American army after the Civil War was also regarded as a tool in defence, with domestic police functions being secondary.[9] This may be borne out in the models in that American internal conflicts with Native Americans did not enter the US army model. The American army, however, lacked the capacity to engage in complex and coordinated actions abroad until the Spanish–American War. The war marked the turning point from being an army that was home-bound, due to organizational and logistical constraints, to being one that was increasingly capable of mobilizing and deploying forces abroad, such as in Cuba, Puerto Rico, the Philippines, China, and Mexico.[10]

It should be noted that imports and lagged exports enter the US army model significantly, though negatively, while the army enters the import model negatively (positive during war) and fails to enter the export model. While mixed, the US army case reflects mostly an inverse relationship with trade. While this situation might support the interdependence point of view, it stands in contrast with the case of the US navy and exports. It is very possible, however, that planners perceived fewer threats (relevant to the use of the army) when trade was expanding.

The Italian army reflects a different set of problems. On paper, the Italian army had four basic missions since 1866: to defend against external enemies; to fight wars abroad; to act as a tool in nation-building and help to 'create Italians'; and to provide domestic support for the state.[11] These four missions reflect the full gamut of roles for an army, but the Italian army was ill-equipped to perform all of these functions, except for the purely domestic one, where it was often quite brutal in the south. Italy was vulnerable along its land borders in the north, however, and along its coasts. By virtue of its geography, Italy had an amphibious orientation towards defence, although there was often divided opinion on what foreign policy priorities should be. The army got priority over the navy, however, and always had significantly larger amounts of expenditure than the navy. While it was probably true that the navy was a more competent force than the army, there is some support for the argument that the navy also suffered from many of the shortcomings that affected the army.[12]

Italian railways were also in a relatively backward state, which severely hampered the army's effort at deployment.[13] To compensate for the weakness in Italian railways, however, the army pursued a policy of distributing fortifications around the country as a way of decreasing vulnerability. Italian troops were also poorly trained, were not well prepared for colonial warfare, and may have lacked in-depth knowledge of overseas enemies.[14] These impediments to the army might imply that its responsiveness to changing threats and perceived vulnerabilities was slower than was true for the other states.

The Italian army did undergo some reform efforts, however, but the most important reforms occurred too late for the First World War. Just prior to the Libyan War of 1911, two year conscription for all branches of the army was adopted (except for the Carabinieri), and recruitment efforts were increased as well. There were improvements in barracks and pay, the northeastern frontier was fortified, the machine gun was introduced into the infantry and cavalry, and the army began to motorize and use aircraft.[15] While these reforms were late in coming, they may indicate that the army became more focused on foreign policy relative to domestic constabulary functions as 1913 approached.

While Russia has always had a large navy, Russia's land orientation has meant that most of its military resources have been dedicated to land defence, with the navy playing a secondary role. Russian leaders periodically saw the potential of naval power, but such views were short-lived. This, together with economic, technological, and geographic constraints, combined to subordinate naval objectives to those of the army.[16] The importance of the army is also a reflection of the fact that the primary military threats confronted by Russia in modern history have largely been from the land. Despite the predominance of the army in Russian defence, however, Russian trade in this time period travelled mostly by sea. The majority of Russian trade by sea, in turn, went to western Europe, which has been the primary source of threat for Russia over land (and sea). In addition, the development of Russian land transport (mostly rails) was partly stimulated by Russian trade with western Europe. Early Russian railway lines connected river cities and connected the capital with the western frontier. In addition, Russian rail development extended from the coasts of the Baltic and Black Seas inland, which aided in the export of oil and grain to Europe.[17]

The role of land transport in Russian trade, then, was to aid sea-borne exports to Europe. Yet the Russian navy was not the primary tool in foreign policy. Aside from the fact that the destination for most of Russia's sea-borne trade was also the principal historical source of threat over land to Russia, the absolute size of Russian trade was small by comparison. Russia's internal transport – by rail, road, and river – was simply inadequate to develop a scale of foreign trade commensurate with its geographic and population size.[18] Though population size alone does not amount to a productive base for exports, nor a ready source of demand for imports. The Russian army, then, was the primary tool of Russian foreign policy. As is discussed below, it was also the primary tool of Russian expansion and war.

Even the Japanese army in the 1870s performed the role of a domestic police force. Japan passed the Conscription Act in 1873, making military service universal from then onward (as opposed to being based on class).[19] The Japanese army would later become a primary tool of foreign policy as well. A classic view of Japanese naval thought illustrates that, despite Japan's island status, the navy acted as a support for the army in Japanese expansion and conquest. It is said that the Japanese navy has historically been a means of defending the country and for military transport through the narrow seas and waterways among the islands. The navy functioned mostly as a means to serve the needs of the army.[20] Consequently, Japanese naval thought appeared to be opposite to that of the classic ideas of Britain, which saw the navy as the primary defensive tool that would be supported by a relatively small army. Japan's navy supported the land objectives of the army, in contrast, which were largely close to the homeland before the First World War.[21] The Japanese navy was also less important than the army for the shaping of Japanese imperial expansion.[22]

While all the navies of the states in this study were oriented towards external relations, then, their armies varied. The Italian and Japanese armies performed domestic police functions, which may have militated against their effectiveness as tools of foreign policy – at least until the final years before the war. The armies of the other states all appear to have performed mainly foreign policy duties, with the American army being the least active here.

One cannot make the simple parallel between strategic orientation between land or sea and trade flows across both environments either. There is a more complex set of interactions between trade and military power regarding environmental orientation. As noted, Russian trade by sea largely went to an area that was the main source of land threat. In addition, the Russian army's actions in the Far East were met by various army expeditions of Britain. While all of Japan's trade was by sea, due to the fact that Japan is an island, the Japanese army was seen as being the main tool of foreign policy. In short, the interaction between sea and land across commerce and military power is more complex than traditional categories of sea power and land power would suggest.

It is also likely that the defensive role of armies is more sensitive and supple an instrument of foreign policy than we might generally believe. The traditional view is to see navies as being a more flexible instrument because they can be employed and withdrawn with relative ease, while the employment of armies implies commitment and a degree of inflexibility (see Chapter 1). The compelling connections between armies and trade, however, lead me to believe that the home defence role of the army is highly sensitive to the external environment, which may be transmitted to army behaviour through a country's trade or foreign threats that interact with trade by accentuating the vulnerability of commerce.

It is also possible, though hardly established, that armies are generally more protectionist and even mercantilist in orientation than navies. Most of the connections between armies and trade in Chapter 4 support a positive relationship between spending and trade, while the navy models offer very mixed results. If we assume that army planning for home defence is influenced by the vulnerabilities due to trade dependence, then we might expect that armies have a tendency to prefer protectionist measures to lessen vulnerability. Armies may prefer a domestic ability to produce military goods, rather than buying them from abroad, and may argue for increased defence needs due to increased external dependence.

It should be noted that the CUST term enters each army model positively, except for the German (CUST fails to enter the Italian army model). Where CUST changes due to conflict or an important date, it becomes positive (with Germany) or stays positive (with Japan) and becomes negative only with Russia. CUST enters all three navy models positively and fails to enter two altogether. There are also two significant changes with CUST in the navy models. CUST enters the French navy model negatively and remains negative (though flatter) after 1872. Germany, however, shows CUST entering negatively and becoming positive from 1890 onward.

Along with trade expansion and mutual rivalry has gone a shift towards naval power on the part of all but perhaps France. As Table 6.5 shows, the proportion of military expenditures that went into navies generally increased during the period, especially in the decade before the war. It may be true that naval competition was not really a domino effect, where, as one author states, France built its ships because Italy built its ships, which was motivated by Austrian ship-building, driven by Russian ship-building, and so on.[23]

There were certainly a wide variety of domestic and international factors involved in naval expansion, but one cannot truly separate the expansionary trade practices of the states from their naval rivalries (and army rivalries) because they are tied together. The specific roles that the navies of the seven states performed in relation to commerce and rivalry differed, however, owing to differences in size, capability, economic circumstances, and even naval ideas.[24]

Table 6.5: Navies as a Percentage of Military Expenditures, 1865–1913

Years	Britain	France	Germany	Italy	Japan	Russia	US
1865	42.08	32.75		24		15.07	
1870	43.72	32.52		13.43		13.86	27.42
1875	42.86	24.27	11.88	17.1	26.89	14.74	34.33
1880	40.48	25.75	9.7	17.07	28.39	14.01	26.2
1885	38	34.02	12.29	24.29	34.36	18.4	27.29
1890	46.79	25.77	9.07	26.8	39.54	17.84	33.04
1895	49.44	29.62	12.92	22.09	57.44	19.25	35.72
1900	37.36	35.65	19.6	31.43	43.78	26.71	29.34
1905	55.76	30.65	26.09	29.61	67.82	30.87	48.25
1910	56.83	28.45	34.32	36	45.28	23.3	39.35
1913	61.24	30.47	28.86	31.82	49.71	42.17	39.73

Source: See Appendix 1.

The movement towards naval power does not necessarily appear in the military data when it is measured as a percentage of national income. The German, Japanese, and US navy models contain negative signs on the intercept time dummies, each of which indicates a possible change after a point in time. These data are in percentage change, however. If we examine the army and navy spending as percentages of national income in their levels, there is a positive association in the army and navy dependence for each state except for Germany. The levels of army and navy spending as percentages of national income all produce positive correlations and show upward moving scatter plots (with a few outliers for times of war). The correlations range from 0.305 for France to 0.601 for Britain, with the rest falling in between. Germany is the peculiar exception, however, with a correlation of –0.558. The German data produce a downward-moving scatter plot that appears to be free of outliers as well.

While the levels of the data of six states show that increases in army and navy dependence occurred together, the German case shows a clear opposite tendency. In examining the data, it appears that dependence on army spending fluctuated with no overall tendency until about 1890, where it began to make clear downward movements. The exception is 1913 itself, where army dependence dramatically increased. Navy dependence data show a smooth flat line up to about 1890 and a clear tendency upward since then.

The above military and trade data show several things. First, the relationships between military power and commerce cut across the grouping between the larger and smaller of the Great Powers (ranked in terms of trade and military expenditures). There appears to be no obvious differences among the countries that relate to differences in the models of Chapter 4.

It is also clear that those states with the largest militaries also had the largest amounts of trade, except perhaps for Russia, whose military was quite large, but whose trade was not. Rather than commercial and military orientations being mutually exclusive, it appears that more of the one goes with more of the other regarding the percentage figures. This does not help us explain negative signs in the models, however, which refer to percentage changes. The general argument of a military orientation as opposed to a commercial one, perhaps like that put forth by Rosecrance, is not evident here.

We might also consider the roles of armies to be more complex than initially assumed. The roles of navies are largely fixed on external relations, although there are certainly great differences in the nature of these external roles. There is also no clear and obvious distinction between sea orientation and land orientation with either military power and trade, as the examples of Russia and Japan make clear. There is no correspondence, then, between trade by mode of transport and the balance of military expenditures between branches. This is further indication that the categories of land power and sea power are too simple, and that countries really exhibit varying degrees of both orientations in their relations.

TRADE, STRATEGY, AND THE GEOGRAPHIC DISTRIBUTION OF TRADE

As is evident from Tables 6.6 to 6.12, there are several patterns in the geographical distribution of trade of the seven states. Western Europe is the location of most world trade. While western Europe is the single largest area for Britain, it has never provided a majority of Britain's trade in this time period (though it perhaps did at an earlier time). In addition, British colonies provided a substantial amount of trade. French colonial trade, in contrast, was a much smaller part of total French trade. The colonial trade of Germany and Italy was not distinguished from the other regions because it was only a marginal portion of their total trade. While Britain began to pursue a system of colonial preferences in its trade during the 1880s, one can still consider Britain to be only moderately dependent on colonial trade, with the other countries being considerably less so. With both Britain and France, however, there was a progressive increase in the percentages of their trade with colonies.

Another pattern evident here is that most of the states began the period with a regional trade orientation towards Western Europe and, as time progressed, evolved into increasingly global trading patterns. British trade patterns, of course, were already global at the beginning of this time period, with sizeable portions of trade going to other regions. The globalization of British trade, indicated by a strong tendency to move away from western Europe to other continents, occurred as far back as the eighteenth century.[25] From about the mid-1850s onward, however, the geographic patterns of British trade remained relatively stable.

Russia is perhaps an exception here because, while it too began the period under consideration with a very regional trade orientation, Russian trade patterns remained overwhelmingly oriented towards western Europe throughout. It must be mentioned, however, that Russian regional trade (Table 6.7) is slightly in error. As with the tables for other states, the residual category of *other* in Russian trade tables, which indicates small amounts of trade not distinguished by country, has been left out of the percentages. At most, however, this omission means that the zero percentages for Africa, Asia, and South and Central America might not be zero – although they would certainly still be well under 1 per cent. The Russian percentages for western and eastern Europe and North America, however, are certainly accurate. Surprisingly, Russian trade with Eastern Europe actually declined by a few percentages during the entire period, which may have something to do with Russian rivalry with Austria and Germany.

Japan also reflects something of an exception. Japan also began the period with a heavy concentration of its trade with Western Europe. As time progressed, however, Japanese trade moved in greater amounts into North America and Asia. It would not be inaccurate to view the changes in the distribution of Japanese trade as reflecting a globalized trading pattern, because Japan still retained a considerable portion of trade with Western Europe and its trade with North America actually increased. But it may also be accurate to view the changes here as being a reorientation of Japanese trade from one regional pattern to another – from the distant region of western Europe to the local one of Asia. A new majority of Japanese trade was with Asia by 1913. It must also be noted that there is some inaccuracy in the Japanese regional trade table (Table 6.12) as well. At various times, the Japanese trade tables would have a fairly large figure for the *other* category. Clearly, there would be slightly larger percentages for Africa, and South and Central America in the Japanese distribution. But the major regions here are accurate.

The proportion of US trade with Europe declined dramatically during the period as well, but never went below 50 per cent of total US trade. The general shift in US trade was towards the Western Hemisphere, Asia, and Africa. While US trade also reflected a tendency to become more global in scope, the United States also showed a substantial regional focus on the Western Hemisphere.

The remaining countries all saw the globalization of their trade. While they were still heavily dependent on Western Europe, the growth of trade to other regions did not entail any other region becoming the conspicuous focus. This is really quite in line with the others above in that the continued regional focus on western Europe with these states amounts to a continued reliance on their local regions, whereas there is an increased focus on the local regions in US and Japanese trade.

The regional trade distributions of Germany and Italy did show dramatic shifts away from western Europe towards other regions, with German trade becoming more global in scope than Italian. Neither Germany nor Italy, however, would ever have less than a majority of their trade with Western Europe before the war. French trade also shifted in its patterns, but its movement away from western Europe was less dramatic than that of Germany and Italy owing to an already substantial presence beyond Europe. The principal area of proportional gain for France was with its colonies, but even colonial trade remained a relatively small amount of total French trade.

As is evident, eastern Europe occupied a relatively minor place in the total trade of all the states (not shown for the United States). The trade of most of the states with Eastern Europe, including that of Russia, actually declined proportionally. Italy's trade with Eastern Europe increased somewhat at the end of the period, but Germany's trade with Eastern Europe significantly increased throughout.

The geographic distribution of trade indicates several things. First, the location of the great majority of the trade of these states was also the source of threat and military rivalry. Conflict and rivalry took place among trade partners. Arguments that cast the Great Powers as being on a competitive quest for colonies in order to gain access to raw materials and markets exaggerate the importance of trade outside of Europe and North America. It is true that rivalries occurred in remote areas, which is likely to have had an affect on trade to those areas, but the value of the trade itself was quite small in many of those cases. As discussed in Chapter 7, the trade of rival Great Powers to remote areas appears to have had more relative importance as a tool of statecraft than it had in terms of trade value. The distribution of regional trade is a good general indicator of areas of strategic importance to states and, consequently, expansionary practices and patterns of conflict.

British trade expansion, as noted, occurred before that of the other states. British economic and military expansion has been described as having grown in a vacuum with little resistance among the major states.[26] Along with the growth of trade, British territorial acquisitions grew from about 1.5 million square miles in 1800 to about 390 million square miles in 1900.[27] Trade was an overt interest in expansion, but military expansion soon followed. Territorial expansion may have served several purposes for British trade. Aside from colonial trade proper, which Britain was moderately dependent upon, expansion also provided Britain with many points of contact that the navy could use to establish a broad network of defence for its trade and shipping more generally. It may be ironic that the connection between British trade and naval power was closest during the period of liberal trade. Mercantilists may have viewed the British colonies as a means of self-sufficiency for Britain,[28] but Britain generally allowed free trade with its colonies. The irony of this, of course, was that the colonies were acquired by force and then brought into a free trade arrangement – a curious mix of liberalism and mercantilism.

In addition, Britain required a vigorous merchant navy, but repealed the Navigation Laws in 1850, which meant that shipping no longer had to be British made (although ships were still British owned and manned). The colonies saw the old Navigation Laws as hindering their trade. British shipping, however, did not lose its supremacy after the new laws, partly because of the advent of iron shipping, in which Britain was already ahead.[29] If British merchant ships were closely guarded, however, then why does merchant tonnage enter the British navy model negatively and with borderline significance? If the British navy protected British trade and British merchant ships carried that trade, then merchant tonnage should enter the navy model positively and significantly. As suggested in Chapter 4, there may be a policy reason behind this result. A more likely possibility is that the merchant ships of other countries also carried British trade which, as indicated in Table 6.6, was more geographically dispersed than that of the other countries (with French trade being the second most dispersed). If this is true, then variation in British trade was not well connected to variation in British merchant tonnage, which is supported by the absence of merchant tonnage in the British trade models.

Table 6.6: British Regional Trade (percentage total), 1860–1913

Years	*W. Eur.*	*E. Eur.*	*Africa*	*Asia*	*N. Amer.*	*C. and S. Amer.*	*Colonies*
1860	34.6	8.5	4.39	5.03	18.04	6.55	23.19
1865	37.54	7.5	6.33	5.29	9.54	8.85	25.24
1870	36.93	8.48	4.89	3.97	14.82	8.53	21.96
1875	38.81	7.13	2.83	4.29	14.44	7.45	24.57
1880	35.61	5.84	2.55	4.31	20.79	5.61	24.95
1885	36.1	6.08	2.83	3.82	18.3	5.34	26.44
1890	36.19	6.78	2.45	3.21	19.18	6.47	25.46
1895	37.5	7.13	2.52	3.06	18.59	6.63	24.43
1900	37.3	5.9	2.95	3.25	20.07	6.21	24.11
1905	34.82	6.63	3.28	3.88	16.74	8.45	25.76
1910	33.38	6.95	3.67	2.91	15.01	10.06	27.04
1913	33.67	6.12	3.14	4.32	14.33	9.58	28.53

Source: Central Statistical Office, *Annual Abstract of Statistics* (London: HMSO), various years.

The strategy that emerged to support British trade was one of acquiring bases, coaling stations, and other access points along the entire logistical spread of British trade. In general, the navy was oriented towards providing a broad defensive function for commerce.[30] Trade routes, straits, canals, and colonies needed protection. By the end of the century, British coaling stations alone numbered at least forty, with about eight in the Western Hemisphere and the rest scattered through the Mediterranean, Indian Ocean, and Pacific.[31]

Along with an enormous defence network of naval power came a relaxed policy on commercial treaties as well. The British government made three types of commercial treaties in its liberal period: reciprocity treaties with European states; open-door treaties with states such as Turkey, Japan, and China; and pure free trade treaties with states such as those in South and Central America.[32] Up to the 1880s, then, the government supported free and fair trade and was reluctant to intervene on behalf of British firms. The government confined itself to defending free trade and seeking commercial treaties. Force was generally frowned upon because it would be immoral 'to open markets at the point of a bayonet'.[33]

This brief summary of what is a very conventional view of the British navy is also not clearly supported by the results in Chapter 4. The summary suggests that both imports and exports would be positively related to navy spending. In fact, the results are mixed and the positive connection seems more secure with the British army. Before attempting to resolve this problem, however, I will discuss it in more detail below. I will also try to refrain from discussing similar incongruities with the other countries until I have discussed the details in their data.

In ways that were smaller than those of large naval forces, however, British military operations were also used coercively to establish secure trading environments and punish aggressive moves against them, despite the above quote. While trade was the primary motive in the early expansion into India,[34] for example, military forces had to follow as the East India Company pursued a series of treaties with local princes, as well as annexations. The Company had raised three of its own armies before the 1857 mutiny.[35] Over time, British military policy in India was transformed into a general tool of British imperial policy. At first, the protection of India itself was the issue, which led to alliances, buffers, protectorates, and the growth of rail networks throughout the country. Later, India itself became the central focus of a larger naval infrastructure that allowed Britain to dominate the Indian Ocean.[36]

In order to arrive at a hegemonic position in the Indian Ocean, however, India itself had to be secured first. If one were to look at a railway map of India just before the First World War, one would notice a relatively even spread of railway lines throughout most of the country, and a dense belt of lines across nearly the entire northern border, from Baluchistan Agency in the northwest straight across the top of India to just south of the corner of Tibet and China. In addition, British railways penetrated the northern border into Baluchistan, Afghanistan, and other neighbouring countries, from which Britain carried on a steady frontier trade with all the countries north of India. Frontier activities, of course, were accompanied by army activities. From 1840 to 1900, Britain conducted at least 110 wars of expedition and military operations on or beyond the borders of India. The refusal of a village to pay revenue (Britain raised finances there to pay for various government expenditures), assaults on people in British territory by natives, theft, raids, and many other actions by native groups pushed the British northward into skirmishes.[37]

While the occupation and settlement practices of Britain in India allowed commerce to flow unchecked, the implied positive association between British military activities there and trade may have been less immediate than the above description suggests. It could also have been that the conflicts that led to military expansion in the area destroyed or disrupted trade, and that only after a settlement had been reached, did trade recover and grow.

As the other states in this study began to industrialize and advance their trade interests, the commercially relevant aspects of British military power would acquire greater dimension. Competition in trade became tied into military rivalry among the other emerging Great Powers, and each reinforced the other. Sometimes military rivalry engendered trade rivalry as well. One of the long-standing conflicts in the nineteenth century, related to British activities in India, was Anglo-Russian rivalry. This conflict has a long history and lasted perhaps up to the 1907 Anglo-Russian Agreement. Russian expansion into Central Asia goes back to about 1860, and mirrors in many ways British expansion on the other side of the frontier. In the mid-1860s, Russia absorbed several key cities in Central Asia, such as Turkestan and Tashkent, and created protectorates over Khiva and Bukhara in 1873. Russia was seeking frontiers that could be defended easily.[38] But competition with the British was also a factor in Russian expansion.

The competitive rail expansion of both Russia and Britain along the frontiers of India, Afghanistan, Persia, and surrounding areas was a central theme in the conflict. Russian railway development in the region began in earnest with the fall of the last independent state in the region, the Kokand Khanate in 1876. The Trans-caspian railway line was started in 1881 to aid military actions against local tribes, but was later extended and reached Tashkent. This route, however, was very limited in its ability to support commerce and did not provide a direct railway line to European Russia.[39] By the mid-1880s, Russian railway development in Asia was seen by Britain as being a menace. Lord Curzon, travelling along the Trans-Caspian, stated that Russian activities in the area no longer resembled pragmatic responses to local threats, but had acquired an imperial character that threatened Britain and Asia.[40]

Britain did tend to overestimate Russian movements east and south. From the end of the Napoleonic Wars onward, Britain periodically complained of the Russian threat to India. In fact, the logistical requirements of any Russian invasion through the vast stretches of territory and mountain passes were well beyond the limits of the possible.[41] Overestimating the Russian strategic potential was, of course, also the business of most geopolitical writers. Russia never lived up to the predictions of Halford MacKinder. It has been argued that significant Russian progress in railway construction did not really even occur until after the turn of the century.[42]

The amount of new railway construction in Russia does not really reflect this last statement. If one looks at Russia each year from 1859 to 1913, the fluctuations clearly show varying amounts of new railway construction throughout with two periods of conspicuous growth. The first was between 1868 and 1878, which saw much greater growth in new construction than beforehand and for several years afterward. The high point in this period was 1871, which saw 2,910 kilometres in new construction. The next period was 1893–1902 and reflects even larger amounts of new railway construction, with the high point being 1899, which saw 5,248 new kilometres. The period 1903–13 generally showed significantly lower amounts of new railway construction.[43]

Despite these earlier spurts in railway growth, however, Russian ability to threaten India was still exaggerated. In addition, Russian trade with the Asian frontier was never dominant in Russian trade. It is true that Russian trade with Persia began to grow in the 1880s, aided by preferential tariffs and government subsidies, which perhaps indicates that Persia was sliding into the Russian sphere of influence.[44] Russian railways also affected trade in that expansion opened up new geographic areas to trade. Sometimes Russian goals for railway development were trade, such as with the export of grain to the West, and sometimes goals were military and strategic, such as strengthening of the empire and competition with Britain.[45]

It is unfortunate that the Russian Imperial Statistical Series (*Statistika Rossiiskoi Imperii*) provides specific trade information with Central Asia only from 1858 to 1867. The series indicates trade with the Kergive Steppes, Khiva, Bukhara, Tashkent, Afghanistan, and so on, but ceases to do so after 1867. Trade with Central Asia was generally small, however. In the year 1867, which reflects the highest amount of trade with Central Asia between 1858 and 1867, Russia's total trade (imports + exports) with the region was at a mere 29.48 million roubles while it was 182.97 million roubles with Britain alone, which makes trade with Central Asia in that year a mere 16 per cent of Russia's trade with Britain. Even though this trade was quite small in comparison to Russian trade with the West, it may very well have moved in step with Russian railway and army development because it was entwined with the Anglo-Russian rivalry. But we cannot know this.

Despite British imperial exaggerations, the conflict between Russia and Britain was certainly a real one. Russian rail development was seen as being detrimental to British interests. In particular, Russian plans for a Trans-Persian line would bring the Russians too close to India, but the British could not stop the plans. The line from Orenburg to Tashkent was completed in 1905, which Britain saw as a threat to Afghanistan. Russia also built railheads approaching the Indo-Persian corridor. The Julfa railhead in Azerbaijan was laid in 1907, later connecting to Tabriz in 1916. One was laid at the Kushka fortress at the end of the main branch line in 1900, joining the Trans-Caspian line at Merv. And a railhead was built on the Afghan border (completed in 1916), and was connected to the Trans-Caspian and Orenburg–Tashkent lines in 1905.[46]

Table 6.7: Russian Regional Trade (percentage total), 1861–1905

Years	W. Eur.	E. Eur.	Asia	Africa	N. Amer.	C. and S. Amer.
1861	81.08	5.88	9.78	0	2.03	1.07
1865	83.01	6.68	8.83	0	0.67	0.12
1870	94.8	3.57	0	0	0.75	0.05
1875	90.9	3.37	0	0	0.93	2.28
1880	91.17	4.28	0	0	0.98	1.54
1885	89.34	3.47	0	1.84	2.81	0.04
1890	85.47	2.69	1.41	1.36	5.49	0.15
1895	83.69	2.62	6.65	1.39	2.59	0.06
1900	83.96	2.02	7.65	1.58	3.54	0.02
1905	83.18	2.01	8.82	0.68	2.59	0.05

Source: *Statistical Tables for Principal and Other Foreign Countries*, House of Commons Sessional Papers (London: HMSO), various years.

Britain responded to Russian railway advances with counter railway expansion, but Britain had always had a far greater amount of railways in Asia than had Russia from the beginning. The competition between Britain and Russia led to a series of boundary agreements in the late 1880s. After the 1885 Pamirs Boundary Commission, where Britain recognized Russian annexations in Central Asia, several agreements followed between 1887 and 1889. But full settlement of the rivalry between the two did not occur until the Anglo-Russian Agreement of 1907.[47] The advent of buffer status for Afghanistan was an outcome of a series of British–Russian antagonisms over the country. As early as 1873, Afghanistan was recognized as a neutral zone by agreement between Russia and Britain. With Russian troops on the border of Afghanistan in 1878 and a local attack on a British party in the Kyber Pass, however, the Second Anglo–Afghan War began. The resulting Treaty of Gandamuk (1879), opened the way for British domination over Afghanistan's foreign policy. From 1880 onward, Afghanistan began to act as a buffer state. Another crisis in 1884 led to the boundary commission noted above, and the recognition of Afghanistan as being in the British sphere of influence.[48]

The 1907 Anglo-Russian Agreement, of course, settled rivalries in Asia between Russia and Britain for the remainder of the period. The agreement also provided an opportunity for Russia and Japan (an ally of Britain since 1902) to settle their differences and thus prevent another war between them.[49] The agreement divided Persia into spheres of influence for Britain and Russia, Chinese control over Tibet was recognized by both parties, Russia conceded Afghanistan as a British interest, and Britain agreed not to interfere in the internal affairs of Afghanistan.[50] From a larger perspective, the agreement was an opportunity for Britain to remove one more competitor from the list of possible enemies, which allowed Britain to concentrate more on the German problem.[51]

Russian trade with Asia as a whole, of course, grew to moderate significance in the years before the war. As noted, the flaws in the Russian table mean that the role of Asia in Russian trade would be slightly higher than shown here. Western Europe was the primary area of trade for Russia, but for at least some of the years Asia was the second largest area.

German military and trade expansion was much more vigorous than Russian, and presented a greater geopolitical problem for Britain. German trade expansion did not actually commence with German victory over France in 1871, but was quite moderate until the middle of the 1880s (see below). As noted, however, German trade expansion was directed towards the rest of the world beyond western Europe.

German naval policy was initially justified on the grounds that Germany needed to protect its trade. The beginnings of German naval policy are perhaps with the 1865 Prussian naval bill, which argued for the need to protect German coasts and trade from other states.[52] The Franco–Prussian War put a damper on naval ambitions in Germany, however, because the army proved to be the primary tool in fighting the war and the navy was nearly irrelevant.[53] German trade expansion and colonial acquisitions, however, continued without a strong navy, which led to a change in policy. In 1884, Germany acquired a host of new territories overseas, including Southwest Africa, Togo, the Cameroons, the Marshall Islands, and others. Germany advanced towards parts of East Africa in 1885 as well. Territorial gains and trade growth allowed Germany to claim with some justification that it needed a strong navy in order to match Germany's position in the world.[54] Not only were German colonies (small by British standards) a potential source of vulnerability, but German trade and shipping required protection from enemies. German competition with Britain really begins in 1890, with the period from 1898 to the war being the most aggressive, as German naval development jumped to a higher level.

Table 6.8: German Regional Trade (percentage total), 1880–1913

Years	W. Eur.	E. Eur.	Africa	Asia	N. Amer.	C. and S. Amer.	Oceania
1880	79.86	9.94	0.37	1.57	6.65	1.28	0.16
1885	82.16	9.07	0.34	1.18	5.05	1.9	0.3
1890	65.18	11.52	0.6	3.37	10.9	6.47	0.94
1895	56.18	12.11	1.15	5.04	11.69	8.42	1.78
1900	58.4	11.04	2.04	5.57	13.78	7.5	1.62
1905	54.61	13.26	2.64	6.21	11.89	9.6	1.64
1910	51.91	14.04	3.65	7.07	11.38	9.62	2.22
1913	51.76	13.25	3.39	7.65	12.22	9.55	2.07

Source: Germany, Kaiserlichen Statistischen Amt, *Statistisches Jahrbuch für das Deutsche Reich* (Berlin: Puttkammer and Muhlbrecht), various years.

The Germans were not strong advocates of the *guerre de course* strategy. As noted in Chapter 1, *guerre de course* is a naval strategy for a second-tier navy, the principal strategic focus of which is to destroy the commerce of an enemy. The commerce-destroying orientation is well suited for a second-tier navy. Germany had few overseas bases and British trade routes were far from German shores, which meant that *guerre de course* would not find many advocates in Germany.[55] Tirpitz would later argue that commerce protection itself could not be very effective without large ships, because even the vessels involved in commerce protection and coastal defence needed protection.[56] I do not want to recount the series of events and naval bills that accompanied German naval policy during the period. Rather, I will confine the discussion here to the geopolitical elements of German rivalry with Britain and show how this rivalry was tied into trade expansion.

Anglo-German military rivalry was not really in full swing until the end of the century. In the 1880s, Germany saw Britain as a potential ally – even encouraging cooperation between Britain and Italy – because France was the main enemy of Germany at the time.[57] But as Britain became the main stumbling block to German expansionary goals, German naval strategy turned towards Britain. The naval strategy that Germany came to pursue was that of risk theory, which was the policy of Tirpitz. The goal of risk was to make the German navy powerful enough to deter the most powerful navy in the region (Britain) from attacking German interests. The German navy was to be a real threat to British supremacy – not powerful enough to defeat the British navy, but too powerful for Britain to attack without significant damage to itself.[58] The British navy dominated the North Sea and the Channel, which effectively meant that German access to the world could be controlled by Britain. The British never really tried to block German access to the rest of the world, but the Germans believed that they were being 'hemmed in' and deprived of a world position commensurate with their economic and diplomatic interests.[59]

The risk theory worked as long as Britain's other competitors in the world remained antagonistic towards Britain, so as to prevent the British fleet from concentrating too much force in its home waters. But the Franco-Russian Alliance (1894), the Anglo-Japanese Alliance (1902), the Anglo-French Entente (1904), the Anglo-Russian Agreement (1907), the destruction of the Russian Pacific fleet by Japan in 1905, and the friendly attitude of the United States towards Britain ruined the risk strategy.[60] As time went on, Britain removed most of the main states from its list of potential enemies, leaving Germany isolated. And Italy would be of no use in the Mediterranean. The risk strategy had counted on the dispersal of the British fleet because this would leave Britain with less naval power to deploy in its home waters to counter the German navy.[61] Unfortunately for the Germans, French–Italian relations were also improving, which meant that the Italian fleet would not even act as a counter to the French fleet in the Mediterranean.[62]

In addition, the German army was in need of enlargement. Since the Franco–Prussian War, German army spending had been positively associated with French army spending, but the German army also turned its attention to Russia. The association between German and French army spending was stronger in the period before 1885. German army spending was also generally larger in amount before 1890 than afterwards. German army increases also began to respond to Russian, especially in the years immediately before the war.[63] While the association between German and Russian army spending is present after 1890, it is generally strongest in the last decade before the war (especially when Russian spending is lagged). Germany is traditionally thought of as being a land power,[64] but it appears that German security requirements were being stretched in both directions, with the pull of maritime interests probably becoming the predominant focus after 1890.

The British certainly acknowledged aggressive economic competition from the United States, but the two were also in competition on the military front. One could even say that Britain had to decide which state – Germany or the United States – was the greater potential threat to British interests. Britain could not maintain a two-power standard against all states, especially with the United States being a potential rival.[65] If one examines the levels of military spending, the United States was routinely the most competitive with Britain in terms of naval expenditure. As the last decade before the war approached, however, the naval expenditures of the other states also began to grow, which meant that Britain could not maintain a two-power standard against all. All the Great Powers were changing the relative position of Britain, of course, not simply the United States. Since the late nineteenth century, as one author states, British sea power has been 'reduced from an indefinite superiority to a three, to a two and now to a one [in 1928] power standard'.[66]

Why should Britain not have decided to find common alliance with Germany, while maintaining a competitive posture towards the United States? Why accept American naval power and oppose German, rather than the opposite? This is quite a reasonable question in light of the fact that the United States was not at all unlike Germany in terms of aggressive competition and expansionary ambitions.

Without relying on any alleged cultural sympathies for an answer to the above question, Britain's choice of the United States over Germany was quite reasonable from a geopolitical standpoint. German naval power was more of a threat to the British by virtue of location. The Germans on the North Sea required passage through the Channel to get to the Atlantic. The United States navy was mostly preoccupied with the Western Hemisphere, except for a small Asian squadron at the time. The British realized that they had to concede the Western Hemisphere to the United States and remove the United States from the list of potential enemies in order to concentrate more effectively on the Germans.[67] Thus Britain appeased the United States at the end of the century by making concessions on several issues, such as the Panama Canal issue and the Alaskan boundary issue.[68]

The Spanish–American War marked the entrance of the United States into Great Power status. While American trade had always been fairly large in amount, the proportions of American trade to Asia began to grow after the war. It should be noted, however, that the Spanish–American War does not seem to mark an increase in US import or export dependence on Asia, as indicated by the lack of the dummy variable D1898 in either trade model.

The United States did very consciously expand its naval access to various regions along with its commerce, which is perhaps most true with US exports. Well before Mahan, American naval officers advocated the expansion of American exports into as many parts of the world as possible as a function of national strategy. The relative strategic significance of areas was tied into whether or not access to markets was under American control.[69] The connection between exports and navy spending supports the presence of this influence. Mahan also thought that those geographic features that benefited trade also benefited strategy. With regard to the Central American isthmus, Mahan states that control over such land 'like the key to a military position, exerts a vital effect upon the course of trade, and so upon the struggle ... for that increase of wealth, of prosperity, and of general consideration, which affect both the happiness and the dignity of nations'.[70] The desirable effects on trade that came from such control, thought Mahan, also led into diplomatic and military rivalries.[71]

It would be no exaggeration to say that American naval officers were the true trade representatives of the US in this period. As US vessels visited the coasts of Africa, sailed along the Indian Ocean, South America, and the Pacific, they sought outlets for American manufactures and upheld the mission of protecting the lives and property of Americans abroad.[72] It has been argued that American expansion was not really driven by a constant drive to expand into overseas markets, and that the general belief in the need to export was only an intermittent one. Instead American expansion, even after 1898, was halting and uncertain.[73] It has also been argued that economic motives were important in American foreign policy, but did not drive policy,[74] although American naval base acquisitions were driven, among other things, by expanding commerce.[75] The connections between exports and naval spending in Chapter 4, however, do argue for the importance of exports in US foreign policy in this period. Imports seem to be conspicuously absent as a foreign policy concern, which might reflect the relative lack of dependence on critical supplies of goods.

Very often military concerns prevailed and economic issues became a tool of military goals. Teddy Roosevelt's interest in the Panama Canal, for example, was largely a function of his concern for bases. Roosevelt saw potential German advances into the Western Hemisphere and Japanese advances towards Hawaii as being a significant threat to the United States. Base acquisition would enable the United States to prevent further European encroachments into the Western Hemisphere and to extend naval protection to American merchant ships in the Pacific.[76] As argued in Chapter 3, however, these military concerns are related to commerce in numerous ways. It is simply not enough to argue that trade gains were not always the driving force in US foreign policy. Even if it was not, there was still a host of connections between military power and commerce that argues for a relationship.

Table 6.9: US Regional Trade (percentage total), 1866–1913

Years	Europe	Americas	Asia	Africa	Oceania
1866	74.01	24.06	3.18	0.57	1.25
1870	68.13	25.41	4.49	0.55	0.77
1875	63.79	25.09	5.09	0.52	0.86
1880	67.53	18.9	5.33	0.56	0.87
1885	65.34	20.43	5.84	0.5	1.85
1890	65.44	21.41	5.83	0.46	1.9
1895	59.18	22.75	5.96	0.7	1.52
1900	60.97	18.57	8.81	1.24	2.88
1905	54.63	24.34	10.84	1.05	1.4
1910	54.47	27.55	8.08	1.01	1.51
1913	52.27	29.59	9.65	1.21	1.56

Source: US Department of Commerce, *Historical Statistics of the United States: Colonial Times to 1970* (Washington, DC: GPO, 1976), Vol. 2.

Earlier interest in a canal across the isthmus, on the other hand, was tied into American export expansion. During the Arthur administration in the 1880s, American grain exports were facing higher tariff walls in Europe, and Britain was importing greater amounts of grain from India. It was clear in the United States that the Suez Canal was draining off American grain exports to Britain. The United States thus sought to put forth a series of reciprocity agreements with states, especially those in the Caribbean and Central America. Such agreements became linked into the effort to secure the land rights over the isthmus in Central America.[77] The United States began to see the possibility of becoming the gatekeeper of European access to Asia between the Atlantic and Pacific Oceans.

Whatever the causes of American export and naval expansion, the two went hand-in-hand. As with the other sea powers, American commercial expansion was followed by the acquisition of bases, coaling stations, and commercial treaties. The commercial treaties could not be entirely separated from security issues. The American commercial treaty with Korea in 1882, for example, was welcomed by China and Korea because the United States could act as a bulwark against Japan.[78] The Treaty of Amity and Commerce had a mixture of commercial and security elements to it. Article I of the Treaty stated that if either party were treated unjustly and oppressively by other powers, the other would come to its aid.[79] The treaty with Korea was the first in a series that Korea soon made with others, such as Britain and Germany, and was the culmination of a long effort by the Powers to find a way into Korea.

The requirements of American commercial expansion contradict-ed any isolationist attitude towards political entanglements.[80] The American support of freedom of the seas would require the force to ensure such freedom, including an international military presence to act as an infrastructure for such support. While the United States acquired sites in Asia, however, its base acquisitions were heavily concentrated in the Western Hemisphere.[81]

In addition, the commercially relevant aspects of naval power on the part of other Great Powers was often the cause of American naval expansion. The British–Italian–German naval blockade against Venezuela in 1902, owing to a default on debts, for example, was seen as being a threat to US security. The result was the formation of a fleet, made up of the North Atlantic, South Atlantic, and Mediterranean Squadrons, and British acceptance of the Monroe Doctrine.[82] The Boxer Rebellion (1900) is another instance where military and commercial interests intersected, resulting in naval expansion. With the Boxer Rebellion, the United States gained the right to station troops in and around Peking.

American policy in Asia was supported by the Asiatic Fleet (Asiatic Squadron before 1902). While the fleet's main mission was to protect American holdings in the Pacific and to execute war plans against Japan in case of war, gunboats also patrolled Chinese rivers, where they could fight against bandits and protect American lives and property.[83] It was a prevailing American attitude that the US navy had the right to go wherever American citizens were in order to protect them. While there are certainly many other examples that one could point to, the point is clear that commercial and military interests were really insepa-rable. An increase in American naval presence, bases, coaling stations, and other assets served both military and commercial purposes.

French trade expansion showed a less dramatic shift away from western Europe than most of the others. As Table 6.10 shows, France has always had a majority of its trade with Western Europe, and the percentage variation is less dramatic than it is for other countries. The areas where French trade gained in percentage terms were in Asia and French colonies – and the percentage increases for these regions were moderate. In short, there are some shifts in the geographic distribution of French trade, but the overall pattern is relatively stable.

Before the Crimean War, French naval strategy was oriented toward 'not dominating, but of preventing all domination of the seas', which, according to Bernard Brodie, was similar to the German strategy under Tirpitz discussed above.[84] In the mid-1840s, France decided that it needed a strong navy, and was expanding into the Pacific.[85] It was classic French mercantilist thinking that colonies should be acquired as a source of raw materials and as a potential market for manufactures. A navy would thus act as a means of protecting French trade, shipping, and colonies.[86] The idea of using the navy as a tool in empire building was given added emphasis during the Second Empire of Louis Napoleon, which meant that the French navy began to become modern and powerful, just in time for the Crimean War.[87]

French expansion from the 1860s onward was pushed forward by young naval officers, especially in Asia, much like their American counterparts in the 1870s.[88] In addition to colonial expansion, the French navy was in competition with the British after the Crimean War. While Britain may have had the advantage of fleet size over France, many of the technological innovations in naval construction came from France in this period. The French bid for parity with the British was to be achieved not by matching Britain ship by ship, but by superior design and speed. Thus France focused on building fast, lightly armoured frigates.[89]

The Franco–Prussian War, however, led to a drastic reduction in the size and importance of the French navy. The army was seen as being more important after the war, as in Germany at the time, and the French navy was reduced to about 200 vessels.[90] In examining French military spending, a depression in the level of naval spending does appear evident in the data for several years after the war, but the growth rates of navy spending do not appear to be very different from army spending after the war itself. The unstable politics of the Third Republic was also bad for the navy, which saw about 30 different ministers of marine between 1871 and 1901.[91] The reduction in the navy's size, despite technological innovations, meant that the French navy would remain a second-order navy, not one truly capable of challenging the command of the seas that the British navy aimed at maintaining. The army was seen as being the primary tool in defence, with the idea that a war of revenge against Germany would be on land.[92]

The French naval strategy that emerged in the nineteenth century, then, was overtly oriented towards commerce – of the enemy. The *Jeune Ecole* school of naval thought, which climbed into prominence in France with the advent of Admiral Aube as Minister of Marine in 1886, propagated the strategy of *guerre de course* for France.[93] The *Jeune Ecole* was against large battleships and in favour of smaller and faster vessels that could defend coasts and attack trade, which contradicted the traditional thinking about command of the sea.[94] Belief in *guerre de course* was based on the idea that 'the effects of war are felt only if commerce is hit'.[95]

French commerce-destroying strategy was focused on Britain as the potential enemy, but France shifted policy when it became clear that Germany and the Triple Alliance were the real enemies. By 1900, then, the *guerre de course* strategy was abandoned and there was, once again, a shift towards building large battleships. The goal here was to have 28 battleships, 20 armoured cruisers, 52 destroyers, and a host of smaller vessels by 1907.[96] French naval policy remained confused in this period, however, with many Ministers of Marine and agitation of the *Jeune Ecole* against the new policy, among other things.[97] French construction plans were upgraded again in 1906, and in 1910 the Minister of Marine decided to create 16 dreadnoughts by 1919, which was too ambitious for French finances to handle. The French navy consequently dropped from second to fifth place among the major navies of the world.[98] In addition, it was not until 1911 that France and Britain began naval cooperation, which allowed Britain to focus even more on Germany.[99] Despite the obvious landward threat posed by Germany, it is interesting to note that the shift in French naval strategy was in some manner related to the German threat, due to the complex nature of Great Power rivalry and to the tangled ways in which land and sea environments interact.

Table 6.10: French Regional Trade (percentage total), 1870–1913

Years	W. Eur.	E. Eur.	Africa	Asia	N. Amer.	C. and S. Amer.	Oceania	Colonies
1870	59.71	7.29	2.08	3.48	9.26	10.51		
1875	66.74	5.96	2.38	3.78	6.13	9.34	0.06	5.59
1880	60.46	6.46	2.17	3.93	12.51	8.27	0.34	5.46
1885	63.82	5.65	1.76	5.01	7.39	9.11	0.31	7.39
1890	60.25	5.71	2.14	5.22	7.89	10.67	0.49	8.05
1895	57.12	5.43	1.3	5.98	8.06	9.87	1.07	10.38
1900	59.04	5.25	1.45	5.44	8.82	8.32	1.16	10.25
1905	57.87	6.17	1.84	5.83	8.31	8.47	1.18	10.43
1910	54.27	5.26	1.97	6.6	8.26	8.63	1.8	12.41
1913	54.68	5.41	2.33	6.19	8.91	8.74	1.96	11.06

Source: *Annuaire Statistique de la France* (Paris: Institut National de la Statistique et des Etudes Economiques), various years.

From a geopolitical standpoint, French power was eclipsed by German power some time after the Franco–Prussian War. French naval strategy progressively turned away from Britain and towards Germany. Pressured by great German land power and vigorous sea power, France gravitated towards Britain for protection. This change in focus provides some intuitive backing for the fact that both branches of the French military enter the German army model.

Italian trade expansion shows a fairly dramatic shift away from western Europe towards other regions. Italian trade gained in percentage terms in every other region, although Oceania was truly marginal for Italian trade. Italian expansion was also conducted with a naval orientation towards local and coastal defence. The Italian navy had little role outside of the Mediterranean. The Italian fleet was focused not on taking command of the Western Mediterranean from the French, but on making French control tenuous,[100] reflecting the state of French–Italian rivalry in the Mediterranean. French naval power in the Mediterranean, however, served several purposes. The French navy also served in the Mediterranean to protect French lines of communication with its empire and as a tool in French colonial rivalry with Britain.[101]

Italian colonial ambitions, however, were oriented towards creating profitable economic activity in Africa and possibly in finding a solution to southern Italy's population problem.[102] However, Italian colonies would never become central to either trade or strategic policy.

Table 6.11: Italian Regional Trade (percentage total), 1865–1913

Years	W. Eur.	E. Eur.	Asia	Africa	N. Amer.	C. and S. Amer.	Oceania
1865	81.75	9.69	0.03	2	0.77	4.18	0
1870	81.88	7.71	0.06	1.17	4.47	3.55	0
1875	85.78	5.1	0	1.57	3.2	4.34	0
1880	79.79	6.36	3.32	2.11	5.53	2.89	0
1885	80.55	6.35	4.25	2.48	4.36	1.99	0.01
1890	73.74	7.77	5.95	1.9	6.84	3.71	0.07
1895	70.76	7.48	4.85	1.93	10.03	4.75	0.2
1900	67.91	7.38	5.87	2.34	11.54	5.53	0.22
1905	68.28	9.23	6.87	2.74	12.55	6.52	0.21
1910	58.56	10.03	7.59	3.1	11.98	7.87	0.52
1913	55.54	7.9	7.5	4.21	13.01	9.18	0.74

Source: *Annuario Statistico Italiano* (Rome: ISTAT), various years.

Eritrea, created in 1890 out of acquisitions around Ethiopia, was seen by Prime Minister Crispi as being the cornerstone of Italian imperial plans.[103] However, Italian colonies did not pay off. As noted above, the Italian army was poorly equipped for colonial expansion. Italy did indeed conduct a steady trade with its colonies, but this trade amounted to a small part of Italian trade as a whole, and Italy never dominated the trade markets of its colonies (until the war). In 1900, Italy had only 2.9 per cent of Eritrean imports and 13.1 per cent of its exports. The figures did climb by 1910 to a share of 30.1 per cent of Eritrean imports and 27.7 per cent of its exports.[104] It would not be until the fascist period that Italy would impose more complete control over Eritrean trade.

To support Italian expansionist goals, the Istituto Coloniale Italiano was set up in 1906 to maximize the benefits of colonial expansion: 'Pacific Italian commercial penetration in the Mediterranean basin must meet ever greater success'.[105] Colonial expansion was also seen as being a substitute for a war with France and irredentist expansion in the north of Italy.[106]

The Italian navy, and army for that matter, did not attempt to traverse the full geographic extent of Italian trade. Outside of Italy's small colonial activities, then, the Italian military was focused on threats posed locally (mostly by France), which seems to accord with the fact that the majority of Italian trade was with Western Europe.

Table 6.12: Japanese Regional Trade (percentage total), 1881–1913

Years	W. Eur.	E. Eur.	Asia	Africa	N. Amer.	C. and S. Amer.	Oceania
1881	51.84	0.11	21.31	0	20.95	0	0.23
1885	41.51	0.47	27.81	0	27.03	0	0.53
1890	39.63	0.86	32.33	0	20.03	0	0.82
1895	39.32	0.07	33.64	0	24.76	0	0.87
1900	34.22	2.13	37.6	0.36	24.38	0.01	1.01
1905	28.96	0.68	42.76	0	25.54	0	1.25
1910	29.29	0.23	44.69	0.54	22.49	0.27	1.53
1913	26.61	0.38	45.82	0.66	23.42	0.37	1.73

Source: *Statistical Tables for Principal and Other Foreign Countries*, House of Commons Sessional Papers (London: HMSO), various years; and Japan, Imperial Cabinet, *Résumé Statistique de l'Empire du Japon* (Tokyo: Bureau of General Statistics), various years.

The expansion of Japanese trade really began with the Sino–Japanese War (1894–95) which, before the war, was at a lower level (see Table 6.12). Japan's foreign trade was cramped by the 'unequal treaties' with the Great Powers, which Japan had been seeking to throw off from 1872 to 1894. The primary issues here for Japan regarding the treaties were extraterritorial jurisdiction and tariff autonomy. A major step in the direction of autonomy was the 1894 Anglo-Japanese Treaty, which promised the ending of extraterritoriality not sooner than five years and modified Japanese import tariffs.[107] While Japan regained domestic autonomy by 1899, it did not gain full tariff autonomy until 1911.[108] Japan's war against China, however, marked the beginning of Japan's ascent to Great Power status, and the beginning of Japanese access to the Asian mainland.[109] From the war onward, Japanese trade would both expand in general and begin moving in greater amounts toward Asia.

In addition, Japanese trade expansion reflected Japanese security concerns. While Japan is an island, its security has always been amphibious in nature, owing to the fact that it has had to guard against both the land power of Russia and China and the sea power of Britain, the United States, Russia, and others.[110] Japan's enemies, then, were seen as having the capacity to cut off Japan's trade routes and conduct a starvation campaign against them.[111] Thus Japan early on came to see Korea as a primary security interest over land and to see the need for naval expansion to protect trade routes over sea. Korea was both Japan's first line of defence and a source of trade, which is why the Japanese army assented to the building of railways in Korea after the war with China.[112] The dual commercial and strategic importance of Korea to Japan drove Japanese efforts to open Korea as far back as the 1870s. Japan tried a range of tactics, from diplomatic pressure to gunboat diplomacy.[113]

While Korea was vital to Japan, however, it was also the locus of strategic concern for Russia, Britain, and the United States. As soon as Japan won over China in Korea, it found itself in near hostilities with Russia. Russia was seeking Port Arthur and its surrounding territory. In 1898 Japan and Russia ultimately came to an agreement, which said that if Russia conceded Korea to Japan, Japan would recognize Russia's new leased territory in South Manchuria (which Japan captured and then lost in 1895, and which the Chinese granted to the Russians in 1897 in order to house their Far Eastern Fleet).[114]

It has been stated that the naval competition around the turn of the century was not driven by economic competition or the quest for colonies, but was more for Great Power gains.[115] While trade with Africa, Asia, and Central and South America may not have been the driving ambition of the Great Powers, especially in light of the fact that trade with these areas was a relatively minor portion of trade for most of the states, trade with these other regions became bound up with strategic issues. Competition and rivalry with other Great Powers and local issues both gave strategic importance to trade.

Trade among Great Powers is a different matter. The great majority of trade, as noted, was located in western Europe. Trade expansion, the aggressive acquisition of market footholds, and protectionist policies fed military rivalry and vice-versa. With perhaps a degree of overstatement, J. F. C. Fuller states of German trade policy that:

> to enforce her economic policy upon her neighbors she had her immensely powerful army; but to enforce her will on her overseas competitors her army was useless, so she built an immensely powerful fleet. Every time a hostile tariff was raised against her she said that she was being encircled, and demanded her place in the sun.[116]

Fuller's statement, while dramatic, is really a picture of how most of the Great Powers dealt with trade expansion. The military was a tool in trade expansion and an instrument in trade conflict as well. In all the rivalries of the Great Powers, trade conflict was knotted up with military. As Britain came to face more and more competitors, British government support of trade also evolved during this period into a more aggressive stance. The British government began the period with a policy of not interfering on behalf of specific commercial interests, but was content to uphold the principle of fair trade for British firms. As competition grew more aggressive, especially after the 1880s, British policy began to change to a more activist role.[117] Joseph Chamberlain stated in 1896 that:

> The Foreign Office and the Colonial Office are chiefly engaged in finding new markets and in defending the old ones. The War Office and the Admiralty are mostly occupied in preparations for the defense of these markets, and for the protection of our commerce.[118]

Most of the governments of the Great Powers sought to support their overseas industries and investments as well. A combination of factors, including increased foreign economic activity, nationalist policies that pointed to restrictions on foreign business, and problems that businesses faced regarding the willingness of foreign governments to live up to their agreements all generated friction between governments.[119] Not only did these problems make businesses more dependent on their home governments for support and protection, but the governments of the Great Powers also wanted to use the foreign business practices of home industries for their own foreign policy goals.[120]

In addition, there was a growing politicization of economic and financial dealings in the late nineteenth century. As tensions between the Triple Alliance and the Entente Powers progressed, the political character of foreign lending also increased. While several countries participated in politically motivated lending practices, France took the forefront here with lending to Russia (see Chapter 7). A great deal of French loans to Russia were spent on war preparations – payment for arms imports from France or on building strategic railways.[121] While France and Britain were able to finance their military rivalry out of the government budget, other states had to borrow to compete. Germany, Austria-Hungary, and Italy relied partly on internal borrowing, while Russia, Turkey, and the Balkan states relied on external borrowing. Russia never paid back any of the loans it received for armament financing, however. It either defaulted on or repudiated its loans during and after the war.[122]

Nevertheless, foreign loans and arms sales were intertwined with diplomacy. Financial dealings were often entangled in diplomatic goals, business deals were aided with the use of force and bribes, and financial dealings were periodically subject to political sabotage.[123] French arms sales competition against Germany, for example, led France not only to impose tariffs against German steel-makers in 1881, but also to lift the ban on foreign arms sales in 1885, which had been hindering French competition against Krupp. French arms-makers would later push the Germans out of the Russian market – aided, of course, by the Franco-Russian Alliance in 1894.[124] French loans to Russia allowed Russia to purchase French arms. French loans also allowed France to out-compete Germany in foreign arms sales in China, Italy, the Balkans, and Central and South America.[125]

THE COMPOSITION OF TRADE: COMMODITY GROUPS

The discussion of commodity trade below is not comprehensive. The goal is to summarize the main features of commodity trade for each state in order to identify the basic areas of trade dependence. The strategic issues involved here are only highlighted, but it should be noted that all the states in this study faced issues of vulnerability and access. The above discussion would apply to the commodity trade figures as well.

If one examines Table 6.13, for example, it is quite clear that Britain was very dependent on the import of agriculture and industrial raw materials. British trade surpluses were in the area of manufactures. Agricultural exports were a very small percentage of exports, and raw materials exports were only a moderate portion of exports.

Table 6.13: British Commodity Trade (percentage total), 1860–1913

Years	Agriculture		Raw materials		Manufactures	
	Imp.	Exp.	Imp.	Exp.	Imp.	Exp.
1860	38.41	5.15	54.32	6.33	7.26	88.52
1865	31.39	4.34	58.98	6.63	9.63	89.03
1870	35.82	4.76	51.58	7.36	12.6	87.88
1875	43.11	4.43	43.67	9.36	13.21	86.21
1880	45.32	5.07	40.38	10.9	14.3	84.04
1885	43.23	5.4	40.75	10.65	16.01	83.95
1890	41.88	4.78	41.36	14.19	16.76	81.02
1895	42.81	5.35	37.39	13.09	19.8	81.56
1900	42.28	4.87	33.05	15.66	24.67	79.46
1905	41.1	5.89	33.39	11.31	25.52	82.8
1910	38.14	6.18	38.66	12.62	23.21	81.2
1913	37.9	6.34	36.81	13.6	25.29	80.05

Source: B. R. Mitchell, *British Historical Statistics* (Cambridge: Cambridge University Press, 1988).

Dependence on the import of raw materials and agriculture conditioned British strategy, especially in terms of conflict and rivalry with other states and the vulnerability to access that this implied. Britain considered its import-dependence for food to be a particular vulnerability, which drove concerns about the possibility of being starved into submission by an aggressive enemy in time of war.[126] The 'starvation theory' pointed to the disastrous effects that being denied access to food imports would have on domestic food prices as well. Commerce protection became critical to British naval policy as a result.[127] As indicated in Chapter 1, the strategy of *guerre de course* threatened not only the denial of access to critical items, but financial and social disruption caused by the resulting shortages. British exports, in contrast, were heavily weighted in favour of manufactures throughout.

French commodity trade (see Table 6.14) indicates a striking dependence on raw materials imports. Agricultural imports for France fluctuated during the period and manufactured imports saw a moderate increase over the years. While agricultural imports declined as a percentage of imports for France, raw materials remained the significant majority of imports during the entire period. The majority of French exports were also in the manufactures category, though not to the extent of British exports.

Table 6.14: French Commodity Trade (percentage total), 1860–1913

Years	Agriculture		Raw materials		Manufactures	
	Imp.	Exp.	Imp.	Exp.	Imp.	Exp.
1860	20.82		76.07		3.11	62.71
1865	18.89		74.6		6.51	54.24
1870	27.97		61.98		10.05	50.86
1875	22.65		66.44		10.91	50.37
1880	39.98	23.39	49.12	23.56	11.9	53.06
1885	35.59	24.29	49.49	22.9	14.92	52.82
1890	32.57	22.78	53.48	23.9	13.95	53.32
1895	27.85	17.52	56.48	25.9	15.67	56.58
1900	17.43	18.72	64.62	26.41	17.94	54.88
1905	17.22	16.05	64.6	27.49	18.18	56.46
1910	19.7	13.76	60.58	30.98	19.72	55.26
1913	21.59	12.19	58.73	27.01	19.69	60.8

Source: *Annuaire Statistique de la France* (Paris: Institut National de la Statistique et des Etudes Economiques), various years.

German commodity trade (see Table 6.15) shows a reliance on all three categories of imports, but raw material imports grew proportionately as time went on, which may reflect the growth of German industrialization. Agricultural imports increased by a few percentages as well, but raw materials saw the greatest gains. Imports did not dominate German strategy, however. As is evident from the above discussion on trade expansion, Germany maintained a vigorous export policy. In addition, German imports do not show a pronounced dependence on any particular category. Like the other industrial states, however, the great majority of exports are in manufactures. Unlike Britain and France, then, Germany did not have a focal point of trade vulnerability in terms of commodities (except perhaps toward the end of the period with raw materials).

Table 6.15: German Commodity Trade (percentage total), 1880–1913

Years	Agriculture		Raw materials		Manufactures	
	Imp.	Exp.	Imp.	Exp.	Imp.	Exp.
1880	25.19	20.13	35.84	14.51	38.96	65.36
1885	23.27	16.31	36.94	14.91	39.79	68.78
1890	25.38	13.73	37.55	15.97	37.07	70.3
1895	25.55	12.46	38.42	15.31	36.02	72.23
1900	26.16	10.58	39.73	16.1	34.11	73.33
1905	29.55	8.47	40.89	15.53	29.57	75.99
1910	26.56	9.81	45.07	15.76	28.36	74.43
1913	27.43	9.92	43.34	15.05	29.23	75.03

Source: Hoffmann, *Das Wachstum der Deutschen Wirtschaft seit der Mitte des 19 Jahrhunderts* (Berlin: Springer-Verlag, 1965).

Italian imports are also spread across the three trade categories here (see Table 6.16), but Italy was most dependent on the import of manufactures and raw materials. Manufactures were also the largest source of Italian exports. Italy was both resource-poor and weakly industrial, which made Italy even more vulnerable than most of the others.

Italy's reliance on manufactured imports made Italy dependent upon the larger European economies for its development, which calls attention to a heightened sense of vulnerability. But dependence on raw materials was partly behind Italian colonial policy. It is true, however, that the Italian navy never acquired much capability beyond the Mediterranean. Not only was Italy's strategic position dominated by Britain, and harassed by France, but Italy would never seek to break out of this position. Instead, Italian policy was reactive to the relations of Britain, France, and Germany.

Table 6.16: Italian Commodity Trade (percentage total), 1880–1913

Years	Agriculture		Raw materials		Manufactures	
	Imp.	Exp.	Imp.	Exp.	Imp.	Exp.
1880	26.37	35.87	29.15	15.85	44.48	48.28
1885	28.42	33.54	26.78	15.67	44.79	50.79
1890	25.3	28.46	33.33	17.41	41.36	54.13
1895	20.47	29.87	38.42	17.05	41.11	53.08
1900	17.06	26.08	40.71	17.64	42.24	56.28
1905	19.84	25.04	36.56	15.31	43.6	59.65
1910	20.33	29.47	36.35	13.27	43.31	57.26
1913	19.28	30.33	38.04	14.37	42.68	55.29

Source: *Annuario Statistico Italiano* (Rome: ISTAT), various years.

The largest portion of Japanese imports were manufactures during most of the time period as well, but raw materials grew rapidly after the turn of the century to occupy between one-third and one-half of Japanese imports. This change in import dependence reflects the rapid nature of Japanese industrialization. Japanese manufactures were also a majority of exports in this period, most of which were labour-intensive goods such as carpets, fans, silk, porcelain, and similar items. Japan was dependent on the import of most minerals and raw materials, although coal and copper were among the larger of its exports.

Raw materials imports and manufactured imports were the critical areas of dependence here for Japan. Most of the raw materials for industry had to be imported, and Japan required more as it industrialized. Manufactured imports included a wide range of commodities, including many industrial items, such as machinery, motors, and railway equipment.

Table 6.17: Japanese Commodity Trade (percentage total), 1885–1913

Years	Agriculture		Raw materials		Manufactures	
	Imp.	Exp.	Imp.	Exp.	Imp.	Exp.
1885	27.65	34.95	11.41	10.74	61.52	54.31
1890	35.64	26.17	12.9	20.22	51.46	53.61
1895	20.47	17.48	12.51	10.41	67.02	72.11
1900	22.73	11.79	17.82	17.51	59.45	70.7
1908	15.6	10.8	35.2	10.9	48.4	77.1
1910	9.7	11.3	49.8	8.8	39.9	79
1913	16.5	9.8	48.5	8.1	34.4	81.1

Source: Department of Agriculture and Commerce, *Japan in the Beginning of the 20th Century* (Tokyo: Tokyo-Shoin, 1904).

Russian commodity trade was not available for every year, but the data in Table 6.18 are enough to indicate the main types of Russian trade dependence. Surprisingly, raw materials were a majority of Russian imports for a number of years before the war, with agriculture and manufactures representing declining portions of imports. In addition, Russian exports are somewhat surprising. Agriculture and raw materials show an opposite trend, with agriculture increasing as a percentage of exports and raw materials decreasing.

Table 6.18: Russian Commodity Trade (percentage total), 1872–94

Years	Agriculture		Raw materials		Manufactures	
	Imp.	Exp.	Imp.	Exp.	Imp.	Exp.
1872	24.63	48.93	44.71	49.01	30.66	2.06
1875	22.21	56.23	47.45	42.66	30.46	1.11
1880	32.86	54.06	48.96	44.91	26.82	1.04
1885	22.54	66.94	58.44	31.58	19.02	1.48
1890	15.92	59.15	64.93	38.09	19.15	2.63
1894	13.35	69.44	61.6	29.48	25.05	1.08

Source: Tawsawentral Nyi Statisticheskii Komitet, *Statistika Rossiiskoi Imperii* (Petrograd), various years.

It must be mentioned here that the manufactures category for Russia should show a slightly higher percentage and raw materials should be slightly lower than it is because semi-manufactures could not be separated from Russian raw materials trade. But agriculture and raw materials dominated Russian exports.

The United States was certainly dependent on manufactured imports, while only being moderately dependent on agricultural and raw materials imports during the period before the war. But American exports were backed up by a vigorous effort at entering into trade markets around the world. In addition, manufactures steadily grew as a percentage of exports throughout, while raw materials exports declined as a percentage of the total. Agricultural exports sharply increased as a percentage of the total, but then declined proportionately.

Table 6.19: US Commodity Trade (percentage total), 1870–1913

Years	Agriculture		Raw materials		Manufactures	
	Imp.	Exp.	Imp.	Exp.	Imp.	Exp.
1870	34.4	24.67	13.07	56.76	52.75	18.57
1875	38.09	37.88	16.7	41.68	45.22	20.44
1880	32.63	55.7	21.26	29.49	46.11	14.81
1885	33.91	44.7	20.76	34.53	45.16	20.63
1890	33.08	42.25	22.81	36.57	44.11	21.18
1895	33.88	40.1	25.68	33.92	40.44	25.98
1900	27.18	39.82	33.18	24.8	39.65	35.38
1905	26.03	26.88	35.42	32.1	38.46	41.02
1910	21	21.58	37.12	33.57	41.94	44.85
1913	22.39	20.71	35.8	30.47	41.75	48.79

Source: US Department of Commerce, *Historical Statistics of the United States: Colonial Times to 1970* (Washington, DC: GPO, 1976), Vol. 2.

American imports of raw materials also grew in percentage terms during the period, despite the great store of industrial raw materials available to the American economy. The United States rapidly acquired the industrial capability to exploit its raw materials as well, while Russia, in contrast, remained relatively backward throughout.

Most of the countries indicated an area of conspicuous dependence in imports, based upon the above commodity trade tables, while also reflecting an emphasis on export dependence. It is also evident from the previous discussion that most of these states pursued military policies that were partly focused on addressing their vulnerabilities. While the previous trade data highlighted vulnerability that was regional in nature, the commodity group data point to vulnerability of critical supplies. Resource dependence takes on a strategic component when it is either crucial for a national economy or when particular areas of resources dependence feed the production of military power. The types of resources that are considered to be strategic, therefore, depend on the states in question. There is no fixed list of what resources are considered to be strategic. Aside from the fact that technological change alters the importance of minerals,[128] *strategic* minerals are whatever minerals that policy-makers think are critical to the economic and military security of their country.[129] From commodity tables, we can obtain a general picture of what groups of goods a country is most dependent on, which may indicate areas of importance for the state.

The traditional geopolitical thinking about resources, as noted, is that a secure and plentiful supply of resources is necessary for Great Power status. The country with a highly developed defence and industrial base and the ability to mobilize its full economic potential is the one that would prevail in time of war.[130] Import dependence for critical items therefore creates problems for a state, and those problems become even worse when the critical supply comes from only a few locations. As one author states, 'essentially, the geopolitics of resources results when consuming nations are not also the producers'.[131]

It could be argued that dependence on external supply for critical items becomes a component in the grand strategy of a state and that the development of trade and transport becomes a function of the power and ambition of states.[132] As noted above, territorial acquisitions, military domination of critical waterways, the use of limited military power to coerce another state, and similar items reflect conflicts of interest that involve both military power and commerce. The overseas economic and military presence of states, whether empires or not, can be seen as being attempts to acquire the security that a hinterland was thought to provide large countries. Hinterlands are the territorial expanses outside the core areas of large states from which resources are drawn.[133] None of the European states had hinterlands. The British Empire, with its centre of gravity in India, the French Empire, the late acquisitions of Germany, Italy, and Japan were perhaps attempts to produce hinterlands that would be held together by international military infrastructures. In addition to such external presence creating locations of vital interest for a state's grand strategy,[134] the connecting infrastructure on land and sea, which allows for communications with areas of external interest, becomes militarily significant. Areas and routes of vital interest, in turn, become a focal point of rivalry. Britain, for example, had to remain constantly aware of the actions of the French in North Africa, Egypt, and the Levant, German overseas activity and rail development to Turkey, and Russian activity in Central Asia.[135]

Without recounting the strategies and rivalries of the states above, it is enough to state here that the composition of trade dependence is a good indicator of the overall vulnerabilities that affect a state. These vulnerabilities, together with the geographic distribution of trade, act as central indicators of the state's interests in terms of their nature and location, which provides the framework for that state's strategic policy. The United States is no exception here, despite the fact that it was not critically dependent on raw materials from abroad. American naval officers promoted a vigorous policy of seeking out export markets instead, which was in line with the belief that the United States had to find outlets for its abundant production. In addition, there was the insistent attitude that the American navy had the right to go wherever American citizens were in order to protect them. The general lack of dependence on external supply for critical items, in addition to the above, meant that exports, not imports, would become the primary focus in American ambitions. This policy appears to be supported by the positive relationship between US naval spending and exports in Chapter 4.

THE SUEZ CANAL

The economic and military expansion of the Great Powers is collectively summarized with the use of the Suez Canal, which was a microcosm of the commercial and military rivalries preceding the First World War. It is common in geopolitical works to state that straits and canals are critical arteries of commerce and military power and that, for the state that controls them militarily, straits and canals become a means for protection of one's own commerce and a potential tool of strangulation of an enemy's.[136] The traditional view is that vulnerable

trade routes require military control and an open threat to them
would be a clear call to war.[137]

The Suez Canal was unique in its importance. The Panama Canal
never attained the importance of the Suez as an artery of world
commerce and military access in this period. The opening of Panama
certainly altered the US geopolitical outlook by broadening defence
requirements and allowing for the movement of the navy from one
ocean to another, but the Panama Canal was most important for
American commerce.[138] The essential difference between Panama and
Suez was that Suez was located in densely populated areas, while
Panama was far from major population centres. Trade routes emerge
in order to connect existing trade centres, which, in turn, emerge
among dense populations.[139] In addition, the Suez route had frequent
fuelling stations, which freed space for cargo, and had many ports,
which allowed for the opportunity of short-haul trade.[140]

The Suez Canal was Europe's gateway to Asia. Not only did it
liberate European commerce from the long and risky journey around
the Cape Route, but it also liberated the Continent from British
domination of access to Asia. It is true that Britain dominated the
Suez, as it did the Cape Route, but Britain feared that its own
commercial centrality would be lost by the canal's opening because the
canal would aid the rise of Britain's main competitors (see Chapter 7).
The canal certainly did aid the economic and military expansion of
the Continent, but Britain's share of Suez traffic remained overwhelmingly dominant during the entire period from 1869 to 1913.
The opening of the canal also changed the importance of African
countries bordering the Red Sea and exposed both Africa and the Far
East to further European expansion later on.[141]

Table 6.20: Shipping through the Suez Canal, 1870–1913

Years	Grs tons (000s)	Net tons (000s)	Ships (no.)	Rate/ton (francs)
1870	654.9	436.6	486	10
1875	2940.7	2010	1494	13
1880	4344.5	3057.4	2026	12
1885	8985.4	6335.8	3624	9.5
1890	9749.1	6899.1	3389	9.5
1895	11833.6	8448.4	3434	9
1900	13699.2	9738.2	3441	9
1905	18810.4	13134.1	4116	8.5
1910	23054.9	16581.9	4533	7.75
1913	27737.2	20033.9	5085	6.25

Source: *Suez Canal: Returns of Shipping and Tonnage*, House of Commons Sessional
Papers (London: HMSO), various years.

The amount of cargo moving through the Suez Canal steadily increased, making the Cape Route less economical. The shipping tonnage through the canal was also increasing at a faster rate than that of cargo, meaning that the ships were getting larger. In addition, the rate per ton charged to vessels moving through the canal steadily declined after an initial increase. Even during the war, the rates declined. The canal opened in 1869 with a rate of ten francs per ton, reaching a high point of 13 francs per ton from 1874 to 1876. The rate would then steadily decline over the years to 6.25 francs per ton in 1913. The 1913 rate remained up to 1915, and over the next two years rose from 6.25 to 8.5 francs per ton.[142] It is surprising that the rate during wartime did not increase until 1916.

While the Suez Canal certainly became the major shipping artery in the world, any concern that Britain's world position was being eroded by the opening of the canal was overdrawn. As noted, Britain dominated both the Cape Route and the canal. As Table 6.21 shows, Britain owned the great majority of all the shipping tonnage that passed through the canal from its opening to the war. There were indeed signs that the other states were gaining in their use of the canal, particularly Germany, but British net tonnage moving through the canal never went below the 1900 level of 57.6 per cent of the total from the opening of the canal to the war. Germany was clearly in second place by the 1890s, in terms of total net tonnage passing through the canal, but the German figures are quite small compared to the British. In addition, the German and Austro-Hungarian amounts disappeared in 1915.

It must also be mentioned that with the signing of the Suez Canal Convention in October of 1888, the principle of free access to the canal was formally assured. The first article of the Convention states that the canal 'shall always be free and open, in time of war as in time of peace, to every vessel of commerce or of war, without distinction of flag'.[143] The convention agreement came out of a British desire to keep the canal open to all ships. Britain became the *de facto* custodian of the canal with the ending of dual French–British control in September 1882. But from 1882 onward Britain sought agreement with the other Powers to keep the canal open and free for all ships (except that Britain also wanted the right to defend the canal against aggression).[144] Earlier French efforts at securing the neutrality of the canal, particularly those of Ferdinand de Lesseps, came to nothing.[145]

Table 6.21: Net Tonnage through the Suez Canal (percentage total), 1870–1913

	Austria	Britain	France	Germany	Italy
1870	4.4	66.4	19.5	0	1.4
1875	3.2	73.5	8	1.6	2.9
1876	2.6	75.2	8.1	1.3	2.9
1880	2.4	79.6	6.1	1.2	2.4
1885	1.9	76.8	9.1	3.1	2.5
1890	1.7	77.3	5.3	7.1	2.1
1895	2	71.8	8	8.2	1.7
1900	3.5	57.6	7.7	15	1.6
1905	3.5	63.6	6.4	16.1	1.4
1910	3.9	62.9	5	15.5	1.3
1913	4.2	60.2	4.6	16.7	1.5

Source: *Suez Canal: Returns of Shipping and Tonnage*, House of Commons Sessional Papers (London: HMSO), various years.

Russia, the United States, and Japan also used the canal in this period, but their figures were not constant and often wavered dramatically from very small amounts to sizeable amounts in the nineteenth century. Generally, however, their amounts of net tonnage through the canal were each routinely under 1 per cent of the total. The United States, Russia, and Japan all experienced increases in their tonnage through the canal during the decade preceding the war, although the US levels tended to remain well below the other two.

In addition to merchant traffic, however, the Suez Canal was also a gateway for European military access to Asia. The ships that travelled through the canal ranged from merchant vessels to warships and government-chartered vessels to mail ships. The military access to Asia afforded by the canal is at least as significant as the commercial access that the canal provided. British domination of the canal gave Britain control over the passageway, which could be used to regulate the movement of its rivals – a role consistent with that of gatekeeper to the smaller navies of Europe, where Britain could literally determine European naval access to the planet. The strategic importance of the canal has actually been highlighted with nearly every international crisis that erupted since its opening, whether the Russo–Turkish War (1877), the Italian colonial activities in Massawa and Abyssinia from 1885 to 1896 (it may or may not be a coincidence that the first Italian colonial acquisition was at Assab on the Red Sea in 1869), the Spanish–American War (1898), the Boxer Rebellion (1900), the Russo–Japanese War (1905–06), and a variety of others. Each crisis opened up the question of whether Britain would close the canal. During the Spanish–American War, for example, Britain denied all effective use of the canal to Spanish warships, refused coal to Spain, and was generally sympathetic to the United States despite the rules of the 1888 Convention.[146]

The canal was especially relevant to the Mediterranean interests of Italy, France, and Germany. In 1906, for example, France sought a way to regain its lost influence in Egypt by encouraging the Sultan of Turkey to assert his sovereign rights over Egypt. The Sultan attempted to order Egyptian troops out of the Sinai Peninsula and hinted at putting a railway across the peninsula to the edge of the canal. Britain saw these moves as being a direct threat to the canal, placed a fleet in Egyptian waters, and thwarted the Sultan's efforts.[147]

There appears to be no indication that Italy ever saw British domination of Suez as being a threat to its security. Italian colonial expansion mainly conflicted with the interests of France, which became Italy's main rival. It is even likely that British control of Suez and its presence in the Mediterranean aided Italy because it too was a counter to France.[148]

The Suez Canal is most interesting here in terms of German strategy against Britain. In particular, the development of an overland rail route to the East, extending from Berlin to Baghdad, and then to the Persian Gulf would allow Germany to counter the effects of British domination of Egypt and the Suez.[149] In addition, a pro-German Turkey could provide a means to push Britain out of Egypt. While the Baghdad Railway issue (see Chapter 7) was more complex than this, part of its significance is that it represented a German land effort to outflank British sea power. In the words of Dr Paul Rohrbach in 1911:

> The loss of Egypt would mean not only the end of her [Britain's] domination over the Suez Canal and of her communications with India and the Far East, but would probably entail also the loss of her possessions in Central and East Africa...Turkey, however, can never dream of recovering Egypt until she is mistress of a developed railway system in Asia Minor and Syria...The stronger Turkey becomes, the greater will be the danger for England, if, in a German–English war, Turkey should be on the side of Germany.[150]

German control of the Berlin–Baghdad route would have also aided German dominance in Eastern Europe and in the Near East.[151] Germany and Britain were not at odds on every issue, of course. Britain encouraged German expansion into Africa (as well as Italian) as a way to restrain the French, particularly in East Africa.[152] In fact, France was Britain's primary rival over the canal before Germany even existed as a united country.

The importance of military access to the Indian Ocean and Asia for Europe can be seen with the composition of passengers moving through the canal. Military passengers through the canal amounted to a majority over civilian passengers on a regular basis (see Table 6.22). Passenger traffic through the canal was organized into the three categories of *military, civilian,* and *other* (*other* refers to emigrants, pilgrims, and convicts). The predominance of military passengers largely reflected troop deployments to Asia carried out by various countries (mostly Britain). It is interesting to note that the percentage of passengers that were military began to decline after the turn of the century right up to the war, to a low of 27.5 per cent in 1912. Civilian passenger traffic would become a majority in 1908 (50.6 per cent), and would remain so up to 1913. With the start of the war, of course, civilian traffic declined both in percentage terms and in amount.

Table 6.22: Passenger Traffic through the Suez Canal, 1876–1913

	Military		Civilian	
	No.	*%*	*No.*	*%*
1876	30420	51	20832	34.9
1880	49493	50	29139	29.5
1885	112230	55.6	47068	23.3
1890	67767	43.5	69479	44.6
1895	118635	54.7	74878	34.5
1900	154249	54.7	102415	36.3
1905	110179	43.6	96637	38.2
1910	76854	32.8	128171	54.8
1913	88748	31.4	169641	60.1

Source: *Suez Canal: Returns of Shipping and Tonnage,* House of Commons Sessional Papers (London: HMSO), various years.

In terms of shipping, however, merchant ships consisted by far the great majority of the traffic through the Suez Canal, except during the war itself. Despite this, most Great Powers maintained a steady level of military traffic through the canal, as evidenced by warship movements. Table 6.23 shows the number and tonnage of warships that went through the canal for a select number of years. While Britain sent more warships through the canal than any other state for most years, France was generally second. Interestingly, the German naval presence in the canal, while generally larger from the end of the century onward than beforehand, never got anywhere near the British amount and was frequently well under the French amount.

Warship movements through the canal reflected a host of interests, such as overseas trade, colonial interests, and mutual competition and rivalry among the Great Powers. As described in Chapter 7 in the context of trade rivalry, the Suez Canal was bound up with rivalry over Turkey during the Baghdad Railway issue.

Table 6.23: Warships through the Suez Canal, Select Years, 1892–1913

Years	Austria		Britain		France		Germany		Italy		Japan		Russia		US	
	No.	Tons	No.	Tons	No.	Tons	No.	Tons	No.	Tons	No.	Tons	No.	Tons	No.	Tons
1892	3	2.87	46	97.8	17	37	1	0.61	10	5.17	2	2.35	5	6.24	0	0
1893	3	2.75	38	80.4	14	38	3	1.38	8	3.61	1	1.28	5	3.75	2	2.37
1895	4	1.8	39	49.2	21	47.8	9	4.84	12	7.68	0	0	7	6.22	3	1.91
1896	4	1.84	28	35.6	13	9.2	0	0	17	7.81	0	0	6	9.71	0	0
1899	6	5.33	28	23	12	11	11	10.7	11	9.4	11	10.1	1	0.17	25	67.6
1900	4	4.65	52	60.2	19	33.6	14	19.2	14	13.7	9	20.2	4	8.9	15	38.7
1902	4	5.6	41	57.1	10	14.3	4	2.16	16	16.9	9	15.3	7	17.8	18	47
1903			40	62.7			4	1.49								
1906			41	79.9			4	8.02								
1907	3	2.39	23	55.7	5	1.98	1	1.04	7	1.61	4	12.5	2	0.34	4	5.1
1908	2	2.75	23	38.5	4	2.69	0	0	3	1.87	0	0	2	2.53	6	15.8
1909	2	0.95	19	40.2	2	5.12	4	9.55	6	2.78	0	0	0	0	27	103
1910	3	3.22	23	54.7	4	8.05	4	6.24	8	17.1	1	4.87	2	1.32	4	5.85
1911	0	0	33	65.6	2	6.88	3	1.25	4	1.93	4	14.2	3	2.89	0	0
1912	2	1.96	38	93.3	1	3.89	0	0	34	18.6	0	0	1	2.26	3	1.25
1913	2	2.74	23	50.3	1	2.98	0	0	9	5.18	0	0	1	3.25	1	3.32

Source: *Suez Canal: Returns of Shipping and Tonnage,* House of Commons Sessional Papers (London: HMSO), various years. Tons in thousands.

CONCLUSION

What can be said from the discussion above regarding the results seen in Chapter 4? The military and commercial indicators in the first section of this chapter do not reveal systematic differences among the states, with the exception of differences in the actual roles played by their armies and navies. There are meaningful differences in the roles of the armies, for example, which help explain why some might be connected to commerce and some not. What is not readily evident from the above, however, is why some of those army and navy terms are negatively related to the trade terms. We could accept the reasoning implied by interdependence to account for this, but we are still left with the question of why there are such differences.

More interesting and possibly more useful are the regional and commodity group trade data. Several deductions can be made from these trade data, which might provide some guidance. First, a large amount of the trade among the states in this book was located either near rivalries or was among rivals themselves. Most of the states in this book were each other's main trade partners. Second, all the states showed changing patterns in their regional trade distributions reflecting, to varying degrees, increased global trading patterns as time went on. British trade, of course, was already global in scope at the beginning of the period. Third, all states showed a continued heavy reliance on trade with Western Europe, regardless of where they were located. Fourth, all states showed either the continued importance of their local regions (if they were in Europe) or the growing importance of their local regions (if they were outside Europe). Fifth, all states showed some pronounced emphasis in their imports and exports regarding commodity group dependence. While commodity group trade may provide strong guidance on the nature of trade vulnerabilities, however, we cannot relate these to specific areas from this data.

Several statements can also be made about the military behaviour of the states in this study. Some states had larger military roles than others, such that they performed both functions that were focused on their regions and functions that were far removed from their localities. Britain had the most geographically dispersed military activities of the period. The smaller militaries performed functions that were mostly local in nature, though it is true that all of them were trying to expand into larger roles as time went on, which reflected the onset of competitive rivalry and, in some cases, aggressive trade expansion. Given that the majority of the states in this study are located in Europe, the local roles of the European militaries were bound up with matters of Great Power rivalry. Vulnerabilities as they related to local trade would also relate to these rivalries.

What about trade with other regions? If regional trade is a good indicator of areas of strategic importance to states, with the major trading regions being the most important areas, then can we separate trade into major and minor categories with the idea being that each will relate to the military power of the state differently? I ask this question because it is both reasonable and possible that the relevant mix of military–commercial connections vary by category of trade. We could argue the same for the commodity groups, but the main problem here is that we do not know which regions these groups are associated with. Given that military power is geographically oriented, the regional breakdowns might be a better indicator. The ideal trade measure would be the commodity group breakdowns by origin and destination, but these are unavailable.

Perhaps the major trade flows, which were also located largely in western Europe, were those most associated with the protection that military power affords. This could be due to the fact that vulnerability may grow with the magnitude of trade (see the discussion of this in Chapter 3) and to the fact that this trade was closest to the major rivalries of the period. Despite the vulnerability to trade posed by these rivalries, however, the Great Powers generally did not destroy each other's trade.

Smaller trade flows in other parts of the world may have experienced more disruption, although much of this disruption was probably local in nature rather than it being due to the intrusions of other Great Powers. The types of military actions employed in response to these types of threats could have encompassed a range of punitive and protective activities, as was the case with the British in India and in the territories to the north, whereas the major arteries of trade could have been accompanied by longer-term military commitments and even larger amounts of military power.

If the above reasoning is sound, then it could be that the aggregate trade and military terms in the models of Chapter 4 reflect all manner of influences, such that the differences in the statistical output reflect the net effects of these influences. If this is true, then using the regional categories of trade might produce more telling estimates.

Two tasks follow in the remaining two chapters of this book. First, in Chapter 7, I attempt to link the rivalry behaviour of the states to their trade relations, giving specific attention to the level of inter-dependence among them. The goal here is to understand the role that trade dependence had in the strategic policies of these states. I am also interested in determining how mutual dependence in trade behaved over time as rivalries progressed. Did the magnitudes of inter-dependence decline among rivals? While the discussion in Chapter 7 focuses on rivalry behaviour, I will avoid repeating what has already been said. The discussion will instead focus on how rivalry and trade relations interacted.

The second task, in Chapter 8, is to estimate a second set of regression models by taking the regional trade groupings into account. This is not done for all countries, as data do not permit. The goal here is to determine whether the results in Chapter 4 give way to a clearer pattern across countries. It is possible that certain categories of trade are more important than others. It is even possible that the nature of the relationships changes by regional category.

NOTES

1. Alfred T. Mahan, *The Problem of Asia and its Effect Upon International Policies* (Boston, MA: Little, Brown and Co., 1900), p. 43.
2. John Gooch, *Armies in Europe* (London: Routledge and Kegan Paul, 1980), pp. 70–2, 80–1, 109–22.
3. William H. McNeill, *The Pursuit of Power: Technology, Armed Force, and Society Since A.D. 1000* (Chicago: University of Chicago Press, 1982), pp. 256–7.
4. Arthur J. Marder, *The Anatomy of British Sea Power: A History of British Naval Policy in the Pre-Dreadnought Era, 1880–1905* (New York: Alfred A. Knopf, 1940), pp. 66–8.
5. Ibid., pp. 68–70.
6. Lt.-Col. P. D. Maud, 'Lord Haldane's Reorganization of the British Army,

1905–1912', in Gordon B. Turner (ed.), *A History of Military Affairs in Western Society Since the Eighteenth Century* (New York: Harcourt, Brace and Co., 1952), pp. 269–74.

7. J. F. C. Fuller, *War and Western Civilization, 1832-1932: A Study of War as a Political Instrument and the Expression of Mass Democracy* (1932; reprint. Freeport, NY: Books for Libraries Press, 1969), pp. 182–3; E. L. Woodward, *Great Britain and the German Navy* (Oxford: Clarendon, 1935), pp. 32–3; McNeill, *Pursuit of Power*, pp. 23–31.

8. See Maud, 'Lord Haldane's' and Fuller, *Western Civilization*, p. 183.

9. Russel F. Weigley, 'The Anglo-American Armies and Peace, 1783–1868', in Joan R. Challinor and Robert L. Beisner (eds), *Arms at Rest: Peacemaking and Peacekeeping in American History* (New York: Greenwood Press, 1987), p. 151.

10. James A. Huston, *The Sinews of War: Army Logistics, 1775–1953* (Washington, DC: GPO, 1966), pp. 305–6.

11. John Gooch, *Army, State and Society in Italy, 1870–1915* (New York: St. Martin's Press, 1989), p. 171.

12. R. J. B. Bosworth, *Italy, The Least of the Great Powers: Italian Foreign Policy Before the First World War* (London: Cambridge University Press, 1979), p. 24.

13. There is the view that Italian railways were not all that backward. A good introduction to the issue is P. M. Kalla-Bishop, *Italian Railways* (Newton Abbot: David and Charles, 1971).

14. Gooch, *Army*, pp. 171–2.

15. John Whittam, *The Politics of the Italian Army, 1861–1918* (London: Croom Helm, 1977), pp. 160–1.

16. Donald W. Mitchell, *A History of Russian and Soviet Sea Power* (New York: Macmillan, 1974), pp. xix–xx.

17. Holland Hunter, *Soviet Transportation Policy* (Cambridge, MA: Harvard University Press, 1957), p. 10.

18. W. Gordon East, *An Historical Geography of Europe* 5th edn, (1966; reprint. London: Methuen, 1967), p. 430.

19. Malcolm McIntosh, *Japan Re-Armed* (New York: St. Martin's Press, 1986), p. 6.

20. Alexander Kiralfy, 'Japanese Naval Strategy,' in Edward M. Earle (ed.), *Makers of Modern Strategy: Military Thought from Machiavelli to Hitler* (Princeton, NJ: Princeton University Press, 1943), p. 483.

21. Ibid., p. 484.

22. W. G. Beasley, *Japanese Imperialism, 1894–1945* (Oxford: Clarendon, 1987), p. 36.

23. James L. Stokesbury, *Navy and Empire* (New York: William Morrow, 1983), p. 283.

24. Ibid., p. 282.

25. Werner Schlote, *British Overseas Trade: From 1700 to the 1930s*, trans. W. O. Henderson and W. H. Chaloner (Oxford: Basil Blackwell, 1952), p. 79.

26. Weigley, 'Armies and Peace', p. 148.

27. Richard A. Preston, Sydney F. Wise, and Herman O. Werner, *Men in Arms: A History of Warfare and its Interrelationships with Western Society* (New York: Fredrick A. Praeger, 1956), p. 219.

28. Robert L. Schuyler, *The Fall of the Old Colonial System: A Study in British Free Trade, 1770–1870* (London: Oxford University Press, 1945), pp. 14–15, 195–9.

29. See A. D. Couper, *The Geography of Sea Transport* (London: Hutchinson University Library, 1972).

30. Robert E. Harkavy, *Great Power Competition for Overseas Bases: The Geopolitics of Access Diplomacy* (New York: Pergamon, 1982), p. 47; Paul M. Kennedy, *The Rise and Fall of British Naval Mastery* (New York: Praeger, 1976), p. 157. See also Preston, *Men in Arms*, p.223; and Schuyler, *Colonial System*, pp. 30–7.

31. T. Miller Maguire, *Outlines of Military Geography* (Cambridge: Cambridge University Press, 1899), pp. 88–9.

32. D. C. M. Platt, *Finance, Trade, and Politics in British Foreign Policy: 1815–1914* (Oxford: Clarendon Press, 1971), p. 86.

33. Ibid., p. 85.

34. Gerald Morgan, *Anglo-Russian Rivalry in Central Asia: 1810–1895* (London: Frank Cass, 1981), p. 213.

35. Eric Carlton, *Occupation: The Policies and Practices of Military Conquerors* (Savage, MD: Barnes and Noble, 1992), pp. 33–4.

36. Phillip Darby, *British Defence Policy East of Suez, 1947–1968* (London: Oxford University Press, for Royal Institute of International Affairs, 1973), pp. 2–4.

37. The figure was obtained from a list of military actions on or beyond the borders of India from 1849 up to about the end of the century in *Sessional Papers for the House of Commons*, Vol. XCVI, 1905, pp. 848–61.

38. Willian C. Fuller, Jr., *Strategy and Power in Russia: 1600–1914* (New York: Free Press, 1992), p. 290.

39. Robert N. Taaffe, 'Transportation and Regional Specialization: The Example of Soviet Central Asia', *Annals of the Association of American Geographers* 52/1 (March 1962), p. 82.

40. George N. Curzon, *Russia in Central Asia in 1889, and the Anglo-Russian Question* (1889; reprint. New York: Barnes and Noble, 1967), p. 44.

41. Morgan, *Anglo-Russian Rivalry*, p. 214.

42. See Milan Hauner, *What is Asia to Us? Russia's Asian Heartland Yesterday and Today* (Boston, MA: Unwin Hyman, 1990) for a good discussion of Russian railway expansion, especially pp. 98–107. Also Fuller, Jr., *Strategy and Power*, contains a good discussion of Russian expansion in general.

43. Paval A. Khromov, *Ekonomicheskoe Razvitie Rossii v XIX i XX Vekakh, 1899–1917* (Moscow: Gospolitizdat, 1950), p. 462.

44. Rogers P. Churchill, *The Anglo-Russian Convention of 1907* (Cedar Rapids, IA: The Torch Press, 1939), p. 7.

45. Hunter, *Soviet Transportation*, pp. 10–11, 161.

46. Hauner, *What is Asia*, pp. 98–9, 101.

47. Thomas E. Ross, 'Buffer States: A Geographer's Perspective', in John Chay and Thomas E. Ross (eds), *Buffer States in World Politics* (Boulder, CO: Westview, 1986), p. 15; Morgan, *Anglo-Russian Rivalry*, p. 1.

48. David B. Jenkins, 'The History of Afghanistan as a Buffer State', in John Chay and Thomas E. Ross (eds), *Buffer States in World Politics* (Boulder, CO: Westview, 1986), pp. 178–81.

49. Churchill, *Anglo-Russian*, pp. 148–9.

50. Jenkins, 'Buffer State,' p. 183.

51. Churchill, *Anglo-Russian*, p. 341.

52. Archibald Hurd and Henry Castle, *German Sea-Power: Its Rise, Progress, and Economic Basis* (1913; reprint, Westport, CT: Greenwood Press, 1971), pp. 88–9.

53. Ibid., pp. 90–2.

54. Ibid., pp. 95, 108–9, 292–4.

55. Theodore Ropp, 'Continental Doctrines of Sea Power', in Edward M. Earle (ed.), *Makers of Modern Strategy: Military Thought from Machiavelli to Hitler* (Princeton, NJ: Princeton University Press, 1943), p. 451.

56. Woodward, *Great Britain*, pp. 32–3; McNeill, *Pursuit of Power*, pp. 32–3.

57. Ivo N. Lambi, *The Navy and German Power Politics, 1862–1914* (Boston, MA: Allen and Unwin, 1984), pp. 27, 44–6, 113–33.

58. Woodward, *Great Britain*, pp. 32–3; McNeill, *Pursuit of Power*, pp. 32–3.

59. Jack Snyder, *Myths of Empire: Domestic Politics and International Ambition* (Ithaca,

NY: Cornell University Press, 1991), p. 66.

60. Peter Padfield, *The Great Naval Race: The Anglo-German Naval Rivalry, 1900–1914* (New York: David McKay, 1974), p. 132; Ropp, 'Continental Doctrines', p. 451; McNeill, *Pursuit of Power*, pp. 304–5.

61. Woodward, *Great Britain*, pp. 73–4.

62. Ibid., pp. 74–5.

63. McNeill, *Pursuit of Power*, p. 305.

64. MacKinder, of course, saw Germany as being as likely a candidate for control over the heartland as Russia.

65. Woodward, *Great Britain*, p. 12; Harold Sprout and Margaret Sprout, *Toward a New Order of Sea Power: American Naval Policy and the World Scene, 1918–1922* (Princeton, NJ: Princeton University Press, 1946), pp. 20–1.

66. M. H. Long, 'Imperial Policies of Great Britain', *Foreign Affairs* 6/2 (January 1928), p. 251.

67. Woodward, *Great Britain*, p. 12; Sprout and Sprout, *Toward a New Order*, pp. 20–1.

68. Kennedy, *Naval Mastery*, p. 212.

69. Kenneth J. Hagan, *American Gunboat Diplomacy and the Old Navy: 1877–1889* (Westport, CT: Greenwood Press, 1973), p. 188.

70. Alfred T. Mahan, *The Interest of America in Sea Power: Present and Future* (1897; reprint. Port Washington, NY: Kennikat Press, 1970), p. 66.

71. Ibid.

72. Ruhl Barlett, *Policy and Power: Two Centuries of American Foreign Relations* (New York: Hill and Wang, 1963), p. 123; Hagan, *Gunboat Diplomacy*, pp. 188–9.

73. David M. Pletcher, '1861–1898: Economic Growth and Diplomatic Adjustment', in William H. Becker and Samuel F. Wells, Jr. (eds), *Economics and World Power: An Assessment of American Diplomacy Since 1789* (New York: Columbia University Press, 1984), p. 127.

74. Ibid., pp. 164–5.

75. George Stambuk, *American Military Forces Abroad: Their Impact on the Western State System* (Columbus: Ohio State University Press, 1963), pp. 15–16.

76. William H. Becker, '1899–1920: America Adjusts to World Power', in William H. Becker and Samuel F. Wells, Jr. (eds), *Economics and World Power: An Assessment of American Diplomacy Since 1789* (New York: Columbia University Press, 1984), pp. 188–9; Barlett, *Policy and Power*, pp. 133, 135.

77. Tom E. Terrill, *The Tariff, Politics, and American Foreign Policy, 1874–1901* (Westport, CT: Greenwood Press, 1973), pp. 73–7.

78. Barlett, *Policy and Power*, p. 130.

79. Kim Key-Hiuk, *The Last Phase of the East Asian World Order* (Berkeley: University of California Press, 1980), p. 314.

80. Preston, *Men in Arms*, p. 232.

81. Ropp, 'Continental Doctrines', p. 448.

82. Edwin B. Hooper, *United States Naval Power in a Changing World* (New York: Praeger, 1988), pp. 102–3.

83. Bernard D. Cole, *Gunboats and Marines: The United States Navy in China, 1925–1928* (Newark: University of Delaware Press, 1983), pp. 24, 26, 28.

84. Bernard Brodie, *Sea Power in the Machine Age* (Princeton, NJ: Princeton University Press, 1941), p. 41.

85. E. H. Jenkins, *A History of the French Navy: From its Beginnings to the Present Day* (London: Macdonald and Jane's, 1973), p. 292.

86. Charles W. Cole, *French Mercantilist Doctrines Before Colbert* (1931; reprint. New York: Octagon Books, 1969), pp. 221–2.

87. Jenkins, *French Navy*, pp. 294–7.

88. Ibid., pp. 303–4.

89. Ibid., pp. 298–9; Maurice Pearton, *Diplomacy, War and Technology* (Lawrence: University Press of Kansas, 1984), p. 61.
90. Jenkins, *French Navy*, p. 303.
91. Ibid.
92. Ropp, 'Continental Doctrines', p. 446.
93. Jenkins, *French Navy*, p. 307.
94. Ibid, pp. 304–5.
95. Brodie, *Sea Power*, p. 102.
96. Jenkins, *French Navy*, pp. 307–8.
97. Ibid., p. 309.
98. Ibid., pp. 308–9.
99. Ibid., p. 310.
100. Ropp, 'Continental Doctrines', p. 448.
101. Marder, *Anatomy*, pp. 145–6.
102. Tekeste Negash, *Italian Colonialism in Eritrea, 1882–1941: Policies, Praxis and Impact* (Uppsala: Almqvist and Wiksell International, 1987), pp. 2–3.
103. Whittam, *Italian Army*, p. 133.
104. Negash, *Italian Colonialism*, p. 39.
105. R. J. B. Bosworth, *Italy, The Least of the Great Powers: Italian Foreign Policy Before the First World War* (London: Cambridge University Press, 1979), pp. 58, 59. Quote on p. 59.
106. Whittam, *Italian Army*, p. 133.
107. Ian H. Nish, *Japanese Foreign Policy 1869–1942: Kasumigaseki to Miyakezaka* (London: Routledge and Kegan Paul, 1977), p. 33.
108. Tatsuji Takeuchi, *War and Diplomacy in the Japanese Empire* (Garden City, NY: Doubleday, Doran, and Co., 1935) p.107; Beasley, *Japanese Imperialism*, pp. 133–4.
109. Giichi Ono, *Expenditures of the Sino-Japanese War* (New York: Oxford University Press, 1922), pp. 7–8, 88–9. This volume also discusses Japanese military expenditures for the war and provides some useful statistics. See also the companion volume, by the same author, *War and Armament Expenditures of Japan* (New York: Oxford University Press, 1922).
110. Nish, *Japanese Foreign Policy*, p. 17.
111. McIntosh, *Japan Re-Armed*, p. 5.
112. Beasley, *Japanese Imperialism*, p. 79.
113. See, for example, Key-Hiuk, *World Order*, pp. 219–28, 231–2, 244–8.
114. Nish, *Japanese Foreign Policy*, p. 51.
115. Herbert Rosinski, 'The Limitations of Mahan and Tirpitz', in Gordon B. Turner (ed.), *A History of Military Affairs in Western Society Since the Eighteenth Century* (New York: Harcourt, Brace and Co., 1952), p. 356.
116. Fuller, *Western Civilization*, p. 190.
117. Platt, *Finance*, pp. 100–4.
118. Quoted in Ibid., p. xvi.
119. Pearton, *Diplomacy*, p. 107.
120. Ibid, pp. 107–8.
121. Paul Einzig, *The Economics of Rearmament* (London: Kegan Paul, Trench, Trubner, 1934), p. 19.
122. Ibid., pp. 15, 25.
123. Karl Polanyi, *The Great Transformation* (New York: Rinehart and Co., 1944), pp. 12–13. This volume is full of classic insights on the interaction between diplomacy and international economics.
124. McNeill, *Pursuit of Power*, pp. 299–300.
125. Ibid., p. 300.
126. Marder, *Anatomy*, pp. 84–6.

127. Ibid., pp. 84–6, 90; Margaret L. Barnett, *British Food Policy During the First World War* (Boston MA: George Allen and Unwin, 1985), p. 5.

128. Hans Gustafsson, Bertil Oden, and Andreas Tegen, *South African Minerals: An Analysis of Western Dependence* (Uppsala: Nordiska Afrikainstitutet, 1990), p. 40.

129. John C. Kraft, 'Strategic Minerals and World Stability', in Gerard J. Mangone (ed.), *American Strategic Minerals* (New York: Crane Russak, 1984), p.9.

130. Ewan W. Anderson, *Strategic Minerals: The Geopolitical Problems for the United States* (New York: Praeger, 1988), p. 3.

131. Ibid., p. 14.

132. Patrick O'Sullivan, *Transport Policy: Geographic and Economic Planning Aspects* (Totowa, NJ: Barnes and Noble, 1980), p. 204.

133. Geoffrey Parker, *Western Geopolitical Thought in the Twentieth Century* (New York: St. Martin's Press, 1985), pp. 141–5.

134. Michael C. Desch, 'The Keys That Lock Up the World: Identifying American Interests in the Periphery', *International Security* 14/1 (Summer 1989), pp. 97–9.

135. Harkavy, *Great Power*, p. 47.

136. Most of the navalist literature cited above in Chapter 1 addresses this and related issues.

137. It may be argued that access can be as efficiently maintained today with political agreements and that states are not as ready to use military force to coerce a smaller state into granting access. Although there are conflicting examples. On the one hand, the closing of the Suez Canal in 1967 did not lead to military action, but the Iraqi threat to the Persian Gulf did.

138. See G. S. Bryan, 'Geography and the Defense of the Caribbean and the Panama Canal', *Annals of the Association of American Geographers* 31/1 (March 1941), pp. 83–94.

139. Geography alone meant that Panama would not be a rival to Suez and that American naval control over Panama would not really be analogous to British control over the narrow seas around Europe and the Suez. Sprout and Sprout, *Toward a New Order*, p. 23; and Eugene van Cleef, *Trade Centers and Trade Routes* (New York: D. Applleton-Century, 1937), pp. 200–4.

140. Cleef, *Trade Centers*, p. 205.

141. R. A. Johns, *Colonial Trade and International Exchange: The Transition From Autarky to International Trade* (London: Pinter Publishers, 1988), p. 64.

142. Great Britain, *Suez Canal: Returns of Shipping and Tonnage in House of Commons, Sessional Papers* (London: HMSO, various years).

143. Quoted in Hugh J. Schonfield, *The Suez Canal in Peace and War: 1869–1969* (Coral Gables, FL: University of Miami Press, 1969), p. 52.

144. Ibid., p. 51.

145. For a discussion of de Lesseps' efforts at securing the neutrality of the canal, see Pierre Crabites, *The Spoliation of Suez* (London: George Routledge and Sons, 1940), pp. 218-29.

146. D. A. Farnie, *East and West of Suez: The Suez Canal in History, 1854–1956* (Oxford: Clarendon Press, 1969), pp. 458–60.

147. Schonfield, *The Suez Canal*, p. 53.

148. Farnie, *East and West of Suez*.

149. Schonfield, *The Suez Canal*, p. 62.

150. Quoted in Ibid., pp. 62–3.

151. Cleef, *Trade Centers*, p. 181.

152. Farnie, *East and West*, p. 432.

7

Trade Interdependence and Military Rivalry

The purpose of this chapter is to analyse the interaction of rivalry among the Great Powers with their international trade. The impact of military rivalry on trade relations is potentially complicated owing to the fact that numerous scenarios of trade relations can be focused on. One could focus on the trade of two rival states with each other or on the trade of two rivals to a third country. The third country could be another Great Power or a country that is itself a focal point of rivalry. One could also focus on the interaction between rivalry and trade multilaterally, which would make the story all the more complicated.

Another complication here is that there were at least 12 lines of rivalry among the states in this study that existed somewhere between the Crimean War and 1913.[1] Each one had its unique features and all were generally complicated interactions that entered military, diplomatic, and economic matters. These rivalries also did not necessarily hinge on a specific issue or line of conflict, but were often generalized states of competition which were the known dispositions of the states involved.

An attempt to model all of the rivalries that existed among the Great Powers would produce a very complicated mess. At least five of the Great Powers were in some form of rivalry with Britain alone, for example, and each of these five had additional rivalries with other Great Powers. A proper model would also need to take into account the alliances of these countries, which were mostly designed to militate against the threats posed by specific lines of rivalry to begin with.

To complicate matters further, the trade conflicts of these states would need to be included in order to combine adequately the interaction of economic conflict with military and diplomatic conflict. This would also include estimating the effects on trade of the alliances as well. Thus we would have a system of 12 bilateral rivalries among states, the intensity and nature of which may vary from one rivalry to another, which would also include alliances and trade relations and perhaps even measures of interdependence. How does one specify a model that captures all of this without making a terrible mess?

What can be done with relative ease, however, is to compare the trade and tariff data of known rivals in order to get a picture of their trade relations. I will present these data below in the context of the rivalries and alliances among the states. My goal is not to present a general outline of Great Power rivalries, but instead to discuss the economic dimensions of these rivalries and relate this to the degree of interdependence among them.

While there were many different episodes of trade conflict in the period leading up to the First World War, we can break them up into two broad patterns. The first pattern was the advent of trade conflict between Britain and most of the other Great Powers. This pattern of trade conflict reflected the rise of aggressive competition against Britain on the part of newcomers, and a changing position of Britain in world trade. The predominant lines of trade conflict with Britain involved Germany, the United States, and France. While there were several episodes when these conflicts seemed to peak and decline, it may also be true that a general state of economic friction persisted over a long period of time. Britain also faced tough competition in Asia from Japan, which became a fiercer competitor against Britain after the Sino–Japanese War of 1894–95 (especially in India and China). Britain watched with concern as Japan's exports to China grew nearly thirteen-fold between 1890 and 1913, while British exports to China remained relatively stable.[2]

The second pattern of trade conflict was among the other Great Powers, without necessarily involving Britain. These conflicts also had specific episodes, but were general states of protracted trade rivalry as well. Russo-German trade conflict, Franco-Italian trade conflict, and Continental fears of American economic competition were among the most prominent examples.

RIVALRY AND AVERAGE TARIFF LEVELS

It would certainly not be accurate to view the relationship between military power and commerce as being a simple function of protectionist trade practices. The states in question spanned the gamut of liberal to protectionist, and very often changed policies. In addition, their trade variables often relate differently to military spending and some also undergo changes. The United States collected by far the largest amount of customs revenue in dollar terms of the seven states, with the rest trailing considerably behind. Japanese customs revenue was quite small in comparison to the other states here, largely because Japan lacked autonomy in its tariff policy (which was not fully regained until 1911).[3] After the Sino–Japanese War, however, Japanese customs revenue began to climb.

The levels of customs as a percentage of imports for the United States are also high in relation to other countries and were quite slow in declining. American tariffs did not come down after the civil war as expected. A series of tariff acts were passed (1883, 1890, 1894, 1897, 1909, 1913) that were either overtly protectionist or, at best, moderately so. The percentages for the United States were higher than those for all other states in this study, except for Russian levels, which surpassed American levels in the late 1880s. Despite their size, however, the American levels began a steady decline around the turn of the century. British average tariff levels were always among the lowest of the seven and, on a regular basis, the lowest. Surprisingly, France and Germany also had fairly low levels, although France, Germany, Austria, Italy, and Russia all had general increases in their levels into the mid-1890s, and then experienced varying amounts of moderate decline up to the war.

Tables 7.1 and 7.2 show the simple correlations of the average tariff in both percentage changes and in their levels forms across eight states. Most of the correlations in Table 7.1 are close to zero or very weak. The notable exceptions are the correlations of Austria with both Italy and Russia and that between Russia and the United States. All three are moderately positive. There are a few correlations that are moderate or weak, but negative as well. In general, then, there was not much co-movement in the growth rates of the average tariff levels. There could be more complicated relationships in the data, however, if lags and other variables were investigated. Tariff conflict does seem to imply co-movement in the data, but these conflicts were probably too short-lived to appear in the correlations.

Table 7.1: Correlations of Average Tariff Rate (percentage change), 1873–1913

	Britain	France	Germany	Italy	Japan	Russia	US
Austria	−0.146	0.112	0.127	0.379	−0.053	0.352	−0.028
Britain		0.107	−0.077	0.057	−0.128	0.195	0.092
France			0.006	0.056	−0.209	0.065	−0.386
Germany				0.018	−0.089	0.292	−0.028
Italy					−0.049	−0.002	−0.283
Japan						0.212	0.184
Russia							0.322

The levels of the data in Table 7.2 show different, though not necessarily expected, results. First Britain, the United States, and Japan have negative correlations with each of the other countries, though

Britain and the US have a moderate positive correlation with each other. The correlations between Britain and the other five countries, however, are negative and generally weak. This reflects a tendency (however weak) for the trends in the data to move away from the British series. US correlations with the others range from weak (Japanese) to strong (Austria, France). Strong negative correlations indicate that the trends of the two series generally moved in opposite directions.

If we view high positive correlations as being superficial indicators of competitive protectionist rivalry, then neither Britain nor the United States appeared to have been in a state of competitive protectionism with any of the other states, not, at least for very long. While the United States was quite protectionist in this period, then, the general levels of customs as a percentage of imports do not significantly move in a positive direction with any of the other states. Japan also shows very low negative correlations with each of the other countries here, with a moderate negative association with Italy.

France, Germany, Austria, Italy, and Russia show a different pattern from the others. All five countries have high positive correlations in the levels of their average tariff rates with each other. This result is fitting in light of the fact that these states were generally oriented towards mercantilist trade policies to a greater extent than the other states. These four states were also involved in trade conflicts with each other. These correlations do not necessarily imply trade conflict, however, because the correlations generally do not appear in the percentage changes of the data. We can only state that there was a tendency for the levels of the data to move in similar ways over time. Any co-movement in the percentage changes is likely for short periods of time only.

Table 7.2: Correlations of Average Tariff Rate (levels), 1872–1913

	Britain	France	Germany	Italy	Japan	Russia	US
Austria	−0.172	0.856	0.696	0.464	−0.097	0.699	−0.783
Britain		−0.29	−0.212	−0.263	−0.114	−0.096	0.347
France			0.867	0.741	−0.124	0.838	−0.757
Germany				0.805	−0.094	0.904	−0.516
Italy					−0.395	0.766	−0.311
Japan						−0.115	−0.152
Russia							−0.435

The existence of trade conflict between two countries also does not necessarily mean that there will be a high positive correlation in their average tariff rates. Germany was involved in trade conflict with Britain, but the correlation between the two above is negligible. Despite the trade rivalry between Britain and Germany, then,

Germany continued to enjoy the benefits of British free trade policy throughout the conflict.

ECONOMIC DIMENSIONS TO RIVALRY

While the imports of trade partners from each other were generally not in opposition to each other, their positions in the markets of third Great Powers reflect a different pattern. There appears to be at least good descriptive evidence below that many rival states saw their trade in opposition in the markets of other Great Powers. The same evidence tends to show that the trade of Great Power rivals with each other does not show polarization, however, or even reflect the complaints of the various states. The major exception here is French–Italian trade (see below).

It was during the 1870s that Britain's trade supremacy began to be challenged. In the 1850s and 1860s, there was a definite trend on the part of the major states towards freer trade. While none followed free trade to the extent that the British did, this trend was evident even in Germany and the United States.[4] France made drastic changes in its trade policy between 1860 and 1867. The French movement toward free trade began with the Anglo-French commercial treaty of 1860 (which was the first in a series of treaties with Europe), followed by a host of measures that reduced duties and restrictions, and ended with legislation in 1866–67 that reduced restrictions of trade with French colonies and ended the surtax on imports from foreign ships and the tonnage duty on foreign-built ships.[5] France even lifted the protectionist policy on its colonies, which was based on reciprocity between France and the colonies, by according tariff autonomy to the colonies in 1866.[6]

As national industries in the United States and on the Continent of Europe grew, however, the governments of the states became more aggressive as they sought to control their home markets and push into foreign markets. Tariffs were readily resorted to, especially after 1875. Governments very willingly supported the development of railways and port facilities, and gave shipping subsidies and favourable navigation restrictions to aid the development of new shipping lines.[7] The turn towards protectionism on the part of Britain's competitors was also driven by depression and, after the Italian and German wars of unification, by the rise of a more militant nationalism.[8] France held on to a free trade policy until 1892, when it adopted a tougher tariff and turned away from the liberal orientation in trade that had existed since 1860.[9] France also reintroduced protectionism into its colonial policy, with the 1892 law that imposed tariff assimilation on the colonies.[10]

As Western Europe and the United States industrialized, they adopted heavy tariffs against British manufactures, while the British maintained a free trade policy and admitted the manufactures of its new competitors duty-free.[11] These protectionist trends implied that British exports to the new competitors would begin a trend of decline, while the share in British imports on the part of its competitors would show a slightly different trend,[12] although these tendencies were not evenly evident across Britain's main trade partners. British exports to the United States, for example, went from about 12.8 per cent of total British exports in 1870 down to 7.1 per cent in 1878. British imports from the United States, in contrast, increased in the same period from about 16.4 per cent of British imports in 1870 to 24.2 per cent in 1878.

From the 1870s onward, however, it seemed in Britain that the industrializing countries of Europe and the United States were injuring British commercial interests through aggressive competition and protectionist practices. There was also the belief that the advancing newcomers were furthered by the opening of the Suez Canal in 1869. While the canal certainly benefited Britain as well, British commercial supremacy was aided before the canal's opening by European dependence on the Cape Route. European trade with Asia had to travel the long route around the Cape before the opening of the canal, which Britain dominated. Not only did the Cape Route make trade with Asia a long-term affair, but there were risks involved in such long journeys, such as the possibility of interruptions of trade due to war. In addition, the various supplies and services needed to support such trade were all provided by Britain. Britain's shipping supremacy, its system of warehousing and distribution, as well as Britain's dominance in trade with the East put Britain in a controlling position. The opening of the canal, coupled with growing use of steamships, opened direct trade routes from southern and eastern Europe to Asia.[13]

Despite increased access to the world afforded to the Continent by the Suez Canal, Britain retained overwhelming dominance of the canal from its opening to 1913. Britain benefited immensely from the trade and military access to the east afforded by the canal as well. It is interesting to note that the increases in German tonnage through the canal in the decade before the war were large enough to make German shipping the second largest through the canal, despite the intensity of Anglo-German rivalry (see Table 6.21). Britain did not deny Germany access to the east.

German trade conflict with Britain, however, was a main line of trade rivalry right up to 1913, and cannot be fully understood outside of the military rivalry of the two as well. Anglo-German trade conflict was in full force by 1885, but perhaps had its roots in policy changes under Bismarck in 1879, which may have begun a reversal of the liberal trend that was under way in Prussian trade policy beforehand.[14] Germany had been on the road to free trade before 1879 with a series of tariff reductions from 1868 to 1873, where there was a near abandonment of protective tariffs (maintaining those for revenue purposes only).[15] The tariff reductions were all in force in 1877, but a reaction followed soon after with a return to protection. Bismarck's changes were designed to give preference to home industries over foreign, to reform the railway system and rates in order to favour the transport of German goods over foreign, and to provide revenue to support the reorganization of state finances.[16] German customs revenue began to grow after 1880, reaching its highest levels between 1895 and 1905, and then declining somewhat before the war.

The British press blamed the 'commercial uprising of the German people' for the economic hardship that Britain experienced in 1885.[17] German trade expansion in the 1880s, however, was moderate. There was a slight decline in imports and exports during the second half of the 1880s, not recovering until the end of the decade.[18] German presence in foreign trade markets was growing, however. British consulates often complained of German government practices in aiding German commerce, including high German tariffs and freight charges. Wherever Britain appeared to be losing a market foothold, the Germans appeared to be gaining. German advances into the markets of southern and eastern Europe during the 1880s, German advances into Asian markets, and German advances into markets in the Western Hemisphere, filled the British Foreign Office with concern.[19]

In 1885, the British Foreign Office issued a questionnaire to its diplomatic and consular personnel around the world to determine what the impediments to British trade were. While there were many reasons for British trade problems, news of German advances into local markets, German houses underselling British houses, German trade representatives having superior foreign language skills, and many other complaints were heard just about everywhere.[20]

It was not until the 1890s, however, that British concern over aggressive German commercial advances became alarmist. British alarm seemed to rise as British trade lagged and to fall as British trade recovered. British protectionists saw German influence seeping into Britain through an open trade door, which fed growing nationalist hostility towards Germany.[21] By 1896, however, the Germans were generally seen as being the greatest commercial menace to Britain in the world, especially by the British press.[22] There were many British charges of unfair practices against Germany. In 1894, a controversy arose over German use of prison labour to produce various goods. One charge was that prisoners made items that were copied from British models and then sent to the British market to undersell domestic producers. In the autumn of 1894, the charges against German prison labour were that over 44,000 convicts were competing with British production in 16 traded items.[23] Joseph Chamberlain added to this accusation by stating that:

> the Germans have actually sent over to this country for models of English manufactures, and they are making them in their prisons. At the present time they are making about 20 different articles in various branches of industry; so that after they have contrived to ruin the brush trade they will go into many other trades.[24]

German protectionism under Bismarck was mostly in agriculture, however, and Germany enjoyed most favoured nation (MFN) status with Britain. Germany had trade agreements that were mutual with states such as Italy, Greece, Spain, and Switzerland; it generally had MFN treatment with Austria-Hungary, Belgium, the Netherlands, Sweden, Norway, and France, which meant that when France negotiated reductions of duties with other countries Germany would enjoy the lower rates. There was some strain over trade issues for Germany with the United States and Russia, both of which wanted to export agriculture and were consequently affected by German tariffs.[25] Indeed, German trade conflict with Russia often seemed to be a greater problem than that with Britain (see below).

While the British were indeed losing market footholds to the Germans, British fears were out of proportion to the facts regarding Britain's home market. There does appear to be some evidence that British trade was being crowded out of certain markets abroad by competitors (see below), but the United States was capturing a much larger portion of the British import market than was Germany, as seen in Chapter 5, and the British trade imbalance with the United States was quite large.

It is also hard to see in the import figures of Chapter 5 that one country's gain in the market of the other was the other's loss in general. If this were true in the British–German case, for example, then we might expect to find that the German position in the British market moved in one direction while the British position in the German market moved in the other. As Tables 7.3 and 7.4 indicate, however, the evidence for this in the British–German case is weak. With a few exceptions, the tables indicate that the shares that trade partners had in each other's imports were generally unassociated. The inclusive dates of each country pair are indicated below each table. Japanese import data are the shortest due to missing data.

The strong negative association is between Britain and Japan. The data show that, each country's imports from the other as a percentage of its total imports clearly move in opposite directions. While Japan's dependence on Britain was large, it generally declined over time. The opposite holds for Britain, with a very small degree of dependence on Japan that generally increased over time. It is surprising not to find strong negative correlations between Britain and most of the other countries given the general movement away from Britain in their imports. The lack of negative correlations indicates that this movement did not occur at both ends of the trade relationship.

Table 7.3: Correlations of Imports by Origin (levels), 1870–1913

	France	*Germany*	*Italy*	*Japan*	*Russia*	*US*
Britain	0.291	–0.241	0.817	–0.769	–0.104	–0.294
France		–0.129	0.924	na	–0.068	0.013
Germany			0.545	0.75	0.341	0.509
Italy				–0.399	–0.221	na
Japan					na	0.825
Russia						na

Russian–Italian correlation, 1870–1906; all correlations with Germany, 1880–1913; all correlations with Japan, 1880–1906.

The remaining correlations in Table 7.3 are either insignificant altogether or are significant and positive. Italy actually has peculiarly strong positive associations with Britain, France, and Germany. Britain and France have no other positive associations like this, although the United States has strong positive correlations with both Germany and Japan. While we might interpret strong negative associations as indicating an asymmetrical change in the relative positions that each country had in the market of the other (and perhaps supporting the sort of complaint that Britain made against Germany above), it is unclear what, if anything, positive associations reflect. Positive associations obviously indicate that each country's import dependence on the other moves in the same direction, but what does this tell us? It is possible, though not indicated by the discussion above, that some of these countries provided access to their home markets on a reciprocal basis.

Table 7.4 shows correlations of the same import data, though in percentage changes. The German and US negative associations with Britain disappear altogether, though a moderate negative association between Britain and France exists. The Italian correlations with Britain, France, and Germany remain positive but much weaker, and the negative association between Italy and Japan remains. The remaining correlations are close to zero.

Table 7.4: Correlations of Imports by Origin (percentage change), 1871–1913

	France	*Germany*	*Italy*	*Japan*	*Russia*	*US*
Britain	−0.338	0.012	0.282	−0.134	−0.096	−0.068
France		0.128	0.203	na	0.019	0.068
Germany			0.314	−0.101	0.156	−0.035
Italy				−0.337	−0.157	na
Japan					na	0.03
Russia						na

Russian–Italian correlation, 1871–1906; all correlations with Germany, 1881–1913; all correlations with Japan, 1881–1906.

While Britain's complaints that competitors were gaining in the British market at the same time Britain was losing in theirs are generally absent from the correlations above, is there evidence of such a polarization in the markets of third countries? What follows below is a discussion of other trade conflicts and related rivalries while examining the correlations of each country's position in the imports of others.

For most of the period in general, Britain was Germany's largest trade partner. There was a drop in German trade with Britain from 1905 to 1910, but trade between the two recovered up to the war. Russia and the United States were the next two largest trade partners with Germany, with Russia surpassing Britain for a few years. Britain, the United States, and Russia were the three primary trade partners of Germany throughout this period and the three primary enemies of Germany during the war. The United States, of course, grew over time to become a primary partner. All three states converge at a similar level of trade, with Germany by 1913 in monetary value, surpassing French and Italian trade with Germany. Is it not ironic that Germany's best trade partners were also its enemies during the war?

If one looks at the percentages of trade between rivals, a slightly different picture emerges. German total trade with Britain as a percentage of German trade rose for a decade or so after 1880, but then steadily declined. The percentage decline reflects the fact that German trade with the world grew at a faster rate than its trade with Britain did. This fact may or may not be related to the onset of rivalry.

Britain started out with an overall trade surplus with Germany in 1870, but had a deficit with the other partners. In addition, the size of the deficit with the United States in 1870 was larger than that of the others and would grow to a high of £124.6 million in 1901, and then decline to £82.2 million by 1913. In addition, Britain had an overall trade surplus with Germany for the entire period between 1870 and 1912, with a deficit in 1913 itself. As aggressive as German trade practices might have been, Britain's real trade imbalance here was with the United States. Britain also had overall trade deficits with both France and Russia, of course, but they never grew to the proportions of Britain's deficit with the United States.

If Germany's gains were not Britain's losses regarding their mutual imports, did Germany's position in the British market stand in opposition to those of other countries? Table 7.5 shows simple correlations of the percentage import figures that were summarized in Table 5.5 for Britain.

Table 7.5: Correlations of British Imports, 1870–1913

	Germany	*Italy*	*Japan*	*Russia*	*US*
France	–0.496	0.489	–0.728	–0.039	0.181
Germany		–0.073	0.382	–0.036	–0.023
Italy			–0.694	0.304	–0.376
Japan				0.066	–0.163
Russia					–0.763

The negative correlations in the table indicate that the German position in the British import market may have grown at the expense of France's, although Japan has a strong negative correlation with France (as well as with Italy). In examining charts of the French and German figures here, the French figure undergoes large fluctuations, but there is an overall downward movement. The German figure is more stable and shows a slight rise over time. The moderate negative correlation between Italy and the United States may also indicate that the US position grew as the Italian declined as well. The US position also appears to have grown at the expense of Russia's. In examining British imports from Russia and the United States, the US figure rises from 1870 as a percentage of British imports while the Russian figure falls moderately. It appears as though the opposite took place as 1913 approached, with a decided fall in the US figure and a slight rise in the Russian.

German economic tensions with Russia were another central line of economic conflict from about the second half of the 1880s until about 1894, although German–Russian economic tensions began earlier after Russo–Turkish War. Because Russia anticipated that the Turkish War would injure its finances, it began collecting its customs duties in gold in 1877, which effectively increased Russian duties.[26] Germany felt a heavy burden from Russia's change in policy, being a primary trade partner with Russia, and began to increase German duties in 1879. The German increases affected Russian grain exports to Germany, with duties on grain increasing to a total of 400 per cent from 1879 to 1885, leading to a decline in Russian grain exports.[27] While Russia's expenditure on the Turkish War was a heavy burden on Russian finances for a few years, however, Russian customs as a percentage of imports in general were quite moderate during the war. Russian duties, and their level as a percentage of imports, would, however, increase dramatically after this period.

Economic conflict between Germany and Russia worsened throughout the second half of the 1880s. A tariff war between the two states was under way as Russia increased its tariff in April 1885 and then again in May 1887 on pig iron, coal, iron ore, metals, machines, and agriculture. Germany then increased its tariff in May 1885 and again in December 1887.[28] Russia's highly protective tariff was raised eight times between 1881 and 1891, culminating in 1891 levels that were the highest since 1850. While Russia's general tariff increases affected all countries, the tariff was discriminatory towards land-borne trade, which injured German competition against Britain to supply Russia with coal, iron, and other items.[29] Prior to this trade conflict, German–Russian economic relations were based on Russia sending agricultural exports to Germany and receiving industrial goods from Germany, coupled with German finance to aid in Russian development. This arrangement changed as both states adopted more restrictive economic policies towards each other.[30]

Germany and Russia began negotiating a solution to their problems towards the end of 1891, but could not come to agreement. Between 1 and 16 August 1893, a tariff war erupted between the two. On 1 August 1893, German goods sent to Russia became subject to the maximum tariff (about 30 per cent on manufactures and 20 per cent on semi-manufactures). Germany responded to this by imposing taxes of 50 per cent on Russian goods that were already subject to customs duties. The duty on Russian bread, for example, was then about 115 per cent higher than on bread from America, Hungary, Rumania, and Argentina. Russia retaliated by raising the tariff on German goods by 50 per cent, raising the shipping dues against German vessels, and extending these measures to Finland. Germany responded with a 50 per cent tax on goods from Finland as well.[31]

Both Germany and Russia sought a solution to the conflict. Russia wanted a treaty with Germany, to be the first in a series, and Germany wanted an agreement with Russia to counter the Franco-Russian Alliance. A treaty was signed in February 1894, from which both sides gained. Russia received MFN status where it obtained lower grain duties and the removal of duties on other items such as flax, oil-seed, and wool. Russia also gained an advantage over the United States in the duty on oil to Germany. Germany, in turn, gained a reduction in duties on 120 items (for example, 20 per cent on leather goods, 17–20 per cent on unwrought iron, 18 per cent on iron machinery, 17–20 per cent on pottery, 17 per cent on paper, 12–30 per cent on woollen tissues).[32] Russia and Germany also agreed not to raise the duties on certain items for ten years. In addition, Russia agreed to discontinue its distinction between sea-borne and land-borne goods, which hindered German competitiveness in Russia, and Germany agreed that Russian goods would no longer be subject to higher rates than domestic goods for transport on Prussian state railways.[33]

German trade with Russia declined in value between 1884 and 1886 as a result of this conflict, though it began to recover during the rest of the decade and experienced a general trend upward (despite fluctuations) until 1913. In percentage terms, German total trade with Russia wavered between 7 per cent and 9 per cent of German trade in the 1880s (with 1886 being a low of 6.8 per cent), but would waver upwards of between 10 per cent and 12 per cent between 1900 and 1913.

Table 7.6: Correlations of German Imports, 1880–1913

	France	Italy	Japan	Russia	US
Britain	0.302	0.073	−0.7	−0.59	−0.51
France		−0.692	−0.8	−0.409	−0.859
Italy			0.396	0.042	0.514
Japan				0.544	0.896
Russia					0.383

If any state's trade was in opposition to British in the German import market, then it was Russian, US, Japanese, or all three, as indicated by the negative correlations between Britain and these states in Table 7.6. In examining the movement of the four country's figures, it appears that the United States and Britain were most clearly in opposition to each other. The British figure initially rises after 1880 and then steadily declines, while the US figure appears to do the opposite. The Russian figure has an overall upward movement, though not a steep one, and fluctuates throughout. It appears to rise when the British figure declines and vice-versa. The Japanese figure, while very small, tends to rise over time as well. The French figure in the German import market also seems to have shifted to each of the other states, with the exception of Britain.

The German table, then, appears to indicate a shift in imports away from Britain and France and towards the United States, Russia, Japan, and perhaps even Italy. We cannot, of course, be certain that the negative correlations indicate that one country's gain was the other's loss. More information about trade would be needed. Given the negative correlations and a visual inspection of the data, however, we can state that German imports had an overall tendency to move away from Britain and France and toward these other countries.

The economic strain between Germany and Russia, and the resulting diplomatic coolness, was the means by which France attempted to become the primary financier of Russian development. Part of France's effort at seeking an alliance with Russia was to counter the German threat. France's role in Russian finance was small, but began to grow during the second half of the 1880s. According to George F. Kennan, French investment in Russia in 1886 was only about 1.5 million francs, which was around 9.4 per cent of French foreign investment. And the French role in lending to the Russian government was approximately 15 per cent of Russian borrowing, while Germany provided about 60 per cent.[34]

Between 1888 and 1889, Russia received three loans from France and a small one from Germany, which dramatically improved conditions for the Russian treasury.[35] The French effort to become a chief source of financing for Russia was the politically motivated economic background to France's effort at seeking an alliance with Russia. France's primary concern was to get Russian guarantees of cooperation against any Triple Alliance power that would threaten the peace. This was an empty gain given that both Russia and France would cooperate in such an event anyway because their security would mandate it.[36]

Tables 7.7 and 7.8 are correlations of French and Russian import figures. The strongest negative correlation in the French table is that between the United States and Britain, although there is a moderate negative one between Britain and Germany and a slightly stronger one between the United States and Italy. We do not see the Russian import position being negatively correlated to that of Germany, which we might expect. Instead, the correlations suggest that the United States was chiefly advancing in the French import market.

Table 7.7: Correlations of French Imports, 1870–1913

	Germany	*Italy*	*Russia*	*US*
Britain	−0.303	0.72	0.016	−0.527
Germany		−0.249	−0.197	0.208
Italy			0.08	−0.45
Russia				0.299

The Russian table shows a strong negative correlation between Germany and the United States and only a weak negative correlation between France and Germany. In examining the German and US figures in Russian imports, it appears that the German figure tended to decline in the early years, reaching lows in the mid-1890s, while the US figure tended to rise in the early years. In the second part of the period, the German figure tended to recover and rise smoothly until it took a sharp downturn in the last year or two before the war. The US figure begins to decline after 1890. If French–German rivalry and the resulting alliance of 1894 affected Russian trade with Germany and France, then, it was slight.

Table 7.8: Correlations of Russian Imports, 1870–1913

	France	*Germany*	*Italy*	*US*
Britain	0.215	0.07	0.5	–0.179
France		–0.285	0.411	0.048
Germany			–0.123	–0.765
Italy				0.084

US and Italy, 1870–1906.

A very clear example of trade polarization between two rivals is seen with France and Italy. While the conflict between these two states was not the primary line of conflict preceding the First World War, France and Italy were in a state of rivalry on several fronts. In terms of trade, relations between Italy and France worsened in 1881 and remained poor throughout the decade. French economic pressure on Italy in 1881, French rejection of a navigation treaty with Italy in 1886, and Italian denunciation of a commercial treaty with France in 1886 (in force since 1881) were some of the main events of this conflict. The Italians were antagonized over the French acquisition of Tunisia and, after the Italian turn towards Germany, the French sought to sever Italian ties to the Triple Alliance and maintained that no commercial agreement between France and Italy would be possible so long as Italy maintained its German connection.[37]

The conflict between France and Italy was perhaps heightened when Britain weakened its Mediterranean fleet in order to concentrate more naval power in its home waters in response to the German challenge in the period. Italy was perhaps more exposed to France as a result and France increased its Mediterranean fleet, which led Italy into even closer ties with the Triple Alliance.[38] As conflict between Italy and France increased, there was even talk of possible war.

The trade conflict between France and Italy, then, was influenced by diplomatic and strategic issues having to do with the alliance politics of the Continent and with colonial matters in North Africa. The result of the trade conflict was a drastic decline in their total trade with each other. Italy was much more dependent on France than France was on Italy. France's trade pattern was more global than Italy's at the time, and France simply had more trade than Italy did in absolute terms. Unlike the other trade conflicts above, however, the decline in trade between France and Italy lasted a long time. Italian total trade with France as a percentage of total Italian trade was 31.2 per cent in 1880, and frequently higher than this beforehand. Trade would decline steadily after that reaching the low of 8.2 per cent of total Italian trade in 1913 itself. Part of this decline in dependence on France is certainly due to the general growth of Italian trade elsewhere, but the shift away from France was more pronounced after 1880.

Table 7.9: Correlations of Italian Imports, 1870–1913

	France	*Germany*	*Japan*	*Russia*	*US*
Britain	0.712	−0.832	−0.602	−0.51	−0.761
France		−0.923	−0.607	−0.691	−0.847
Germany			0.695	0.527	0.854
Japan				−0.027	0.724
Russia					0.468

Table 7.9 indicates a more extreme situation with France than does the Italian position in Table 7.7, probably because Italy was more dependent on France than the reverse. The British and French figures in Table 7.9 have very high negative correlations with Germany and the United States, as well as strong negative correlations with Japan and Russia. Germany, Japan, Russia, and the United States all have strong positive correlations with each other in the Italian market (except for Russia and Japan), which indicates that each country's position generally increased over time, despite fluctuations and differences in magnitude. While the British and French declines in Italian imports are steady throughout, the French figure becomes drastic after the onset of the trade conflict with Italy.

The final tables are for the United States and Japan (Tables 7.10 and 7.11) which also contain correlations of the import percentages of main trade partners. The strongest negative correlations in the US table include the British–German and the British–Japanese. The British figure appears to decline steeply and smoothly for most of the years, whereas the other two show smooth rises, although both are below the magnitudes of the British figure.

Table 7.10: Correlations of US Imports, 1870–1913

	France	*Germany*	*Japan*
Britain	0.021	−0.733	−0.843
France		−0.201	−0.241
Germany			0.585

Finally, the Japanese table again shows strong negative correlations of Germany with both Britain and France, although Britain and France also have strong negative associations with Russia and the United States. Italy also has strong negative associations with Germany, Russia, and the United States. The British figure contains the sharpest decline while the French declines more smoothly. The US figure shows the sharpest rise over time, followed by the German.

Table 7.11: Correlations of Japanese Imports, 1880–1906

	France	Germany	Italy	Russia	US
Britain	0.899	–0.761	0.834	–0.704	–0.747
France		–0.708	0.797	–0.503	–0.705
Germany			–0.843	0.594	0.56
Italy				–0.708	–0.505
Russia					0.52

GREAT POWER TRADE TO TARGETS OF RIVALRY: THE TURKISH AND
EGYPTIAN CASES

The third trade scenario to look at is among Great Powers to another area or country. Only two cases are examined here (Turkey and Egypt) in order to spare the reader another long string of tables. The reasoning behind this type of focus on trade is to determine whether the trade positions of rival Great Powers were in opposition to each other in countries that were economically and militarily smaller and were also the focal points of rivalry.

The data below show that the trade positions of rivals in Turkey and Egypt does show patterns different from the trade positions of non-rivals in those countries. The trade position of Germany and those of Britain and France in Turkey, for example, are negatively associated, while the position of Britain and those of France and Russia in Turkey are not. The evidence presented below is selective and the methods, like the above, are descriptive. These correlations can tell only what the general tendencies are in the levels of the data. The evidence is also somewhat superficial.

The first case here involves Turkey and the trade issues surrounding rivalry during the Baghdad Railway question. This issue itself is a classic example of how diplomatic, economic, and military concerns combine in peacetime rivalries. In addition, the conflict surrounding the Baghdad Railway is a microcosm of three major lines of rivalry that preceded the war – Anglo-German, Russo-German, and Anglo-Russian. The Baghdad Railway issue, of course, is not discussed in full here. I merely summarize the basic diplomacy of the conflict and attempt to tie these issues into trade relations.

The Baghdad Railway issue begins in the late 1880s when the Turkish Sultan approached the Germans with an offer of a concession to extend the Anatolian rail system. The issue grew over time into a major contention among a handful of states and tied into the larger rivalries, strategies, and trade positions of all of them. While the concession was primarily an economic question at the time, however, the German Foreign Office became interested in the matter. News of the concession to the Germans also led to proposals by British, French, and Belgian companies.[39]

Britain and Russia also opposed the German concession in Turkey, ostensibly for different reasons. The British maintained that the planned line to be built (Konia to Constantinople) would cut through two British lines in Smyrna. The British even indicated a possible naval demonstration against the line, but the Germans and British ultimately resolved the issue.[40] Russia was opposed to all groups seeking concessions because it did not want to strengthen Turkey at all.[41] The concession was ultimately signed in February 1893, however, and the Konia line was completed in 1896.

The Turks sought further extension of the Anatolia Railway and had a definite preference for the Germans. The Germans actually tried to play down any diplomatic gains they might obtain in order to avoid turning the railway issue into a diplomatic struggle.[42] While the Germans saw the potential military advantages, as well as the diplomatic prestige to be gained in the region, they also wanted to spread the financial risk and leave the project open in order to show the world that the Germans were not aggressively expanding into Turkey.[43]

The Deutsche Bank asked Turkey for another concession in 1899 to extend the railway from Konia to Baghdad, and this was ultimately granted. The Russians, previously satisfied with the German role in Turkey, grew alarmed as German economic and political interests advanced in Turkey. Russia ultimately sought a concession from Turkey to have exclusive rights to build railways in the Black Sea Basin, which the Turks granted (exempting themselves).[44]

Over time, negotiations on the project became quite complicated and entangled in the politics of the Continent after the turn of the century. The negotiations broke down in 1903, for example, after which the rail issue escalated from being an economic issue to one entangled in diplomatic and strategic questions. From then on, the rail issue would be the concern of the statesmen of Europe, whereas before it was a matter for various bankers and the Turkish Sultan.[45] Germany started off being willing to involve other states in the project to avoid making it a political matter, but the interests of Russia and Britain came to clash with each other and with those of Germany.

The Russians were against the idea of strengthening Turkey through rail, which would militate against Russian influence there and perhaps even open the Persian market to western Europe.[46] British interest in the rail project did not become a decidedly strategic one until after the turn of the century, when Germany became the primary rival of Britain. While Britain was interested in keeping Germany and Russia at odds, the project did not become entangled with the larger issue of British control of access to the east until after the Boer War. A German-controlled rail route to the Persian Gulf could undercut the British position.[47] The German position also changed. At first, the issue of rail development in Turkey was economic to Germany. But as these interests were assailed by rivals, German rail development in Turkey became entangled in the larger issues of strategy. While German trade with Turkey was small, it symbolized German penetration into the east.[48] The interests of Russia and Britain were simply not compatible with these developments. French interests, in contrast, were not entirely clear on the rail issue. French financiers had money in the project, but France took the official line of maintaining loyalty to its alliance with Russia (1894) and it followed the policy of Britain and Russia on the matter.[49]

The rail issue in Turkey, then, came to reflect several lines of conflict. First, there was the issue of Anglo-Russian rivalry, where each state would oppose the strengthening of the other in Turkey. Second, there was the Russo-Turkish conflict. Russia was wary of anything that would increase Turkish power. Third, there was the earlier British goal of keeping Russia and Germany at odds, which meant that Britain did not like anything that promised German–Russian cooperation. Fourth, and most importantly, the rail issue became a function of Anglo-German rivalry after the Boer War, where the German effort at obtaining a land route to the Persian Gulf threatened to undercut British domination of the shortest route to the east.

On the trade front, Britain and France feared that 'Turkey was being drawn into the orbit of the Central Powers by force of trade'.[50] In general, trade with Turkey represented a small part of the trade of the main rivals here. In terms of percentages, Turkey never reached 5 per cent of Russian trade in this period, never reached 4 per cent of French trade, has only reached the high of 1 per cent of German trade in 1910 and 1911, and never went beyond 2.58 per cent (in 1870) of British trade. Russian trade with Turkey was the least stable of the four. In 1877, owing to the Turkish War, Russian trade with Turkey plummeted to less than 1 per cent of Russian trade, but recovered the next year to just over 2 per cent. The next decade would see Russian trade with Turkey fluctuate dramatically, and then stabilize somewhat thereafter. The general trend in Russian trade to Turkey as a percentage of Russian trade, however, was downward. The same was true for British and French trade with Turkey. While the levels of British and French trade with Turkey were very stable in amounts during the period, the general directions of their corresponding percentages were both downward.

Table 7.12: Great Power Trade with Turkey (percentage), 1870–1913

Years	Britain	France	Germany	Russia
1870	2.58	3.49	0	2.78
1875	1.97	2.67	0	2.96
1880	1.59	2.1	0	4.11
1885	1.79	2.55	0.14	2.75
1890	1.62	2.36	0.57	1.83
1895	1.62	2.02	0.8	na
1900	1.28	1.79	0.6	1.5
1905	1.28	1.53	0.92	1.32
1910	1.11	1.26	1.05	na
1913	0.95	1.16	0.82	na

Note: Figures represent each countries trade (imports + exports) with Turkey as a percentage of its total trade.
Source: See Appendix 1 for various national series.

A similar picture of trade positions emerges when one looks at the trade of the same countries with Turkey as a percentage of Turkish trade (see Table 7.13). The British and French portions of the Turkish market, while substantial throughout, generally declined. Britain had 46.6 per cent of Turkish trade in 1878, but declined to less than half that amount in 1913, with just under 20 per cent. Likewise, France began with over 20 per cent of the Turkish market in 1878 and ended with just over 12 per cent in 1913.

Table 7.13: Turkey's Trade with Main Partners (percentage), 1878–1913

Years	Britain	France	Germany	Russia	Other
1878	46.6	20.48	0.18	6.22	26.52
1880	38.32	21.13	0.17	6.87	33.51
1885	41.62	18.88	0.08	6.7	32.73
1890	40.93	18.24	0.5	5.41	34.93
1895	37.32	17.11	1.75	5.35	38.47
1900	35.86	18.47	3.23	6.54	35.91
1905	33.96	14.66	5	4.73	41.64
1910	21.31	12.82	8.01	5.7	52.16
1913	19.98	12.32	9.25	6.79	51.65

Note: Percentages are of Turkey's total trade.
Source: B. R. Mitchell, *International Historical Statistics: Africa and Asia* (New York: New York University Press, 1982).

Table 7.14: Correlations of Turkish Imports, 1878–1900

	France	Germany	Russia	World
Britain	0.626	−0.801	−0.107	−0.912
France		−0.551	−0.082	−0.801
Germany			−0.129	0.76
Russia				−0.167

The Russian portion of Turkish trade fluctuated, but remained between 5 per cent and 7 per cent. The German portion of Turkish trade, however, increased steeply after the turn of the century, but never reached 10 per cent of total Turkish trade. Clearly, Turkey began the period with a strong trade orientation towards Britain and, to some extent, France, but turned towards other states as time went on. What is interesting here is that the portion of Turkish trade with the rest of the world (*Other* in the table) grew to become a majority of Turkey's trade. Despite British and French fears that Germany was seeking to control Turkish trade, Germany occupied a relatively small place in total Turkish trade. Britain and France lost more of the Turkish market to the rest of the world than they did to Germany.

A descriptive picture of the relative gains and losses in the Turkish market can be seen from the correlations in Table 7.14. The correlations above are of the percentages that each of the states has in Turkish imports (that is, the import side of the figures in Table 7.13). Britain and France have a strong positive correlation with each other, but both have strong negative correlations with the German figure. Britain and France also have strongly negative correlations with the rest of the world. While these correlations are at least consistent with the view that Turkey was being pulled into the German orbit at the expense of Britain and France, Turkey's trade was also expanding elsewhere.

The Egyptian case is presented below mainly because it is tied into the Turkish case. Egypt is important in its own right, of course, being the location of the Suez Canal, but the role of the canal as the shortest route to the east was also tied into the Turkish issue for two major reasons. One is that Turkey was the nominal suzerain over Egypt and the other is that the railway line issue was, at least in rhetoric, a land route around British control of the sea. The German effort to acquire a land route to the east was, at least partially, a function of the German effort at escaping the British grip on German access. A land route to the Persian Gulf was such a possibility. In addition, close German–Turkish ties could be a means by which the British hold on Egypt could be weakened or, at least, threatened.

I will not make too much of the geopolitics of the Baghdad Railway issue and how it ties into Egypt. It is quite easy to overstate such matters. It will suffice to state here that Egypt was also a focal point of rivalry. Well before the Germans came along, of course, France and Britain were rivals in the area, and Russia had an interest there as well. In fact, Egypt is the only African country that is regularly reported in Russian trade tables for Africa. The rest of Africa, if there is any Russian trade there at all, is simply housed together as *other*. While Germany has been a focal point in this study, in terms of rivalry and trade relations, then, there are other possibilities as well that could be reflected in the data below.

Table 7.15: Great Power Trade with Egypt (percentage), 1880–1913

Years	Britain	France	Germany	Italy	Russia
1880	1.77	1.1	0.16	1.65	na
1885	1.95	0.75	0.13	1.27	1.84
1890	1.58	0.65	na	1.16	1.35
1895	1.84	0.69	0.3	0.96	1.37
1900	2.14	0.79	0.52	1.35	1.58
1905	2.37	1.18	0.68	1.51	0.68
1910	2.47	1.03	0.78	1.5	na
1913	2.23	0.98	0.77	1.23	na

Note: Figures represent each countries trade (imports + exports) with Egypt as a percentage of its total trade.
Source: See Appendix 1 for various national series.

As shown in Table 7.15, British import dependence on Egypt was generally small, but larger than that of the others. In value, Britain had and maintained the largest amount of trade with Egypt during the entire period by far. France was the second largest trader with Egypt of the five until Germany surpassed France towards the end of the period. Italy and Russia were also main traders with Egypt, but neither ever reached the French levels. Like the example above, the role of Egyptian trade was small in the trade of all these states. Although trade with Egypt surpassed 2 per cent of British trade on a regular basis after the turn of the century.

In terms of Egypt's imports (see Table 7.16), Britain declined from having an overwhelming majority position in Egyptian import dependence to having less than 38 per cent in 1913. France and Italy retained about the same position in Egyptian imports, although the Russian figure declines in the earlier years and then stays about the same as well. Germany experienced continual growth until it became the second largest of Egypt's import partners by the end of the period, although the German position in Egypt's imports still remained small compared to the British.

Table 7.16: Egypt's Trade with Main Partners (percentage), 1880–1913

Years	Britain	Russia	France	Germany	Italy	Other
1875	69.75	1.57	13.52	na	4.43	10.73
1880	59.05	3.94	10.89	na	3.96	22.16
1885	52.32	8.31	9.77	0.25	6.15	23.23
1890	53.81	6.65	8.7	0.33	4.96	25.56
1895	47.43	7.55	9.36	3.14	3.49	29.03
1900	47.32	5.82	8.9	4.98	4.08	28.91
1905	42.35	4.22	9.58	6.4	4.2	33.25
1910	41.2	4.27	9.78	8.21	3.76	32.78
1913	37.7	5.32	9.21	9.65	4.27	33.87

Note: Percentages are of Egypt's total trade.
Source: B. R. Mitchell, *International Historical Statistics: Africa and Asia* (New York: New York University Press, 1982).

The correlations below, then, show similar results to the Turkish case above. Germany has a strong negative correlation with Britain, though not with France, despite the strong positive correlation between Britain and France. Germany also has a strong negative correlation with Russia, although Britain and France do as well.

Table 7.17: Correlations of Egyptian Imports, 1874–1913

	France	*Germany*	*Italy*	*Russia*	*World*
Britain	0.802	–0.731	–0.085	–0.525	–0.953
France		0.001	–0.052	–0.762	–0.852
Germany			0.837	–0.728	0.069
Italy				–0.241	–0.155
Russia					0.603

Germany, 1884–1913.

The Italian figure has a strong positive correlation with Germany, but has no association with Britain and France and only a weak negative correlation with Russia. Finally, Britain and France also have very strong negative correlations with the rest of the world. While the evidence suggests that it is possible that Britain and France lost position to Germany in the Egyptian market, it is also possible and likely that they lost to the rest of the world.

CONCLUSION

While the evidence presented above is largely descriptive, it is reasonable to suggest that the imports of Great Power rivals from each other were not really in opposition as complaints might suggest, but that their import positions in third country markets were. One could elevate this discussion to a more analytical level by estimating models of the relationship between conflict and trade using the type of trade data reported above. Most of the conflict and trade models use simple aggregates of bilateral trade, but more interesting measures that capture different trade scenarios could be used. The main difficulty here, especially with historical data, would be to define an appropriate set of regressors for such a project. While general conflict terms might be useful, for example, conflict that is specific to the trade market and/or the two rival states would be most interesting.

The above discussion has also indicated that the trade positions of the states were entwined with the larger issues of conflict and rivalry. Military/strategic issues, such as control of the sea routes to Asia, were both commercial and military matters. It is clear from the above and from Chapter 6, however, that the interactions between military power and commerce among these states was a messy story.

NOTES

1. These rivalries would include Anglo-Russian, Anglo-French, Anglo-German, Anglo-American, Anglo-Japanese, Russo-Japanese, American–Japanese, German–French, German–Russian, French–Italian, Italo-Austrian, and Austro-Russian.
2. Ian H. Nish, *Alliance in Decline: A Study in Anglo-Japanese Relations, 1908–1923* (London: The Athlone Press, 1972), p. 10.
3. Tatsuji Takeuchi, *War and Diplomacy in the Japanese Empire* (Garden City, NY: Doubleday, Doran and Co., 1935), p. 107; W. G. Beasley, *Japanese Imperialism 1894–1945* (Oxford: Clarendon Press, 1987), pp. 133–4.
4. Albert H. Imlah, *Economic Elements in the Pax Britannica: Studies in British Foreign Trade in the Nineteenth Century* (Cambridge, MA: Harvard University Press, 1958), p. 193.
5. Michael S. Smith, *Tariff Reform in France, 1860-1900: The Politics of Economic Interest* (Ithaca, NY: Cornell University Press, 1980), p. 28.
6. Arthur Girault, *The Colonial Tariff Policy of France* (Oxford: Clarendon Press, 1916), p. 6.
7. Ross J. Hoffman, *Great Britain and The German Trade Rivalry: 1875–1914* (New York: Russell and Russell, 1964), pp. 12–13.
8. Imlah, *Pax Britannica*, p. 194.
9. Smith, *Tariff Reform*, p. 196.
10. Girault, *Colonial Tariff*, pp. 6–7.
11. Werner Schlote, *British Overseas Trade: From 1700 to the 1930s* (Oxford: Basil Blackwell, 1952), p. 82; Imlah, *Pax Britannica*, p. 195.
12. Schlote, *British Overseas Trade*, p. 83.
13. Hoffman, *Trade Rivalry*, p. 70.
14. Imlah, *Pax Britannica*, pp. 193–4.
15. Percey Ashley, *Modern Tariff History: Germany–United States–France* (London: John Murray, 1910), pp. 52–3.
16. Ibid., pp. 58–9.
17. Hoffman, *Trade Rivalry*, p. 74.
18. See Ashley, *Tariff History*, pp. 80–4 for a discussion of this.
19. Hoffman, *Trade Rivalry*, p. 74.
20. Ibid., see Appendix I, pp. 305–24, which contains responses to the questionnaire.
21. See Paul M. Kennedy, *The Rise of the Anglo-German Antagonism, 1860–1914* (London: Ashfield Press, 1980). There is discussion throughout on trade conflict between Britain and Germany, but there is particular mention of these issues in the latter 1890s and early 1900s on pp. 261–6.
22. Hoffman, *Trade Rivalry*, pp. 224–31.
23. Ibid., pp. 236–8.
24. Quoted in ibid., p. 238.
25. Ashley, *Tariff History*, p. 83.
26. George F. Kennan, *The Decline of Bismarck's European Order: Franco-Russian Relations, 1875–1890* (Princeton NJ: Princeton University Press, 1979), pp. 226–31.
27. Ibid.

28. Dietrich Geyer, *Russian Imperialism: The Interaction of Domestic and Foreign Policy, 1860–1914* (New Haven, CT: Yale University Press, 1987), p. 152.
29. Ashley, *Tariff History*, pp. 92–3.
30. Geyer, *Russian Imperialism*, p. 60.
31. Ashley, *Tariff History*, pp. 94–5.
32. Ibid., p.97.
33. Ibid., p.98.
34. Kennan, *European Order*, pp. 236–7.
35. Ibid., p. 401.
36. William L. Langer, *The Franco-Russian Alliance: 1890–1894* (Cambridge, MA: Harvard University Press, 1929), pp. 187, 399–400.
37. Ibid., pp. 115–16.
38. R. J. B. Bosworth, *Italy, the Least of the Great Powers: Italian Foreign Policy Before the First World War* (London: Cambridge University Press, 1979), p. 268.
39. J. B. Woolf, *The Diplomatic History of the Bagdad Railroad* (1936; reprint. New York: Octagon Books, 1973), p. 16.
40. Ibid., pp. 16–17.
41. Ibid., p. 16.
42. Ibid., pp. 10–1, 35–8, 48–52.
43. Ibid., pp. 19–22. Kennedy notes that German banks could not raise the large amounts of capital needed for the project and thus needed British and French involvement. See Kennedy, *Anglo-German Antagonism*, p. 260.
44. Woolf, *Bagdad Railroad*, pp. 24–8.
45. Ibid., p. 64.
46. Ibid.
47. Ibid., pp. 64–5.
48. Ibid., pp. 65–6.
49. Ibid., p. 64.
50. Ibid., p. 9.

8

Military Spending and Regional Trade:
Six Exploratory Models

This chapter presents six exploratory models that make use of trade data by region. As indicated in the last two chapters, better models might be estimated with trade variables that reflect regional or commodity-wide breakdowns. Fortunately, most of the countries in this study have adequate data along these lines to estimate such models. The data do vary according to sample size and there are a few cases where the data are inadequate.

The major problem in estimating these models is one of guidance. While the arguments outlined in earlier chapters might provide general guidance on specifying a model, and the detailed discussion of each state's behaviour might also provide some guidance, the truth is that considerable differences across countries could exist in the data with no obvious indications as to why that might be. Specific policy analysis might produce some clarity in these cases, but even this is no guarantee. Before discussing the particulars of the models, then, I will note several important points that should condition how the reader views the models.

First, only six models were estimated: three army and three navy models. The British, French, and US army and navy models in Chapter 4 provide the basis for the six models below. The rest of the countries were not estimated for different reasons. Germany and Japan have the smallest sample of regional trade data available (both are from 1880 to 1913), and the Japanese data have some missing years. Italy and Russia do have more years of regional trade data to be included, but there are some problems. With Italy there are some years of trade with Asia that were zero (1870–77), although this did not occur before or since. These zero values were reported in the early editions of *Annuario Statistico Italiano* (that is, no values reported for Asian countries during these years in the tables on trade by origin and destination), but it is uncertain whether the values were actually zero or whether there was an interruption in reporting. This is not a serious problem for Italy, but it makes the Asian data less certain and the growth rates of the points 1869–70 and 1877–78 troublesome. Russian data also has missing years for Asia and Africa, which may or may not be legitimately zero, and the regional trade reporting generally stops in the year 1906.

Britain, France, and the US have the least troublesome regional trade data. There is a problem with the regional quantities for Oceania in the French data and I have decided to exclude Oceania as a variable for consideration from the models below. There were several missing years for the Oceania data for France, although the total amount of Oceania trade here was very small. For some of the earlier years available, the values were under one million francs. Thus the category was excluded altogether. Oceania is included in the colonial category for Britain, however, and so there was no attempt to exclude it. Colonial trade for Britain is of general interest here.

There is one point of inconsistency. French colonial trade was generally not distinguished from the totals from 1868 to 1874. French colonial trade is an important category that I am very interested in including in the French models (if it enters significantly) in order to compare it with the British. Given that the amount of trade to Oceania for several years after 1874 was quite tiny, I used an estimate of French colonial trade in the period 1868–74 based upon subtracting the imports and exports of each of the remaining regions from total imports and exports. The remainder includes colonial and Oceania trade, with the Oceania part likely being very small. The estimates are also very similar in magnitude to the colonial trade values in the remaining years of the 1870s. The remaining French colonial trade data from 1875 to 1913 are as the data record reports.

Another point to note is that the trade by commodity group is not used for the models below. My choice was to use either regional or commodity trade in the models, but not both. Including both would generate severe collinearity given that the two sets of trade data sum to the same amount. Separate models with regional and commodity group trade would also needlessly duplicate substantially similar results. The best of all data would be commodity group trade by region, but this information is generally not available. There are individual commodities by origin and destination readily available, but not for all commodities traded.

In addition, the only models estimated below are those with military variables as dependent variables. Models with the regional trade figures on the left-hand side are equally interesting, but given all of the regressors at hand, there would be more needless and probably less illuminating multiplication of models, each with the same set of regressors in them. New regressors, particularly those related to a particular region, would probably be needed for such models as well.

The most important point to note about the models below is that there is a degree of opportunism in the way that I built them, which may draw some criticism. The specification for the army and navy models of each country in Chapter 4 was the starting point. The aggregate trade variables were removed and the regional import and export values were put in their place. The resulting models reflect two important features. One is that the trade variables were tested with and without lags and included when they made a contribution to the model. Thus a specific regional trade figure would be excluded when it made no contribution to the model. In the French cases, I have restricted the sample to 1874–1913 in order to exclude the extreme army values during the Franco–Prussian War and to test French spending for relationships with German and Italian military spending terms as well. This also allows me to avoid using all but the last year (1874) of the estimates for French colonial trade.

Second, the degree of multicollinearity in the models was a potential problem. To cut down on this problem, I chose to combine the regional trade figures when appropriate. I would combine the regional trade variables when each variable had a similar influence on the dependent variable (that is, the same sign and similar magnitudes on the coefficients) and when either no change in any of the variables was detected or the same type of change in each was detected with the use of dummy variables. In the British army model below, for example, imports from South and Central America are combined with colonial imports. While the reader may be critical of this decision, it is not as unreasonable as might at first appear. If all of the regional trade data for a country were added up, the result would equal the total trade figures. There is no conceptual problem, then, in summing a few regional trade figures while leaving others separate. As long as the signs and magnitudes on the coefficients for the individual regional trade variables are similar, including them as a sum serves to reduce multicollinearity while posing no conceptual problems.

Finally all of the trade variables used (defined below) were prepared in an identical manner to the aggregate import and export figures used in Chapter 4. Each was deflated with the WPI for each country, then made a percentage of national income, and then the percentage change of that measure was taken. In the cases where regional trade figures were combined, the values as percentages of national income were added first and the percentage changes were then taken (that is, the percentage change of a sum was taken, rather than the sum of percentage changes).

DEFINITION OF TRADE VARIABLES

All non-trade variables in the models below are as defined in Chapter 4. There are three dependent variables for army spending and three for navy spending, which are the same as those used in Chapter 4. BRA_t and BRN_t are the growth rates of British army and navy spending as percentages of national income, for example, with the French and US variables being defined similarly. Abbreviations are also used in the models for the regional trade variables. Generally NA = North America, SA = South and Central America, AS = Asia, AF = Africa, WE = Western Europe, EE = Eastern Europe, EU = Europe, and CO = Colonies and the subscripts t and t-1 refer to unlagged and lagged values respectively.

The following terms refer to imports from and exports to regions in the British, French, and US models. All have been made percentages of national income and the percentage changes of these measures have been taken.

British models

ASSAE = Asian + South (and Central) American exports
COE = Colonial exports
EEASI = East European and Asian imports
NAE = North American exports
SACOI = South (and Central) American + colonial imports
WEASE = West European and Asian exports
WEE = West European exports

French models

AFE = African exports
ASI = Asian imports
EEASAFCOI = East European + Asian + African + colonial imports
NACOI = North American + colonial imports
NAE = North American exports
NASACOE = North American + South (and Central) American + colonial exports
WEE = West European exports
WEI = West European imports

US models

AFE = African exports
AME = American exports (all of the Americas)

AMI = American imports (all of the Americas)
ASE = Asian exports
ASI = Asian imports
EUAMAFI = European + American + African imports (all of Europe)
EUAME = European and American exports (all of Europe and the Americas)
EUASE = European and Asian exports (all of Europe)
EUASI = European and Asian imports (all of Europe)

Because the trade terms are defined differently for each model, tabular presentation is inefficient. Thus each model is presented in equation form below. Finally, the discussion below will be confined to the commercial terms in the models only.

THE ARMY MODELS

Each of the army models below indicate variations in how the commercial terms relate to army spending. With the British army model, South and Central American and colonial imports (SACOI) and colonial exports (COE) enter lagged and negatively, though weakly in both cases. East European and Asian imports (EEASI) are positive, though weak. The conspicuous strength in the British army model is West European and Asian exports (WEASE), which enters strongly and positively. Both regional trade values also change in the relationship to army spending after 1889. The dummy D1889 takes the value of 1 from 1857 to 1889 and 0 afterwards. The slope dummy coefficient for WEASE indicates that the relationship between these regional trade figures and army spending was weakly positive up to 1889 (the sum of the two coefficients is 0.329). From 1890 onward, however, the value is strongly positive.

The strongest positive term, then, involves areas that accounted for the largest single portion of British trade (Western Europe, see Chapter 6) and regions that involved considerable rivalry (both Western Europe and Asia). The rivalry issues of Britain in Asia do not appear to be conspicuously different from those in Africa, except perhaps for the presence of India, however, which was the focal point of the Empire. It is possible that rivalry issues in Asia were more important to Britain owing to the centrality of India and the fact that Russia, Japan, and perhaps even the United States were the most relevant rivals of Britain in Asia. But this is unclear.

$$BRA_t = 4.316 - 0.5891SACOI_{t-1} + 0.383EEASI_t + 2.122WEASE_{t-1} - 0.463COE_{t-1}$$
$$(-1.522) \qquad (1.882) \qquad (3.346) \qquad (-1.487)$$

$$+ 0.857BRC_t + 0.466NAVY_t - 8.292CON_{t-1} + 22.73WAR1_t + 0.942D1889$$
$$(2.351) \qquad (1.981) \qquad (-1.519) \qquad (2.322) \qquad (0.139)$$

$$- 1.793D1889*WEASE_{t-1} + 0.283AR(1)$$
$$(-2.052) \qquad (1.612)$$

Adj. R^2 = 0.456
DW = 1.977
Period: 1857–1913
N = 57

The French army model also shows mixed results, although all trade terms enter the model significantly. Most of the trade terms are negative, although the conspicuously positive case is imports from western Europe (WEI) in both unlagged and lagged forms. Lagged imports from North America and colonies (NACOI) and those from Asia (ASI), as well as exports to Africa (AFE) and lagged exports to North America (NAE) all enter negatively and significantly. The negative relations, then, involve trade that amounts to the smaller fraction of French regional trade (see Chapter 6). The positive import terms are both the major area of imports (western Europe) and the area where all of France's rivals were located (Britain, Germany, Italy). The rest of the world was a smaller portion of total French trade and more peripheral to French rivalry issues.

$$FRA_t = 6.83 + 0.285WEI_t + 0.642WEI_{t-1} - 0.15NACOI_{t-1} - 0.223ASI_{t-1} - 0.154NAE_{t-1}$$
$$(2.673) \qquad (6.719) \qquad (-3.722) \qquad (-5.001) \qquad (-4.691)$$

$$- 0.154AFE_t + 0.215FRC_t - 4.826CON_{t-1} - 2.277WAR2_t + 0.107GRN_{t-1} + 0.286ITA_{t-1}$$
$$(-3.772) \qquad (2.418) \qquad (-3.365) \qquad (-1.459) \qquad (2.576) \qquad (3.76)$$

$$- 0.294ITN_{t-1} - 0.507GNP_t - 0.202GOV_{t-1}$$
$$(-4.958) \qquad (-3.468) \qquad (-1.82)$$

Adj. R^2 = 0.762
DW = 1.943
Period: 1874–1913
N = 40

All of the trade terms in the US army model, except for one, initially enter negatively, although three of them indicate a change. The exception is imports from Asia (ASI), which is insignificant (though positive). This term becomes strongly significant and positive, however, from 1898 onward, as indicated by the slope dummy $D1898*ASI_{t-1}$. Exports to Africa (AFE) also enter insignificantly, though they become significant and positive from 1898 onward ($D1898*AFE_t$). The last trade term to undergo a change is exports to the Americas (AME), which initially enter negatively, but become positive during times of conflict (CON_t*AME_t).

In the US army case, then, it appears that most of the trade terms are negatively related to army spending, but several become positive during times of conflict and/or rivalry. The period since 1898 is generally one of greater rivalry than beforehand.

$$USA_t = -3.744 - 1.137AMI_{t-1} - 0.592EUASI_t + 0.2ASI_{t-1} - 0.509EUASE_{t-1} - 0.064AFE_t$$
$$(-3.579) \qquad (-3.464) \qquad (0.779) \qquad (-2.612) \qquad (-0.828)$$

$$-0.759AME_t + 0.667USN_{t-1} - 0.605GOV_{t-1} - 0.242BRA_t + 68.537WAR2_t - 4.987D1898$$
$$(-1.745) \qquad (4.018) \qquad (-1.817) \qquad (-2.41) \qquad (4.678) \qquad (-1.103)$$

$$+ 1.087D1898*ASI_{t-1} + 2.471CON_t + 1.209CON_t*AME_t + 0.475D1898*AFE_t$$
$$(2.729) \qquad (0.397) \qquad (2.273) \qquad (2.248)$$

Adj. R^2 = 0.805
DW = 2.176
Period: 1868–1913
N = 46

THE NAVY MODELS

The navy models show similar, though not identical, patterns to the army models. In the British navy model, imports from South and Central America and the colonies (SACOI) enter negatively, as do lagged exports to North America (NAE). Lagged exports to Asia and South and Central America (ASSAE), however, are positive. The case of exports to Western Europe (WEE) indicate a change, where they are positively related to navy spending up to 1881 and become insignificantly negative from 1882 onward, as indicated by the slope dummy $D1882*WEE_t$ (the sum of the two coefficients is –0.077). D1882 takes the value of 1 from 1882 to 1913 and 0 beforehand.

In the British army model above, exports to western Europe and Asia were strong and positive during the period of rivalry and insignificant beforehand. With navy spending, however, it appears to be the opposite with west European exports.

$$\text{BRN}_t = 10.906 - 0.334\text{SACOI}_t + 1.138\text{WEE}_t - 1.215\text{D1882*WEE}_t - 0.075\text{NAE}_{t-1}$$
$$\quad\quad (-2.056) \quad\quad (4.422) \quad\quad\quad (-4.376) \quad\quad\quad\quad (-1.969)$$

$$+ 0.208\text{ASSAE}_{t-1} - 10.217\text{WAR2}_t - 0.081\text{FRA}_t + 0.608\text{ARMY}_t + 2.102\text{D1882}$$
$$\quad (2.403) \quad\quad\quad (-3.988) \quad\quad\quad (-2.857) \quad\quad (5.136) \quad\quad\quad (0.855)$$

$$- 0.682\text{D1882*ARMY}_t + 7.324\text{WAR1}_t - 1.174\text{MERC}_t + 0.14\text{BRC}_t + 0.38\text{AR(1)}$$
$$\quad (-4.892) \quad\quad\quad\quad (2.301) \quad\quad\quad (-2.328) \quad\quad (1.117) \quad\quad (2.716)$$

Adj. R^2 = 0.751
DW = 1.989
Period: 1857–1913
N = 57

The French navy model again shows that the positive trade term is imports from western Europe (WEI), whereas lagged exports to western Europe (WEE) and the trade terms of other regions are negative. Most of the French trade terms had such a similarity in how they related to navy spending that several could be combined. EEASAFCOI$_t$, for example, reflects imports from eastern Europe, Asia, Africa and the colonies.

$$\text{FRN}_t = -3.208 - 0.476\text{WEE}_{t-1} - 0.414\text{EEASAFCOI}_t + 0.729\text{WEI}_t - 0.606\text{NASACOE}_t$$
$$\quad\quad\quad (-3.255) \quad\quad\quad (-3.91) \quad\quad\quad\quad (4.047) \quad\quad\quad (-6.44)$$

$$- 0.405\text{BRN}_{t-1} + 10.823\text{WAR2}_t - 0.634\text{GNP}_t + 1.02\text{MERC}_{t-1} + 0.174\text{GRN}_{t-1}$$
$$\quad (-3.397) \quad\quad\quad (4.272) \quad\quad\quad (-2.665) \quad\quad (3.476) \quad\quad\quad (2.216)$$

$$+ 0.337\text{GOV}_{t-1} + 0.957\text{FRA}_{t-1} - 1.405\text{WAR2}_t\text{*FRA}_{t-1} + 0.16\text{FRC}_t + 0.801\text{AR(1)}$$
$$\quad (2.076) \quad\quad\quad (2.43) \quad\quad\quad\quad (-3.329) \quad\quad\quad\quad (1.005) \quad\quad (6.018)$$

Adj. R^2 = 0.729
DW = 1.743
Period: 1875–1913
N = 39

Finally, the US navy model shows Asian imports (ASI) entering positively, but weakly, European and American exports (EUAME) entering positively and significantly, and lagged Asian exports (ASE) entering negatively and significantly. The term EUAMAFI (European, American, and African imports) undergoes a change. The term enters strongly and negatively, but becomes flatter (though still negative) during times of conflict, as the slope dummy CON$_t$*EUAMAFI$_t$ indicates. If the US navy acted as a support to exports, as earlier naval

literature suggests (see Chapter 1), then this support appears to have
been concentrated on Europe and the Americas, which were the
largest destinations for US exports at the time.

$$\text{USN}_t = -3.609 + 0.27\text{ASI}_t - 0.176\text{ASE}_{t-1} + 0.355\text{EUAME}_t - 2.479\text{EUAMAFI}_t$$
$$(1.472)(-2.908)(2.39)(-8.47)$$

$$+ 0.262\text{USC}_{t-1} - 0.323\text{GNP}_{t-1} - 0.295\text{BRM}_t + 3.699\text{MERC}_t + 4.456\text{CON}_t$$
$$(1.459)(-1.55)(-3.894)(7.541)(1.301)$$

$$+ 1.34\text{CON}_t*\text{EUAMAFI}_t - 5.476\text{D}1898 - 0.693\text{AR}(1)$$
$$(5.139)(-2.336)(-6.166)$$

Adj. R^2 = 0.747
DW = 2.006
Period: 1869–1913
N = 45

CONCLUSION

The models above suggest that there is more complexity in how
military spending and trade relate than the aggregate trade terms in
the models of Chapter 4 indicate. What is immediately interesting
about the above models is that the positive terms for trade generally
involve trade with the major regions of the world, although this is not
exclusively true. Some of the trade terms with western Europe were
also negative and a few trade terms to other regions were positive.
British navy spending is positively related to exports to Asia and South
and Central America, for example, which are not the major portions
of British regional trade. There are also some positive terms with other
regions in the US models, especially with the army model. It is
generally true, however, that the major regional trade flows (such as
western Europe) offer most of the positive trade terms.

There are two key points to note here. One is that, if
interdependence theory offers an accurate guide to how military
power and commerce relate, then why are the negative trade terms
concentrated mostly in the regions outside of the major economies?
Why are both colonial imports and exports negatively related to British
army spending and colonial imports negatively related to British navy
spending? Was there a process at work with British colonies where, as
their trade with Britain increased, conflict with Britain fell, which
would have led military spending to fall?

The negative signs about British colonial trade are not necessarily intelligible from the perspective advanced here either. Given British dependence on its colonial imports (as indicated by Table 6.6), we might have expected a positive relationship. Even a radical point of view, which would argue for an exploitation scenario, would lead to an expectation of a positive relationship between military spending and colonial trade. It may very well be that the term for colonial imports in the British model reflects the net effects of the relationship, since colonial trade was geographically dispersed. If we broke British colonial trade into its proper regions, it is likely that each component would be small. It might be that each regional component to colonial trade was more related to what was effecting the non-colonial trade with those regions.

We can ask similar questions about the other trade terms. Why are so many trade terms negative if military spending and commerce are positively related? And why are most of the positive terms in areas that have the most trade and most of the negative terms in areas that have the smaller portions of trade if interdependence theory is an accurate guide?

There are two points to keep in mind in addressing the above questions. First, the six models above are examined alone. There are no corresponding trade models to compare the military models with, for reasons addressed above. This implies that, while the above results are interesting and suggestive, we cannot be certain of the full story here. It could very well be that some of the negative trade terms above reflect the cases argued for in Chapter 3 where a negative term combined with a positive term indicate a positive overall relationship, but we cannot know this. A correct trade model of these regional terms would certainly require additional regressors, ones that are perhaps specific to conditions in those regions. We do know that some of the terms above are indeed negative, which implies an inverse relationship.

It does not appear likely at face value that the negative relationships reflect the argument that as trade expands the military loses its role and thus declines. I say this because the regions that contain most of the negative terms were the subject of very aggressive military behaviour of the Great Powers for a long time. We do not see Great Power military behaviour declining, for example, as their trade with Africa grew because expanding trade gave countries an incentive to cooperate. African countries were subjected to Western colonial control, where no decision-making on the part of colonized countries entered into the issue. Strangely, characterizations of the pre-First World War period as an era of liberalism tend to ignore the fact that this liberalism also came with predatory mercantilist behaviour regarding colonized territory.

A possible partial explanation for these negative terms is that there could have been a trade-off between military spending proper and military spending for specifically colonial purposes. British colonial military expansion may have been positively related to Britain's colonial trade, for example, and this colonial military expansion may have been at the expense of British army and navy spending proper. This is not a terribly convincing explanation and would certainly need to be tested, but some trade-off could have existed between the military spending of a state, on the one hand, and its local military spending in Africa, Asia, and elsewhere, on the other.

It may be more likely that trade itself was driven down by military behaviour, and perhaps military rivalry among the Great Powers themselves, which would be the other side to the interdependence view. Thus rather than arguing that increasing trade causes military power to fall, we might argue the opposite line of causality: that military expansion (and perhaps rivalry) adversely affected Great Power trade to these regions. If this were true, then we might discover that the types of military activities conducted by these states in Asia, Africa, colonies, and in other areas where the trade flows were generally smaller were largely coercive, intrusive, and perhaps even punitive in nature. Punitive actions against local commerce or even a localized disruption to commerce would, for example, injure trade flows. There are still two problems with this line of reasoning. First, military spending is the dependent variable in the above models and thus does not reflect this argument. Second, why did military expansion not lead to the same results everywhere?

The second issue noted above is that most of the positive terms are also in regions (western Europe) where the majority of Great Power rivalry occurred. Why do we not see positive terms with North American trade in the British and French models? If rivalry is the issue, of course, then the United States was not really a contender until the latter part of the period.

Could it be that the positive relationship between military power and trade existed when there was an overall climate of military rivalry, which may have called forth a military role to protect commerce? The reasoning here might be that the rivalry and competition among the major states produced a military role to protect and advance trade (that is, the protective and regulative functions), but in areas where Western colonial expansion prevailed, the rivalry was of a different character. There was no real territorial expansion in Europe itself during the time period, whereas Africa, Asia, and elsewhere saw much expansion. In terms of sheer number, there were far more colonial wars than major ones in the period as well. It is possible that Great Power rivalry in regions outside of Europe or in regions where trade flows were smaller (not to mention conflicts between these states and local peoples) exerted a different influence on the relationship than did rivalry in Europe proper or in regions where trade flows were larger because there was a real difference in the types of military activities associated with these different trade flows.

The term containing west European exports in the British army model (with Asian exports) becomes strongly positive from 1890 onward, for example, although the positive west European terms in the other models do not indicate this type of change. There are terms in the US army model, however, that become positive during times of conflict, but these include other regions of the world.

Conclusion

This book has analysed the interaction between military power and commerce among the Great Powers prior to the First World War. There are two clear, but not so easy to understand, results in the regression models above. One is that military spending and trade are positively related in some cases and the other result is that military spending and trade are negatively related in other cases. All of the results in this book are complicated, however, and can be broken roughly into four groups. While the evidence produced offers rich information about how military power and commerce were related among the Great Powers, how these relationships varied among them and how conflict and rivalry interacted with their trade dependence, there are more questions about these relationships than clear answers. Each group of results provides some insight and some guidance with respect to the questions posed in the beginning of this book, but the clear injunction from the evidence is to continue this research programme.

The first set of results concerns the evidence reflected in the 28 regression models in Chapter 4. It was argued that, while the results were mixed, most of them appeared to support a direct relationship between military power and commerce. It is not clear from these results, however, why there are differences both across countries and in the models of single countries, nor are patterns evident in these differences that might offer explanations. While some of these results coincide consistently with state policies, others do not. The strong and positive connection between the US navy and exports, for example, is consistent with the export orientation of the American state and with American naval ideas on supporting exports. Britain's focus on its import vulnerabilities and the role of the British navy in protecting its trade, however, unexpectedly coincides with mixed results that tend to suggest a negative connection between the navy and imports.

We could accept the idea that the results in Chapter 4 provide support for both arguments outlined in Chapters 2 and 3. Thus far I have presented the idea that military power and commerce are directly related in contrast to the argument that they are inversely related as if they were necessarily mutually exclusive across all countries. Is it possible that the relationship could be direct with some countries and inverse with others, or even direct with one branch of the military or trade indicator and inverse with others? If so, then there is need of an explanation for why one process would operate on one country or set of indicators (leading to a direct relationship) and another process would operate on another country or set of indicators (leading to an inverse relationship). The toughest cases here would be those where there are mixed results within a single country's data.

If such an explanation is possible, it is likely to be rooted in deeper details about military and commercial behaviour. Recalling the numerous types of connections between military power and commerce outlined in Chapter 3, there could be wide variations in state behaviour here. The nature and location of threats vary, as do the magnitudes, types, and locations of trade dependence. The deeper the detail about military and commercial behaviour, the more complex the patterns could be of military–commercial interactions. This would likely modify either point of view above and perhaps allow for more intricate hypotheses about relationships. All the literature in Chapters 1 and 2 is quite general in nature. While many of the connections between military power and commerce are established in the navalist literature, for example, they remain general, descriptive characteristics of naval behaviour. The argument in Chapter 3 tried to develop these connections further, but the intricacies of the connections between the variables are clearly more complicated than this argument or the alternative suggest.

The argument that the growth in economic interdependence leads to a decline in military power, for example, is cast in general terms, whereas we could envision a situation where a state actively protects and supports trade in one region, while its military role in another region declines while its trade expands there. It is probably more likely, especially in the period before the First World War, that we would find a case where a state protects and supports its trade in one region while its military behaviour in another region is aggressive and disruptive enough that it adversely affects trade, which would also account for a negative relationship (though in a different way from that suggested by the interdependence argument).

The second set of results concerns an attempt to find at least some of these deeper details. The most potentially telling information from Chapter 6 concerns the regional and commodity group breakdowns in trade for each country. Aside from the fact that rival states were also among each other's best trade partners (as indicated by the data in

Chapter 5), each set of regional and commodity group trade data indicated areas of pronounced dependence for each country as well as a general pattern of change described by increasingly global trade patterns as 1913 approached. A key issue here is whether we could match the major and minor areas of trade dependence with different types of military behaviours. The discussion of Great Power behaviour that accompanied the trade data shed some light on the matter, but the possibilities here are still speculative in nature. While it may be true that the geographic distribution of a country's trade acts as a good indicator of areas that are most important to a country, it is not exactly clear that there were systematic differences in military behaviour along these lines, though this possibility seems likely.

The main speculation here was that the major trade flows, which mostly occurred in proximity to the Great Powers, required the most protection due to increased vulnerability, which itself was due to rivalry behaviour and the larger magnitudes of these trade flows. Smaller trade flows, which were to and from different regions, may have been less protected, subject to local disruption, and may even have been advanced through force of arms (which was certainly true in some cases). The implication of this line of reasoning is to test models with regional or commodity group breakdowns rather than aggregate trade data.

The third group of results is in Chapter 7 and is focused on describing the extent to which the trade of two states that were known to be in rivalry stood in opposition to each other. My concern here was to uncover any asymmetries in mutual dependence that might be bound up with rivalry behaviour. Generally, despite the complaints heard at the time, the mutual import dependence levels of two rivals were not in opposition. The Germans were not gaining in the British import market while the British lost in the German market. While German trade dependence on Britain did decrease over the years, as was true of most of the others, there was not a corresponding increase in British dependence on Germany.

There did appear to be such asymmetries, however, when it came to the trade of the two rivals in a third country market. This type of focus is particularly interesting because the shifting trade dependence of the third country might coincide with the third country's alliance with one of the rivals (as appears to be evident with Italy) or, if the third country was itself a focal point of rivalry, the trade of the two rivals in the third country market could itself become a tool of rivalry. In the Italian case, for example, we can clearly relate French–Italian conflict to the decline in French–Italian trade, while the increase in German–Italian trade may be linked to the Triple Alliance (which itself was directed against France and was related to both French–Italian and French–German conflict).

Even in the import markets of the other states in this study, how-ever, there appeared to be a general opposition between the positions of Germany, Japan and the United States against Britain and France. The overall picture one gets is that the emerging newcomers were advancing in trade at the expense of the older states in third country markets. Much more could be done with trade interdependence data, but the above results present good descriptive indication that the process of rivalry did have implications for trade, though not in a straightforward way.

The last group of results concerns the regression models of Chapter 8, where regional trade data were used in place of aggregate trade data. While army and navy spending were the only dependent variables here and only three countries were included, there are some provocative, if tentative, results. The most interesting contrast is that most of the positive terms for the trade variables involve the major trade regions and that most of the negative trade terms are with the smaller trade regions. While this is not perfectly true, it does appear to be a pattern in the output. The speculation in Chapter 8 about why this output varies the way it does might prove interesting, but the earlier suspicion that different types of military behaviour may have occurred with different trade flows is probably correct, where protective and regulative behaviour would mostly accompany the major arteries of commerce and punitive, coercive and intrusive behaviour would mostly accompany the smaller trade flows.

It appears unconvincing to assert that the interdependence argument operates with small amounts of trade to a distant region, while a direct relationship pertains with the major arteries of trade. While direct relationships between military spending and the major arteries of trade make sense in terms of the argument in Chapter 3, why would interdependence cause the role of military power to decline with the smaller trade flows and not the major trade flows? The reverse pattern might have been easier to argue – that inter-dependence was operating in the major trade flows and a direct relationship in the minor ones, but that is not the pattern we have in Chapter 8. As stated in the conclusion to Chapter 8, however, a more consistent story might be that the aggressive military behaviour of the Great Powers in distant regions drove trade to these regions downward, which might account for the negative association, but this cannot be inferred from the six models themselves due to the fact that military spending is the dependent variable in all of them.

The obvious direction for future research on these relationships among the Great Powers is towards highly detailed historical data. In particular, more specific military variables are needed in conjunction with more detailed trade data. There are some more detailed military measures readily available, such as data on colonial military spending and colonial military manpower, but other measures are more difficult to come by. Constructing a data set on military actions to particular regions or countries for this time period would be valuable, though difficult. There are some examples of historical data on the frequency of military access, but they are generally not complete. The best available is military personnel and warship movements through the Suez Canal, but these data are patchy when collected by country. If more specific military measures could be constructed and analysed in conjunction with equally specific trade and conflict measures, then a more revealing story might emerge.

It is generally easier to acquire more detailed trade data than military data. While getting data on commodity groups by origin and destination might prove impossible, there are individual commodities available by origin and destination. There are also highly detailed trade data on very specific locations over a period of time as well as a great wealth of colonial trade statistics. It is even relatively easy to acquire commodity trade by quantity and value separately, such that one could make accurate price indexes for trade.

While more detailed data is likely to deepen our understanding of the connections between military power and commerce among the Great Powers, it is also possible, even likely, that the statistical results of any models would vary based upon how the data were prepared and how the models were specified. The data used here are time series. All but the exceptions noted have been made percentages of national income and, on all of the data, percentage changes have been taken. If I had used the Hodrick-Prescott filter to estimate the trend and then de-trended the data accordingly, for example, the results may have been different and even less complicated. I chose growth rates because they are intuitive and they do achieve the goal of making the data stationary because the numerator in the growth rate is the first-difference of the series.

Cross-sectional data would also probably produce different results. There is no issue of a trend in cross-sectional data. It is thus common for the data points in a cross-sectional model to be in levels form. If cross-sectional models were estimated here, where data were gathered across a handful of states for a single year or even two or three years, then the results might be less complicated than those from percentage changes. There are not enough Great Powers to estimate such a model with a single year, of course. An earlier article that I wrote used cross-sectional data in the postwar period. While the models were much simpler than those in this book, the results offer less complexity.[1]

The most interesting step to take for research here is to focus on the period after the Second World War. From a data point of view, there are many time series and cross-sectional data sets that could be collected. There are also a greater variety of military measures to choose from. Detailed military spending breakdowns, military manpower, naval tonnage and other military equipment measures, and even frequency of access information are available widely. On this last measure, for example, US data on the number of military personnel by branch who are stationed in various parts of the world are available over most of the Cold War period.

From a substantive point of view, however, little is known about how military behaviour and commercial behaviour interact in most of the countries in the world today. We can take a cursory look at US behaviour and find many examples, but what about the small and medium-sized countries of the world? Moreover, while the United States has a plethora of connections between military power and commerce, none of these connections reflect the aggressive and acquisitive uses of military power that were common practice among the Great Powers. The defensive uses of US military power (as with protecting trade routes) and the punitive uses (as with embargoes) are evident, but the more aggressive uses of military power for commercial ends are absent.

Today's major states do not engage in this type of activity. We are apt to think of such activity as being outmoded by some aspect of modernity or just being plain old-fashioned. I think that smaller states, especially those that are ambitious, are likely to engage in these behaviours on a smaller scale. What do we know of all of the states in Africa, for example? Interactions among these states in areas of trade and military power are hard to come by because they are never present in the literature. We can ask the same question of other regions. What of Chinese naval behaviour in the South China Sea? While oil resources are the crucial issue there, how do Chinese naval movements and China's aggressive ambitions relate (if at all) to Chinese trade flows there? I am strongly interested in building a data set on such activity of states that are usually left out of the question. The present study has focused on Great Powers, but the rest of the world may yield interesting information, especially today.

NOTE

1. Michael P. Gerace, 'State Interests, Military Power and International Commerce: Some Cross-National Evidence', *Geopolitics* 5/1 (Summer 2001), pp. 101–24.

APPENDIX 1

A Note on Data Sources and Problems

The chief sources of statistical material in this study were the statistical series of the various governments, although I have also used some secondary works. I relied wholly on secondary materials for the traditional description and analysis portions of the work.

SOURCE MATERIAL

I pursued several avenues for obtaining the statistical data in this study. The first was to search through the national statistical series of each country. Most countries have a yearly publication that is akin to the *Annuaire Statistique de la France*. Fortunately, I had access to the British, French, German, Italian, Japanese, Russian, and American series going back to their first issues. Boston Public Library actually has the series of all of the above countries, except for Russia, from their first issues up to the time when the series ended or up to the present. Boston Public Library even has the Austro-Hungarian Empire's series, which ended in 1918. In addition, I used other government sources to fill gaps in the information left by the national series. The majority of the data, however, were retrieved from each national series. The exceptions are noted below.

All of these official statistical series are identical in their formats, except for a few differences. The German series, for example, aggregated trade by commodity in the same way that all the others had (agriculture, raw materials for industry, semi-manufactures and finished manufactures) for only a few years. The German commodity trade had to be obtained from Walther G. Hoffmann, *Das Wachstum der Deutschen Wirtschaft seit der Mitte des 19 Jahrhunderts* (Berlin: Springer-Verlag, 1965). Germany also did not distinguish trade by origin and destination before 1880, and distinguished trade by mode of transport for only a few years.

The British *Statistical Tables for Principal and Other Foreign Countries,* which was accessed through Sessional Papers for the House of Commons, was especially useful (the series ran from 1860 to 1912). Specifically, *Statistical Tables* allowed me to acquire Russian trade by origin and destination. The Russian series, *Statistika Rossiiskoi Imperii,* reported Russian trade by commodity group, but was very scanty on trade by origin and destination. Russian military expenditures and customs revenue were also available in both *Statistika Rossiiskoi* and *Statistical Tables,* which allowed for some cross-referencing, though Russian military expenditures for 1912 and 1913 were not available in these two series. I decided instead to use the military spending data reported in Pavel A. Khromov, *Ekonomicheskoe Razvitie Rossii v XIX i XX Vekakh, 1899-1917* (Moscow: Gospolitizdat, 1950). These data are identical to that reported in the imperial series, except that they are less rounded, and Khromov reports extraordinary military expenditures comprehensively as well.

I was also able to use *Statistical Tables* to fill gaps in the French data. The *Annuaire Statistique de la France* only reports trade by origin and destination back to 1875, while *Statistical Tables* allowed me to fill in these numbers back to 1870. The *Annuaire Statistique de la France* also only reports French military expenditures back to 1868 (indeed later editions report them back only to 1871 in historical tables – Résumé Retrospectif). The French series starts in 1878 (like the Italian series), and even the first edition reports military expenditures back only to 1868. The British *Statistical Tables* had French revenues and expenditures by detailed category back to 1855 (with the exception of 1862, which seems to be generally unavailable).

The *Annuario Statistico Italiano,* which also starts in 1878, was remarkably complete. Like all the national series, the further back in time the issue, the more generous it was. The data reporting in all the national documents seems to get less generous in the twentieth century. The Italian series had data right back to 1861 on most items (otherwise 1862), and a considerable amount of data for earlier periods. Like the German and Japanese series, the Italian series reported continuous tables for naval ships (type, number, and tonnage) for a large number of years. Unfortunately, the other countries were not so generous with continuous naval tonnage. The British *Annual Abstracts of Statistics,* which starts in 1854, only reported naval ship and tonnage information for the interwar period. The modern issues of the British series all report naval manpower, but none of the issues in the British series do so for the pre-1913 period – although they continuously report army manpower. For continuous British naval tonnage and naval manpower, one would have to scour Sessional Papers for a large number of years.

Japanese statistics came from two main sources. The volume *Japan in the Beginning of the 20th Century*, published by the Japanese government in English, and the series *Résumé Statistique de l'Empire du Japon* (in both French and Japanese), which ran from 1886 to 1916, were immensely useful. Another series sponsored by the Japanese government, *The Japan Yearbook*, has useful interwar data, but is very scanty for the pre-1913 period. The British *Statistical Tables* periodically reported Japanese trade and military data, as well, but none of this was used.

With the United States, *Statistical Abstracts of the United States* are available from 1878 onward. While select individual statistics, such as military expenditures and customs revenue, can be obtained all the way back to the beginning of the period under study from earlier editions of *Statistical Abstracts*, trade by origin and destination is not available from the end of the Civil War into the late 1870s. There are other series available for the United States, which report trade data far back enough for this study, but the *Historical Statistics of the United States: Colonial Times to 1970* has trade already organized by region going all the way back to 1790, not to mention continuous data on commodity trade, government expenditures, and nearly every other relevant statistic for this study.

In short, the national series of each of the countries were a treasure trove of information. As noted, however, some of them left critical gaps in the information, which I was able to fill with other sources.

Several excellent secondary materials were also used to fill gaps (as well as cross-reference data). There were a few series by B. R. Mitchell that were invaluable. For Britain, there are three editions on British historical statistics (the latest being *British Historical Statistics*, 1988). The data in this series was as reliable as the national series and was used for all of British military expenditures. The *Annual Abstracts of Statistics* report detailed tables of expenditure, but sometimes the amounts reported for military expenditures included the cost of collecting the revenue and sometimes they did not. While the resulting inconsistencies are small, the Mitchell series appears to report the data consistently.

Other Mitchell series that were used were *European Historical Statistics: 1750-1975* and *International Historical Statistics: Europe, 1750–1988, International Historical Statistics: Africa and Asia,* and *International Historical Statistics: the Americas, 1750-1988*. In addition to cross-references provided by these series, I used the wholesale prices indexes in them when they were not available in the national series. In all the Mitchell series, there is a high degree of correspondence with the various national series on data reported.

A NOTE ON MILITARY EXPENDITURES

The military expenditures of these states, except for the United States, counted spending in two categories: ordinary and extraordinary expenditures. This was actually true for all categories of government spending. Thus total military expenditures are ordinary plus extraordinary expenditures. Ordinary expenditures were the planned amounts that were produced by the governments each year and the extraordinary amounts were unplanned amounts that were mostly due to crisis and war. It would seem that most secondary accounts of these military expenditure data use only the ordinary amounts. Ordinary military expenditures produce a smoother time series than should be the case because the main changes in spending due to crisis and war are left out of the data.

Germany, for example, had no war between 1872 and 1913 (excluding colonial involvements), but the cost of the Franco–Prussian War was a set of rolling army and navy expenditures that lasted until 1882. These amounts are entirely in the extraordinary category. The same is true of the other countries. With Russia, the Russo–Turkish War, the China Expedition and the last several years before the First World War all contain significant amounts of extraordinary expenditure.

The totals for army and navy spending used in this study, then, are both the ordinary and extraordinary amounts combined.

TRADE BY REGION AND COMMODITY GROUP

The trade by region was mostly aggregated by myself from trade tables by origin and destination. The major exception is the US regional data, which came from *Historical Statistics of the United States*, as noted. For the remaining cases, I aggregated the trade by region by examining the trade tables of each state for each of the years in the study. Two points bear noting.

First, estimates for trade (or any other statistic) would change with later editions of the series because the data were updated. If we were seeking a trade table for the year 1890, for example, then the series dated 1891 would contain the data. Most of the editions of the official statistical series reported trade by origin and destination for two years at a time. The 1891 edition would then have trade for 1889 and 1890. The following edition, 1892, would have trade tables for 1890 and 1891, with the 1890 values differing slightly from those in the earlier edition. In all cases, I used the latter estimate of trade by origin and destination by working backward in time with the tables. Thus the trade data used in this study reflect the most updated version of the data.

The second point to note is that the definitions of the regions (western Europe, North America, and so on) are very conventional. Sometimes the trade tables would segment the countries out by region and, on a few occasions, they would also add the trade for the region as well. Otherwise I would place the countries in their regions myself and add up the trade of all countries traded with in a particular region.

The American regional trade in *Historical Statistics* was already aggregated, but did not distinguish between western and eastern Europe and aggregated all Western Hemisphere trade into the category *the Americas.* With all other countries, the regional breakdowns were the same. British and French documents went to the trouble of distinguishing their colonial trade from the rest of the world as well, which made it very easy to separate out from their trade with the rest of the world. This does, of course, mean that the Asian, African, and South and Central American trade values in the British and French regional trade tables are absent of their colonial trade.

The commodity group trade was a similar story. Sometimes a commodity trade table segmented out the commodities into groups (and sometimes it even summed each group), otherwise I would segment the groups out myself among trade tables that listed imports and exports with each commodity traded by year (following the earlier examples) and sum the groups.

SPECIFIC PROBLEMS WITH THE DATA

As noted in the text, all data are in percentage change form (except for the dummy variables). For all government spending and trade variables (except for Russia and Japan), the data were first made percentages of national income and then percentage changes were calculated. There are a few problems to note about the resulting data.

First, French military spending for 1862 was simply not available. Neither the *Annuaire Statistique* nor the *Statistical Tables* report the value for that year. I have thus estimated the amount by simply taking the average of the values for 1861 and 1863.

Japanese military spending poses two problems. The first is that the extraordinary amounts for the Russo–Japanese War (1904–05) are not available for both branches of the military, although the ordinary amounts are. This absence produces a very noticeable dent in the series for these two years, where the values are much too low for 1904–05. I have thus estimated the extraordinary amounts for 1904 and 1905 as follows. First, I took the average of the total amount spent on the military for 1903 and 1906. Then I subtracted 1904's ordinary amount from this and considered the remainder to be an estimate of the extraordinary growth for 1904. Then I calculated the proportions of ordinary army and navy spending for 1904 by simply dividing the actual total ordinary amounts into the branches. I then multiplied the estimated extraordinary growth by these proportions to apportion the amount of extraordinary growth between the branches for 1904. Then I calculated the growth rate between 1903 and the new aggregate 1904 value and, on the basis of this proportion, I let 1905's total value grow by the same amount. I then subtracted the actual ordinary amount of 1905 from this new aggregate value for 1905, and considered the remainder to be the estimated extraordinary growth for 1905. I then apportioned this extraordinary amount to the army and navy based upon the proportions of ordinary army and navy spending of total ordinary spending for 1905. By estimating the values this way, I let the 1905 amount grow by exactly the same percentage as the 1904 value (with respect to the 1903 value). The average extraordinary amount between 1903 and 1906 is just the starting point.

The second problem concerns Japanese army data only. The growth rate of the series produces an exceedingly high amount for 1895 (during the Sino–Japanese War). The growth rate for total army spending in 1895 was about 385 per cent, whereas it was under 5 per cent for 1894 and 1.5 per cent for 1896. This outlier actually improved the army model, but probably had undue influence on the model and so was removed. The averages of the two growth rates for 1894 and 1896 respectively were used instead.

There were a few other cases, particularly with the regional trade data, where a single year produced a large outlier. In these cases, I generally did nothing if the model did not change appreciably with and without the outlier. Otherwise, I calculated the average amounts for the periods before and after the outlier.

APPENDIX 2

Specifications for Models in Chapter 4

The regression tables in Chapter 4 (Tables 4.1–4.4) may cause some confusion owing to the fact that sometimes the lags in the variables have been indicated in the tables and sometimes they have not. The reason for presenting the data in the tables in this way is simply one of convenience. While I have mentioned what variables are lagged and unlagged in the discussion of the models in Chapter 4, the full specifications of each model are presented below. I will merely list the variables that are in each model with their names (as defined) and the period (t or t-1) in an equation without, however, including coefficients or signs. The terms in the regressions in Chapter 8 are fully explained there.

ARMY MODELS

Britain: 1854–1913
$ARMY_t$ = Constant, IMP_t, IMT_{t-1}, EXP_{t-1}, $CUST_t$, GNP_t, $NAVY_t$, CON_{t-1}, $WAR1_t$, D1889, D1889*EXP_{t-1}, AR(1)

France: 1858–1913
$ARMY_t$ = Constant, IMP_t, EXP_{t-1}, $CUST_t$, $BRITNAVY_t$, GNP_t, GOV_t, $WAR1_t$, CON_{t-1}, $WAR2_{t-1}$, CON_{t-1}*IMP_t, AR(1)

Germany: 1875–1913
$ARMY_t$ = Constant, IMP_t, EXP_t, $CUST_t$, $FRENCHMIL_{t-1}$, $RUSMIL_{t-1}$, CON_{t-1}, CON_{t-1}*$CUST_t$, D1894, AR(1)

Italy: 1865–1913
$ARMY_t$ = Constant, IMP_t, EXP_t, $NAVY_t$, CON_t, $WAR1_t$, GNP_{t-1}, GOV_t, AR(1)

Japan: 1875–1913

$ARMY_t$ = Constant, IMP_t, JPE_{t-1}, $RUSMIL_t$, $CUST_{t-1}$, $NAVY_t$, D1904, $D1904*CUST_{t-1}$, GOV_t, $WAR2_t$, AR(1)

Russia: 1864–1913

$ARMY_t$ = Constant, IMP_t, IMP_{t-1}, $CUST_{t-1}$, D1878, $D1878*NAVY_t$, $NAVY_t$, $D1878*IMP_t$, GOV_t, $D1878*CUST_{t-1}$, AR(1)

United States: 1869–1913

$ARMY_t$ = Constant, IMP_t, EXP_t, EXP_{t-1}, $CUST_{t-1}$, $NAVY_{t-1}$, $BRITNAVY_{t-1}$, GNP_{t-1}, GOV_{t-1}, D1898, $D1898*IMP_t$, AR(1)

NAVY MODELS

Britain: 1854–1913

$NAVY_t$ = Constant, IMP_t, EXP_{t-1}, $CUST_t$, $MERC_t$, $ARMY_t$, $WAR2_t$, $D1882*ARMY_t$, CON_{t-1}, $WAR2*IMP_t$, D1882, $CON_{t-1}*EXP_{t-1}$, GNP_{t-1}, AR(1)

France: 1857–1913

$NAVY_t$ = Constant, IMP_t, EXP_t, $CUST_{t-1}$, GOV_t, $WAR1_t$, $WAR2_t$, $BRITNAVY_{t-1}$, D1872, $D1872*ARMY_{t-1}$, $WAR1_t*EXP_t$, $ARMY_{t-1}$, $D1872*CUST_{t-1}$, $MERC_{t-1}$

Germany: 1874–1913

$NAVY_t$ = Constant, IMP_t, EXP_{t-1}, $CUST_t$, $WAR2_{t-1}$, GNP_t, D1882, $D1882*EXP_{t-1}$, $FRENCHARMY_t$, D1890, $D1890*CUST_t$, $MERC_{t-1}$

Italy: 1864–1913

$NAVY_t$ = Constant, IMP_t, IMP_{t-1}, $CUST_t$, $ARMY_t$, D1882, GOV_t, $MERC_{t-1}$

Japan: 1874–1913

$NAVY_t$ = Constant, IMP_t, CON_{t-1}, GOV_t, $MERC_t$, $ARMY_t$, D1895, $D1895*ARMY_t$, $D1895*IMP_t$

Russia: 1864–1913

$NAVY_t$ = Constant, IMP_{t-1}, EXP_t, CON_{t-1}, $WAR2_t$, $BRITNAVY_{t-1}$, $CON_{t-1}*IMP_{t-1}$, D1878, $D1878*EXP_t$, AR(1)

United States: 1869–1913

$NAVY_t$ = Constant, IMP_t, EXP_t, $CUST_{t-1}$, GNP_t, $BRITMIL_t$, $MERC_t$, CON_t, CON_t*IMP_t, D1898, AR(1)

IMPORT MODELS

Britain: 1854–1913
IMP_t = Constant, $ARMY_t$, $ARMY_{t-1}$, $NAVY_t$, $NAVY_{t-1}$, EXP_t, $CUST_t$, PD/PF_t, $WAR1_t$, CON_t, $WAR3_t$, CON_t*ARMY_t, $WAR3_t*NAVY_{t-1}$, GNP_t, AR(1)

France: 1857–1913
IMP_t = Constant, $ARMY_t$, $NAVY_{t-1}$, EXP_t, $CUST_t$, GNP_t, PD/PF_{t-1}, CON_t, $WAR1_{t-1}$, $MERC_t$

Germany: 1875–1913
IMP_t = Constant, $ARMY_{t-1}$, $CUST_t$, EXP_t, GNP_{t-1}, PD/PF_t, $NAVY_t$, D1890, D1890*$NAVY_t$, $MERC_t$, AR(1)

Italy: 1865–1913
IMP_t = Constant, $ARMY_t$, $ARMY_{t-1}$, $NAVY_t$, $NAVY_{t-1}$, EXP_t, $CUST_t$, CON_t, PD/PF_t, GNP_{t-1}, AR(1)

Japan: 1874–1913
IMP_t = Constant, $NAVY_{t-1}$, EXP_{t-1}, CON_t, $CUST_t$, PD/PF_t, $MERC_t$, AR(1)

Russia: 1864–1913
IMP_t = Constant, $ARMY_{t-1}$, EXP_{t-1}, $CUST_t$, D1878, D1878*$ARMY_{t-1}$, AR(1)

United States: 1869–1913
IMP_t = Constant, $ARMY_t$, $NAVYPROXY_t$, $CUST_t$, PD/PF_{t-1}, GNP_{t-1}, $WAR1_{t-1}$, $WAR1_{t-1}*ARMY_t$, CON_t, AR(1)

$NAVYPROXY_t$ = Residuals from regression of navy term on the remaining regressors, as indicated in Chapter 4.

EXPORT MODELS

Britain: 1853–1913
EXP_t = Constant, $ARMY_t$, $ARMY_{t-1}$, $NAVY_t$, PF/PD_t, IMP_t, GNP_t, D1882, D1882*$ARMY_t$, D1882*$NAVY_t$, $WAR1_t$, $WAR2_t$

France: 1856–1913
EXP_t = Constant, $ARMY_t$, $NAVY_t$, GNP_t, CON_t, PF/PD_t, $WAR1_t$, D1870, D1870*$ARMY_t$, CON_t*NAVY_t, $MERC_t$

Germany: 1874–1913
EXP_t = Constant, $ARMY_t$, GNP_t, PF/PD_t, $WAR2_t$, IMP_{t-1}, $NAVY_t$, D1890, D1890*$NAVY_t$

Italy: 1865–1913
EXP_t = Constant, $ARMY_t$, $ARMY_{t-1}$, $NAVY_{t-1}$, IMP_t, GNP_{t-1}, PF/PD_t, $WAR2_t$, $MERC_{t-1}$, AR(1)

Japan: 1875–1913
EXP_t = Constant, $ARMY_{t-1}$, IMP_t, PF/PD_t, D1895, D1895*$ARMY_{t-1}$, AR(1)

Russia: 1863–1913
EXP_t = Constant, $ARMY_{t-1}$, $NAVY_t$, D1878, D1878*$ARMY_{t-1}$, D1890, D1890*$NAVY_t$

United States: 1869–1913
EXP_t = Constant, $NAVY_t$, $NAVY_{t-1}$, PF/PD_t, GNP_t, $WAR2_{t-1}$, AR(1)

Bibliography

STATISTICAL SOURCES

France: *Annuaire Statistique de la France*, Paris: Institut National de la Statistique et des Etudes Economiques, various years, 1878–1966.

Germany: Kaiserlichen Statistischen Amt. (1880–1918), Statistisches Reichsamte (1918–1942). *Statistisches Jahrbuch für das Deutsche Reich*, Berlin: Puttkammer and Muhlbrecht, various years, 1880–1942.

Great Britain: Central Statistical Office, *Annual Abstract of Statistics*, London: HMSO, various years, 1853–1939.

—*Statistical Tables for Principal and Other Foreign Countries*, House of Commons Sessional Papers, London: HMSO, various years, 1860–1912.

—*Suez Canal: Returns of Shipping and Tonnage*, House of Commons Sessional Papers, London: HMSO, various years, 1876–1918.

Hoffmann, Walther G., *Das Wachstum der Deutschen Wirtschaft seit der Mitte des 19 Jahrhunderts*, Berlin: Springer-Verlag, 1965.

Italy: *Annuario Statistico Italiano*, Rome: ISTAT, various years, 1878–1939.

Japan: Imperial Cabinet, *Résumé Statistique de l'Empire du Japon*, Tokyo: Bureau of General Statistics, various years, 1888–1916.

—Department of Agriculture and Commerce, *Japan in the Beginning of the 20th Century*, Tokyo: Tokyo-Shoin, 1904.

Khromov, Pavel A., *Ekonomicheskoe Razvitie Rossii v XIX i XX Vekakh, 1899–1917*, Moscow: Gospolitizdat, 1950.

Mitchell, B. R., *European Historical Statistics: 1750–1975*, New York: Facts on File, 2nd and rev. edn, 1980.

— *International Historical Statistics: Africa and Asia*, New York: New York University Press, 1982.

—*British Historical Statistics*, Cambridge: Cambridge University Press, 1988.

— *International Historical Statistics: Europe, 1750–1988*, New York: M Stockton Press, 3rd edn, 1992.

— *International Historical Statistics: The Americas, 1750–1988*, New York: M Stockton Press, 1993.

Russia: Tawsawentral Nyi Statisticheskii Komitet, *Statistika Rossiiskoi Imperii*, Petrograd, various years, 1886–1916.

United States: Department of Commerce, *Historical Statistics of the United States: Colonial Times to 1970*, Washington, DC: GPO, 1976, 2 vols.

—Department of Commerce, *Statistical Abstracts of the United States*, Washington, DC: GPO, 2000.

GENERAL REFERENCES

Alam, M. Shahid, *Poverty from the Wealth of Nations: Integration and Polarization in the Global Economy Since 1760*, New York: St. Martin's Press, 2000.

Alford, Jr. H. and H. Neill, *Modern Economic Warfare: Law and the Naval Participant*, Washington, DC: GPO, 1967.

Anderson, Ewan W., *Strategic Minerals: The Geopolitical Problems for the United States*, New York: Praeger, 1988.

Angell, Sir Norman, *Raw Materials, Population Pressure and War*, Boston, MD: World Peace Foundation, 1936.

Ashley, Percey, *Modern Tariff History: Germany–United States–France*, London: John Murray, 1910.

Balassa, Bela, *The Theory of Economic Integration*, Homewood, IL: Richard D. Irwin, 1961.

Baldwin, David, 'Power Analysis and World Politics: New Trends Versus Old Tendencies', *World Politics* 31/2 (January 1979), pp. 161–94.

— *Economic Statecraft*, Princeton, NJ: Princeton University Press, 1985.

Barbieri, Katherine and Gerald Schneider, 'Globalization and Peace: Assessing New Directions in the Study of Trade and Conflict', *Journal of Peace Research* 36/4 (July 1999), pp. 387–404.

Barlett, Ruhl, *Policy and Power: Two Centuries of American Foreign Relations*, New York: Hill and Wang, 1963.

Barnett, L. Margaret, *British Food Policy During the First World War*, Boston MA: George Allen and Unwin, 1985.

Beasley, W. G., *Japanese Imperialism, 1894–1945*, Oxford: Clarendon Press, 1987.

Becker, William H., '1899–1920: America Adjusts to World Power', in William H. Becker and Samuel F. Wells, Jr. (eds), *Economics and World Power: An Assessment of American Diplomacy Since 1789*, New York: Columbia University Press, 1984, pp. 173–223.

Borrus, Michael and John Zysman, 'Industrial Competitiveness and American National Security', in Wayne Sandholtz, et al. (eds), *The*

Highest Stakes: The Economic Foundations of the Next Security System, New York: Oxford University Press, 1992, pp. 7–52.

Bosworth, R. J. B., *Italy, the Least of the Great Powers: Italian Foreign Policy Before the First World War*, London: Cambridge University Press, 1979.

Brodie, Bernard, *Sea Power in the Machine Age*, Princeton, NJ: Princeton University Press, 1941.

— *A Guide to Naval Strategy*, Princeton, NJ: Princeton University Press, 1944.

— *Strategy in the Missile Age*, Princeton, NJ: Princeton University Press, 1959.

Bryan, G. S., 'Geography and the Defense of the Caribbean and the Panama Canal', *Annals of the Association of American Geographers* 31/1 (March 1941): pp. 83–94.

Brzezinski, Zbigniew, *Game Plan: How to Conduct the US–Soviet Contest*, Boston, MD: Atlantic Monthly Press, 1986.

Bull, Hedley, 'Sea Power and Political Influence', in Jonathan Alford (ed.), *Sea Power and Influence: Old Issues and New Challenges*, London: IISS, 1980, pp. 3–11.

Cable, James, *Gunboat Diplomacy: Political Applications of Limited Naval Force*, New York: Praeger, 1971.

— *Navies in Violent Peace*, New York: St. Martin's Press, 1989.

Caporaso, James A., 'Interdependence and the Coordination of Foreign and Domestic Policies in the Atlantic World', in Wolfram Hanrieder (ed.), *Economic Issues and the Atlantic Community*, New York: Praeger, 1982, pp. 1–14.

Carlton, Eric, *Occupation: The Policies and Practices of Military Conquerors*, Savage, MD: Barnes and Noble, 1992.

Chan, S. 'The Impact of Defense Spending on Economic Performance: A Survey of Evidence and Problems', *Orbis* 29/2 (1985), pp. 403–34.

— 'The Political Economy of Military Spending and Economic Performance: Directions for Future Research', in A. L. Ross (ed.), *The Political Economy of Defense: Issues and Perspectives*, NY: Greenwood, 1991, pp. 203–22.

Choucri, Nazli and Robert C. North, *Nations in Conflict: National Growth and International Violence*, San Francisco, CA: W. H. Freeman and Co., 1975.

Churchill, Rogers P., *The Anglo-Russian Convention of 1907*, Cedar Rapids, IA: The Torch Press, 1939.

Cleef, Eugene van, *Trade Centers and Trade Routes*, New York: D. Applleton-Century, 1937.

Cohen, Benjamin J. *In Whose Interests? International Banking and American Foreign Policy*, New Haven, CT: Yale University Press, 1986.

Cohen, Saul B., *Geography and Politics in a World Divided*, New York: Oxford University Press, 1973.

Cole, Bernard D., *Gunboats and Marines: The United States Navy in China, 1925–1928*, Newark: University of Delaware Press, 1983.

Cole, Charles W., *French Mercantilist Doctrines Before Colbert*, 1931, reprint. New York: Octagon Books, 1969.

'Continuity and Change in the Westphalian Order', special issue of *International Studies Review* 2 (Summer 2000).

Conybeare, John A. C., *Trade Wars: The Theory and Practice of International Commercial Rivalry*, New York: Columbia University Press, 1987.

Couper, A. D., *The Geography of Sea Transport*, London: Hutchinson University Library, 1972.

Crabites, Pierre, *The Spoliation of Suez*, London: George Routledge and Sons, 1940.

Crawford, Beverly, 'The New Security Dilemma Under International Economic Interdependence', *Millennium* 23 (Spring 1994), pp. 25–55.

Curzon, George N., *Russia in Central Asia in 1889, and the Anglo-Russian Question*, 1889, reprint. New York: Barnes and Noble, 1967.

Darby, Phillip, *British Defence Policy East of Suez, 1947–1968*, London: Oxford University Press for the Royal Institute of International Affairs, 1973.

Deger, S. and R. Smith, 'Military Expenditure and Growth in Less Developed Countries', *Journal of Conflict Resolution* 27/2 (1983), pp. 335–53.

DeGrasse, R. W., *Military Expansion and Economic Decline: The Impact of Military Spending on US Economic Performance*, Armonk, NY: ME Sharpe, 1983.

Delucchi, Mark and James Murphy, 'US Military Expenditures to Protect the Use of Persian Gulf Oil for Motor Vehicles', (April 1996), at www.uctc.net/papers/325.pdf.

Desch, Michael C., 'The Keys That Lock Up the World: Identifying American Interests in the Periphery', *International Security* 14/1 (Summer 1989), pp. 86–121.

Deudney, Daniel, *Whole Earth Security: A Geopolitics of Peace*, Washington, DC: Worldwatch Institute, July 1983.

Drucker, Peter F., 'The Global Economy and the Nation-State', *Foreign Affairs* 76 (September–October 1997), pp. 159–71.

Earle, Edward M., 'Adam Smith, Alexander Hamilton, Fredrich List: The Economic Foundations of Military Power', in Edward M. Earle (ed.), *Makers of Modern Strategy: Military Thought from Machiavelli to Hitler*, Princeton, NJ: Princeton University Press, 1943, pp. 117–54.

East, W. Gordon, *An Historical Geography of Europe*, 1966, reprint. 5th edn, London: Methuen, 1967.

Ebinger, Charles K., *The Critical Link: Energy and National Security in the 1980s*, Cambridge: Ballinger, 1982.

Eckes, Alfred E., Jr., *The United States and the Global Struggle for Minerals*, Austin: University of Texas Press, 1979.

Einzig, Paul, *The Economics of Rearmament*, London: Kegan Paul, Trench, Trubner, 1934.

— *Economic Warfare*, London: Macmillan, 1940.

Ekelund, Robert B., *Mercantilism as a Rent-Seeking Society: Economic Regulation in Historical Perspective*, College Station, TX: Texas A and M University Press, 1981.

Emeny, Brooks, *The Strategy of Raw Materials: The Study of America in Peace and War*, New York: Macmillan, 1934.

Evans, Douglas, *The Politics of Trade: The Evolution of the Superbloc*, New York: John Wiley and Sons, 1974.

Evans, Peter, 'The Eclipse of the State: Reflections on Stateness in an Era of Globalization', *World Politics* 50 (October 1997), pp. 62–87.

Farnie, D. A., *East and West of Suez: The Suez Canal in History, 1854–1956*, Oxford: Clarendon Press, 1969.

Frederiksen, P. C. and R. E. Looney, 'Defense Expenditures and Economic Growth in Developing Countries', *Armed Forces and Society* 9/4 (1983), pp. 633–45.

Fuller, J. F. C., *War and Western Civilization, 1832–1932: A Study of War as a Political Instrument and the Expression of Mass Democracy*, 1932, reprint. Freeport, NY: Books for Libraries Press, 1969.

Fuller, Jr., William C., *Strategy and Power in Russia: 1600–1914*, New York: Free Press, 1992.

Gasiorowski, Mark, 'Economic Interdependence and International Conflict: Some Cross-National Evidence', *International Studies Quarterly* 30/1 (March 1986), pp. 23–38.

Gasiorowski, Mark and Solomon W. Polackek, 'Conflict and Interdependence: East–West Trade and Linkages in the Era of Détente', *Journal of Conflict Resolution* 26/4 (December, 1982), pp. 709–29.

Gerace, Michael P., 'State Interests, Military Power and International Commerce: Some Cross-National Evidence', *Geopolitics* 5/1 (Summer 2001), pp. 101–24.

Geyer, Dietrich, *Russian Imperialism: The Interaction of Domestic and Foreign Policy, 1860–1914*, New Haven CT: Yale University Press, 1987.

Gilpin, Robert, *US Power and the Multinational Corporation: The Political Economy of Foreign Direct Investment*, New York: Basic Books, 1975.

— *War and Change in World Politics*, Cambridge: Cambridge University Press, 1981.

— *The Political Economy of International Relations*, Princeton, NJ: Princeton University Press, 1987.

— *The Challenge of Global Capitalism: The World Economy in the 21st Century*, Princeton, NJ: Princeton University Press, 2000.

Girault, Arthur, *The Colonial Tariff Policy of France*, Oxford: Clarendon Press, 1916.

Gooch, John, *Armies in Europe*, London: Routledge and Kegan Paul, 1980.

— *Army, State and Society in Italy, 1870–1915*, New York: St. Martin's Press, 1989.

Gorg, Christoph and Joachim Hirsch, 'Is International Democracy Possible?' *Review of International Political Economy* 5 (Winter 1998), pp. 585–615.

Gorshkov, S. G., *The Sea Power of the State*, Oxford: Pergamon Press, 1979.

Gottmann, Jean, 'Bugeaud, Gallieni, Lyautey: The Development of French Colonial Warfare', in Edward M. Earle (ed.), *Makers of Modern Strategy: Military Thought from Machiavelli to Hitler*, Princeton, NJ: Princeton University Press, 1943, pp. 234–59.

Gowa, Joanne, *Allies and Adversaries, and International Trade*, Princeton, NJ: Princeton University Press, 1994.

Gray, Colin S., *The Geopolitics of Superpower*, Lexington, KY: University of Kentucky Press, 1988.

— *The Leverage of Sea Power: The Strategic Advantage of Navies in War*, New York: The Free Press, 1992.

Gregory, Paul R., *Russian National Income: 1885–1913*, Cambridge: Cambridge University Press, 1982.

Grove, Eric J., *The Future of Sea Power*, Annapolis, MD: Naval Institute Press, 1990.

Guehenno, Jean Marie, 'The Impact of Globalisation on Strategy', *Survival* 40 (Winter 1998/99), pp. 5–19.

Gustafsson, Hans, Bertil Oden, and Andreas Tegen, *South African Minerals: An Analysis of Western Dependence*, Uppsala: Nordiska Afrikainstitutet, 1990.

Hagan, Kenneth J., *American Gunboat Diplomacy and the Old Navy: 1877–1889*, Westport, CT: Greenwood Press, 1973.

Haglund, David G. (ed.), *The Defence Industrial Base and the West*, New York: Routledge, 1989.

Ham, Rose Marie and David C. Mowery, 'Enduring Dilemmas in US Technology Policy', *California Management Review* 37 (Summer 1995), pp. 89–107.

Hanks, Robert J., *The Unnoticed Challenge: Soviet Maritime Strategy and the Global Choke Points*, Cambridge, MA: Institute for Foreign Policy Analysis, 1980.

— *The Cape Route: Imperiled Western Lifeline*, Cambridge, MA: Institute for Foreign Policy Analysis, 1981.

Harkavy, Robert E., *Great Power Competition for Overseas Bases: The Geopolitics of Access Diplomacy*, New York: Pergamon, 1982.

Hartshorne, Richard, 'Political Geography in the Modern World', *Journal of Conflict Resolution* 4/1 (March 1960), pp. 52–66.

Hauner, Milan, *What is Asia to Us? Russia's Asian Heartland Yesterday and Today*, Boston, MD: Unwin Hyman, 1990.

Hawtrey, R. G., *Economic Aspects of Sovereignty*, London: Longmans, Green and Co., 1930.

Heckscher, Eli F., *Mercantilism*, rev. edn., trans. Mendel Shapiro, E. F. Soderlund (ed.), Vol. 2, London: George Allen and Unwin, 1955.

Heilperin, Michael A., *The Trade of Nations*, New York: Alfred A. Knopf, 1947.

Hirschman, Albert O., *National Power and the Structure of Foreign Trade*, Berkeley: University of California Press, 1945.

Hoffman, Ross J., *Great Britain and The German Trade Rivalry: 1875–1914*, New York: Russell and Russell, 1964.

Holton, Robert, *Globalization and the Nation-State*, New York: St. Martin's Press, 1998.

Hooper, Edwin B., *United States Naval Power in a Changing World*, New York: Praeger, 1988.

Howard, Michael, 'Order and Conflict at Sea in the 1980s', in Jonathan Alford (ed.), *Sea Power and Influence: Old Issues and New Challenges*, London: IISS, 1980, pp. 74–79.

Hu, Patricia S., 'Estimates of 1996 US Military Expenditures on Defending Oil Supplies from the Middle East: Literature Review', (August 1997), at www-cta.ornl.gov/Publications/military.pdf.

Huang, C. and F. W. Hoole, 'Military Burden and Economic Hegemonic Decline: The Case of the United States', in A. Mintz (ed.), *The Political Economy of Military Spending in the United States*, London: Routledge, 1992, pp. 238–58.

Huisken, Ron, *The Meaning and Measurement of Military Expenditures*, SIPRI Research Report No. 10 (Stockholm: SIPRI, 1973).

Hunter, Holland, *Soviet Transportation Policy*, Cambridge, MA: Harvard University Press, 1957.

Hurd, Archibald and Henry Castle, *German Sea-Power: Its Rise, Progress, and Economic Basis*, 1913. reprint. Westport, CT: Greenwood Press, 1971.

Huston, James A., *The Sinews of War: Army Logistics, 1775–1953*, Washington, DC: GPO, 1966.

Ikenberry, G. John, 'Why Export Democracy? The "Hidden Grand Strategy", of American Foreign Policy', *The Wilson Quarterly* 23/2 (Spring 1999), p. 56, available at wwics.si.edu/OUTREACH/WQ/WQSELECT/IKENB.HTM

Imlah, Albert H., *Economic Elements in the Pax Britannica: Studies in British Foreign Trade in the Nineteenth Century*, Cambridge, MA: Harvard University Press, 1958.

Jean, Carlo, 'The Role of the Nation State in Providing Security in a

Changed World', *International Spectator* 33/1 (January–March 1998), pp. 67–77.

Jenkins, David B., 'The History of Afghanistan as a Buffer State', in John Chay and Thomas E. Ross (eds), *Buffer States in World Politics*, Boulder, CO: Westview, 1986, pp. 171–89.

Jenkins, E. H., *A History of the French Navy: From its Beginnings to the Present Day*, London: Macdonald and Jane's, 1973.

Johns, R. A., *Colonial Trade and International Exchange: The Transition From Autarky to International Trade*, London: Pinter Publishers, 1988.

Jones, Jr., Joseph M. *Tariff Retaliation: Repercussions of the Hawley-Smoot Bill*, Philadelphia: University of Pennsylvania Press, 1934.

Jones, Stephen B., 'The Power Inventory and National Strategy', *World Politics* 6/4 (July 1954), pp. 421–52.

Kaiser, David E., *Economic Diplomacy and the Origins of the Second World War: Germany, Britain, France, and Eastern Europe, 1930–39*, Princeton, NJ: Princeton University Press, 1980.

Kalla-Bishop, P. M., *Italian Railways*, Newton Abbot: David and Charles, 1971.

Kaloudis, George, 'The Search for Global Order', *International Journal on World Peace* 15 (March 1998), pp. 3–21.

Kennan, George F., *The Decline of Bismarck's European Order: Franco-Russian Relations, 1875–1890*, Princeton, NJ: Princeton University Press, 1979.

Kennedy, Paul M., *The Rise and Fall of British Naval Mastery*, New York: Praeger, 1976.

— *The Rise of the Anglo-German Antagonism, 1860–1914*, London: Ashfield Press, 1980.

— *The Rise and Fall of the Great Powers: Economic Change and Military Conflict From 1500 to 2000*, New York: Random House, 1987.

Keohane, Robert O., and Joseph S. Nye, *Power and Interdependence*, 2nd edn., Boston, MD: Scott, Foresman and Co., 1989.

Key, Helmer, *The New Colonial Policy*, London: Methuen, 1927.

Kieffer, John E., *Realities of World Power*, New York: David McKay Co., 1952.

Kim, Key-Hiuk, *The Last Phase of the East Asian World Order: Korea, Japan, and the Chinese Empire, 1860–1882*, Berkeley, CA: University of California Press, 1980.

Kiralfy, Alexander, 'Japanese Naval Strategy', in Edward M. Earle (ed.), *Makers of Modern Strategy: Military Thought from Machiavelli to Hitler*, Princeton, NJ: Princeton University Press, 1943, pp. 457–84.

Kissinger, Henry A., *Diplomacy*, New York: Simon and Schuster, 1994.

Klein, Burton H., *Germany's Economic Preparation for War*, Cambridge, MA: Harvard University Press, 1959.

Knorr, Klaus, *The War Potential of Nations*, Princeton, NJ: Princeton University Press, 1956.

— 'The Concept of Economic Potential for War', *World Politics* 10/1 (October 1957), pp. 49–62.

— *Military Power and Potential*, Lexington, MA: Heath Lexington Books, 1970.

— *The Power of Nations: The Political Economy of International Relations*, New York: Basic Books, 1975.

Koburger, Jr., Charles W., *Narrow Seas, Small Navies, and Fat Merchantmen: Naval Strategies for the 1990s*, New York: Praeger, 1990.

Kraft, John C., 'Strategic Minerals and World Stability', in Gerard J. Mangone (ed.), *American Strategic Minerals*, New York: Crane Russak, 1984.

Kranold, Herman, *The International Distribution of Raw Materials*, London: George Routledge and Sons, 1938.

Krasner, Stephen D., 'State Power and the Structure of International Trade', *World Politics* 28/3 (April 1976), pp. 317–47.

— *Defending the National Interest: Raw Materials Investments and US Foreign Policy*, Princeton, NJ: Princeton University Press, 1978.

Lambi, Ivo N., *The Navy and German Power Politics, 1862–1914*, Boston, MD: Allen and Unwin, 1984.

Langer, William L., *The Franco-Russian Alliance: 1890–1894*, Cambridge, MA: Harvard University Press, 1929.

Leith, C. K., J. W. Furness, and Cleona Lewis, *World Minerals and World Peace*, Washington, DC: Brookings Institution, 1943.

Lim, D., 'Another Look at Growth and Defense in Less Developed Countries', *Economic Development and Cultural Change* 31/2 (1983), pp. 377–84.

Long, M. H., 'Imperial Policies of Great Britain', *Foreign Affairs* 6/2 (January 1928), pp. 245–68.

Luttwak, Edward N., *Strategy and History, Collected Essays*, Vol. 2, New Brunswick, NJ: Transaction Books, 1985.

— *Strategy: The Logic of War and Peace*, Cambridge, MA: Belknap Press, 1987.

McCwire, Michael, 'Maritime Strategy and the Super-Powers', in Jonathan Alford (ed.), *Sea Power and Influence: Old Issues and New Challenges*, London: IISS, 1980, pp. 56–65.

McIntosh, Malcolm, *Japan Re-Armed*, New York: St. Martin's Press, 1986.

McNaugher, Thomas L., *Arms and Oil: US Military Strategy and the Persian Gulf*, Washington, DC: Brookings Institution, 1985.

McNeill, William H., *The Pursuit of Power: Technology, Armed Force, and Society Since AD 1000*, Chicago: University of Chicago Press, 1982.

MacKinder, Halford, *Democratic Ideals and Reality, With Additional Papers*, New York: W. W. Norton, 1962.

Maguire, T. Miller, *Outlines of Military Geography*, Cambridge: Cambridge University Press, 1899.

Mahan, Alfred T., *Armaments and Arbitration: Or the Place of Force in the International Relations of States*, New York: Harper and Brothers, 1912.

— *The Influence of Sea Power Upon History: 1660–1783*, 1890, reprint, New York: Sagamore Press, 1957.

— *The Interest of America in Sea Power: Present and Future*, 1897, reprint. Port Washington, NY: Kennikat Press, 1970.

— *The Problem of Asia and its Effect Upon International Policies*, Boston, MD: Little, Brown and Co., 1900.

Makinda, Samuel M., 'Sovereignty and Global Security', *Security Dialogue*, 29 (September 1998), pp. 281–92.

Mansfield, Edward D. and Rachel Bronson, 'Alliances, Preferential Trading Arrangements, and International Trade', *American Political Science Review*, 91/1 (March 1997), pp. 94–107.

Mansfield, Edward D., Jon C., Pevehouse, and David H. Bearce, 'Preferential Trading Arrangements and Military Disputes', in Jean-Marc F. Blanchard, Edward D. Mansfield and Norrin M. Ripsman (eds), *Power and the Purse: Economic Statecraft, Interdependence and National Security*, London: Frank Cass, 2000, pp. 92–118.

Marder, Arthur J., *The Anatomy of British Sea Power: A History of British Naval Policy in the Pre-Dreadnought Era, 1880–1905*, New York: Alfred A. Knopf, 1940.

Marshall, Robert, 'Autonomy and Sovereignty in the Era of Global Restructuring', *Studies in Political Economy* 59 (Summer 1999), pp. 115–47.

Mastanduno, Michael, 'Economics and Security in Statecraft and Scholarship', *International Organization* 52/4 (Autumn 1998), pp. 825–54.

— 'Economic Statecraft, Interdependence, and National Security: Agendas for Research', in Jean-Marc F. Blanchard, Edward D. Mansfield and Norrin M. Ripsman (eds), *Power and the Purse: Economic Statecraft, Interdependence and National Security*, London: Frank Cass, 2000, pp. 288–316.

Maud, Lt.-Col. P. D., 'Lord Haldane's Reorganization of the British Army, 1905–1912', in Gordon B. Turner (ed.), *A History of Military Affairs in Western Society Since the Eighteenth Century*, New York: Harcourt, Brace and Co., 1952, pp. 269–74.

Maull, Hans W., *Energy, Minerals and Western Security*, Baltimore, MD: Johns Hopkins University Press, 1984.

Mitchell, Donald W., *A History of Russian and Soviet Sea Power*, New York: Macmillan, 1974.

Mitchell, William, *Winged Defense: The Development and Possibilities of*

Modern Air Power – Economic and Military, New York: G. P. Putnam's Sons, 1925.

Moberg, Erik, 'The Protection of Resources', in Jonathan Alford (ed.), *Sea Power and Influence: Old Issues and New Challenges*, London: IISS, 1980, pp. 19–23.

Moore, Rebecca R., 'Globalization and the Future of US Human Rights Policy', *Washington Quarterly* 21 (Autumn 1998), pp. 193–212.

Moran, Theodore H., *American Economic Policy and National Security*, New York: Council on Foreign Relations Press, 1993.

Morgan, Gerald, *Anglo-Russian Rivalry in Central Asia: 1810–1895*, London: Frank Cass, 1981.

Morgenthau, Hans J., *Politics Among Nations*, 6th edn., revised by Kenneth W. Thompson, New York: McGraw-Hill, 1985.

Morrow, James D., Randolph M. Siverson and Tressa E. Tabares, 'The Political Determinants of International Trade: The Major Powers, 1907–90', *American Political Science Review* 92/3 (September 1998): pp. 649–61.

Mueller, M. J. and H. S. Atesoglu, 'A Theory of Defense Spending and Economic Growth', in J. E. Payne and A. P. Sahu (eds), *Defense Spending and Economic Growth*, Boulder, CO: Westview, 1993, pp. 41–53.

Nardenelli, C. and G. B. Ackerman, 'Defense Expenditures and the Survival of American Capitalism: A Note', *Armed Forces and Society* 3/1 (1976), pp. 13–16.

Negash, Tekeste, *Italian Colonialism in Eritrea, 1882–1941: Policies, Praxis and Impact*, Uppsala: Almqvist and Wiksell International, 1987.

Nichols, Albert L. and Richard Zeckhauser, 'Stockpiling Strategies and Cartel Prices', *Rand Journal of Economics* 8/1 (Spring 1977), pp. 66–96.

Nish, Ian H., *Alliance in Decline: A Study in Anglo-Japanese Relations, 1908–1923*, London: The Athlone Press, 1972.

— *Japanese Foreign Policy 1869–1942: Kasumigaseki to Miyakezaka*, London: Routledge and Kegan Paul, 1977.

Nye, Jr., Joseph S., *Bound to Lead: The Changing Nature of American Power*, New York: Basic Books, 1990.

— 'Soft Power', *Foreign Policy* 80 (Autumn 1990), pp. 153–71.

O'Connor, Raymond G., *Force and Diplomacy: Essays Military and Diplomatic*, Coral Gables, FL: University of Miami Press, 1972.

Olson, Jr., Mancur, *The Economics of Wartime Shortage: A History of British Food Supplies in the Napoleonic War and in the World War I and II*, Durham, NC: Duke University Press, 1963.

Oneal, John R. and Bruce Russett, 'Assessing the Liberal Peace with Alternative Specifications: Trade Still Reduces Conflict', *Journal of Peace Research* 36/4 (1999), pp. 423–42.

Ono, Giichi, *Expenditures of the Sino-Japanese War*, New York: Oxford University Press, 1922.

— *War and Armament Expenditures of Japan*, New York: Oxford University Press, 1922.

Osgood, Robert E., 'Military Implications of the New Ocean Politics', in Jonathan Alford (ed.), *Sea Power and Influence: Old Issues and New Challenges*, London: IISS, 1980, pp. 12–18.

O'Sullivan, Noel, 'Concept and Reality in Globalization Theory', in C. P. Rao (ed.), *Globalization, Privatization and Free Market Economy*, Westport, CT: Quorum, 1998.

O'Sullivan, Patrick, *Transport Policy: Geographic and Economic Planning Aspects*, Totowa, NJ: Barnes and Noble, 1980.

Padfield, Peter, *The Great Naval Race: The Anglo-German Naval Rivalry, 1900–1914*, New York: David McKay, 1974.

Parker, Geoffrey, *Western Geopolitical Thought in the Twentieth Century*, New York: St. Martin's Press, 1985.

— *The Geopolitics of Domination*, London: Routledge, 1988.

Pearton, Maurice, *Diplomacy, War and Technology*, Lawrence: University Press of Kansas, 1984.

Pedraja, Rene de la, *The Rise and Decline of US Merchant Shipping in the Twentieth Century*, New York: Twayne Publishers, 1992.

Platt, D. C. M., *Finance, Trade, and Politics in British Foreign Policy: 1815–1914*, Oxford: Clarendon Press, 1971.

Pletcher, David M., '1861–1898: Economic Growth and Diplomatic Adjustment', in William H. Becker and Samuel F. Wells, Jr. (eds), *Economics and World Power: An Assessment of American Diplomacy Since 1789*, New York: Columbia University Press, 1984, pp. 119–71.

Polackek, Solomon W., 'Conflict and Trade', *Journal of Conflict Resolution* 24/1 (March 1980), pp. 55–78.

Polackek, Solomon W., John Robst and Yuan-Ching Chang, 'Liberalism and Interdependence: Extending the Trade-Conflict Model', *Journal of Peace Research* 36/4 (July 1999), pp. 405–22.

Polanyi, Karl, *The Great Transformation*, New York: Rinehart and Co., 1944.

Pollins, Brian M., 'Does Trade Still Follow the Flag?' *American Political Science Review* 83/2 (June 1989), pp. 465–80.

— 'Conflict, Cooperation, and Commerce: The Effect of International Political Interactions on Bilateral Trade Flows', *American Journal of Political Science* 33/3 (August 1989), pp. 737–61.

Pounds, Norman G., 'A Free and Secure Access to the Sea', *Annals of the Association of American Geographers* 49/3 (September 1959), pp. 256–68.

Preeg, Ernest H., *Economic Blocs and US Foreign Policy*, Washington, DC: National Planning Association, 1974, Report No. 135.

Preston, Richard A., Sydney F. Wise, and Herman O. Werner, *Men in*

Arms: A History of Warfare and its Interrelationships with Western Society, New York: Fredrick A. Praeger, 1956.

Ram, R., 'Conceptual Linkages Between Defense Spending and Economic Growth and Development: A Selective Review', in J. E. Payne and A. P. Sahu (eds), *Defense Spending and Economic Growth*, Boulder, CO: Westview, 1993, pp. 19–39.

Rensburg, W. C. J. and D. A. Pretorius, *South Africa's Strategic Minerals: Pieces on a Continental Chess Board*, Johannesburg: Valiant Publishers, 1977.

Reuveny, Rafael and Heejoon Kang, 'International Trade, Political Conflict/Cooperation, and Granger Causality', *American Journal of Political Science* 40 (August 1996), pp. 943–70.

— 'Bilateral Trade and Political Conflict/Cooperation: Do Goods Matter?' *Journal of Peace Research* 35 (September 1998), pp. 581–602.

Ropp, Theodore, 'Continental Doctrines of Sea Power', in Edward M. Earle (ed.), *Makers of Modern Strategy: Military Thought from Machiavelli to Hitler*, Princeton, NJ: Princeton University Press, 1943, pp. 446–56.

Rosecrance, Richard, *The Rise of the Trading State: Commerce and Conquest in the Modern World*, New York: Basic Books, 1986.

— *America's Economic Resurgence: A Bold New Strategy*, New York: Harper and Row, 1990.

— 'Regionalism and the Post-Cold War Era', *International Journal* 66/3 (Summer 1991), pp. 373–93.

Rosenau, James N., *The Study of Global Interdependence: Essays on the Transnationalization of World Affairs*, London: Frances Pinter, 1980.

Rosinski, Herbert, 'The Limitations of Mahan and Tirpitz', in Gordon B. Turner (ed.), *A History of Military Affairs in Western Society Since the Eighteenth Century*, New York: Harcourt, Brace and Co., 1952, pp. 352–57.

Ross, Thomas E., 'Buffer States: A Geographer's Perspective', in John Chay and Thomas E. Ross (eds), *Buffer States in World Politics*, Boulder, CO: Westview, 1986, pp. 11–28.

Royal Institute of International Affairs, *Raw Materials and Colonies*, New York: Oxford University Press, 1936.

Sandholtz, Wayne and John Zysman, 'Europe's Emergence as a Global Protagonist', in Wayne Sandholtz, et al. (eds), *The Highest Stakes: The Economic Foundations of the Next Security System*, New York: Oxford University Press, 1992, pp. 81–113.

Sayrs, Lois W., 'Reconsidering Trade and Conflict: A Qualitative Choice Model with Censoring', *Conflict Management and Peace Science* 10/1 (Spring 1988), pp. 1–19.

— 'Expected Utility and Peace Science: An Assessment of Trade and Conflict', *Conflict Management and Peace Science* 11/1 (Spring 1990), pp. 17–44.

Scharfen, John C., *The Dismal Battlefield: Mobilizing for Economic Conflict*, Annapolis: Naval Institute Press, 1995.

Schlote, Werner, *British Overseas Trade: From 1700 to the 1930s*, trans. W. O. Henderson and W. H. Chaloner, Oxford: Basil Blackwell, 1952.

Schmidt, Vivien A., 'The New World Order Incorporated: The Rise of Business and the Decline of the Nation-State', *Daedalus* 124/2 (Spring 1995), pp. 75–106.

Schmoller, Gustav, *The Mercantile System and its Historical Significance*, 1897, reprint. New York: Augustus M. Kelly, 1967.

Schonfield, Hugh J., *The Suez Canal in Peace and War: 1869–1969*, Coral Gables, FL: University of Miami Press, 1969.

Schuyler, Robert L., *The Fall of the Old Colonial System: A Study in British Free Trade, 1770–1870*, London: Oxford University Press, 1945.

Sen, Gautam, *The Military Origins of Industrialisation and International Trade Rivalry*, New York: St. Martin's Press, 1984.

Seversky, Alexander P. de, *Victory Through Air Power*, New York: Simon and Schuster, 1942.

Singer, J. David, *Models, Methods, and Progress in World Politics*, Boulder, CO: Westview, 1990.

Singer, Max and Aaron Wildovsky, *The Real World Order: Zones of Peace, Zones of Turmoil*, Chatham, NJ: Chatham House, 1993.

Smith, Michael S., *Tariff Reform in France, 1860–1900: The Politics of Economic Interest*, Ithaca, NY: Cornell University Press, 1980.

Smith, R. P., 'Military Expenditures and Capitalism', *Cambridge Journal of Economics* 1 (1976), pp. 61–76.

Snyder, Jack, *Myths of Empire: Domestic Politics and International Ambition*, Ithaca, NY: Cornell University Press, 1991.

Soros, George, *The Crisis of Global Capitalism: Open Society Endangered*, New York: Public Affairs, 1998.

Spiegel, Henry W., *The Economics of Total War*, New York: Appleton-Century, 1942.

Sprout, Harold and Margaret Sprout, *Toward a New Order of Sea Power: American Naval Policy and the World Scene, 1918–1922*, Princeton, NJ: Princeton University Press, 1946.

Spykman, Nicholas J., *The Geography of the Peace*, New York: Harcourt, Brace and Co., 1944.

Spykman, Nicholas J. and Abbie A. Rollins, 'Geographic Objectives in Foreign Policy, I', *American Political Science Review* 33/3 (June 1939), pp. 391–410.

— 'Geographic Objectives in Foreign Policy, II', *American Political Science Review* 33/4 (August 1939), pp. 591–614.

Staley, Eugene, *Raw Materials in Peace and War*, New York: Council on Foreign Relations, 1937.

— *World Economy in Transition: Technology Vs. Politics, Laissez Faire Vs.*

Planning, Power Vs. Welfare, New York: Council on Foreign Relations, 1939.

Stambuk, George, *American Military Forces Abroad: Their Impact on the Western State System*, Columbus: Ohio State University Press, 1963.

Stokesbury, James L., *Navy and Empire*, New York: William Morrow, 1983.

Strange, Susan, *States and Markets*, London: Pinter Publishers, 1988.

Sullivan, Michael, *Power in Contemporary International Politics*, Columbia: University of South Carolina Press, 1990.

Taaffe, Robert N., 'Transportation and Regional Specialization: The Example of Soviet Central Asia', *Annals of the Association of American Geographers* 52/1 (March 1962), pp. 80–98.

Takeuchi, Tatsuji, *War and Diplomacy in the Japanese Empire*, Garden City, NY: Doubleday, Doran, and Co., 1935.

Terrill, Tom E., *The Tariff, Politics, and American Foreign Policy, 1874–1901*, Westport, CT: Greenwood Press, 1973.

Thompson, W. Scott, *Power Projection: A Net Assessment of US and Soviet Capabilities*, New York: National Strategy Information Center, 1978.

Till, Geoffrey, *Maritime Strategy and the Nuclear Age*, New York: St. Martin's Press, 1982.

Tracy, Nicholas, *Attack On Maritime Trade*, Toronto: University of Toronto Press, 1991.

Valencia, Mark J., 'Northeast Asia: Petroleum Potential, Jurisdictional Claims and International Relations', *Ocean Development and International Law* 20/1 (1989), pp. 35–61.

Vanberg, Viktor, 'Globalization, Democracy, and Citizens' Sovereignty: Can Competition among Governments Enhance Democracy?' *Constitutional Political Economy* 11 (March 2000), pp. 87–112.

Villiers, Cas de (ed.), *Southern Africa: The Politics of Raw Materials*, Pretoria: Foreign Affairs Association, 1977.

Viner, Jacob, *The Customs Union Issue*, New York: Carnegie Endowment for International Peace, 1950.

Voronkov, Lev, 'Regional Cooperation: Conflict Prevention and Security through Interdependence', *International Journal of Peace Studies* 4/2 (July 1999), pp. 83–93.

Wallace, Benjamin and Bruce and Lynn Ransey Edminster, *International Control of Raw Materials*, Washington, DC: Brookings Institution, 1930.

Warner, Edward P., 'Douhet, Mitchell, Seversky: Theories of Air Warfare', in Edward M. Earle (ed.), *Makers of Modern Strategy: Military Thought from Machiavelli to Hitler*, Princeton, NJ: Princeton University Press, 1943, pp. 485–503.

Waltz, Kenneth N., *Theory of International Politics*, New York: Random House, 1979.

Weber, Steve and John Zysman, 'The Risk That Mercantilism Will Define the Next Security System', in Wayne Sandholtz, et al. (eds), *The Highest Stakes: The Economic Foundations of the Next Security System*, New York: Oxford University Press, 1992, pp. 167–96.

Weigley, Russel F., *The American Way of War: A History of United States Military Strategy and Policy*, Bloomington: Indiana University Press, 1973.

— 'The Anglo-American Armies and Peace, 1783–1868', in Joan R. Challinor and Robert L. Beisner (eds), *Arms at Rest: Peacemaking and Peacekeeping in American History*, New York: Greenwood Press, 1987, pp. 133–59.

Whittam, John, *The Politics of the Italian Army, 1861–1918*, London: Croom Helm, 1977.

Whittlesey, Derwent, *The Earth and the State: A Study in Political Geography*, New York: Henry Holt, 1939.

William J. Casey Institute of the Center for Security Policy, 'Terms of "Engagement": Lugar Anti-Sanctions Measure Could Preclude Important US Security Policy Options', *Casey Institute Perspectives* No. 98-C 117 (William J. Casey Institute of the Center for Security Policy), 22 June 1998, at www.security-policy.org/papers/1998/98-C117.html

Winton, John, *Convoy: The Defense of Sea Trade, 1890–1990*, London: Michael Joseph, 1983.

Woodward, E. L., *Great Britain and the German Navy*, Oxford: Clarendon, 1935.

Woolf, J. B., *The Diplomatic History of the Bagdad Railroad*, 1936, reprint.New York: Octagon Books, 1973.

Wu, Yuan-Li, *Economic Warfare*, New York: Prentice-Hall, 1952.

Index